The Road to Academic Excellence

The Road to Academic Excellence

The Making of World-Class Research Universities

Philip G. Altbach and Jamil Salmi
Editors

THE WORLD BANK
Washington, D.C.

ISBN: 978-0-8213-8805-1
eISBN: 978-0-8213-8806-8
DOI: 10.1596/978-0-8213-8805-1

Library of Congress Cataloging-in-Publication Data
The road to academic excellence: the making of world-class research universities / edited by Philip G. Altbach and Jamil Salmi.
    p. cm. — (Directions in development)
    Includes bibliographical references and index.
    ISBN 978-0-8213-8805-1 (alk. paper) — ISBN 978-0-8213-8806-8
    1. Education, Higher—Economic aspects. 2. Economic development—Effect of education on. 3. Universities and colleges—Research. 4. Higher education and state. 5. Education and globalization. I. Salmi, Jamil. II. Altbach, Philip G.
    LC67.6.R63 2011
    378.3'8—dc23
                                                                            2011017058
Cover photo by: Gary Wayne Gilbert
Cover photo of Linden Lane and Gasson Hall, Boston College
Cover design: Naylor Design, Inc.

Contents

Figures

Tables

Preface

Education, or more specifically, higher education, is the pathway to the empowerment of people and the development of nations. Knowledge generation has replaced ownership of capital assets and labor productivity as the source of growth and prosperity. Innovation is seen as the mantra for development. This realization is so pervasive that nations are scrambling to create institutions and organizations that would facilitate the process of knowledge creation. Knowledge creation requires a network of scholars actively engaged in its pursuit because the search for the unknown is a product of engaged minds, constantly challenging the known in an enabling environment. The modern university is the ideal space for the ecosystem of scholars to search for new ideas in a spirit of free inquiry.

In human history, the university has been one of the great institutions that has emerged and endured. Its structure, however, has changed over the centuries. The Akademons in the age of Plato and Aristotle was a center for dialogue and discussion to understand humanity and its place in society. Abstract thought through philosophy and mathematics was the dominant paradigm. The institution of the university emerged in the time of Abélard, in part as a theocratic space where questions confronting the established religious order were debated. Scholastic methods were employed to understand legal statutes and reasoning, supporting complex political institutions in Bologna and Paris. The concept of the university as a research institution arose in 19th-century Germany, at a time when the Industrial Revolution had crept upon the world in the age of explosion of new ideas. This required empirical research to be undertaken in laboratories before results could be validated for new technology to emerge. The primacy of research over teaching was solidified in the Humboldtian version of the university, with the quest for knowledge as an ongoing enterprise. The discernable aspect of the modern university was the provision of substantial public funding to support research.

The modern research university has also encouraged deep specializations structured around disciplines. Dividing knowledge into disciplines and fields provides depth of understanding in an increasingly complex world. However, a growing understanding has appeared that the problems of the 21st century require a holistic understanding of knowledge, in its various aspects. New knowledge today materializes at the boundaries of existing disciplines, and cross-fertilization of disciplinary understanding occurs in myriad ways. The necessity to relate research to the needs of society has also emerged as a dominant paradigm of the policy discourse in higher education. To quote Gurudev Rabindranath Tagore, a Nobel laureate and sage scholar of India, "The highest education is that which does not merely give us information but makes our life in harmony with all existence." Whether the institutional structure of the modern research university is flexible enough to accommodate learning across disciplines and to harmonize education with the needs of society is yet to be tested. The world today is ripe for another tectonic shift in our understanding of the university as an institution.

India is set to reform its higher education structure. India can emerge as a knowledge power only if an appropriate architecture for higher education is put in place. Indian youth have demonstrated their inventiveness and energy in the past. Higher education that channels this capacity for innovation will unleash the latent potential of India's demographic dividend. India is in the process of establishing Universities for Innovation that are positioned to be at the cutting edge of research fostered through the teaching-learning process.

In the world of higher education policy research, the editors of this volume are preeminent scholars. Their ideas have already influenced nations striving for academic excellence. The compilation of the case studies of research universities in developing and transition economies—which together constitute the aspirations for the future—by prominent thinkers and scholars within the world of academia will help reflect beyond the boundaries of accepted wisdom as nations strive toward academic excellence, discovering new pathways to progress and development. The world is eagerly awaiting the emergence of the next big idea in the governance of academia and the metamorphosis of the university as a place of learning.

I consider it my privilege to have been associated with this book, for which I am immensely grateful to the editors—Philip G. Altbach and Jamil Salmi—for having provided me with this opportunity.

Kapil Sibal
Minister of Human Resource Development
Government of India

Acknowledgments

This book is the result of a collaborative effort. Of greatest importance are the authors of the case studies—they have produced well-researched and incisive case studies that extend knowledge of this important topic. In November 2009, the entire research group met to discuss the work at the Shanghai Jiao Tong University's Graduate School of Education (GSE). The editors are indebted to Dean Nian Cai Liu and his colleagues at GSE. This research was co-sponsored by the Center for International Higher Education (CIHE) at Boston College with funding from the Ford Foundation and by the World Bank's Human Development Network. At Boston College, the team is indebted to Liz Reisberg for staff assistance and to Edith Hoshino, CIHE's publications editor, for assistance with the preparation of this book. At the World Bank, special thanks are owed to Roberta Malee Bassett for helpful comments and suggestions. The book was finalized under the helpful guidance of Elizabeth King (Education Director) and Robin Horn (Education Sector Manager). Full responsibility for errors and misinterpretations remains, however, with the authors and the editors.

Philip G. Altbach
Chestnut Hill, Massachusetts

Jamil Salmi
Washington, DC

About the Authors

Philip G. Altbach is the J. Donald Monan, S. J. University Professor and the director of the Center for International Higher Education in the Lynch School of Education at Boston College. He was the 2004–06 Distinguished Scholar Leader for the New Century Scholars initiative of the Fulbright program. He has been a senior associate of the Carnegie Foundation for the Advancement of Teaching. He coauthored *Turmoil and Transition: The International Imperative in Higher Education, Comparative Higher Education, Student Politics in America* (Paris: United Nations Educational, Scientific, and Cultural Organization, 2009), and other books. He coedited the *International Handbook of Higher Education* (Dordrecht, the Netherlands: Springer, 2006). His most recent book is *World Class Worldwide: Transforming Research Universities in Asia and Latin America* (Baltimore: Johns Hopkins University Press, 2007). He holds a bachelor's degree, master's degree, and PhD from the University of Chicago. He has taught at Harvard University, the University of Wisconsin–Madison, and the State University of New York at Buffalo; has been a visiting scholar at the Sciences Po in Paris, France, and the University of Mumbai in India; and is a guest professor at Peking University in China.

Andrés Bernasconi is an associate professor and vice-rector for research and graduate programs at Universidad Andrés Bello in Chile. His field of study is the sociology of higher education, and he has done research on higher education law, university governance, the development of the academic profession, and privatization, with a regional focus on Latin America. His works have been published in *Higher Education, Comparative Education Review, Journal of Education, Journal of Education Policy,* and *Journal of Interamerican Studies and World Affairs.* A lawyer by training, he holds a master's of public policy degree from Harvard University and a PhD in sociology of organizations from Boston University.

Isak Froumin is a lead education specialist at the World Bank, based in Moscow. His World Bank experience includes projects in Afghanistan, Kazakhstan, the Kyrgyz Republic, India, Nepal, and Turkmenistan. Since March 2008, he has been a strategic development adviser for the Higher School of Economics in Moscow. He is supervising the university's strategic planning and educational research program.

Narayana Jayaram is professor of research methodology and dean of the School of Social Sciences at the Tata Institute of Social Sciences in Mumbai, India. He has been director of the Institute for Social and Economic Change in Bangalore. He is managing editor of the *Sociological Bulletin* and has written widely on higher education issues in India.

Nian Cai Liu is the dean of the Graduate School of Education and the director of the Center for World-Class Universities at Shanghai Jiao Tong University in China. He took his undergraduate studies in chemistry at Lanzhou University in China. He obtained his master's degree and PhD in polymer science and engineering from Queen's University in Kingston, Canada. His current research interests include world-class universities, science policy, and strategic planning of universities. He has published extensively in both Chinese and English journals. *The Academic Ranking of World Universities,* an online publication of his group, has attracted attention from all over the world.

Francisco Marmolejo is the executive director of the Consortium for North American Higher Education Collaboration and assistant vice president for Western Hemispheric programs at the University of Arizona. Previously, he was an American Council on Education fellow at the

University of Massachusetts–Amherst and academic vice president at the Universidad de las Américas in Mexico. He has been part of the Organisation for Economic Co-operation and Development (OECD) and World Bank peer review teams conducting evaluations of higher education in Europe, Latin America, Africa, and Asia. At the University of Arizona, he is an affiliate faculty member at the Center for Latin American Studies and affiliated researcher at the Center for the Study of Higher Education.

Peter Materu is a lead education specialist at the World Bank, where he focuses on tertiary education and skills development. Prior to joining the World Bank, he was a professor of electrical engineering at the University of Dar es Salaam in Tanzania, where he also served as dean of the faculty of engineering and later as director for postgraduate studies. He holds graduate degrees in both engineering and education.

Hena Mukherjee earned a bachelor's degree with honors from the University of Singapore, a diploma and a master's of education from the University of Malaya, and a doctor of education from Harvard University, where she was a Fulbright Scholar. She retired as lead education specialist from the World Bank where she had been responsible for developing and managing basic and higher education reform projects in South and East Asia, particularly in China. Before joining the World Bank, she was chief education program officer at the Commonwealth Secretariat in London, responsible for programs in enterprise training, teacher education, and higher education in Commonwealth countries. She had moved to London from the faculty of education at the University of Malaya in Kuala Lumpur, where she had been associate professor and founding head of the Social Foundations Department. She continues to consult for the World Bank and is currently working on tertiary education programs in South and East Asia. Formerly a Singaporean, she is now a Malaysian national.

Pai Obanya was on the academic staff of his alma mater, the University of Ibadan in Nigeria, from 1971 to 1986. Appointed full professor of education in 1979, he served as director of the Institute of Education of the university from 1980 to 1983. At the international level, he was program coordinator for education with the World Confederation of Organizations of the Teaching Profession from 1986 to 1988. Thereafter, he joined the United Nations Educational, Scientific, and Cultural Organization

(UNESCO) Secretariat as deputy director of the UNESCO Regional Office for Education in Africa.

Gerard A. Postiglione is professor and head of the division of policy, administration, and social sciences at the Faculty of Education and director of the Wah Ching Center of Research on Education in China at the University of Hong Kong. He has published more than 100 journal articles and book chapters and 10 books. He has advised nongovernmental organizations and international foundations, including the Carnegie Foundation for the Advancement of Teaching, on the academic profession in Hong Kong SAR, China. He also served as senior consultant at the Ford Foundation's Beijing office for one year to establish a grants framework for China on educational reform and cultural vitality.

Byung Shik Rhee is assistant professor of higher education at Yonsei University in Seoul, the Republic of Korea. He previously served as a visiting scholar at the Higher Education Research Institute at the University of California, Los Angeles. He has served as advisory member of the Presidential Committee on Education Innovation and the Education Policy Committee of the Korean Ministry of Education, Science and Technology. He holds a PhD in higher education from the University of Michigan.

Petra Righetti is an education consultant for the Africa Education Unit of the World Bank. She currently coordinates the World Bank Tertiary Education Program for Africa and leads the preparation of the information and communications technology component for the Ghana Skills and Technology Development Project. She has a graduate degree in international relations and economics from the Johns Hopkins School of Advanced International Studies in Washington, D.C.

Jamil Salmi, a Moroccan education economist, is the World Bank's tertiary education coordinator. He is the principal author of the Bank's tertiary education strategy titled "Constructing Knowledge Societies: New Challenges for Tertiary Education." For the past 17 years, he has provided policy advice on tertiary education reform to the governments of more than 60 countries in Europe, Asia, Africa, and South America. He is a member of the governing board of the International Institute for Educational Planning of UNESCO, the International Reference Group of the Leadership Foundation for Higher Education in London, and the editorial advisory group of the OECD's *Journal of Higher Education Management and Policy*. His latest book, published in February 2009, is *The Challenge of Establishing World Class Universities* (Washington, DC: World Bank, 2009).

Qi Wang is a lecturer at the Graduate School of Education of Shanghai Jiao Tong University in China. She received her master's degree in education (international education) and PhD in education from the University of Bath in the United Kingdom. Her research interests include the building of world-class universities, skill formation and national development, and comparative and international education.

Qing Hui Wang is a PhD candidate at the Graduate School of Education of Shanghai Jiao Tong University in China. He was a visiting fellow at the Boston College Center for International Higher Education. His research interests focus on the role of department chairs in research universities and the building of world-class universities in China. His work includes the chapter "Growth of Scientific Elites for an Innovation-Oriented Country" in the strategic research project funded by the Science and Technology Committee of the Ministry of Education in China.

Poh Kam Wong is professor at the National University of Singapore Business School and director of the Entrepreneurship Centre. He also holds a professorship appointment (by courtesy) at the Lee Kuan Yew School of Public Policy and the National University of Singapore Engineering School. He obtained two bachelor's degrees, a master's degree, and a PhD from the Massachusetts Institute of Technology. He has published widely on innovation management, technology entrepreneurship, and science and technology policy in leading international journals including *Organization Science, Journal of Business Venturing, Entrepreneurship Theory and Practice, Research Policy, Journal of Management,* and *Scientometrics.* He has also consulted widely for international agencies such as the World Bank, major government agencies in Singapore, and many high-tech firms in Asia. He was a Fulbright Visiting Scholar at the University of California, Berkeley, and received the Public Administration Medal (Bronze) from the Singapore government in 2005 for his contribution to education in Singapore.

Abbreviations

ARES	Academic Reputation Survey
ARWU	Academic Ranking of World Universities
CBSE	Central Board of Secondary Examination
CONACYT	National Science and Technology Council
CRUCH	Consejo de Rectores de las Universidades Chilenas (Council of Rectors of Chilean Universities)
FONDECYT	Fondo Nacional de Desarrollo Científico y Tecnólogico (National Fund for Scientific and Technological Development)
GDP	gross domestic product
HEEACT	Higher Education Evaluation and Accreditation Council of Taiwan
HKUST	Hong Kong University of Science and Technology
HSE	Higher School of Economics (Russian Federation)
ICT	information and communications technology
IIT	Indian Institutes of Technology
INSEAD	Institut Européen d'Administration des Affaires (European Institute of Business Administration)
ITESM	Instituto Tecnológico y de Estudios Superiores de Monterrey (Technological Institute of Higher Education Studies of Monterrey)

ITRI	Industrial Technology Research Institute
JEE	Joint Entrance Examination
K–12	kindergarten–12th grade
KEDI	Korean Educational Development Institute
LAOTSE	Links to Asia by Organizing Traineeship and Student Exchange
MEST	Ministry of Education, Science and Technology
NUS	National University of Singapore
OPEC	Organization of the Petroleum Exporting Countries
RDC	Research and Development Corporation
POSTECH	Pohang University of Science and Technology
PUC	Pontificia Universidad Católica de Chile (Pontifical Catholic University of Chile)
RIST	Research Institute of Industrial Science and Technology
SACS	Southern Association of Colleges and Schools
SCI	Science Citation Index
SETARA	Rating System for Malaysian Higher Education Institutions (local acronym)
SJTU	Shanghai Jiao Tong University
SSCI	Social Sciences Citation Index
STPM	Malaysian Higher School Certificate (local acronym)
THE	Times Higher Education
TIMSS	Trends in International Mathematics and Science Study
UANL	Autonomous University of Nuevo Léon
UCH	Universidad de Chile (University of Chile)
UM	University of Malaya
UNAM	Universidad Nacional Autónoma de México (National Autonomous University of Mexico)
UNESCO	United Nations Educational, Scientific, and Cultural Organization

Introduction

Philip G. Altbach and Jamil Salmi

For middle-income and developing countries—as well as some industrial nations—a major challenge for building and sustaining successful research universities is determining the mechanisms that allow those universities to participate effectively in the global knowledge network on an equal basis with the top academic institutions in the world. These research universities provide advanced education for the academic profession, policy makers, and public and private sector professionals involved in the complex, globalized economies of the 21st century. In addition to their contribution to economic development, these universities play a key societal role by serving as cultural institutions, centers for social commentary and criticism, and intellectual hubs.

The positive contribution of tertiary education is increasingly recognized as not limited to middle-income and advanced countries, because it applies equally to low-income economies. Tertiary education can help these countries to become more globally competitive by developing a skilled, productive, and flexible labor force and by creating, applying, and spreading new ideas and technologies.

The availability of qualified professionals and technicians and the application of advanced knowledge indispensably help developing countries achieve the Millennium Development Goals and build the institutional

1

capacity essential to reduce poverty. Progress in agriculture, health, and environmental protection, for example, cannot be achieved without highly qualified specialists in these areas. Similarly, Education for All cannot be reached without qualified teachers trained at the tertiary education level.

A recent study on how to accelerate economic growth in Sub-Saharan Africa spells out the crucial contribution of tertiary education in supporting this endeavor (World Bank 2008). It observes that the key for success in a globalized world increasingly lies in how effectively a country can assimilate available knowledge and build comparative advantages in areas with higher growth prospects and how it can use technology to address the most pressing environmental challenges. Higher-level institutions in Sub-Saharan Africa that are equipped to provide quality education and conduct relevant applied research can play a key role in producing workers with the skills to assimilate technology and make effective decisions that help industry to diversify into a broader range of products. Good-quality and relevant tertiary education is also key to stimulating innovations to produce new varieties of crops and new materials and to develop sources of energy that can facilitate progress toward reducing poverty, achieving food security, and improving health.

Within the tertiary education system, research universities play a critical role in training the professionals, high-level specialists, scientists, and researchers needed by the economy and in generating new knowledge in support of the national innovation system (World Bank 2002). A recent global study of patent generation has shown, for example, that universities and research institutes, more than firms, drive scientific advances in biotechnology (Cookson 2007). In this context, an increasingly pressing priority of many governments is to ensure that their top universities are actually operating at the cutting edge of intellectual and scientific development.

Research universities are considered among the central institutions of the 21st-century knowledge economies. This issue has been covered in two recent books—*World Class Worldwide: Transforming Research Universities in Asia and Latin America* (Altbach and Balán 2007) and *The Challenge of Establishing World-Class Universities* (Salmi 2009). This book extends the analysis to the next level by examining the recent experience of 11 universities in nine countries that have grappled with the challenges of building successful research institutions in difficult circumstances and learning from these experiences.

The few scholars who have attempted to define what separates elite research institutions from the rest have identified a number of basic features—highly qualified faculty; excellence in research results; quality of teaching and learning; high levels of government and nongovernment sources of funding; international and highly talented students; academic freedom; well-defined autonomous governance structures; and well-equipped facilities for teaching, research, administration, and often student life (Niland 2000, 2007; Altbach 2004; Khoon et al. 2005).

Recognizing the importance of the role of research universities in the fast-growing regions of Asia and Latin America, Altbach and Balán (2007) examined the development of these institutions in seven countries, focusing on what it takes to build research universities in challenging environments. The paths to research excellence were discussed, indicating many problems and possibilities involved with university development in Asian and Latin American contexts.

To propose a more manageable definition of top-research universities and to understand the foundations and circumstances of successful research universities, Salmi (2009) made the case that the superior results of these institutions—highly sought graduates, leading-edge research, and dynamic knowledge and technology transfer—could essentially be attributed to three complementary sets of factors at play in top research universities: (a) a high concentration of talent (faculty members and students); (b) abundant resources to offer a rich learning environment and to conduct advanced research; and (c) favorable governance features that encourage leadership, strategic vision, innovation, and flexibility and that enable institutions to make decisions and manage resources without being encumbered by bureaucracy. It is the dynamic interaction among these three groups of features that makes the difference as the distinguishing characteristic of high-ranking research universities, as illustrated in figure I.1.

Salmi (2009) also identified three major approaches that governments intent on setting up such institutions could follow. The first consists of upgrading a few existing universities that have the potential to excel (picking winners). The second relies on encouraging several existing institutions to merge and transform into a new university that would achieve the type of synergies corresponding to a world-class institution (hybrid formula). Finally, governments can decide to create new world-class universities from scratch (clean-slate approach).

The main chapters of this book are nine case studies that illustrate what it takes to establish and sustain research universities and help validate the analytical model outlined above, including the paths to building research excellence.

Figure I.1   Characteristics of a World-Class University: Alignment of Key Factors

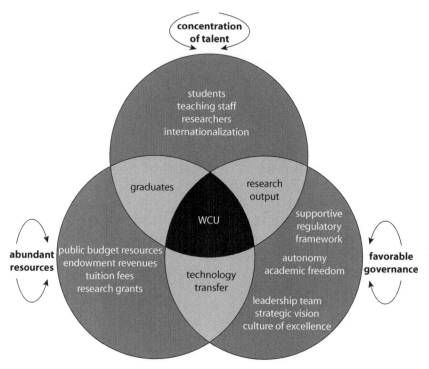

Source: Salmi 2009.
Note: WCU = world-class university.

The editors specifically selected these case studies with several criteria in mind. First, we tried to achieve a good regional balance by including examples from at least five regions on four continents: Latin America (Chile and Mexico), South Asia (India), East and Southeast Asia (China; Hong Kong SAR, China; the Republic of Korea; Malaysia; Singapore), eastern Europe (the Russian Federation), and Africa (Nigeria). Second, we included both public and private institutions. Third, we wanted the case studies to represent a mix of strategies, including upgrading existing universities and establishing entirely new institutions within the past two decades. Fourth, we selected institutions with a variety of academic configurations—some operating with a predominant focus on science and technology, others being comprehensive universities, and one of them stressing the social sciences. Finally, we selected three case studies with special emphases: chapter 8 on Chile compares the top two universities in the country, one public and one private; chapter 5 on the University of Malaya and the National University of Singapore offers a historical comparison, where two institutions were initially created as separate campuses of the same university and have had significantly different experiences since then; and chapter 7 on Nigeria, where the University of Ibadan represents an example of a flagship university that underwent a serious deterioration and is now embarking on a path back to excellence.

The institutions chosen for the case studies also represent a wide range of results regarding their scientific production and their position in the global university rankings, as illustrated by tables I.1 and I.2. Notwithstanding the methodological limitations of the rankings, they indicate the relative achievements of the various institutions studied in this book, showing that only seven out of the 11 institutions have already achieved a place in one of the top global rankings.

Different lessons emerge from the analysis of these case studies. Among the themes that seem to be important are leadership, government policy and funding, the ability to continually focus on a clear set of goals and institutional policies, development of a strong academic culture, and

Table I.1   Evolution of the Research Production of the Selected Institutions, 1999–2009

Institution	Number of articles published in top journals	
	1999	2009
University of Ibadan (Nigeria)	132	568
Shanghai Jiao Tong University	650	7,341
Pohang University of Science and Technology (Republic of Korea)	706	1,516
University of Chile	548	1,186
Pontifical Catholic University of Chile	385	1,153
Indian Institutes of Technology[a]	345	939
Hong Kong University of Science and Technology	949	1,857
University of Malaya	257	1,565
National University of Singapore	2,101	4,614
Monterrey Institute of Technology (Mexico)	55	242
Higher School of Economics (Russian Federation)	3	38

Source: Scopus database. The editors wish to thank SciVerse Scopus for graciously providing the data for this table.
a. The only Indian Institute of Technology (IIT) appearing in the rankings is the Kharagpur ITT, at 401–500 in the Academic Ranking of World Universities (ARWU).

Table I.2   Position of the Institutions Selected in the 2010 ARWU, HEAACT, and *THE* Rankings

Institution	ARWU	HEEACT	THE
University of Ibadan (Nigeria)	Not ranked	Not ranked	Not ranked
Shanghai Jiao Tong University	201–300	183	Not ranked
Pohang University of Science and Technology (Republic of Korea)	301–400	331	28
University of Chile	401–500	439	Not ranked
Pontifical Catholic University of Chile	401–500	428	Not ranked
Indian Institutes of Technology[a]	401–500	Not ranked	Not ranked
Hong Kong University of Science and Technology	201–300	323	41
University of Malaya	Not ranked	Not ranked	Not ranked
National University of Singapore	101–50	Not ranked	34
Monterrey Institute of Technology (Mexico)	Not ranked	Not ranked	Not ranked
Higher School of Economics (Russian Federation)	Not ranked	Not ranked	Not ranked

Sources: ARWU, http://www.arwu.org/ARWU2010.jsp; HEEACT, http://ranking.heeact.edu.tw/en-us/2010/TOP/100; *THE,* http://www.timeshighereducation.co.uk/world-university-rankings/2010-2011/top-200.html.
Note: ARWU = Academic Ranking of World Universities, HEEACT = Higher Education Evaluation and Accreditation Council of Taiwan, THE = Times Higher Education. Annex IA describes the methodology of these three leading rankings.
a. The only Indian Institute of Technology (IIT) appearing in the rankings is the Kharagpur ITT, at 401–500 in ARWU.

quality of the academic staff. These cases show that it is possible, in sometimes unpromising locations and against difficult challenges, to build successful research institutions. Some of the cases also illustrate that, because of unfavorable circumstances or other problems in the wider political, social, and economic context, efforts end in at least partial failure.

Annex IA Summary of the Methodology of the Three Leading International Rankings

The Academic Ranking of World Universities (ARWU), prepared by Shanghai Jiao Tong University, analyzes 3,000 universities and ranks the top 500 among them. Each institution is given an overall points scale and ranked relative to other institutions. ARWU uses the following indicators:

- Quality of education: alumni of an institution winning Nobel Prizes and Fields Medals (10 percent)
- Quality of faculty: (a) staff of an institution winning Nobel Prizes and Fields Medals (20 percent) and (b) highly cited researchers in 21 broad subject categories (20 percent)
- Research output: (a) papers published in *Nature and Science* (20 percent); and (b) papers indexed in Science Citation Index-expanded and Social Science Citation Index (20 percent)
- Per capita performance: per capita academic performance of an institution (10 percent) (defined as the weighted scores of the other five indicators divided by the number of full-time equivalent academic staff members)
  Academic Ranking of World Universities, http://www.arwu.org/AR-WU2010.jsp.

The Higher Education Evaluation and Accreditation Council of Taiwan (HEEACT) ranks 500 universities. An overall score is calculated for each university for each of eight indicators; for each indicator, the university with the highest number receives the maximum points; the other universities' numbers are subdivided and converted decimally into their respective scores. (HEEACT 2010).

The ranking is based on the following indicators:

- Research productivity: number of articles in the past 11 years (1998–2008) (10 percent); number of articles in the current year (10 percent)
- Research impact: number of citations in the past 11 years (10 percent)
- Number of citations in the past 2 years (10 percent)
- Average number of citations in the past 11 years (10 percent)
- Research excellence: H-index in the past 2 years (20 percent)
- Number of highly cited papers (15 percent)
- Number of articles in the current year in highly cited journals (15 percent)

Higher Education Evaluation and Accreditation Council of Taiwan, http://ranking.heeact.edu.tw/en-us/2010/TOP/100

Times Higher Education (THE) ranks 200 universities. An overall score is calculated for each university using 13 indicators classified into five categories:

- Industry income—innovation: institution's research income from industry scaled against the number of academic staff members (2.5 percent of the final ranking score)
- Teaching—the learning environment (five separate indicators): results of a reputational survey on teaching (15 percent); staff-to-student ratio (4.5 percent); ratio of PhD to bachelor's degrees awarded by each institution (2.25 percent); number of PhDs awarded by an institution, scaled against its size as measured by the number of academic staff members (6 percent); and institutional income scaled against academic staff numbers (2.25 percent)
- Citations—research influence: number of times a university's published work is cited by academics (32.5 percent)
- Research—volume, income, and reputation: results of a reputational survey (19.5 percent); university's research income, scaled against staff numbers and normalized for purchasing power parity (5.25 percent); number of papers published in the academic journals indexed by Thomson Reuters per staff member (4.5 percent); and public research income against an institution's total research income (0.75 percent)
- International mix—staff and students: ratio of international to domestic staff members (3 percent); and ratio of international to domestic students (2 percent)
  Times Higher Education, http://www.timeshighereducation.co.uk/world-university-rankings/2010-2011/analysis-methodology.html.

References

Altbach, Philip G. 2004. "The Costs and Benefits of World-Class Universities." *Academe* 90 (1): 20–23. http://www.aaup.org/AAUP/pubsres/academe/2004/JF/Feat/altb.htm.

Altbach, Philip G., and Jorge Balán. 2007. *World Class Worldwide: Transforming Research Universities in Asia and Latin America.* Baltimore: Johns Hopkins University Press.

Cookson, Clive. 2007. "Universities Drive Biotech Advancement." *Financial Times Europe*, May 6.

HEEACT (Higher Education Evaluation and Accreditation Council of Taiwan). 2010. "2010 by Subject Performance Ranking of Scientific Papers for World Universities: Score Calculation and Sorting." HEEACT, Taipei City, Taiwan, China. http://ranking.heeact.edu.tw/en-us/2010%20by%20Subject/Page/Score%20Calculation%20and%20Sorting.

Khoon, Koh Aik, Roslan Shukor, Osman Hassan, Zainuddin Saleh, Ainon Hamzah, and Rahim Hj. Ismail. 2005. "Hallmark of a World-Class University." *College Student Journal* 39 (4): 765–68. http://findarticles.com/p/articles/mi_m0FCR/is_4_39/ai_n16123684. Accessed April 10, 2007.

Niland, John. 2000. "The Challenge of Building World Class Universities in the Asian Region." On Line Opinion, February 3. http://www.onlineopinion.com.au/view.asp?article=997. Accessed April 10, 2006.

———. 2007. "The Challenge of Building World-class Universities." In *The World-Class University and Ranking: Aiming Beyond Status*, ed. Jan Sadlak and Nian Cai Liu, 61–71. Bucharest: UNESCO-CEPES.

Salmi, Jamil. 2009. The Challenge of Establishing World-Class Universities. Washington, DC: World Bank.

Scopus (database). Elsevier, Amsterdam. http://www.scopus.com/home.url.

World Bank. 2002. *Constructing Knowledge Societies: New Challenges for Tertiary Education*. Washington, DC: World Bank.

———. 2008. *Accelerating Catch-up: Tertiary Education for Growth in Sub-Saharan Africa*. Washington, DC: World Bank.

CHAPTER 1

The Past, Present, and Future of the Research University

Philip G. Altbach

Research universities stand at the center of the 21st-century global knowledge economy and serve as flagships for postsecondary education worldwide. *The Road to Academic Excellence* analyzes how research universities have developed and matured in 10 countries. They are elite, complex institutions with multiple academic and societal roles. They provide the key link between global science and scholarship and a nation's scientific and knowledge system. Research universities produce much of the new information and analysis that not only leads to important advances in technology but also contributes, just as significantly, to better understanding of the human condition through the social sciences and humanities. They are both national institutions that contribute to culture, technology, and society and international institutions that link to global intellectual and scientific trends. They are truly central institutions of the global knowledge society (Salmi 2009). This chapter provides a historical and global context to understand the development of the research universities reviewed in the case studies in this book.

As national institutions, research universities serve only a minority of undergraduate students, usually the nation's best and brightest, and employ the best-qualified academics. They are the central universities for educating students at the doctoral level and produce the bulk of the research output. Smaller countries may have only one research university, whereas larger nations may have many, although they are only a minority of the total tertiary education institutions in the country. In the United States, for example, there are perhaps 150 globally relevant research universities out of about 4,800 postsecondary institutions; India may have 10 such universities out of its 18,000 tertiary institutions, and China about 100 among its 5,000 or so postsecondary institutions.

Research universities produce the bulk of original research—both basic and applied, in most countries—and receive the most funding for research. Their professors are hired on the basis of their qualifications to conduct research and are rewarded for research prowess and productivity. The organization, reward structures, and, indeed, the academic culture of these universities focus on research. In the hierarchy of academic values, research ranks highest, although teaching and advisory services remain important. Most of the academic community, including the undergraduate students, often has the opportunity to participate in research and is exposed to the research culture.

Because of their unique academic mission, research universities require sustained support and favorable working conditions. Their budgets are larger than those of other universities and the cost per student is greater. Their financial support—largely from public sources in most countries—must be sustained if the institutions are to succeed. A considerable degree of autonomy—to make decisions about degrees, programs, and other academic matters—must be provided, and academic freedom is central.

To understand contemporary research universities, one should examine their global context in the 21st century, their historical underpinnings, recent developments, and future challenges.

The 21st-Century Global Context

Research universities are integral parts of the global higher education and societal environment (OECD 2009; Altbach, Reisberg, and Rumbley 2010). Key 21st-century realities for tertiary education worldwide include the massification of enrollment, the role of the private sector and the privatization of public higher education, the ongoing debate concerning public versus private good in higher education, the rise of Asian countries as academic centers, and, quite recently, the global economic crisis and its effect on higher education.

With annual enrollments in tertiary education of at least 30 percent of the eligible age cohort, massification of enrollment has been the central higher education reality of the past half-century. Since 2000, postsecondary enrollments have increased from 100 million to well over 150 million (OECD 2008) worldwide, and expansion continues in much of the world. Half of enrollment growth in the next two decades will occur in just two countries, China and India, but because these countries enroll only 22 percent and 10 percent, respectively, of the age group, they have considerable scope for expansion (Altbach 2009). Global expansion has been fueled by demand from an ever-growing segment of the population for access to the degrees believed to hold the promise of greater lifetime earnings and opportunities, and by the needs of the knowledge-based global economy. The implications of massification have been immense, however, with major financial implications, infrastructure challenges, questions about quality, and potentially diminished returns in labor markets with more university graduates than the economy can sustain.

The next notable phenomenon, private higher education, is not new, but its forms and effect are evolving quite rapidly. The nonprofit private sector has dominated much of East Asia for generations; Japan, the Republic of Korea; the Philippines; and Taiwan, China have educated between 60 and 80 percent of their students in private universities. The nonprofit private sector has been strong in the United States and many Latin American countries as well. Globally, Roman Catholic universities and other religious schools have long been key participants, often serving as the flagship quality institutions in their countries. In the United States, for example, the 217 Catholic four-year institutions account for 20 percent of enrollment in four-year private colleges and universities. Nearly 1,900 Roman Catholic colleges and universities operate worldwide.

A newer phenomenon is the for-profit private institutions that focus on teaching to meet the demands of students for specific fields of study, filling a niche that many public universities could not (Altbach 1999). Because research universities—except those in Japan and the United States—are almost exclusively public institutions, the rise of the private sector presents some challenges, mostly in terms of regulations and quality assurance, although private institutions seldom aspire to be research intensive. The challenge of ensuring that private higher education broadly serves the public interest is a key policy issue in tertiary education in the 21st century (Teixeira 2009).

It remains unclear how the economic crisis that started in 2008 will affect higher education in general and research universities in particular. There are examples in several countries of severe cutbacks in the funding of higher education generally, including the 20 percent budget cutbacks in the United Kingdom in 2010 and 2011 and the continuing state-imposed cuts in most of the U.S. states. Other than Japan, most Asian countries have not cut higher education budgets, and in fact, both China and India have responded to the crisis by adding funds to their tertiary education spending, particularly for research and development. Further, despite economic strains, continental Western Europe has not trimmed higher education budgets significantly.

The result of these spending decisions in the face of the economic crisis is unclear. The research universities subsector may be weakened, at least temporarily, in higher education systems in the major Anglo-Saxon countries—where public research universities prevail—while there is continuing strength in Asia and, to some extent, in continental Western Europe. The slow shift in the balance of academic strength from North America and Europe to East Asia may, in fact, be accelerated by these current economic trends and by differing approaches to spending on education, research, and development during a recession.

The relentless logic of the global knowledge economy and the realities of cross-border academic mobility also influence the direction of higher education generally and of the research university specifically (Marginson and van der Wende 2009a). The need for advanced education for a growing segment of the population, combined with the salience of research for economic development, has increased the profile of research universities. Both faculty members and students are increasingly recruited internationally, and mobility is now an established fact of contemporary higher education, especially affecting research universities.

Historical Background

Research has not always been a key function of academic institutions (Ben-David and Zloczower 1962). In fact, the contemporary research university dates back only to the beginning of the 19th century—specifically to Wilhelm von Humboldt's reformed University of Berlin (Fallon 1980). Before that, universities were largely devoted to teaching and to the preparation of professionals in fields such as law, medicine, and theology. Although the Humboldtian model brilliantly focused on research, it stressed research for national development and applied work as much as, if not more than, basic research. From this research model, the disciplinary structures emerged—with the development of fields such as chemistry and physics, as well as the social sciences, including economics and sociology.

Humboldt's university was a state institution—financed by the Prussian government. Academic staff members were state civil servants and had high social prestige and security of tenure. The structure of the academic profession was hierarchical and based on the chair system. The Humboldtian ideas of *Lernfreiheit* (freedom to learn) and *Lehrfreiheit* (freedom to teach) enshrined a great deal of autonomy and academic freedom in the university.

The Prussian government was supportive of this new university model because it promised to assist in national development and help Prussia— and, later, Germany—to achieve international power and influence. It is significant that the two countries that most enthusiastically adopted the Humboldtian model were Japan and the United States; both, particularly in the 19th and 20th centuries, were committed to national development and saw higher education as a contributor to that development.

The American variant of the German research university is particularly relevant (Geiger 2004a). In the latter 19th century, following the Land Grant acts, U.S. universities began to emphasize research, focusing on harnessing science for agriculture and its emerging industry. The U.S. research university varied from the German model in several important respects: (a) it emphasized service to society as a key value; (b) the organization of the academic profession was more democratic, using discipline-based departments rather than the hierarchy of the chair system; and (c) its governance and administrative arrangement was more participative (by the faculty) and more managerial (by deans and presidents who were appointed by trustees or governing boards rather than elected by peers).

The U.S. research university became the predominant global model by the middle of the 20th century (Geiger 1993, 2004a). Through a combination of significant expenditure on research—provided in part by the U.S. Department of Defense and related to Cold War military technology— strong support from the states, effective academic governance, creation of a differentiated academic system in most states that identified research universities at the top, and a vibrant nonprofit academic sector, U.S. research universities became the international "gold standard."

The "Spirit" of the Research University

A research university is not only an institution, but also an idea (Ben-David 1977; Shils 1997a). Creating and sustaining an institution based on a concept is not easy. At the heart of the research university is its academic staff, which must be committed to the idea of disinterested research—knowledge for its own sake—as well as to the more practical elements of research and its use in contemporary society.

A research university is elite and meritocratic in such areas as hiring and admissions policies, promotion standards, and degree requirements for staff members and students. However, terms like *elite* and *meritocratic* are not necessarily popular in a democratic age when access has been the key rallying cry of proponents of higher education for decades. Yet, for research universities to be successful, they must proudly proclaim these characteristics. Research universities cannot be democratic; they recognize the primacy of merit, and their decisions are based on a relentless pursuit of excellence. At the same time, they are elite institutions in the sense that they aspire to be the best—as often reflected in a top ranking—in teaching, research, and participation in the global knowledge network.

Students, too, are a central element of the spirit of the university. Not only are they, ideally, selected in a meritocratic way from among the brightest young people in society, and perhaps worldwide, but they also must have a commitment to the university's goals and to its academic ethos. A high level of performance is expected.

Although the research university is a central institution in the knowledge economy, it is also an institution that must allow time for reflection and critique and for a consideration of culture, religion, society, and values. The spirit of the research university is open to ideas and willing to challenge established orthodoxies.

And because research universities are firmly linked to society, they are not "ivory towers," a frequent criticism. Von Humboldt purposefully tied the university closely to the needs of state and society. An early president of the University of Wisconsin–Madison, a distinguished U.S. research university, claimed that "the border of the university is the border of the state" (Veysey 1965, 108–9). This statement symbolizes the ideal of serving the needs of society as well as the creation and dissemination of knowledge.

Another central element of the spirit of the research university—alongside its staff members and students—is the principle of academic freedom (Shils 1997b; Altbach 2007). Without academic freedom, a research university cannot fulfill its mission, nor can it be a *world-class* university. The traditional Humboldtian ideal of academic freedom is the freedom of academic staff members and students to pursue teaching, research, publication, and expression without restriction. In most parts of the world, the ideal of academic freedom has expanded to include expression on any topic or theme, even beyond the confines of specific scientific or scholarly expertise. The key element of academic freedom is the concept of open inquiry as a core value of the university.

A research university, especially one that aspires to the highest world standards, is a special institution based on a unique set of ideas and principles. Without a clear and continuing commitment to its own spirit, a research university will not succeed.

The Language of Science and Scholarship

Because universities are international institutions, with an openness to faculty and student flows and to borderless knowledge creation and dissemination, the language of science and scholarship is of central importance. For teaching and publishing, the earliest European universities used a common language—Latin. Even at that time, the universities saw themselves as international institutions, serving students from throughout Europe and often hiring professors from a variety of countries. Knowledge circulated through the medium of Latin. Two key tasks in those early years were translating books from Arabic and Greek into Latin and introducing this knowledge to Europe. Later, as a result of the Protestant Reformation, national languages began to dominate universities in their home countries, and the universities became national, rather than international, institutions.

French was a central language of scholarship during the Age of Enlightenment and the Napoleonic Era. German became a key scientific language with the rise of the research university in the 19th century, and many of the new scientific journals were published in German. Following World War II, English slowly gained influence as the major language of scientific communication with the rise of the U.S. research university and the expansion of university systems in (a) English-speaking countries such as Australia, Canada, New Zealand, and the United Kingdom; and (b) former British colonies including India and Pakistan in South Asia and Ghana, Kenya, Nigeria, South Africa, and Zimbabwe in Africa. In Asia, Hong Kong[1] and Singapore emerged as academic powerhouses that used English in their universities.

By the beginning of the 21st century, English had emerged as the nearly universal medium of scientific communication (Lillis and Curry 2010). Today, universities in non-English-speaking countries are to varying degrees using English as a language of instruction in certain fields.

For example, in many Arabic-speaking countries, as well as in China and Korea, English is used as the language of instruction in scientific areas and in professional fields such as business administration. In Malaysia, which previously had emphasized the use of Bahasa Malaysia as the language of instruction, English has returned as a major teaching language. On the European continent, English is used for teaching in fields deemed most globally relevant and mobile, such as business and engineering.

Most influential academic journals and scientific websites are published in English, and universities in many parts of the world encourage or even demand that their professors publish in English-medium journals as evidence of quality scholarship. Many arguments exist concerning the advisability of this emphasis on the use of English for communication and academic advancement. Yet, in fact, English is now the global language of science and scholarship and is likely to remain dominant for the foreseeable future. Some analysts (Lillis and Curry 2010) have pointed out that academics worldwide are forced to use the methodologies and paradigms of the main English-medium journals, which reflect the values of the editors and boards in the United Kingdom, the United States, and other metropolitan countries. For authors whose first language is not English, acceptance of their work by these influential publications is notably more difficult. The top-ranking journals are increasingly selective, accepting only 5 to 10 percent of submissions, as universities worldwide demand that their scholars and scientists publish in these journals.

The influence of English on research, teaching, and scholarship in the 21st century is one of the realities of research universities worldwide, as illustrated by several case studies presented in this book. In some ways, English is also the language of academic neocolonialism in the sense that scholars everywhere are under pressure to conform to the norms and values of the metropolitan academic systems that use English.

A Special Kind of Professor

The academic community, as noted previously, is the steward of any research university. Thus, the academics need to be well educated to perform their teaching and research responsibilities at the highest levels. Their commitment to the culture of research requires a strong resolution as well. Academic staff members of research universities typically hold a doctorate or its equivalent, usually having studied at the top universities in their home countries or abroad—not the norm for the academic profession in many countries.

The research university professor, like the institution itself, is both competitive and collaborative. These academics are imbued with a desire to contribute to science and scholarship both to advance the field and to build a career and reputation. At the same time, they often work in teams, especially in the sciences, and understand the importance of collaboration.

Research university professors contribute by far the largest amount of scholarly and scientific research articles and books. Their publication rates are far above the average for the academic profession (Haas 1996). Indeed, perhaps 90 percent of the articles appearing in the top-ranked academic journals are likely written by professors in the research-intensive universities.

In a world where many academics work part-time and do not enjoy much job security, research university professors have full-time employment, for the most part with reasonable security of tenure, and are paid adequate if not lavish salaries that can support themselves and their families. In other words, research university professors are, in comparison to their peers, privileged academics. For a research university to be successful, the academics must enjoy conditions of employment that will permit them to do their best work.

Research university professors typically have modest teaching responsibilities; they are given the time to undertake and publish research. In most developed-country research universities, teaching responsibilities seldom include more than two courses per semester and, in some institutions and in some disciplines, can be fewer than two. Where teaching assignments are greater, as is the case in many developing countries, research commitment and productivity tend to be lower.

Research university professors tend to be international in their consciousness and often in their work. They increasingly collaborate with colleagues in different countries and are sometimes internationally mobile, accepting jobs where working conditions, salaries, and facilities are best. This situation contributes to a "brain drain" from developing countries. However, as begun in recent years, internationally minded academics function in more than one country, sometimes holding academic appointments in two or more countries. At the same time, research university professors operate in a national environment—they are, of course, employed by national institutions—and they are expected to fulfill local and national responsibilities. Like the ancient Roman god Janus, they must look in several directions at once.

These academics are also cosmopolitan rather than local in their interests and activities (Gouldner 1957). Their professional ties tend to be with colleagues in their discipline around the world rather than with col-leagues at their home university. They participate directly in the global knowledge network by attending scientific conferences, working jointly with colleagues abroad, and participating actively in cross-border scientific communication. Typically, they are less loyal to their home universities and are willing to move, sometimes abroad, if better working conditions, salaries, or higher prestige is offered. And because of their scientific visi-bility, they often have greater opportunities for such mobility. Sociologist Burton Clark once noted that academics inhabit "small worlds, different worlds" (Clark 1987).

Academics working at research universities are a small but extraor-dinarily key part of the total academic profession. Despite their small numbers, they produce most of the important research. In many countries, they educate most of the academic profession. Thus, their orientations and perspectives have considerable influence on the academic profession as a whole. They are, indeed, a rare and special breed.

Governance and Leadership

Governance, as distinct from management, concerns how academic deci-sions are made. Postsecondary institutions of all kinds are both managed and led. Moreover, they are, at their best, communities of scholars. Universities are, of course, increasingly large bureaucracies with complex management needs (Shattock 2010); yet, they differ significantly from other large organizations in several key ways. First, to be successful, uni-versities must include those who teach and do research (the academic community) in the decision making (the governance) of the institution (Rosovsky 1990). Research universities especially need the full involve-ment of the academic staff in the key decision-making arrangements of the institution. Research universities typically have a greater degree of professorial power and stronger guarantees of academic autonomy than other academic institutions. Second, students, although not necessarily involved directly in governance, must also be included as key stakeholders in the academic community.

Academic leadership is of increasing importance in an era of complex and highly visible academic organizations. The role of the university president, vice chancellor, or rector is managerial and academic. Some have argued that university presidents should be top scholars, whereas others favor successful managers, sometimes from outside of academe, as university leaders (Goodall 2009). In research universities, presidents must have academic credibility and must display a deep knowledge of and respect for the academic mission of the institution. At the same time, they must be able to represent the university in society and must make the case for the centrality and importance of the institution. Modern academic leadership is an increasingly complex and multifaceted task, and finding talented leaders is difficult.

The substantive academic prerogatives—control over admittance, the hiring and firing of professors, the curriculum, and the awarding of degrees—are at the core of professorial responsibilities. The best contemporary universities have shared governance, with the academic community in control of essential academic decisions and the administrators and managers responsible for resources, facilities, and other administrative matters. Academic governance models vary across research universities. Representative bodies of the academic community, sometimes including students, are typical. The traditional European model of control by the senior professors, who also elected the rector from among their ranks for short terms of office, is perhaps no longer practical, in light of the myriad skills (noted previously) demanded of an effective university leader. Regardless, for assurance of the primacy of scholarship, teaching, and research, the academic community must have a significant role in shaping and supervising the key academic elements of the research university.

Basic versus Applied Research

Research universities conduct research in many fields and disciplines. They are the main sources of basic research, joined in a few countries by private corporations (such as pharmaceutical companies) and scientific academies, and thus have key responsibility for the scientific advancement. Basic research is a quintessential public-good function; no one earns a direct profit from basic science. Moreover, fundamental research, particularly in the hard sciences and biomedical fields, is often expensive. The funding of basic science has become problematical in many countries. In the social sciences and humanities, where research is less expensive, questions have nonetheless been raised about its usefulness.

At the same time, there has been more stress on applied research, on university-industry links, and, in general, on income-producing research products. Conflict between the traditional academic goals of the university and the desire to earn income from research, often from corporate enterprises, has created conflicts of interest and occasionally inappropriate relationships (Slaughter and Rhoades 2004). Shaping an appropriate balance to avoid downgrading basic research in the rush for financial stability will be a difficult task.

The California Master Plan for Higher Education

The U.S. research university model is widely considered the gold standard and is emulated globally. The quintessential U.S. public research universities are those of the University of California system. The California Master Plan for Higher Education of 1960 constitutes an effective way of organizing a differentiated public higher education system to cater to research excellence as well as to access and massification. Clark Kerr, chancellor of the University of California, Berkeley, campus and, later, president of the University of California system between 1952 and 1967, was central to both the creation of the Master Plan and the development of the University of California system and its flagship Berkeley campus (Kerr 2001; Pelfrey 2004).

The California Master Plan established the three-tiered California public higher education system, with three systems clearly differentiated by function but linked through system articulation. This arrangement has successfully operated for more than a half-century. At the top tier of the system are the 10 campuses of the University of California. These universities, led by the Berkeley campus, admit the top eighth of high school students in the state and have a research mission. The next tier consists of the 23-campus California State University system, which enrolls about 433,000 students. These institutions offer bachelor's and master's degrees, but not doctorates, and academic staff members are not expected to maintain a research intensity on par with the academics in the University of California system. The third tier, the community-college system, has 112 campuses with 3 million students—the largest such system in the United States. Colleges in this tier have teaching and service at their core and little to no research capacity or expectations. Funding patterns, missions, and governance all differ among the three tiers of the California system, and state regulation has maintained the different missions of the public colleges and universities. The Master Plan imposed differentiation across California public higher education and remains a defining and effective innovation that has served the state well for more than a half-century. By distributing resources with a core ideal of efficiency, the Master Plan also institutionalized a commitment to excellence in its best research universities, such as the University of California, Berkeley.

Clark Kerr, the architect of the Master Plan, had a vision of the key characteristics for the system's research universities, and these elements are central to the University of California, Berkeley, one of the world's finest universities. First, the internal governance of the university is mainly in the hands of the professors; key decisions concerning academic policy and direction, even if initiated by administrators, receive input from the academics. This concept of shared governance is central to the idea of the university. Second, the Berkeley campus is rigorously meritocratic in all its actions—appointment and promotion of faculty, student admissions, and other aspects. Third, although research and teaching are intertwined, research has the upper hand. Fourth, academic freedom is a central value of the academic community. Fifth, the service mission of the university has always been of central importance. From the beginning, the university has been engaged with society, particularly with the state of California.

Until recently, the University of California has received relatively generous funding from the state of California, with each campus funded independently, according to institutional mission and size. Now, with recent budget cuts, the state contribution to the Berkeley operating budget is approximately a quarter of what is needed, although it does pay the salaries of almost all faculty members. The university's remaining income derives from student tuition and fees, research grants and income, the sale of intellectual property, and other sources. This level of state support is now typical of some of the top-ranked public universities and is indicative of a decline in state support for public higher education in the United States. California is, of course, not alone in facing severe, and probably long-lasting, financial and other problems (Lyall and Sell 2006), and the negative effect of the current financial crisis has been seen throughout its entire higher education system.

Like most research universities, the University of California, Berkeley, is simultaneously international, national, and local. It has a wide international reach, recruiting staff members and students from around the world. The university's academic departments and centers are concerned with international issues in all disciplines. Its national influence includes engaging in research supported by national agencies and hosting laboratories sponsored by the federal government. Less well known are the university's efforts to provide service to the statewide and local communities through special educational programs including nondegree courses, community outreach, and similar efforts.

Clark Kerr was aware of the challenges of his model of the university. In an epilogue to his classic book, *The Uses of the University* (2001), he pointed to, among other things, what he called "state penury" in the context of expansion of both enrollments and research, the effect of information technology, the rise of the for-profit private sector, demographic changes, variations in the economic benefits of academic degrees, and other challenges.

The Present Circumstances of the Research University

To paraphrase Charles Dickens, these are the best of times and the worst of times for research universities. There is widespread recognition of the importance of the research university in almost every country. The salience of international academic connections and the role of research in the global knowledge economy are understood as central to sustainable economic growth and stability. However, many countries do not recognize the complexity of and the resources needed for building and sustaining research universities (Salmi 2009).

The early 21st century is now a period of emergence of research universities in countries where they have not existed before and the strengthening of current institutions. It is also a time of the internationalization of the research university.

Some of the characteristics of successful research universities, as defined by their placement in top echelons of the global rankings, can be outlined as follows:

- All successful research universities are part of a differentiated academic system in which they stand at the top of an academic hierarchy and receive appropriate support for their mission.

- Research universities, except in Japan and the United States, are overwhelmingly public institutions. The private sector can seldom support a research university, although private research universities are emerging among some of the Roman Catholic universities in Latin America and in Turkey.

- Research universities are most successful where little or no competition arises from nonuniversity research institutes or where strong ties exist between the universities and such institutes. Although this situation may appear counterintuitive, because competition could be good for sparking innovation in research, the dilution of research between universities and research institutes can also weaken the talent pool, removing top researchers from the classroom and the campus and limiting capacity for interdisciplinary work. The academy of science system in countries such as China and the Russian Federation, the Centre National de la Recherche Scientifique in France, and some other models of distinct research institutes generally lack such connections to universities. There are efforts in some countries to better integrate research institutes and top universities—in some cases, merging them—with the goal of strengthening the universities.

- Research universities are expensive institutions. They require more funding than other universities to attract the best staff members and students and to provide the infrastructure necessary for top research and teaching. The cost per student is inevitably higher than the average across an entire higher education system. Adequate salaries for faculty, well-equipped libraries and laboratories, and scholarship assistance for bright but needy students are examples of the expenditures required.

- Research universities must have adequate and sustained budgets; they cannot succeed on the basis of inadequate funding or severe budgetary fluctuation over time.

- At the same time, research universities have the potential for significant income generation. Students are often willing to pay higher tuition and fees to these institutions because of the prestige attached to their degrees, the high quality of academic programs, and access to the best professors. Current debates in the United Kingdom and in some U.S. states, concerning higher tuition for education at research universities than at other postsecondary institutions, reflect both the need for more revenues and the likely success of differential tuition fees. Research universities also generate intellectual property and other discoveries and innovations that have value in the marketplace. In addition, in some countries research universities—in part because of their prestige—can generate philanthropic gifts to help build an endowment for the university.

- Research universities require physical facilities commensurate with their missions, which means expensive teaching spaces, libraries, and laboratories. Sophisticated information technology is also required. The infrastructures of research universities are both complex and expensive to build, maintain, and periodically upgrade.

The requirements of a research university are manifold, as noted previously: They are physical and human, but also contain principles relating to academic work, including teaching, research, service, and academic standards.

Current and Future Challenges

Research universities face many of the same challenges as higher education generally, although with somewhat different characteristics. The issues discussed here, of course, affect countries and institutions in different ways but will, to some extent, be felt everywhere. Much that can be learned from national and comparative experiences in dealing with these and other issues.

Funding

Central to the success of a research university is adequate and stable funding. Research universities will increasingly be challenged to raise their own funds from potential donors, through the sale of intellectual products and consulting, and increasingly from student tuition and fees. Research universities have more potential to charge higher tuition than do other postsecondary institutions. The private research universities in the United States already do so. However, most public research universities worldwide are not permitted to charge higher fees because of historical compacts or legislative restrictions even in light of the higher costs of education and the willingness of students to pay more for a better and more prestigious degree from a research university. As noted earlier, a debate about these issues is taking place in the United Kingdom and in some U.S. states. It is clear that research universities cost more and that they need to be able to raise funds without relying entirely on the largess of government.

The global economic crisis of the early 21st century has had a significant effect on research universities. As noted earlier, its effects vary across the globe, but the overall result may potentially be a boost to East Asia's universities. East Asian countries have weathered the economic storm in better shape than their Western counterparts, and they seek to join the top ranks of the global research elite. For example, India has increased its higher education investment by 31 percent since 2010, and China has continued to fund its excellence programs in support of the nation's leading universities.

Autonomy

In an era of growing accountability, research universities will be challenged to maintain their management autonomy and to control their essential academic decision making. Research universities are in the uncomfortable position of being, for the most part, state institutions subject to bureaucratic rules and parts of complex bureaucratic academic systems. Although research universities require autonomy in charting their own paths to excellence and in managing their resources, accountability pressures to prove value added and relevance to their myriad stakeholders are encroaching on historic autonomy norms for many research universities.

The Best and the Brightest

National research universities will be increasingly challenged to attract top talent, both professors and students, in an increasingly competitive global academic marketplace. Universities compete not only with other universities, but also with a growing and often well-paid knowledge sector outside the campus, and they find that academic salaries often do not match remuneration outside the universities. Top academics are lured abroad from developing and middle-income countries, as well. In recent years, the best students have also been attracted to top universities overseas by scholarships, excellent academic conditions, and prestige. Although it is difficult to retain professors, universities that can offer at least modestly competitive salaries and good working conditions can be reasonably successful in keeping superior talent. But it is a constant struggle in every country.

Privatization

Research universities, as has been noted, are public institutions in almost all countries. The pressures toward the privatization of the public universities—as a result of reduced public funding—exist nearly everywhere. This trend is for the most part damaging to the research universities because these institutions are mainly engaged in public-good activities such as basic research and the instruction of students in a wide range of disciplines. If research universities are forced to look to the market to pay professors and cover associated expenses, this policy has the genuine potential to damage the quality and focus of their research and detract from their core missions (Geiger 2004b). The tension between fundraising and academic autonomy must be managed carefully.

Globalization

Globalization is both a benefit and a curse to research universities (Knight 2008; Marginson and van der Wende 2009b). Research universities are at the center of global knowledge communication and networks. They funnel new ideas and knowledge into the higher education system and the country as well, and they permit the academic community to participate in international science and scholarship. In the age of the Internet, individuals anywhere can take advantage of global knowledge, but the resources and academic community of research universities make international participation easier and more effective. In many countries, research universities may be the only institutions adequately linked to global networks. Thus, research universities provide a two-way street for scientific participation.

At the same time, for many universities globalization constitutes a challenge. The global academic marketplace for professors and students means that the best students and staff members can be enticed away. Overreliance on international core journals for promotion and research criteria may place professors in peripheral research universities at a disadvantage. Globalization tends to favor universities at the center over others; it does not necessarily contribute to the democratization of science and scholarship.

The Future of the Research University

Because research universities are central institutions in any knowledge- and technology-intensive society and because they are seen as the key to a world-class higher education system, their future is reasonably bright. The fact is that modern societies cannot do without them.

Those who argue that the contemporary university will be fundamentally transformed by distance education and technology, mass enrollments, increasing vocationalization, privatization, or the current financial crisis have a point. The early 21st century is a period of both crisis and transformation for higher education globally. And it is entirely possible that some sectors of higher education will change fundamentally.

However, one sector of higher education is unlikely to be dramatically altered—the research universities. These institutions have the power of tradition, and they are quite good at what they accomplish. They will, without doubt, be changed in some ways, but the research university in 2050 is unlikely to be fundamentally different from such institutions today.

Establishing research universities in countries where they do not exist or upgrading existing universities to serve as research universities is a worldwide phenomenon (Mohrman, Ma, and Baker 2008). This is not at all surprising. To fully participate in the global knowledge economy and to benefit from science and scholarship, countries and academic systems believe they must have at least one research university that is able to function at a world-class level (Deem, Mok, and Lucas 2007). Thus, the community of research universities is rapidly expanding from the traditional academic centers in Europe and North America to developing and emerging economies worldwide (Liu, Wang, and Cheng 2011). Whether this provides the most-efficient means for development in countries at differing stages of economic growth is an important consideration often lost in the race to build a great university in every country. In small and fragile states, for instance, economies of scale may point toward greater efficiencies through excellent regional institutions. Regardless, the recognition of the importance of research universities is nearly universal.

There are no secrets concerning creating or sustaining research universities. Not surprisingly, many countries seeking to establish such institutions look to successful research universities in the academic centers. As a result, an informal global research model has emerged—emulating the U.S. research university especially. Appropriately, the global model inevitably takes on national characteristics to reflect the particular academic and societal realities of local circumstances. The variations that can be seen among successful new research universities reflect this informal global model with national and local variations. Regardless of the problems and challenges facing higher education in the coming period, the research university will remain a central element of every higher education system and a requirement of most economies.

Note

1. Hong Kong is used in historical contexts prior to July 1, 1997.

References and Other Sources

Altbach, Philip G., ed. 1999. *Private Prometheus: Private Higher Education and Development in the 21st Century.* New York: Praeger.

———. 2007. "Academic Freedom: International Realities and Challenges." In *Tradition and Transition: The International Imperative in Higher Education,* 49–66. Rotterdam, The Netherlands: Sense.

————. 2009. "The Giants Awake: The Present and Future of Higher Education Systems in China and India." In *Higher Education to 2030*. Vol. 2 of *Globalization*, ed. Organisation for Economic Co-operation and Development (OECD), 179–204. Paris: OECD.

Altbach, Philip G., Liz Reisberg, and Laura E. Rumbley. 2010. *Trends in Global Higher Education: Tracking an Academic Revolution*. Rotterdam, The Netherlands: Sense.

Ben-David, Joseph. 1977. *Centers of Learning: Britain, France, Germany, United States*. New York: McGraw-Hill.

Ben-David, Joseph, and Awraham Zloczower. 1962. "Universities and Academic Systems in Modern Society." *European Journal of Sociology* 3 (1): 45–84.

Clark, Burton R. 1987. *The Academic Life: Small Worlds, Different Worlds*. Princeton, NJ: Carnegie Foundation for the Advancement of Teaching.

————, ed. 1993. *The Research Foundations of Graduate Education: Germany, Britain, France, United States, Japan*. Berkeley: University of California Press.

————. 1995. *Places of Inquiry: Research and Advanced Education in Modern Universities*. Berkeley: University of California Press.

Deem, Rosemary, Ka Ho Mok, and Lisa Lucas. 2007. "Transforming Higher Education in Whose Image? Exploring the Concept of the 'World-Class' University in Europe and Asia." *Higher Education Policy* 21 (March): 83–98.

Fallon, Daniel. 1980. *The German University: A Heroic Ideal in Conflict with the Modern World*. Boulder: Colorado Associated University Press.

Geiger, Roger L. 1993. *Research and Relevant Knowledge: American Research Universities Since World War II*. New York: Oxford University Press.

————. 2004a. *To Advance Knowledge: The Growth of American Research Universities, 1900–1940*. New Brunswick, NJ: Transaction.

————. 2004b. *Knowledge and Money: Research Universities and the Paradox of the Marketplace*. Stanford, CA: Stanford University Press.

Goodall, Amanda H. 2009. *Socrates in the Boardroom: Why Research Universities Should Be Led by Top Scholars*. Princeton, NJ: Princeton University Press.

Gouldner, Alvin. 1957. "Cosmopolitans and Locals: Toward an Analysis of Latent Social Roles–I." *Administrative Science Quarterly* 2: 281–303.

Haas, J. Eugene. 1996. "The American Academic Profession." In *The International Academic Profession: Portraits of Fourteen Countries*, ed. Philip G. Altbach, 343–90. Princeton, NJ: Carnegie Foundation for the Advancement of Teaching.

Kerr, Clark. 2001. *The Uses of the University*. Cambridge, MA: Harvard University Press.

Knight, Jane. 2008. *Higher Education in Turmoil: The Changing World of Internationalization*. Rotterdam, The Netherlands: Sense.

Lillis, Theresa, and Mary Jane Curry. 2010. *Academic Writing in a Global Context: The Politics and Practices of Publishing in English*. New York: Routledge.

Liu, Nian Cai, Qi Wang, and Ying Cheng, eds. 2011. *Paths to a World-Class University: Lessons from Practices and Experiences*. Rotterdam, The Netherlands: Sense.

Lyall, Katherine C., and Kathleen R. Sell. 2006. *The True Genius of America at Risk: Are We Losing Our Public Universities to de Facto Privatization?* Westport, CT: Praeger.

Marginson, Simon, and Marijk van der Wende. 2009a. "Europeanization, International Rankings, and Faculty Mobility: Three Cases in Higher Education Globalization." In *Higher Education to 2030*. Vol. 2 of *Globalization*, ed. Organisation for Economic Co-operation and Development (OECD), 109–41. Paris: OECD.

———. 2009b. "The New Global Landscape of Nations and Institutions." In *Higher Education to 2030*. Vol. 2 of *Globalization*, ed. Organisation for Economic Co-operation and Development (OECD), 17–62. Paris: OECD.

Mohrman, Kathryn, Wanhua Ma, and David Baker. 2008. "The Research University in Transition: The Emerging Global Model." *Higher Education Policy* 21 (March): 5–28.

Nerad, Maresi, and Mimi Heggelund, eds. 2008. *Toward a Global PhD? Forces and Forms in Doctoral Education Worldwide*. Seattle: University of Washington Press.

OECD (Organisation for Economic Co-operation and Development). 2008. *Higher Education to 2030*. Vol. 1 of *Demography*. Paris: OECD.

———. 2009. *Higher Education to 2030*. Vol. 2 of *Globalization*. Paris: OECD.

Pelfrey, Patricia. 2004. *A Brief History of the University of California*. Berkeley, CA: University of California Press.

Rosovsky, Henry. 1990. *The University: An Owner's Manual*. New York: Norton.

Salmi, Jalmi. 2009. *The Challenge of Establishing World-Class Universities*. Washington, DC: World Bank.

Shattock, Michael. 2010. *Managing Successful Universities*. Maidenhead, U.K.: McGraw-Hill.

Shils, Edward. 1997a. "The Academic Ethos Under Strain." In *The Order of Learning: Essays on the Contemporary University*, ed. Edward Shils, 99–136. New Brunswick, NJ: Transaction.

———. 1997b. "Academic Freedom." In *The Order of Learning: Essays on the Contemporary University*, ed. Edward Shils, 217–47. New Brunswick, NJ: Transaction.

Slaughter, Sheila, and Gary Rhoades. 2004. *Academic Capitalism and the New Economy: Markets, State, and Higher Education.* Baltimore: Johns Hopkins University Press.

Teixeira, Pedro. 2009. "Mass Higher Education and Private Institutions." In *Higher Education to 2030.* Vol. 2 of *Globalization,* ed. Organisation for Economic Co-operation and Development, 231–58. Paris: OECD.

Veysey, Laurence R. 1965. *The Emergence of the American University.* Chicago: University of Chicago Press.

Walker, George E., Chris M. Golde, Laura Jones, Andrea Conklin Bueschel, and Pat Hutchings. 2008. *The Formation of Scholars: Rethinking Doctoral Education for the 21st Century.* San Francisco: Jossey-Bass.

CHAPTER 2

Building World-Class Universities in China: Shanghai Jiao Tong University

Qing Hui Wang, Qi Wang, and Nian Cai Liu

A research university with world-class capacity, often called a *world-class university*, is regarded as a central part of any academic system and is imperative to developing a nation's competitiveness in the global knowledge economy. The Chinese government (in this chapter, China, or Chinese, refers to mainland China), with no exception, has stated its goal to develop a tertiary education system of international stature with a number of research universities and research centers of excellence. In response to this policy agenda and Shanghai's strategic plans, Shanghai Jiao Tong University (SJTU), a leading Chinese university, is dedicated to achieving a quality standard that transcends national borders and to building itself into a world-class research and higher education institution. This chapter explores how SJTU has developed in the past 10 years in the context of the growing imperatives of the globalized knowledge economy and national policy directives.

National Perspectives and History

The development of world-class research universities has been a dream of the Chinese people that can be traced to the end of the 19th century, when a few of the earliest Chinese universities were established to promote higher education and to develop the nation. The specific goal to build up globally prominent universities has been strongly advocated over the past 10 years in China. The Chinese government adopted that goal as a national policy priority in 1998, and success is considered plausible in several regions of the country. First, the higher education expansion in the past 20 years has produced a great quantity of highly skilled workers. However, only one-tenth of the engineering graduates are qualified to work in multinational companies, according to the *McKinsey Quarterly* (Lauder, Brown, and Ashton 2008). Thus, China is unable to compete in higher-value industries. In that sense, research universities can develop knowledge and train talent to compete in the global knowledge economy (Wang 2008). Second, knowledge is the most important factor in developing a nation's competitiveness in the era of the global knowledge economy. According to *The Global Competitiveness Report 2009–2010* (Schwab 2009), China, in general, showed progress in its economic development prospects; however, the report indicated that improvement was needed in the areas of higher education training, technological readiness, financial market sophistication, and innovation. Improvement, particularly of the competitiveness pillar of innovation, will depend on the role of research universities in creating and managing knowledge. Third, from the perspective of higher education development, China currently has more doctoral students enrolled in its universities than anywhere in the world. Despite the significant size by international standards, the quality of graduate education in China is still in doubt. The development of a number of world-class research universities can further enhance the overall quality of graduate education in the country. With this goal in mind, the government has launched a group of specific national initiatives, including the 211 Project and the 985 Project.

In 1995, the Ministry of Education and the Ministry of Finance issued a document called "The '211 Project' Planning." The 211 Project aims at developing 100 universities by the early 21st century that will take a leading position in the country's economic and social development and in international competition. This national initiative focuses mainly on four aspects of development: disciplinary and interdisciplinary programs, digital campuses, faculty, and university infrastructure. The central government, local governments, and selected universities themselves invested Y 36.83 billion (about US$5.44 billion)—Y 19.61 billion (about US$2.90 billion) in the first phase of the project (1996–2000) and Y 17.22 billion (about US$2.54 billion) in the second phase (2002–07). The total support from the central government was Y 7.84 billion (about US$1.16 billion). For the period 1996–2007, 45 percent of the total financial support was invested in disciplinary development, 29 percent in infrastructure development, 19 percent in digital campus development, and 7 percent in faculty development (Ministerial Office of 211 Project 2007). Currently, the 211 Project is in its third phase.

To further enhance the public funds for higher education, the government launched the 985 Project. That project again reflects the government's goal and efforts to develop a tertiary education system of international stature. On May 4, 1998, President Jiang Zemin declared that "universities should play a critical role in implementing the strategy of invigorating the country through science, technology and education," and "China should have several world-class universities of international standard." To put this idea into practice, the Ministry of Education (1998) issued "The Action Plan for Education Revitalization for the 21st Century" and developed the 985 Project to establish a number of research universities and key research centers of excellence.

The 985 Project has thus far supported 39 selected universities, with financial investment from both the central government and the local government. The project has been implemented in two phases. The first phase ran from 1999 to 2001, and the second from 2004 to 2007. As stated in the accompanying policy document, nine of these universities, considered the "Chinese Ivy League," were on the top of the list and were designated to be developed into "world-class" universities.[1] The remaining 30 institutions were expected to become "world-known" universities (that is, they would have a slightly lower level of achievement but would maintain an international reputation) (Ministry of Education 2008). The total financial support from the central government created Y 14.0 billion (about US$2.07 billion) and Y 18.9 billion (about US$2.79 billion), respectively, in these two phases. More than half of the central government funding in the 985 Project was invested in the top nine universities.

The 985 Project has provided the participating institutions with governance autonomy to improve their national and international competitiveness and to narrow the gap in academic achievement, research performance, and science innovation with other leading research universities in the world (Liu, Liu, et al. 2003). Reforms have been carried out to develop the universities' governance, in terms of administration, management, and staff capacity. Teaching and research have been improved. For example, the participating institutions focus on enhancing their specialized subject areas and on developing their capacity to meet world-class standards. Key national research bases for humanities and the social sciences and major national science and engineering laboratories were established to enhance future research. The top nine universities have also drastically increased the number and quality of their international publications.[2] In turn, the top nine institutions have greatly improved their world rank.[3] These experiences and achievements reached in the first two 985 Project phases are critical for the realization of further development in the third phase. More detailed data and cases in relation to SJTU will be examined later in the chapter.

In general, implementation of the 211 Project and the 985 Project has had significant effects on the development of higher education in China and of higher skills. The projects have created a culture of excellence and have built an awareness of international competition and competitiveness in Chinese universities. The selected universities have played an increasingly critical role, both in rejuvenating higher education as a whole and in implementing socioeconomic reform in China. Their development offers the opportunity for an open discussion to improve higher education quality and explore potential routes to build research universities in China.

Overview of SJTU and Its Practices

Founded in 1896, SJTU is one of the oldest universities in China. The Ministry of Education of China and the Shanghai municipal government jointly operate the university. It is one of the top five universities in China and one of the top two universities in the city of Shanghai, according to the recent major national rankings, and was selected as one of the top nine universities in the first phase of the 985 Project.

From the early to mid-20th century, SJTU was an engineering-focused institute, specializing in transportation, post and telecommunications, print technologies, and national security and defense. Nurturing top engineering talents, SJTU was known as "the Eastern MIT" in the 1930s. In 1956, it was significantly rearranged when the central government decided to transfer a large number of faculty members to Xi'an to build another top engineering school in Shaanxi Province, in northwest China.

Following this rearrangement, the university was officially named Shanghai Jiao Tong University. During the 1960s and 1970s, SJTU was affiliated to the Commission of Science, Technology and Industry for National Defense, developing relevant research and human resources in national defense. After a period of stagnation during the Cultural Revolution, the university was directly subordinated to the Ministry of Education in 1982. Since the 1980s, SJTU has been conducting a series of reforms and development efforts in governance, teaching and research, and infrastructure. Its subject areas have been rebuilt and expanded, and it currently boasts 21 academic schools and departments and 65 subject areas covering economics, law, the arts, social sciences, natural sciences, engineering, agriculture, medicine, and management. The university supports 60 undergraduate programs, 152 master's programs, and 93 doctoral programs. At present, it has about 18,500 undergraduate students, 11,326 master's students, 4,576 doctoral students, and more than 10,000 professional students. SJTU has 3,130 full-time teaching and research staff members, 65 percent of whom have a PhD.

In 1996, during its centennial, SJTU put forward a "three-step" plan to develop into a world-class research university by the mid-21st century. Since then, the university has been continuously creating and modifying a series of institutional strategic plans. The individual schools and departments were also required to create their specific developmental programs. The university denoted 2004 as "the year of strategy planning" and produced a policy for 2010 that focused on the medium- and long-term development of the university to become a comprehensive, research-oriented, internationalized higher education institution. The steps toward achieving world-class status include laying a solid foundation for SJTU's further development into a research university by 2010, "breaking into" the top 100 ranking of universities by 2020, and achieving its overall world-class status and being well-positioned in the top 100 by 2050. Since 1998, SJTU has progressively developed in the areas of disciplinary development, teaching and research, science innovation, faculty quality, and financial resources. The following sections provide detailed analysis and evaluation of SJTU's practices toward becoming a research university with world-class capacity.

Strategic Plans and Goals

At the institutional level, the establishment of a world-class research university requires strong leadership, a vision of the institution's mission and goals, and a clearly articulated procedure to translate the vision into concrete programs and targets (Salmi 2009). These steps play a critical role in commanding and guiding SJTU's development. The university first proposed its mission and goals in 1996 and has designed and undertaken strategic planning accordingly. The Office of Strategic Planning, established in early 1999, is responsible for directing the institution's line of development and policies. It was the first Office of Strategic Planning established among leading universities in China.

Trajectories of Ten-Year Planning

In early 1998, the Shanghai municipal government issued a report that clearly stated the goal of building and developing one or two universities with international stature in Shanghai to enhance the city's global competitiveness. SJTU has been perceived as one of the top two universities in Shanghai; however, university leaders were concerned about its relatively poor academic performance, which might threaten its status among other higher education institutions. More than 30 leading professors in each of SJTU's schools and departments were gathered to provide constructive suggestions to improve this situation. After three rounds of discussions, they proposed ideas to guide SJTU's progress toward becoming a world-class university. The 985 Project, developed by the central government in May 1998, further strengthened SJTU's determination to reform. The Office of Policy Studies was established in January 1999 and was made a specialized department responsible for planning the university's development. Following the administrative structural reform, the Office of Policy Studies was renamed the Office of Strategic Planning in September 1999. Since then, the office integrates accountability, evaluation, and institutional research to outline direction for and to provide essential support to university leaders and other university divisions (a) to implement SJTU's mission of building a university with a capacity for world-class research and education and (b) to improve the university's programs and services.

The efforts were implemented on two levels in STJU. At the university level, the office benchmarked SJTU with its domestic peers, such as Fudan University, Nankai University, Peking University, and Tsinghua University. A range of performance indicators was identified at the university level, including subject areas, faculty structure, student capacity, research-funding investment, quality and quantity of publications, citation index, and other factors. At the second level, all departments and schools were required to analyze their own status quo and to set up their own policies and performance indicators based on the university's mission and goals. By doing so, each department and school clarified its responsibilities.

In 2004, the university concentrated on carrying out and modifying its institutional actions. This exercise encouraged SJTU to identify its status among universities in China and in the world, to define its developmental goals for the next five years (2005–10), and to seek paths and approaches to achieve these goals. The resulting "Strategic Plan for 2005–2010" was approved by the University Council, a management and administrative unit in SJTU (Li, Liu, et al. 2005). Five articulated strategies to translate the university's mission and goals into a definitive process were constructed. The first concept is to develop the university capacity through improving the quality of faculty. The university aims to rapidly increase the number of internationally competitive faculty members and to improve the quality of managerial and technical staff members. SJTU strives to build a pool of leading scholars. The second concept is to strengthen the fundamental sciences by putting new approaches into place. SJTU seeks to employ scholars who formerly held leadership positions, to adopt a performance evaluation system, and to set up natural science foundations. Third, the university encourages interdisciplinary research in different subject areas. In response to the needs of national development and the cutting-edge sciences, SJTU intends to integrate various resources, restructure research organization, and create an interdisciplinary academic atmosphere. The fourth concept is to promote the institution's internationalization. The university strives to improve its governance (a) by introducing advanced concepts and ideas from abroad and from highly talented personnel with international backgrounds, (b) by attracting international experts and those with doctoral degrees from world-class universities, (c) by encouraging the faculty to actively engage in international academic organizations and to participate in international collaborations, (d) by further developing international education for overseas students to China, and (e) by enhancing international collaboration and exchange programs to broaden students' horizons. Finally, the university actively collaborates with the government, other Chinese universities, research organizations, and industries and seeks and integrates diversified public resources to serve the demands for socioeconomic development in Shanghai and in China.

After 10 years of such practices, SJTU has made progress. For example, compared with its performance in 1998, its teaching and research currently cover a wider range of subjects, which have allowed SJTU to transition from an engineering-focused institution to a comprehensive university. The number of high-quality published papers written by SJTU staff members and students has increased tremendously, from 113 in 1997 to 2,331 in 2008 for SCI (Science Citation Index) publications, from 364 to 2,748 for Engineering Index publications, and from 2 to 59 for SSCI (Social Science Citation Index) publications. In terms of its profile and academic performance, SJTU regained its leading position in the Chinese higher education system.

At the beginning of 2008, the university was highly aware that the next five years, from 2008 to 2013, would be a crucial transition period. A new round of planning was begun after assessing the implementation of the Strategic Plan for 2005–2010. Eventually, the Strategic Plan for 2013 was drafted by the Office of Strategic Planning and approved by the University Council.

To carry out the plan and to enhance the quality of SJTU's profile and academic performance to meet the world standard, the office bench-marked and evaluated the university's performance based on its international counterparts. The performance indicators cover seven aspects: university, school, and department scale (for example, the total number of teaching and research staff members, undergraduate students, and postgraduate students), talent capacity building (for example, the proportion of international students, visiting scholars, and courses taught in a bilingual approach), leading academics (for example, the number of highly cited authors, editors for recognized international journals,[4] and Chinese Science Academy members), internationalization of teaching and research staff (for example, the proportion of staff with PhD degrees from overseas institutions and with degrees from world-class universities, foreign staff, and the number of international conferences held in the school), research funding (for example, the amount of research funding from government-funded projects and the volume of international research collaboration), research achievements (the number of journal articles published in *Nature and Science*, the high-citation indicators, and the number of patent applications), and disciplinary development (for example, the number of key disciplines and of key national laboratories and research centers accredited with national and international recognition). As mentioned earlier, each department and school was required to create its own goals and performance indicators in the departmental strategic planning—a task related to its benchmarking and evaluation exercise. This exercise will be analyzed in detail in the section titled "Governance Structure and Management Reform."

Elements of Strategic Planning and Challenges

George Keller (2006) identifies a range of elements of good strategic planning. Universities and colleges need to emphasize the policy of strong management and clear purposes for development, focus on cost and revenue seeking, adopt flexible strategies, widen their network for "clustering," and look beyond strategic actions while avoiding too vast a structural change. These elements can also be seen in the development of SJTU's visions and policies.

Strong management has been advocated in SJTU. The university leaders play a principal role in the planning process and have organized an expert group that forms a strong management team. The university organizes seminars, conferences, and workshops with both university policy makers and university faculty members for their opinion and revises the plans continuously. The enactment process combines strong leadership with faculty input and involvement and unifies different ideas, both top-down and bottom-up suggestions.

SJTU's "three-step" goal also shows clear purpose, a planned sequence, and great flexibility. With carefully defined university goals and missions, a range of purposes and performance indicators are identified at both the university and the faculty levels. Time is an important factor in the activities of the aspiring world-class university (Salmi 2009). SJTU realizes that developing a culture of excellence is not a one-time exercise. The university's mission and plans have sought an appropriate sequence of interventions and careful balance among the various targets. Steps have been taken to build world-class subject areas, departments, institutions, and then the university. The plans provide a solid foundation and sound operation measures to carry out the second phase of the 985 Project, playing a guiding role in SJTU's strategy by providing a basic direction for the university's development.

Another element can be described as "clustering" (Keller 2006)—that is, using and combining various supporting elements and resources to move toward excellence in STJU's case. For example, the university invited experts from both inside and outside the university to design the procedures and policies. The internal expert panel consists of those with hands-on experience in managing the university: university leaders, directors of major management divisions, and deans of schools and departments. The external panel includes members from the China International Engineering Consulting Corporation. The external experts were expected to have an independent and critical view to analyze the university's situations and to offer constructive suggestions and measures.

Finally, the program of action in SJTU has been highly cost-conscious. Funding has been carefully planned and allocated to different departments, institutes, and projects.

In spite of the university's progressive development, SJTU also shares some challenges and problems with other universities in China. It is difficult to optimize the connection between current planning and unforeseeable changes in the future, because higher education, along with the society itself, is under rapid development. These transformations involve thinking about the future without predicting it or changes, which forms a potential challenge (Dobbins n.d.). To reach the desired future, the scheme must adhere to the university's long-term goals and ensure adequate space for future development and for flexible modification if necessary. From the government's perspective, few governance organizations or departments coordinate and organize the detailed tactics in Chinese higher education institutions. The relevant governmental department only proposes that universities implement the planning and, in reality, offers little guidance and requirements on how to implement such planning. Another possible restraint of these essential activities in SJTU or Chinese higher education is that little relevant literature or research is available on the value, methodology, procedures, and implementation of these policies. Likewise, little experience has been drawn from overseas counterparts.

Governance Structure and Management Reform

Strong leadership facilitates the development of a research university. Furthermore, implementation of strategic planning relies on effective governance and management systems of the university.

The governance structure of Chinese universities usually comprises administrative and academic units. The general management system adopted by universities can be summarized as the president taking charge of the university under the leadership of the University Council (Xi 2005; Li 2007). The organizational structure of SJTU comprises the president; Party secretary, whose function (except for Party affairs[5]) is supposed to be equivalent to the chairman of a university board in Western countries; and deans of schools, departments, and research institutes and centers; as well as directors of administration divisions.

The university president is the legal representative of the university and the ultimate symbol of executive power. The president is usually appointed by the government or is elected by the academic community and subsequently approved by authorities. This appointment system might prevent the university from selecting the most suitable leaders for its development (Zhao and Zhou 2006). In response to this situation, SJTU allows vice presidents and the president to share the authority and responsibilities for implementing policies and decisions made by the University Council regarding teaching, research, administration, and other issues.

The Academic Council

The power structures and boundaries of Chinese universities are not as clear as those of Western universities. More often than not, in the West, the academic council (for example, faculty senates), as the academic authority, generally plays a key role in the university management. The university president, as the council president, coordinates the administrative and academic power and implements the council's decisions. At Chinese universities, academic power is usually superseded by administrative authority. From the university's perspective, such an arrangement might promote efficient decision making and policy implementation.

To strengthen academic decision making, SJTU established its Academic Council in December 2008. The council aims to fully develop the roles of teaching and research staff, to strengthen academic management, to improve academic regulations, to enhance teaching and research quality, and to support SJTU's development as a research university (Dong 2008). The Academic Council comprises four subject divisions—humanities and social sciences, physical sciences, engineering science, and life and medical sciences. The duties of the Academic Council include reviewing various policies regarding institutional development, creating academic standards, and consulting on major academic issues (Dong 2008).

Benchmarking and Evaluation

To maintain and strengthen its rapid development, SJTU realizes that it must review the university's performance in a global dimension; that is, all aspects of university performance in SJTU—such as faculty quality, research excellence, and talent cultivation—should be evaluated and compared by international standards. This benchmarking approach organizes the overall goal of the university into specific performance indicators and, ultimately, enables the university to define its current position, to have clear goals and directions for future development, and to design measures accordingly. SJTU has carried out medium- and long-term department and school evaluation since 2007 (Liu, Yang, et al. 2008).

The first evaluation was conducted in the Department of Physics and the Department of Mathematics.

The evaluation exercise was to be conducted in three stages. Stage one was self-evaluation by each department. Departments prepared reports and materials on department indicators and their academic development, including academic environment, the international reputation of its subject areas, representative doctoral dissertations in the past five years, and other aspects. The reports were also to reflect the department's research and teaching capacity, compared to its counterparts, both at home and abroad. The departments were asked to predict their potential development in the future. In stage two, experts read the reports. Feedback was provided in stage three. The experts presented the evaluation results to the university management officials. According to the experts' feedback, each department and school planned their improvement and implemented new measures after approval by the university. The benchmarking and evaluation process allowed the departments to assess their current situation, compared to the national and international counterparts, and, in turn, to analyze their own strengths and weakness.

The evaluation process has had a significant effect on SJTU and on its departments and schools. The process has inspired changes and development in the university. First, the university has adopted the "international standard" as benchmarking for future evaluation. Although the notion of developing a world-class university was raised several years ago, few departments and schools can clearly define such a university. This medium- and long-term evaluation process has offered insight to understanding the concepts and ideologies. Second, the concept that "quality is most important" is reinforced. When analyzing the evaluation documents, SJTU puts great emphasis on quality indicators, such as world-famous professors, high-level research achievements, and influence of publications, while giving less significance to the quantity of published papers and of research funds. In addition, each department and school can list only five scientific research projects and their achievements in the self-evaluation report. In other words, the experts make judgments based on the representative research achievements. By doing so, faculty members are expected to focus on quality improvement and originality in their future research work. Third, for science departments in particular, the evaluation helps to form a clear understanding of the nature, orientation, and contribution of various fields of science. Through the evaluation process, faculty members have realized that fundamental sciences can play a significant role in enhancing undergraduate education and improving the university's status. It has laid a solid basis for the university's future poli-cy-making and management reform.

Campus Development

Campus development can be regarded as another aspect of the manage-ment reform in SJTU. At present, SJTU has five campuses in Shanghai—the Fahuazhen Road, Minhang, Qibao, South Chongqing Road, and Xuhui campuses. Initially, the main campus was located in the Xuhui district, one of the business and commercial centers in Shanghai. During the 1980s, space shortages and high-management costs in Xuhui prompted the university to begin investing heavily in the development of the Minhang campus, which is about 20 kilometers from Xuhui. After significant expansion during the 1990s, the Minhang campus became the main university campus in the early 21st century. The campus has also been equipped with advanced educational resources and facilities.

This campus restructuring laid a solid infrastructure base for adapting the university's strategic development goals, improving teaching and research quality, and meeting the expanding enrollment (Zhou 2001). The campus development has also allowed for the integration of educa-tional resources. For example, the School of Electronic, Information and Electrical Engineering had been scattered in five separate offices around the Xuhui campus, which inhibited the development of integrative and efficient management structures. In Minhang, the new building houses all those departments, facilitating internal management and communication and allowing the departments to share resources, to develop interdisci-plinary research, and to pursue a coordinated external relations strategy. Also, the location of the Minhang campus facilitates university-industry cooperation. For example, SJTU has expanded its collaboration with the Zizhu Science-Based Industrial Park, which is located just south of the Minhang campus. This park includes the research and development centers of Intel, ST Microelectronics, Microsoft, and other high-tech companies.

Improvement of Faculty Quality

Since the late 1990s, various measures have been implemented in SJTU to improve faculty quality. Before 1998, SJTU had 1,753 teaching and research staff members, of whom only 25 percent had a professorship and only 15 percent had a PhD degree. The university has a series of programs to recruit academically talented scholars, including Chair Professors

Program, Distinguished Professors Program, Distinguished Researchers Program, and the Morning Star Program for young scholars. More specifically, faculty development has been conducted in four aspects: employment policies, promotion schemes, expert recruitment, and global recruitment.

SJTU has gradually strengthened the requirements and criteria for selecting faculty members since the 1990s. All academic staff members first employed by SJTU after 2000 are required to have a doctoral degree or the highest degree in the field. In addition, since January 1, 2010, the university has encouraged its departments and schools to employ staff with PhD degrees from research universities abroad or with overseas work experience. However, such focus on an overseas degree restrains the opportunities for elite applicants with only Chinese degrees. This recruiting policy can also undermine the value of Chinese higher education degrees.

Compared to previous policies, a new professorship promotion program (adopted since 2003) has set up two major differences regarding promotion and hiring practices. Rather than simply being promoted (on the basis of work experience and academic qualifications) to a higher rank, internal candidates must compete with external ones for higher positions. Since 2003, both internal and external applicants, at home and abroad, have been offered equal opportunities to compete for professorships and associate professorships. In addition, the program of professor promotion stipulates that applicants can apply for the same position (professor or associate professor) only once every two years, for a maximum of three times.

The university is actively engaged in attracting academic talent and experts, such as Changjiang Scholars, distinguished professors, and distinguished researchers. The university also promotes the Morning Star Program to encourage and attract young scholars. In addition, the Green Passage system provides a fast and prompt mechanism to respond to and deal with such applications. This system helps to quickly resolve issues—such as salary negotiation, welfare, and living expenses—that would have taken much longer by traditional procedures. After implementing this policy, for example, the university recruited about 70 scholars through the Green Passage system in 2008.

SJTU clearly stated within its strategic plan the goal to further develop global recruitment by end-2003. It first published about 400 vacancies on the Internet, including positions for 170 professors and 229 associate professors and 20 technical positions. Altogether, 961 applications were received. By end-2004, vacancies involving 87 full professors and 210 associate professors were filled. More than half of those hired had studied or taught abroad for one year or more. It is worth noting that, by following the principle of "selecting the best," SJTU prefers to leave vacancies unfilled rather than to fill them with inadequately skilled staff (Xiong 2004).

The recruitment measures discussed above have effectively improved the quality of faculty. First, the number of faculty members has satisfied the university's need as it develops. At present, there are over 2,900 full-time faculty members, including about 700 professors and 1,200 associate professors, and the ratio of students to teachers is about 15 to 1 (Zhang 2008).

Second, the competency of faculty members has improved. In terms of qualifications, 85.4 percent of faculty members have master's degrees and 64.4 percent have PhD degrees. In terms of special titles, SJTU has 33 academicians who are members of the Chinese Academy of Sciences and the Chinese Academy of Engineering, 72 professors and chair professors who are Changjiang Scholars, and 57 recipients of the National Outstanding Youth Fund. These high-level talents have contributed to the development of research excellence in SJTU.

Third, the number of university faculty members with international credentials has significantly increased. For example, the percentage of faculty members holding PhD degrees from foreign universities has increased from 5 percent in 2004 to 12 percent in 2008, and most faculty members have studied or taught abroad.

Despite the achievement of attracting high-quality faculty, the university realizes challenges and difficulties lie in such recruitment. Various recruitment measures and programs have been implemented to cater to the university's demand for rapid development. However, such human resource management reform is relatively new in SJTU's practice, with no previous lessons to draw upon. Policy adjustment and readjustment are required to respond promptly to issues such as working contracts, living environment, and other housing requirements (including the Shanghai housing registration system[6]). From the perspective of faculty members, financial remuneration might enable the university to attract qualified faculty. However, for the sake of economic benefits, conflicts can exist or be triggered among various groups. For example, conflicts may arise between overseas returnees and the domestically trained staff, as well as between recent returnees and those who repatriated many years ago (Liu 2010). How the university can help overseas returnee scholars to efficiently build up their research network in Chinese academia remains another concern (SJTU 2010). There is little literature or experience to rely on in dealing with these challenges. The university and its Human Resources Division realize that further research, discussion, and communication with faculty members are necessary (SJTU 2010).

The university aims to develop a world-class faculty by 2020, with a group of academicians and talented young people who are in great demand for national strategic development and who participate in international cutting-edge research of science and technology. More specifically, it will continue to adjust and improve its faculty structure, with an estimated target of 3,400 full-time teachers, more than one-third of whom are at the world-class level. The university will continue to focus on attracting highly talented individuals, with an estimated target of 200 academicians who are members of the Chinese Academy of Sciences and the Chinese Academy of Engineering, 400 distinguished professors, and 800 distinguished researchers.

Encouragement of Academic Discipline Development and Research Excellence

SJTU aims at developing into a comprehensive research university that covers 12 disciplinary fields: natural sciences, engineering, medicine, management, law, economics, agriculture, social sciences, humanities, education, history, and military studies. To further promote quality education and consolidate university capacity, the university has been continuously developing its academic discipline focus and structure and encouraging its research excellence.

Development of Academic Disciplines

Throughout SJTU's history, the university has focused on science and technology subjects. To strengthen its academic dimension, SJTU has taken various approaches to develop different subject areas.

With governmental support, the university promoted mergers with an agriculture university and a medical university in the region in 1999 and 2005, respectively, with the explicit goal of evolving into a larger and more comprehensive research university and enriching its academic disciplines. These mergers enable the participating institutions to share teaching and research resources, consolidate academic capacity, and improve their international prestigious reputation. Challenges that arise when undertaking a merger include conflicting needs and interests and clashing academic cultures (Salmi 2009). However, SJTU has greater chances for success because the push for mergers is occurring within the context of the participating institutions' common goal to create the world-class academic culture and transformation of vision, which in turn brings about internal coherence. In addition, SJTU has ensured relatively independent management in the other two institutions.

Since 2007, the university has proposed new goals and strategies for the development of its academic disciplines. The methods include sustaining the eminence of its flagship departments and their disciplinary development, strengthening its basic disciplinary programs and departments, providing its feature disciplines with special provisions, bolstering underperforming departments and their disciplinary development, and encouraging interdisciplinary research.[7] The university has particularly focused on the strategy of bolstering underperforming departments and their disciplinary development, such as social sciences subjects.

Relatively weak development of social science disciplines has become a bottleneck problem that prevents science and technology institutions from joining SJTU to develop into a comprehensive university. In addition, the majority of the top management staff has a science and technology background. To some extent, this characteristic is favorable for the development of the science disciplines (for example, in terms of teaching and research resource allocation). However, it also restricts students from gaining a more comprehensive education (Ma and Chen 2005). Under these circumstances, the Social Sciences Administration Office was set up in 2002 to develop and manage social sciences disciplines, to organize research-funding applications for social sciences subjects, to advance academic culture, and to coordinate the journal publications. The office proposes specific principles to develop social sciences–related disciplines—that is, strengthening the basic and special role of social sciences in SJTU's disciplinary development, introducing leading professors from China and abroad in the social sciences fields to build research capacity, promoting diversified research to serve the societal needs, and developing international partnerships with institutions around the world to learn from its counterparts.

With these policies and strategies, the academic disciplinary structure has been expanded and enriched and its quality has been improved. In the National Evaluation of Academic Disciplines, SJTU has 6 disciplines ranked among the national top 3 and 11 disciplines ranked among the top 10.

Encouragement of Research Excellence

SJTU encourages its faculty to conduct research at an international level. The university strives to integrate research achievements with the development of key enterprises, to work closely in the development of future industries, and to aid in the construction of an innovation system in China. The university is also engaged in the advanced study of international issues and advises the government in policy making. Through knowledge transfer, the university endeavors to solve scientific and technological issues in industry development and to inspire the research and talent development of the university. Specifically, the university has adopted four main options—rewarding international publications, supporting research of an international standard, encouraging applied research and technology transfer, and using research resources for talent development to enhance its research excellence.

Rewarding international publication. Publication in internationally published journals and books has been significant in the evaluation of research excellence in China. SJTU also has proposed policies and regulations to improve the quality of papers published. First, a policy to reward papers indexed in SCI was issued in 1999. A reward of Y10,000 (about US$1,480) is offered for each SCI paper, of which 90 percent funds further research and 10 percent is a financial reward for the researcher. Second, the Graduate School of SJTU issued a policy that requires all doctoral students in science and engineering to publish internationally. Thus, students pursuing a PhD in sciences must publish at least one SCI paper, and students pursuing a PhD in engineering must publish at least one SCI paper or one paper in English indexed in the Engineering Index, before they may apply for a doctoral degree. Moreover, the policy states clearly that only a published paper with the student's name as the first author can be counted as one full paper. Further papers cannot be counted if the student is the third or latter author. This policy has subsequently been adopted by other departments and schools. Third, the university has focused on the quality of the published papers, rather than the quantity. For example, the number of SCI papers increased to 2,331 in 2007, reaching similar standards as some top 100 world-class universities.

The stature of publications also increased to some extent, but still lagged those of other world-class universities (Zheng 2008). Great emphasis has been placed on developing high-quality and innovative research to inspire further development in specific subject areas as well as at the university in general. To encourage quality publications and improve their international influence, in 2007 SJTU introduced a new reward and evaluation system for papers. The new system decreases the reward for SCI and Engineering Index papers of average quality (Y 1,000 [about US$148] for each SCI paper and Y 800 [about US$120] for each Engineering Index paper), while high-quality papers with more influence are rewarded as before (SJTU 2006).

Encouraging applied research and technology transfer. The university encourages research achievements and technology transfer and provides advice on governmental policy making and local economic development. It encourages faculty members to commercialize their patents through its establishment of a technology transfer center, creation of a patent information platform, and permission for the faculty to invest personally and benefit from this commercialized investment. Technology transfer has brought many economic benefits and promotes the development of future technologies. With the support of the 985 Project throughout the decade, the team members of a research and development project based on a high-definition television functional prototype system have contributed significantly to that technological development in China.

In addition, SJTU emphasizes the development of social science research. As a result, the university consults with the government and local organizations regarding regional and community socioeconomic development. For example, the Graduate School of Education of SJTU has conducted a series of influential government consultations on building world-class universities and developing science and technology policy. Since 2003, the school has published the Academic Ranking of World Universities annually, which has received wide recognition from the international community (SJTU 2008).

Using research resources for talent development. SJTU has strived to enhance its research resources by greatly increasing the level of research funding, collaborating with industry and other research institutions, and promoting higher education and research standards at undergraduate and graduate levels. These approaches have been highly recommended by experts from the Ministry of Education.

The university has established experimental programs and courses for undergraduate education and professional education with high-quality resources and facilities. Additionally, research has been integrated into teaching and learning. The university developed 400 comprehensive and innovative courses, accounting for 85 percent of the total number of the experimental courses. It has also increased its investment in the teaching of experimental programs and implements Participation in Research Program projects and innovative research projects for students. As a result, students' innovation skills have constantly improved, and they have shown their talents in science and technology competitions. In 2010, an SJTU student team won the world championship in the ACM (Association for Computing Machinery) International Collegiate Programming Contest.

STJU takes advantage of university-industry research collaboration in postgraduate education. This university-industry partnership, a relatively new development in Chinese higher education, provides crucial support to improve university development and to build a world-class university (Ma 2005). The long-term goal of these partnerships is to improve the quality of postgraduate education by integrating theory into practice. University-industry research collaboration enables students to develop their innovation skills and to gain hands-on experience (Shen et al. 2009). SJTU has established several university-industry research collaboration programs. Supported by Zizhu Science-Based Industrial Park and other research-based enterprises, the university is further developing its postgraduate education programs. Students are offered internship opportunities on important projects run by the enterprises. At the same time, experienced engineers in industry are invited to teach and supervise postgraduate students at SJTU.

For example, since 2004 SJTU has been developing its partnership with the Shanghai Baoshan Iron and Steel Company. Experts from the company are invited to supervise graduate students, and the company's technology staff is actively engaged in teaching and helping students. In the past five years, this collaborative program has trained 79 master's degree students and 13 doctoral students, and 50 experts have participated in teaching and supervising. According to the SJTU's self-evaluative report in 2009, an increasing number of students have chosen to study with experts from industry (SJTU 2009).

This education and training model has been affirmed by the Ministry of Education and the Shanghai Education Commission and was selected as part of the 2003–2005 Graduate Education Innovation Plan. The local government has advocated developing this model at other universities across Shanghai.

Promotion of Internationalization Strategies

A university can transform into a research university by using internationalization strategies effectively (Salmi 2009). SJTU has worked extensively to provide training of innovative talents with international competitiveness and to establish an international-standard higher education system with advanced education concepts. Specifically, the internationalization strategies are designed in relation to students, faculty, research, and programs. The policies regarding faculty and research development have been discussed earlier. The following analysis will focus on the aspects of students and programs.

Bilingual Teaching and Learning

Bilingual education has been advocated in SJTU since 1998. It is intended to improve students' English-language skills as well as their Chinese-language skills. From 1998 to 2005, about 135 bilingual courses were offered to 11,000 students by 132 teachers. These bilingual courses represented approximately 10 percent of the disciplinary courses offered by SJTU. This proportion increased to 15 percent by 2010 (SJTU Team for GEE 2006). Also, special financial support is offered for bilingual courses. For example, each new bilingual course will receive total support funding of Y 5,000–Y 8,000 (about US$740–US$1,180). In addition, SJTU students are required to take a minimum of 16 credits of English-language courses (SJTU 2007). However, little research has been conducted on the effectiveness of the delivery of bilingual courses in the university. It would be useful to investigate how staff members deliver bilingual teaching and how students experience such teaching and thus to explore any gap between the policy orientation and its implementation.

Summer Schools, Exchange Students, and Internships

To broaden the international experience of its students, the university offers a series of programs that encourage and support students at all levels to study in and visit foreign nations.

At the undergraduate level, the university offers various study tours and helps elite students participate in degree programs abroad and in semester-long study-exchange programs, three-month overseas internships, and summer training programs with foreign universities. SJTU hopes to provide various opportunities for students to travel the world and experience different cultures. The university believes that such international opportunities will enrich the study and work experience of students, making them more internationally competitive. Up to 2008, 19.4 percent of SJTU undergraduate students participated in those study tours. By 2010, the number had increased to 25 percent." According to the university's strategic plans, the number is expected to increase to

50 percent by 2020 (SJTU 2007). In addition, for those students who might not be able to afford such study opportunities, the university has offered scholarships since 2008. This is SJTU's first financial support in China to help undergraduate students with financial difficulties study abroad (SJTU Educational Affairs Office 2009).

SJTU is the first Chinese university to be awarded the International Association for the Exchange of Students for Technical Experience (IAESTE) Scholarship for Overseas Internship. The IAESTE scholarship program offers grants to junior and senior undergraduate students as well as to postgraduate students in the fields of chemical engineering, chemistry, materials, master of business administration, and financial management (SJTU Educational Affairs Office 2007).

At the doctoral level, the university encourages students pursuing a PhD to visit and study at world-class universities to engage in cutting-edge research, to enhance their research capacity, and to improve their international competitiveness (SJTU Graduate School 2007). Selected students will be granted scholarships by SJTU—including tuition fees, travel costs, and living expenses—and will be jointly monitored by their supervisors in SJTU and abroad. Currently, 15 percent of SJTU's doctoral students have had such experience.

According to research conducted by SJTU's Graduate School of Education, students who studied abroad were satisfied and shared positive feedback on their international experience and its influence on their university (Yang et al. 2008). In 2008, 46.3 percent of these students perceived their international experience as a great opportunity for learning cutting-edge knowledge in their field, compared with only 7.4 percent of students who claimed no influence at all; 47.9 percent of students strongly believed they improved their language abilities through the programs, compared with only 5.3 percent who did not agree; 41.5 percent of students were highly aware of their enhanced confidence as a result of the activities, compared with 7.4 percent of students who did not feel the same. Also, 39.9 percent of students found consideration for other cultures.

Dual Degree Programs and Joint Institutes

SJTU is actively engaged in collaborating with internationally prestigious universities by forming dual degree programs and joint institutes. Exploring and using optimal educational resources, the university aims to learn from other research universities with world-class standards, to draw reference to those institutions' governance and management, to experience their curriculum design, and to develop a high-skilled workforce with international competitiveness.

The dual degree programs include SJTU's collaboration with the Berlin Technical University, École Centrale (Lille, Lyon, Marseille, Nantes, and Paris), École des Mines de Nantes (France), Georgia Institute of Technology, and University of Michigan. In 2007, SJTU also cooperated with the Massachusetts Institute of Technology to launch the China Leaders for Manufacturing program (Tong 2008). In China, it is the first and the only degree program at the graduate level for training the next generation of leaders for manufacturing industries (SJTU Team for GEE 2006).

SJTU encourages its departments and schools to collaborate with overseas universities and institutions. Under this policy, a few joint institutes have been built. For example, an agreement to reconstruct SJTU's School of Mechanical Engineering in collaboration with the University of Michigan was signed in August 2000. The project aimed at further developing the School of Mechanical Engineering into a world-famous institute. A "4+2+3" model (four-year undergraduate, two-year master's degree, and three-year doctoral programs) was proposed in the agreement. In 2006, the two universities set up the University of Michigan–Shanghai Jiao Tong University Joint Institute, which has been a successful collaboration between a Chinese and a world-class university (SJTU 2009).

In addition, other joint institutes have been built. For example, the Sino-US Environmental Law Teaching and Research Center, in collaboration with Pace University, intends to build long-term academic exchanges with other elite universities. The collaboration between Columbia University and STJU's School of International and Public Affairs has developed their long-term strategic partnership to train master of public administration personnel highly demanded in the era of globalization (Du 2008).

SJTU's internationalization strategies have also extended overseas. The university's master of business administration programs have been conducted in cooperation with educational institutions in Singapore for 14 years, yielding more than 400 graduates. In 2002, SJTU was approved by the Ministry of Education to set up its overseas campus in Singapore. It is the first overseas university campus established by a Chinese university. At the same time, SJTU is the ninth university with which the Singaporean government would like to build up global collaboration.

Meanings of Internationalization
In summary, the internationalization strategy has been integrated into all aspects of SJTU's development, including activities and programs in

students' capacity building, discipline development, curriculum design, teaching and research resources, and governance and management. In the past, the internationalization strategy focused on a wide range of only import-oriented activities. But SJTU now aims at developing an in-depth mode of internationalization, with both import-oriented and export-oriented activities and programs. For the university's development, the internationalization policy suggests drawing reference from other world-class universities' experience, integrating different concepts of university governance and management, introducing international standards to improve quality in all aspects, and raising awareness of global competition and of cultural diversity among staff members and students.

Diversification of Financial Resources

Like other state universities in China, SJTU's funding comes from diverse resources—government funding, research income, tuition fees, university-run enterprises, and donations from both individuals and social organizations.

Both central and local governments allocate regular educational funding to national universities based on the number of students (Liu 2009). SJTU's regular educational funding is allocated mainly by the central government.

Selected as one of the key participating universities, SJTU has been awarded extra funding by the 211 Project and the 985 Project. Funding from the 211 Project targets three main areas—improvement of institutional research capacity, development of key disciplinary areas, and development of digital campus and infrastructure. The 985 Project funding supports university activities in the following major areas: research capacity building, infrastructure and campus development, talent recruitment and faculty development, and international collaboration. Within the central government funding, 25 percent has been invested in faculty development, 60 percent in research capacity development, 5 percent in undergraduate and postgraduate teaching, 5 percent in digital campus development, and 5 percent in international collaboration.

Research income is another funding source for SJTU. Research is largely supported by government agencies and the industrial sector for development of the university's research capacity. Since the reform of cost-sharing in the higher education sector, tuition fees have been introduced. They now account for a significant proportion of total university revenue. Donations and other sources of private support to SJTU have also become a significant source of university revenue. Many of SJTU's new buildings have been financed with donations from alumni or social celebrities. Furthermore, the Beijing Zizhu Pharmaceutical Co., Ltd., a private business enterprise, has offered the university about Y 1 billion in financial support. This amount is the largest single donation to a university by a private business enterprise in China.

The total budget of SJTU has more than quadrupled in the past 10 years. For a typical year, SJTU's revenue comprises 20 percent regular funding from the government; 20 percent special funding from government initiatives, such as the 985 Project and the 211 Project; 30 percent research income; 20 percent tuition fees; and 10 percent other resources, including donations and income from university-run enterprises.

Conclusion

Constructing research universities is a thought-provoking and time- and resource-consuming endeavor for any institution in any country (Shi 2009). There is no universal formula for developing such universities (Salmi 2009). SJTU has turned its particular conditions into opportunities for the establishment of a research university at an international standard and has made significant progress in many aspects.

The university has changed its management style, from traditional administration to strategic management. This modification enables SJTU to envision the most worthwhile future, to create a bold vision of mission and goals, and, accordingly, to design a series of procedures as blueprints for daily activities. The university takes into account the external environment as well as SJTU's organizational capabilities, overall purposes, and development direction and integrates different management activities, such as medium- and long-term performance evaluation of schools and departments, diversification of financial resources, and innovative employment policies.

The focus of SJTU's development has shifted from domestic to international standards and from domestic to international competition. Recognizing the gap between SJTU and international elite universities, SJTU has encouraged its schools and departments to benchmark their performance with that of their international counterparts, to evaluate their performance by international indicators and standards, to foster research to engage in the international academic world, and to recruit globally for faculty with internationally recognized credentials to strengthen its human resources. These tactics enable SJTU to examine any differences with other research universities and to establish clear targets to close these gaps.

The emphasis of SJTU's development has changed from quantity oriented to quality oriented and from infrastructure building to enhancement of teaching, learning, and research. For example, SJTU now encourages and rewards faculty members and students for quality papers published in top international journals in relevant fields, whereas the university previously encouraged and rewarded them simply for the number of their papers appearing in international publications.

Despite its progress, SJTU's desire to further develop and to achieve its goal of becoming a research university involves a long road ahead. SJTU needs to focus on establishing the long-term global vision of a world-class research university, supported by specific short-term goals, needs, and perspectives. Another challenge is to transform SJTU's organizational culture into a true quality culture, instead of an indicator- or ranking-oriented approach. Although achieving particular rankings is mentioned in the university vision, development needs to focus on improving the quality of education, research, and services.

Notes

1. These top nine universities, selected in the beginning of phase one of the 985 Project, are Fudan University, Harbin Institute of Technology, Nanjing University, Peking University, SJTU, Tsinghua University, University of Science and Technology of China, Xi'an Jiaotong University, and Zhejiang University.

2. For papers written by these nine universities' staff members and students that were published internationally, the average number indexed in the Thomson Scientific Database increased to 2,400 in 2008, 10 times more than in 1999. The performance of staff members and students has also improved significantly, in terms of highly cited researchers and published papers in *Nature and Science*.

3. For example, according to the *Academic Ranking of World Universities* (SJTU 2008), the number of Chinese universities in the top 300 increased from 0 in 2000 to 6 in 2008, and the number of Chinese universities in the top 500 increased from 4 to 18 in the same period.

4. These journals are indexed by the Social Sciences Citation Index, the Science Citation Index Expanded, and the Arts & Humanities Citation Index.

5. Most of the Party secretaries, in practice, are directly involved in the university's daily management and administration. In some cases, they act like copresidents.

6. The housing registration system is a residency permit system. All individuals must be registered as residents of a particular city, town, or village. Through this registration system, they have access to services such as health care and schooling.

7. According to SJTU's documents and information, its flagship departments include engineering, life sciences, and economics and management; its basic discipline is natural sciences; and its feature departments include law, agriculture, social sciences, and humanities. The social sciences and humanities departments are considered relatively underperforming in SJTU's disciplinary development; however, these departments have a range of specialized disciplines and thus play an important role in SJTU's development into a world-class research university.

References

Dobbins, Craig. n.d. "Strategic Planning: External Environmental Scanning." Center for Food and Agricultural Business, Purdue University, West Lafayette, IN. http://www.agecon.purdue.edu/extension/sbpcp/resources/exscan.pdf. Accessed March 5, 2010.

Dong, S. X. 2008. "The New Decision-making Department for Academic Issues: The First Academic Committee Founded." [In Chinese]. *SJTU News*. http://www.sjtu.edu.cn/news/shownews.php?id=18873. Accessed September 1, 2009.

Du, X. 2008. "Training Talent of Excellence with SJTU Characteristics." [In Chinese]. *SJTU E-Journal* 3. http://sjtu.cuepa.cn/show_more.php?doc_id=120991. Accessed September 1, 2009.

Keller, George. 2006. "Higher Education Management: Challenges and Strategies." In *International Handbook of Higher Education*, ed. James F. Forest and Philip G. Altbach, 229–42. Dordrecht, Netherlands: Springer.

Lauder, Hugh, Phillip Brown, and David Ashton. 2008. "Education, Globalization, and the Future of the Knowledge Economy." *European Educational Research Journal 7* (2): 131–56.

Li, J., S. X. Liu, P. Chen, and H. Y. Huang. 2005. "Strategic Development of Higher Education." [In Chinese.] *Education Development and Research 3*: 94–96.

Li, W. 2007. "A Discussion on Power Organization in Chinese Higher Education." [In Chinese.] Master's thesis, Shanxi Normal University, Xi'an, China.

Liu, Nian Cai. 2009. *Building Up World-Class Universities: A Comparison*. Hiroshima, Japan: Research Institute for Higher Education, Hiroshima University.

Liu, N. C., L. Liu, Y. Cheng, and T. T. Wan. 2003. "'985 Project' Narrows Down the Gap between Chinese Top Universities and Other World-Class Universities." [In Chinese.] *Chinese Higher Education* 17: 22–24.

Liu, N. C., J. Yang, Y. Wu, and Y. Cheng. 2008. "Medium- and Long-term Performance Evaluation: The Case of Shanghai Jiao Tong University." [In Chinese.] Vol. 1. of *Case Studies on Chinese Higher Education*, ed. X. J. Liu. Wuhan, China: Huazhong University of Science and Technology Press.

Liu, R. J. 2010. "The Study about Living Environment and State of Overseas Returnees in Chinese Universities." [In Chinese]. Master's thesis, Shanghai Jiao Tong University, Shanghai.

Ma, D. X. 2005. "Promoting Talent Training through University-Industry Research Collaboration." [In Chinese.] *Wenhui Newspaper*, December 20. http://gfb .sjtu.edu.cn/yjcg_read.jsp?id=47&page=1. Accessed September 1, 2009.

Ma, R. S., and Z. F. Chen. 2005. "The Influence of Habitual Thinking in the Way of Liberal Arts Education in the Science and Engineering Institutions." [In Chinese.] *Journal of Henan Vocation-Technical Teachers College* 2: 17–18.

Ministerial Office of 211 Project, China. 2007. *Report on 211 Project 1995–2005*. Beijing: Higher Education Press.

Ministry of Education, China. 1998. "The Action Plan for Education Revitalization for the 21st Century." [In Chinese.] Ministry of Education, Beijing. http:// www.moe.gov.cn/edoas/website18/level3.jsp?tablename=208&infoid=3337. Accessed July 1, 2009.

———. 2008. "985 Project." [In Chinese.] Ministry of Education, Beijing. http:// www.moe.gov.cn/edoas/website18/level3.jsp?tablename=1476&infoid=1223 534999341199. Accessed July 1, 2009.

Salmi, Jamil. 2009. *The Challenge of Establishing World-Class Universities*. Washington, DC: World Bank.

Schwab, Klaus, ed. 2009. *The Global Competitiveness Report 2009–2010*. Geneva: World Economic Forum.

Shen, C., P. P. Li, W. D. Shi, and R. G. Liu. 2009. "The Application of Contingency Theory in the Collaborative Education of Graduate Students among Government, Business, University and Institutes." [In Chinese.] *Journal of Jiangsu University (Social Science Edition)* 11 (2): 83–86.

Shi, Jing Huan. 2009. "Combining Vision, Mission and Action: Tsinghua's Experience in Building a World-Class University." In *The World-Class University as Part of a New Higher Education Paradigm: From Institutional Qualities to Systemic Excellence*, ed. Jan Sadlak and Nian Cai Liu, 307–24. Bucharest, Romania: United Nations Educational, Scientific, and Cultural Organization–European Centre for Higher Education.

SJTU (Shanghai Jiao Tong University). 2006. "Guidelines for Scientific Achievements Rewarding and Intellectual Property Management." SJTU, Shanghai. http://me.sjtu.edu.cn/bszn_kygl.asp?lanmu=bszn&name=%E7%A 7%91%E7%A0%94%E7%AE%A1%E7%90%86. Accessed September 1, 2009.

———. 2007. "Regulations on Adopting Bilingual Education Approach in Teaching and Learning." SJTU, Shanghai. http://cc.sjtu.edu.cn/Able.Acc2. Web/Page_TeachFileDownload.aspx?ID=38. Accessed September 1, 2009.

———. 2008. *Academic Ranking of World Universities* [In Chinese.] http://www .arwu.org/ranking(ch).htm. Accessed September 1, 2009.

———. 2009. "Ten Years On: Development of Shanghai Jiao Tong University." Unpublished manuscript, SJTU, Shanghai.

———. 2010. "Improving Higher-Level Faculty." [In Chinese.] Internal report, SJTU, Shanghai.

SJTU (Shanghai Jiao Tong University) Educational Affairs Office. 2007. "IAESTE Scholarship for Overseas Internship." SJTU Educational Affairs Office, SJTU, Shanghai. http://jwc.sjtu.edu.cn/article.asp?id=609. Accessed September 1, 2009.

———. 2009. "Study Tour for Undergraduate Students." SJTU Educational Affairs Office, SJTU, Shanghai. http://www.jwc.sjtu.edu.cn/toplistb .asp?id=221. Accessed September 1, 2009.

SJTU (Shanghai Jiao Tong University) Graduate School 2007. "Financial Support for Doctoral Students' Study Tour." SJTU Graduate School, SJTU, Shanghai. http://www.gs.sjtu.edu.cn/home.ahtml. Accessed September 1, 2009.

SJTU (Shanghai Jiao Tong University) Team for GEE. 2006. "Global Engineering Excellence Study–SJTU Report." [In Chinese.] SJTU Team for GEE, SJTU, Shanghai.

Tong, X. 2008. "Strategic Management in Chinese Higher Education: The Case Study of Shanghai Jiao Tong University." [In Chinese.] *Journal of Technology College Education 27* (5): 40-42.

Wang, Y. J. 2008. "Expanding the Higher Education System and Building World-Class Universities: China's Response to Globalization and the Knowledge Economy." *European Educational Research Journal 7* (2): 147–53.

Xi, Y. M. 2005. "University Governance Facing Challenges and Its Possible Improvement." [In Chinese.] *Xi'an Jiao Tong University Journal (Social Science) 3.*

Xiong, B. Q. 2004. "SJTU Global Recruitment for Professorship." [In Chinese.] *SJTU News.* http://www.sjtu.edu.cn/news/shownews.php?id=491. Accessed September 1, 2009.

Yang, J., Y. Y. Jiang, J. P. Zhang, and W. Liu. 2008. "The Development of Internationalization in Shanghai Jiao Tong University." Internal report, Graduate School of Education, Shanghai Jiao Tong University, Shanghai.

Zhang, Y. B. 2008. "Employment and Talent Training Reform." [In Chinese.] *Research on Human Resources in Chinese Higher Education* 3: 35–37.

Zhao, W. H., and Q. L. Zhou. 2006. "The Meanings and Values of Vision and Mission in Higher Education Strategic Management." [In Chinese.] *Education Development and Research* 3: 61–64.

Zheng, M. 2008. "SJTU Ranks Third in China in SCI Publications." [In Chinese.] *SJTU News*. http://www.sjtu.edu.cn/news/shownews.php?id=19049. Accessed September 1, 2009.

Zhou, L. 2001. "Strategic Development of Multicampus Universities: A Comparative Study." [In Chinese.] *Journal of Higher Education* 22 (2): 61–64.

CHAPTER 3

The Rise of Research Universities: The Hong Kong University of Science and Technology

Gerard A. Postiglione

"Rome wasn't built in a day."

Before the end of the 19th century, the president of Harvard University, Charles Eliot, counseled John D. Rockefeller that US$50 million (about US$5 billion in today's currency) and 200 years would be required to create a research university (Altbach 2003). After the turn of the century, and with Rockefeller's more than US$50 million, the University of Chicago needed only 20 years to attain top standing. In Asia just before the turn of this century, the newly established Hong Kong University of Science and Technology (HKUST) took only 10 years and less than a tenth of Eliot's figure to become one of Asia's top 10 research universities.[1]

Globalization has quickened the establishment of a research university and shortened the time that nations with rapidly rising economies are willing to wait for such an achievement. For this reason, the current models of world-class research universities have in part shifted away from those institutions that took a century or more to mature toward those that accomplished the feat in a shorter period and within the new rough-and-tumble era of competitive knowledge economics. Even in the "post-American" world with the rise of the rest—notably India and China, where ancient civilizations and extensive national histories are treasured—it seems that a century is far too long to wait for a new research university to ripen (Zakaria 2009). Thus, nations have come to consider establishing new research universities while at the same time strengthening the research capacity of traditional national flagship universities. As this chapter will show, a two-pronged strategy is more sensible for an economy on the move rather than a conventional approach that concentrates resources in already established flagship institutions (Ding 2004; Altbach and Balán 2007; Salmi 2009).

This chapter examines a case in Hong Kong SAR, China, in higher education—the establishment and development of HKUST and its unprecedented achievement of becoming an internationally ranked research university within a decade of its establishment in 1991. This university's rapid rise hinges on a number of factors. Although impossible to duplicate elsewhere, such an array of factors is worthy of detailed consideration. These examples illustrate how a successful research university can be established if the institution is accurate in its perception of opportunity within a rapidly changing economic and political environment; proactive in its approach to capitalizing on potential support and overcoming potential hurdles in society; and skillful in planning first-tier faculty recruitment, highlighting its uniqueness, and devising a way to settle into the existing system of higher education. Selected patterns in this case study will resonate with conditions in other emerging economies. Nevertheless, the complex and interwoven nature and process within a changing environment will make any effort to set out specific conditions for establishing world-class research universities a fruitless endeavor. After identifying the main factors surrounding the establishment and development of HKUST, the chapter provides further discussion about the larger issue of establishing research universities.

Key Factors for HKUST

HKUST took advantage of the sunset years of a colonial administration to nest a U.S. research university culture within the British colonial system of higher education. As Hong Kong's other universities remained wedded to their institutional ethos and heritage, this university distinguished itself from the status quo with foresight about the potential role of a science and technology university in the forthcoming Hong Kong SAR, China. It launched several measures that would eventually be seen in other universities. These measures include putting research on an equal footing with teaching, relying on an entrepreneurial approach to development, appointing rather than electing deans, and requiring students to enroll in social science and humanities courses outside their science and technology specialization.[2] In fact, this policy occurred as part of the general trend of globalization in higher education.

The university's establishment coincided with the founding of the Hong Kong Research Grants Council, which provided funds to strengthen research capacity at colleges and universities in Hong Kong (UGC 2000) Today, the Research Grants Council remains the primary source of research funds, which has nudged the traditionally teaching-focused universities of Hong Kong SAR, China, toward more research. Yet, HKUST had a faster launch. The amount of funding it received gradually rose to award levels comparable with other universities and today remains ahead in the proportion of successful grant applications. For example, in 2009 its application success rate was 47 percent, ahead of 36 percent for the other two top research universities. The amount awarded per faculty member is almost twice as much as that at any other university. Thus, with the establishment of the Research Grants Council, the timing of HKUST's establishment as a research university was ideal.

As the 1990s approached, the four Asian "tigers" (Hong Kong; the Republic of Korea; Singapore; and Taiwan, China) were bleeding manufacturing to nearby Asian countries with lower production costs. With increasingly educated populations, the tigers upgraded their domestic industries toward more value-added production. During this industrial upgrading, the governments of Singapore; Korea; and Taiwan, China set the course for high-technology-intensive industries. Although labor-intensive industries from Hong Kong began moving across the border to the Chinese hinterlands, the government eschewed publicly funded high-technology initiatives, choosing instead to rely on market economics as the driving force. It limited itself to the support of infrastructural investment, including a university of science and technology, which quickly made HKUST a symbolic centerpiece of Hong Kong's high-technology upgrading. Its focus on science and technology in a rising Asia resonated with the popular vision of knowledge transfer for a modern China. That vision was enhanced by HKUST's faculty of business and management in a commercial city like Hong Kong. Unfortunately, the government's reliance on market forces failed to make Hong Kong a high-technology center and thereby limited the potential role of the new university to be a catalyst for Hong Kong's rise in that sector. The powerful property and real estate sectors as well as the second-tier civil servants who were perched to lead Hong Kong after the handover to China in 1997 did little to support Hong Kong's development as a center of high technology, thereby driving that opportunity northward where Shanghai became the proactive benefactor.[3]

HKUST's rapid rise was also assisted by the timing of its establishment, shortly after the government's decision in November 1989 to double enrollments in degree-place higher education. This decision occurred in the wake of the Tiananmen Square event when many potential scientists, who would have studied at this university when it opened in 1991, headed instead for overseas universities to further their study. When annual emigration from Hong Kong began to increase during the 1990s, reaching a high in one year of about 65,000, including highly educated residents, the government moved to double university enrollments. This expansion of higher education enrollments would have been more difficult to achieve without the university's establishment in 1991. Return migration rates of these Hong Kong residents increased in the mid- to late 1990s as they felt secure enough to return, with or without overseas residency or passports.[4]

HKUST's most important success factor was the recruitment of outstandingly talented scholars and scientists. All faculty members had doctorates, and 80 percent received doctorates from or were employed at 24 of the top universities in the world. The university recruits this caliber of academic staff from among the senior scholar generation of the Chinese diaspora. The generation of Chinese scholars who left China for Taiwan, China, and then studied overseas, usually in the United States, was riveted on the changes taking place in China during its first decade of economic reform and the opening to the outside world that began in December 1978. The growing number of China's overseas scholars at U.S. universities reached a tipping point. HKUST recruited heavily from this vast pool of talented academics born in Taiwan, China, or mainland China and trained overseas mostly at U.S. universities, something that the other universities in Hong Kong were less inclined to do at that time.

Woo Chia-wei, the university's first president, was a member of this unique generation of Chinese academics. A physicist by training, Woo had also been president of a major research university in the United States. In fact, he was the first ethnic Chinese person to head a major U.S. university. He was also part of an extensive network of Chinese research scientists in the United States. It was highly significant for HKUST that a senior generation of scientists who had attained international reputations in their fields of expertise felt secure enough in their careers to leave their established posts and move to Hong Kong. This shift indicated a certain faith in President Woo, who not only oversaw the establishment and early development of HKUST, but also was instrumental in assembling an outstanding and internationally renowned academic faculty. As HKUST's first president, Woo set the pace for the next two presidents.

To continue its trajectory toward becoming the premier university of science and technology in Asia, HKUST chose Paul Ching-Wu Chu as its second president. Chu was a pioneer in the field of high-temperature superconductivity. While the T. L. L. Temple Chair of Science at the University of Houston and founding director of the Texas Center for Superconductivity, he also served as a consultant and a visiting staff member at Bell Laboratories, Los Alamos National Laboratory, the Marshall Space Flight Center, Argonne National Laboratory, and DuPont. Chu received the 1988 National Medal of Science, the highest honor for a scientist in the United States, was named Best Researcher in the United States by *U.S. News and World Report* in 1990, and was appointed by the White House to be one of 12 distinguished scientists to evaluate the National Medal of Science nominees. One of his major contributions to HKUST was the establishment of the Institute for Advanced Study. Succeeding Paul Ching-Wu Chu, who retired in late 2009, was Tony Chan, who had been assistant director of the U.S. National Science Foundation in charge of the mathematical and physical sciences directorate. In that position, he guided and managed research funding of almost HK\$10 billion (US\$ 1.29 billion) a year in astronomy, physics, chemistry, mathematical science, material science, and multidisciplinary activities. Although he is just beginning his term as president of HKUST, he is expected to combine his skills as a preeminent scholar and scientist and a world-class administrator.

A key consideration for potential recruits to HKUST in the mid to late 1990s was the surge of prosperity in the economy, as investment from China pushed the economy to record levels. This development helped HKUST gain a fair amount of financial resources from the government, although the amount would still pale in comparison to that of top research universities in the United States. Like other universities in Hong Kong, HKUST received a regular injection of funds on a triennial basis from the University Grants Committee and research funding from the newly established Research Grants Council. However, unlike the other universities, HKUST did not have alumni who could support the university with private donations.

Academic salaries reached levels compatible with those offered in other developed countries, which made the decision of recruited staff to relocate to Hong Kong easier, though salary was not the key factor in the equation for top-rung recruitment. For many distinguished academics, relocation meant moving from a spacious U.S.-style house to smaller apartment-style living quarters in Hong Kong, plus a separation from family studying or working nearby.

The approaching date for sovereignty retrocession represented an important and historical turning point for Chinese academics that intensified their emotional attachment to China. The scientific talent that was stored by Taiwan, China, for three decades and that led the economy's successful drive in high technology production was for the first time being focused on Hong Kong's development, specifically in expanding its higher education system. For Chinese-American academics, this change in focus signified an important opportunity to make a significant contribution to U.S.-China relations.

In short, scholars with a strong emotional attachment to China were elated by the increased openness and economic progress of the country. For them, this progress provided an opportunity to take part in a significant event and play a role in China's modernization. In this sense, timing was crucial for staff recruitment. If HKUST had been established a decade earlier, when it was not yet clear that the colonial status of Hong Kong would end in 1997, then most of that university's Chinese academics would not have chosen to work in Hong Kong. An important factor to these scholars, HKUST ensured a degree of academic freedom as yet unavailable in mainland China.

Thus, HKUST created a valuable niche, which it projected through its institutional vision and supported by recruiting two generations of overseas-based Chinese scholars. It presented a unique historical opportunity to work in a dynamic economy and rapidly expanding university system. It established a robust scholarly climate adjoining a globally emergent and reformist China, coinciding with the systematic upgrading of publicly funded research in Hong Kong's universities.

Although the speed in launching a new research university can be hastened by such key factors, some are not easily duplicated elsewhere. Factors such as a dynamic economy, academic freedom, and proximity to the Chinese mainland contributed to the common development of the entire system of higher education in Hong Kong. Each higher education system has unique conditions, some of which can be turned into opportunities for the establishment of research universities. A world-class research university cannot be created in a vacuum. HKUST is nested in a system in which it identified a niche, but projects its vision far beyond Hong Kong's academy.

Although universities in Hong Kong SAR, China, currently are financed by the government, their autonomy is protected by law.[5] In the late 20th century, competition among the top three research universities (the University of Hong Kong, the Chinese University of Hong Kong, and HKUST) for financial support and academic status from the same government coffers also created a new dynamic in higher education in Hong Kong SAR, China. To some extent, this approach contributed to the rise of the economy's entire university system. After HKUST was established, the government's funding allocation pie resource was enlarged. Yet, these funds were still disbursed on a competitive basis. Rather than using a conventional strategy of concentrating resources in one or more already established flagship institutions, Hong Kong used a two-pronged development strategy in which resources were not concentrated in one institution at the expense of others. It uses a strategy for creating research universities in which, at least in theory, the universities complement one another and thereby strengthen the entire system's research capacity. The University Grants Committee asserts a systemwide approach

> developing an interlocking system where the whole higher education sector is viewed as one force . . . values a role-driven yet deeply collaborative system of higher education . . . committed to extensive collaboration with other institutions. (UGC 2010b)

The extent to which this approach is realized in practice is certainly open to debate. Still, some observers credit this strategy, at least in part, for the reason that four of the eight universities in Hong Kong SAR, China, are ranked in the top 10 in Asia (Times Higher Education 2008). The rest of this chapter examines the HKUST case in more detail. The factors unique to its establishment and development receive the most attention, and the chapter concludes with a reassertion of the conditions for the establishment of research universities in emergent economies.

The HKUST Context

New universities, whether public or private, are part of a society and its higher education system. HKUST was established in a highly mobile society, with a system that had not yet made the transition from elite to mass higher education. Hong Kong SAR, China, remains a relatively small region of 422 square miles with some of the most densely populated areas in the world. The ethos of higher education was shaped by its history as a British colony from 1842 to 1997, after which it returned to China in a one-country–two-system arrangement (So and Chan 2002). Although most research is conducted in English, there are two official languages: Chinese (Cantonese dialect) and English. The University of Hong Kong was established in 1911 and the Chinese University of Hong Kong in 1963.[6] The proportion of the age cohort that had access to higher education was 2 percent in 1981 and 8 percent by 1989, when an executive decision was made to double enrollment to 16 percent by 1994 (UGC 1996). During that period, four colleges and polytechnics were upgraded to university status, and by end-1997, Hong Kong SAR, China, had seven universities (UGC 1999). The Asian financial crisis that began in 1998 crippled any discussion about further expansion. When expansion finally occurred, it was largely through privately funded two-year associate-degree programs at community colleges (Postiglione 2008, 2009). The universities have since upgraded research capacity, preserved academic freedom, and converted from a three- to a four-year bachelor-degree program, thus bringing the system into line with the two main trading partners of Hong Kong SAR, China—mainland China and the United States (UGC 2002a, 2004a, 2004b). The four-year system permits HKUST to deepen its original initiative, set in 1991, of providing all students with a significant amount of humanities and social sciences, more than had been offered at the other comprehensive universities in Hong Kong SAR, China.

Basic Characteristics of HKUST

The following describes the fundamental attributes of HKUST: its placement in several of the global rankings of universities; and its roles, goals, and objectives.

Global Rankings

Because this book focuses on the establishment of world-class research universities, it is notable that HKUST has achieved an impressive score on several international league tables (HKUST 2010d): (a) number 35 of the world's top 200 universities in 2009; (b) number 26 of the world's top 100 universities in engineering and information technology in 2008 and in technology in 2008 (Times Higher Education 2008); (c) number 2 of the world's top 200 Asian universities in 2010; (d) number 39 of the world's top 100 universities in engineering and technology and computer sciences (number 1 in "Greater China") in 2010; and (e) number 52–75 of the world's top 100 universities in social sciences (number 1 in "Greater China") in 2010.[7]

HKUST's Roles, Goals, and Objectives

The Hong Kong University of Science and Technology (a) provides a range of programs leading to the award of First Degrees and postgraduate qualifications; (b) includes professional schools, particularly in the fields of science, technology, engineering, and business; (c) offers courses in humanities and social sciences only at a level sufficient to provide intellectual breadth, contextual background, and communication skills to an otherwise scientific or technological curriculum and for limited postgraduate work; (d) offers research programs for a significant number of students in every subject area; and (e) provides scope for academic staff members to undertake consultancy and collaborative projects with industry in areas where they have special expertise. (UGC 2008)

HKUST emphasized the importance of being unique at a time when Hong Kong SAR, China still viewed its universities as elite institutions. HKUST professed to become a "leading force in higher education," "a global academic leader," "an agent of change," and "a catalyst for significant progress in science and technology research and education in Hong Kong, and the Mainland" (HKUST 2010e). This focus supports Jamil Salmi's assertion that a world-class research university "should be based on a forward-looking vision that is genuinely innovative" (Salmi 2009, 57). Nevertheless, some of HKUST's goals echo those of research universities around the world:

- Give all students, undergraduate and postgraduate alike, a broadly based university experience that includes superior training in their chosen fields of study; a well-rounded education that enhances the development of their creativity, critical thinking, global outlook, and cultural awareness; and a campus life that prepares them to be community leaders and lifelong learners.
- Provide a dynamic and supportive working environment in which faculty and staff may continually develop intellectually and professionally.
- Provide an open environment and atmosphere conducive to the exchange of knowledge, views, and innovative ideas among students, faculty and staff members, and visiting scholars.

- Be a leading institution for research and postgraduate study, pursuing knowledge in both fundamental and applied areas and collaborating closely with business and industry in promoting technological innovation and economic development.
- Promote and assist in the economic and social development of Hong Kong SAR, China, and enrich its culture (HKUST 2010b).

Students and Academic Staff Members

The initial student recruitment in 1991 for the newly established university was one of HKUST's most crucial activities, because in the eyes of the public, it had yet to gain a reputation. In this respect, it adopted a proactive approach focused on bringing the university into direct contact with many sectors of the population. It opened itself to the community by taking advantage of its spectacular campus and facilitating access and visits, especially by potential students and their families. Its newly designed campus with impressive architecture and a panoramic view of the surrounding mountains and seaside was a major attraction. About 250 secondary schools were invited to each send two student representatives on the day the new university's foundation stone was laid.

Aside from opening the campus to the public, the university arranged exhibitions throughout Hong Kong. Professors met prospective students on an individual basis to provide general information, though these exhibitions did not include recruitment. Students were formally selected through a Hong Kong–wide recruitment system that came to be known as the Joint University Programmes Admissions System. This main route assisted senior secondary school students with the results of their Hong Kong Advanced Level Examinations to apply for admission to the bachelor's degree programs offered by the seven public universities and the Hong Kong Institute of Education.

Before HKUST opened, it developed a plan for the number of students allocated to the three major faculties: science students would constitute 25 percent, engineering 40 percent, and business administration 35 percent. Also, 20 percent of all students would be postgraduate students (Kung 2002, 5). These proportions remained stable through 2009 (see table 3.1). However, the student body of the university remains below 10,000. Initial impressions suggest that this figure is in keeping with an economy of scale and helps retain a particular institutional ethos. However, faculty numbers can confound the picture (see table 3.2). In 1991, the University Grants Committee resourced HKUST to enroll 7,000 students, even

Table 3.1   Students at Hong Kong University of Science and Technology, 2010

Program or area of study	Undergraduate	Postgraduate	Total
Science	1,431	476	1,907
Engineering	2,310	1,489	3,799
Business and management	2,132	1,189	3,321
Humanities and social sciences	—	280	280
HKUST Fok Ying Tung Graduate School	—	2	2
Interdisciplinary programs	137	69	206
Total (as at January 2010)	6,010	3,505	9,515

Source: Reprinted by permission from Hong Kong University of Science and Technology.
Note: — = not available.

Table 3.2   Faculty of Hong Kong University of Science and Technology, 2009

Program or area of study	Regular	Visiting	Total
Science	100	19	119
Engineering	149	15	164
Business and management	126	12	138
Humanities and social sciences	54	6	60
Division of Environment[a]	7	1	8
Total (as at January 2009)	436	53	489

Source: Reprinted by permission from Hong Kong University of Science and Technology.
a. The Division of Environment is under the Interdisciplinary Programs Office.

while the other two research universities grew to 12,000 students. During the administration of HKUST's second president, student numbers grew toward 10,000 based on a government promise to support a student-faculty ratio of 12 to 1.[8] The government's promise went unfulfilled while student numbers continued to rise. The unfulfilled promise stifled the planned proportionate rise in the student-faculty ratio, thereby adding to the burden on faculty. Such a disproportionate rise reduced faculty research time and was detrimental to faculty morale.[9] When the ratio rose to 19 to 1, it had a significantly adverse effect on research productivity. HKUST operated with a relatively high student-faculty ratio and a lean professoriat. However, HKUST's currently diversified student population of full-time undergraduates, full-time research postgraduates, and full-time and part-time postgraduates, requires a significant number of adjunct faculty members. This development, in turn, has moved the student-faculty ratio in the direction of 15 to 1 or even 14 to 1.

The top three research universities in Hong Kong SAR, China, draw their largest grants from the same public source. Thus, a rapid expansion in the numbers of faculty members and students at one institution over another would be unlikely. Likewise, faculty-student ratios would be proportionate across research universities. Universities in Hong Kong SAR, China, receive block grants that can be allocated with a degree of flexibility. Although fund allocation formulae within specific institutions may vary, student admission numbers and faculty hiring usually adhere to what was promised in proposals to the University Grants Committee. In short, maintaining stability in the proportionate rise of students and faculty across institutions is seemingly in the best interest of a public system of research universities.

This stability could be considered a strategic factor in the establishment of a research university within a group of public universities. Yet, private research universities generally set their own targets for staff and student recruitment. Rather than block grants, their main sources of income are student tuition, alumni funding, other donations, and research grants from government and corporate sponsorship. In the United States, top public research institutions still draw a significant amount of their main public funding from government budgets. Therefore, such allocations are usually made in the context of preserving the state's system of research universities. Those arrangements could also work in reverse—such as when a state legislature closes a local undergraduate college in its system, but the top research universities in the system usually survive.

The same adverse effects held true for Hong Kong in the early years of HKUST, when an action that seemed equitable in a systemwide context worked against the mission of a research university. In the case of HKUST, its planning committee chair has stated in retrospect:

> Regrettably, the University Grants Committee has since strayed from the principle of giving priority to needs and values, but instead, allocated funds "equitably" to all the varsities. Consequently, UST was not able to offer more places at the postgraduate level in past years as its mission stipulated. This, to me, is unfortunate and a retrograde policy that has caused Hong Kong to lag behind the competition in advanced science and technology. (Chung 2001, 54)

HKUST's Inauguration and Commencement

Appreciation of HKUST's ascent into the research university stratosphere rests heavily on understanding its preestablishment plan and takeoff (Woo 2006). In 1984, the Sino-British Joint Declaration[10] on Hong Kong's future was signed, and China established the adjacent Shenzhen Special

Economic Zone. As the border began to blur and Hong Kong's manufacturing and investment flowed into the Shenzhen zone, Sir Edward Youde, governor at the time, saw this new symbiosis with China as leading to an economic and technological transformation that would continue to relocate Hong Kong's manufacturing industries to south China. The governor expressed a new vision in which Hong Kong would become technologically upgraded. In September 1985, he asked the University and Polytechnic Grants Committee to explore the feasibility of a third university that would augment the existing setup of two low enrollment universities, two polytechnics, and two colleges. At a meeting of the governor's Executive Council in March 1986, the committee responded positively, confirming that the new university would focus on science and technology, management, and postgraduate training (Chung 2001, 148–58).

Planning and Construction

A planning committee was established in 1986, chaired by Sir Chung Sze-yuen of the governor's Executive Council. Its terms of reference included building a campus with a funding allocation from the Royal Hong Kong Jockey Club.[11] The first enrollments were planned for 1994. However, the new campus opened on October 2, 1991, with 600 students. Nine years later, HKUST was ranked seventh in Asia according to *Asia Week*. In 2001, the HKUST business school was ranked the best in Asia by the *Financial Times* and 48th in the world. By 2010, the *Financial Times* ranked the HKUST master of business administration program ninth in the world, tied with the University of Chicago Booth School of Business. This ranking also becomes significant for understanding HKUST's extensive collaboration with business and industry, as noted later in this chapter.

In 1987, the Royal Hong Kong Jockey Club, a nonprofit community organization, pledged HK$1.50 billion (US$192 million) for a project estimated to cost HK$1.93 billion (US$247 million), inflation included (Flahavin 1991). The figure was based on unit costs from the then recent building of the urban campus of the City Polytechnic of Hong Kong. Although this estimate was useful, the fact remained that City Polytechnic was advantaged by its urban environment—unlike HKUST, which was built in a rural area lacking basic infrastructure such as utilities and sewage as well as specific requirements for conducting research in fields such as microelectronics and biotechnology laboratories.

Nevertheless, cost-overrun concerns were raised on May 4, 1988, when HKUST came before the Legislative Council for approval. Because funds for the campus came from the Jockey Club, supplemented by the government, a review by the legislature was required before approval. The government's initial cost estimate for capital construction was conservative and was made public. As campus construction proceeded and was put on a fast track to permit an earlier opening date, building engineers recognized the project's complexity and consulted with the government and the Jockey Club. The exchange of views led to a common understanding of the gap between the originally publicized estimate and the project's cost increase because of both inflation and faster pace of construction. In this context, the new president and his team noted inadequacies in laboratory facilities and building area. The University and Polytechnic Grants Committee expanded the area of the campus, and by June 1990, the budget was increased to HK$3.548 billion (US$455 million), a figure approved by the Legislative Council without objections (Chung 2001, 157). Phases I and II of the construction were completed on schedule in 1993 for HK$3.224 billion (US$413 million), 8.6 percent less than the estimate without overruns (Walker 1994).

In general, the establishment and development of new research universities in developing societies can periodically be plagued by cost overrun issues because of the vast sums required to build a research university. If not handled correctly, these issues can affect the public's view of a new institution. In the case of HKUST, the effort to speed the building process in the interest of facilitating the overall expansion of access to higher education in Hong Kong was overshadowed for a time by building costs. Such cost issues are often quite detailed, and their complexities are not easily presented to the public. Thus, a country's system of governance, especially its legal system and accounting transparency, is critical when establishing a new research university. Today, a developed society like Hong Kong SAR, China—with its vigorous legal and financial accounting systems held in high regard by the international community—commonly has extensive oversight on such large government projects. With the freest press media in Asia, Hong Kong SAR, China, has a literate public kept informed during every step of the process about any questions in the cost of large public projects. Yet, the financial issues surrounding such a large enterprise are often open to multiple interpretations by the media and can become convoluted by the politics of a particular era. Nevertheless, a high degree of transparency is essential for establishing a new research university despite the risks of multiple interpretations. Although the public continues to question major expenditures, past and planned—including a cyberport, a Disneyland, and a high-speed railway—this association of ideas does not include HKUST.

Presidential Search

The name of the university was chosen in 1986 and was officially proposed in the first report of the planning committee in September 1987. HKUST was formally incorporated in April 1988 and immediately sponsored the first meeting of its University Council. After a global search, the first president was appointed in November 1988. Forty-four applications were received, and 47 other names were put forward. More than half came from England (25 applications and 35 names put forward); nine applications from the United States and Canada plus seven other names put forward; two applications from Australia plus one other name put forward; five applications from Hong Kong with seven other names put forward; and three applications from other countries with three other names put forward. Of these, 14 applicants were interviewed, and five of them (from Australia, Hong Kong, the United Kingdom, and the United States) were selected for final consideration (Kung 2002, 5). Though selection committee members, Chung Sze-yuen and Lee Quo-wei, suggested the new president be a person of Chinese descent, the governor would agree only that the final choice must be a candidate who was president of a top Western university. The final choice, put forward and reported to the governor on September 21, 1987, was Woo Chia-wei, a distinguished theoretical physicist and president of San Francisco State University (which had 25,000 students). The choice was approved on October 10, 1987, and publicly announced on November 5. He was well-known in Hong Kong and spoke the commonly used Cantonese dialect as well as the national language of Mandarin. It was highly significant that Woo Chia-wei was the first person of Chinese descent to head a major university in the United States. This distinction would translate as a tremendous boost to the HKUST recruitment of academic staff, a key factor in its rapidly won success.

The government provided HKUST and its new president with an initial vision statement:

> To advance learning and knowledge through teaching and research, particularly: (i) in science, technology, engineering, management and business studies; and (ii) at the postgraduate level; and to assist the economic and social development of Hong Kong. (HKUST 2010)

President Woo appreciated that this vision generally provided the proper guidance and was worded loosely enough to allow the founding faculty to interpret it more forcefully. When he assumed the presidency, he requested that the university be allocated a larger percentage of graduate students. Although this request was not granted, he nevertheless succeeded, on the basis of the words "social development," to upgrade the university's General Education Centre into a School of Humanities and Social Sciences that granted master and PhD degrees.

Elements of HKUST

Language of Instruction

Instruction at HKUST was to be delivered in English. The University of Hong Kong had always adhered to the principle that all instruction be delivered in English, though the campus life of students reflected the bilingual nature of society.[12] The Chinese University of Hong Kong permitted its teachers to use either Chinese (Cantonese or Mandarin) or English as their instructional language. The new university's orientation toward science and technology contributed to this uncontroversial decision to adhere to English-language instruction, despite the upcoming reunion of Hong Kong with China. Most senior professors had been accustomed to teaching in English, and most could not lecture in Cantonese, which was the lingua franca of Hong Kong.

The global university rankings indicate that the language of instruction does not automatically determine the ranking of a research university. For example, Tokyo and Kyoto universities (Japan), where much funding is allocated to translation of English-language journals, are among the world's top-rated Asian universities. There are other top universities, but the issue of language of instruction in world-class universities is complex and has been discussed elsewhere. For example, Jamil Salmi (2009, 61) mentions 11 non-native-speaking higher education systems where some graduate programs are offered in English. Although Hong Kong SAR, China, where most graduate programs are in English, is not mentioned within this group, its higher education system receives a special distinction within China and has two official languages, Chinese and English. Although some of mainland China's top universities use English in selected courses and programs, the only examples of English-language universities on the mainland are relatively new joint ventures: the University of Nottingham Ningbo, China; Xi'an Jiaotong-Liverpool University in Suzhou; and United International College (Hong Kong Baptist University and Beijing Normal University) in the Zhuhai Special Economic Zone adjoining Hong Kong SAR, China.

The language of instruction has implications for HKUST's aim to internationalize its student recruitment, which already extends far beyond Hong Kong SAR, China—including mainland China and overseas. In fact, HKUST has the highest percentage of nonlocal students among its counterparts (UGC 2010a). Although the figures for students from overseas and other parts of Asia are comparable to those at other universities, the percentage of students from the Chinese mainland surpasses other universities, which will probably have a long-term effect of strengthening future partnerships and collaborations. Although most graduate students are from the mainland, the proportion of undergraduate students from the mainland matches that at other universities and will continue to do so as HKUST adopts a four-year university system—in 2012—similar to that on the Chinese mainland.

Innovations in Governance

A key innovation of HKUST that contributes to its maxim "be unique and not duplicate" is the manner in which administrators are chosen. All deans are appointed by recommendations from search committees, and the search committees are dominated by faculty members, rather than appointed by the administration or elected from within a school or faculty, as was the case in the universities of Hong Kong at the time. This process was innovative within the context of Hong Kong, which had a system that adhered closely to the British model of higher education. The HKUST system was a U.S. model in terms of academic field appointments and reflected the U.S. corporate system in which faculty governed the academic part of the university. HKUST also triggered a change at other universities in Hong Kong away from traditional academic titles (lecturer, senior lecturer, and reader and professor) to those used in the United States and elsewhere (assistant professor, associate professor, and professor). Similarly, the current customary administrative titles in universities in Hong Kong SAR, China (vice-chancellor, deputy vice-chancellor, and pro-vice-chancellor) are also undergoing some change with increased use of the titles president, provost, and vice president.

A potentially valuable advantage is created when (a) a new research university is to be established and nested within a particular model of higher education and (b) the system provides enough autonomy for it to develop a particular edge over other long-established institutions of the system by innovating its governance or academic structure in accordance with a unique vision. This project also represents a system to speed up the process of introducing reforms in other top institutions, among which ethos and long history prevent any radical changes that would be risky to the identity and long-established brand of the university.

This type of innovation is a potential advantage in the establishment of research universities. HKUST was established during the sunset years of the British administration and at a time when the United States and mainland China were Hong Kong's major trading partners. Not only were most major universities in the world located in the United States, but the higher education system in mainland China also operated more closely to the U.S. model of higher education, and most of China's prospective academics who studied overseas did so in the United States. This situation gave HKUST a tremendous advantage. HKUST's adaptation of innovations from the U.S. university system made it unique. Meanwhile, the British style of higher education in other institutions, although well established and successful, had more inertia toward change than a newly established university. Thus, the timing of HKUST's establishment, something that "may be difficult to duplicate elsewhere," contributed a great deal to its rapid rise (Wong 2010).

Another factor contributing to HKUST's innovative character was the relatively autonomous nature of higher education in Hong Kong at the time. Although HKUST has been a public institution from the beginning, it possessed a high degree of autonomy in most respects and could freely innovate in academic research and instructional delivery. Though it did not have to await approval by government or the University Grants Committee, it adhered to several basic conventions followed by the other two government research universities, especially in terms of student recruitment. Beginning in 2012, all universities in Hong Kong SAR, China, will move to a standard four-year undergraduate program and will begin to recruit from "senior secondary form six."

Academic Staff—Key to the Academic Kingdom

Although there is a global trend toward recruiting part-time academic staff, HKUST instead sought full-time academic staff, as was the case in Hong Kong's university system. The initial planning of academic staff followed a distinct strategy for faculty: (a) 214 engineering faculty members—21 professors, 54 associate professors, and 139 assistant professors; (b) 171 science faculty members—17 professors, 43 associate professors, and 111 assistant professors; and (c) 160 business administration faculty members—16 professors, 40 associate professors, and 104 assistant professors.[13] This structure differed from the single professor chair system used by departments in Hong Kong's other universities at the time (Chung 2001, 5–6).

HKUST recruited practically all academic staff from outside Hong Kong, most of whom were born in China. If the staff had been recruited largely from the traditional expatriate and local academic pools, that practice would have detracted from the uniqueness of HKUST. This is another point worthy of consideration by universities in a developing country that have a large contingency of students and scholars who study overseas for doctorates but have yet to return home in great numbers. Jamil Salmi (2009, 61) considers this issue but does not mention that Hong Kong SAR, China, probably has the largest proportion of returned diaspora academic staff members, though many are originally from other parts of China. Korea, for example, has been able to attract back a significant number of its overseas academics, though they largely populate second-tier universities. However, Mongolia has not yet been successful in luring them home. The establishment of a new and well-endowed research university can be an attraction. For example, if Mongolia's newly discovered precious mineral deposits tip its economy forward as predicted for future years, it may be able to consider such an initiative. There are other potential examples from the ranks of developing countries.

Another distinguishing characteristic of HKUST concerns the qualifications of its academic staff and the academic centers from which faculty are recruited. Not only do all of HKUST's faculty members possess doctorates from universities around the world, but at least 80 percent also have worked or earned doctorates at renowned research universities— such as California Institute of Technology; Carnegie Mellon University; Columbia University; Cornell University; Harvard University; Imperial College London; Massachusetts Institute of Technology; Northwestern University; Princeton University; Purdue University; Stanford University; University of British Columbia; University of California, Berkeley; University of California, Los Angeles; University of Cambridge; University of Chicago; University of Illinois; University of London; University of Michigan; University of Oxford; University of Toronto; University of Wisconsin–Madison; and Yale University. These qualifications are not only an indication of the caliber of academic staff, but also represent a wellspring of academic capital that is used to build transnational research collaborations among networks of scholars from similar institutions.

Working Environments: The Best of Both Worlds

The adage about Hong Kong SAR, China, being a meeting point between East and West turns out to be more than a cliché for the academic born in China and trained as a scholar and scientist in the West. The Hong

Kong SAR, China, work environment carries many advantages not available elsewhere for some Chinese academics. These advantages include living in a Chinese society and working in an English-language university, teaching in English to Chinese students, conducting research with methods learned in the West and applying them to China's development, publishing in Western academic journals and attaining international recognition, and having their work translated into Chinese for a much larger audience. It also means avoiding the glass ceiling sometimes experienced by Chinese academics overseas and avoiding the restrictions on academic freedom on the mainland. Hong Kong SAR, China, represents a relatively easy adjustment to both academic and societal culture and provides a unique and advantageous environment for innovative academic work. Moreover, a large number of academic staff members at HKUST and at other universities in Hong Kong SAR, China, are foreign nationals, some of whom have Chinese heritage though they may have been born or naturalized overseas. The United Kingdom, for example, has a high proportion (27 percent) of foreign-national academic staff (Salmi 2009, 61). However, in a recent international survey, Hong Kong SAR, China, ranked second (after Australia) in the proportion of foreign nationals.

Multigenerational Recruitment from the Top Down

As mentioned earlier, the first president of HKUST took a major role in recruitment and is quoted as saying: "You've got to start from the top because only first-class people can attract other first-class people. In fast-moving fields like science, engineering, and management, you are either first class or without class" (Course 2001, 8). The academic pillars of HKUST began with those age 50 or younger who were born on the mainland; whose families left for Taiwan, China, in the 1940s; and who had gone to the United States for study and had remained there to start families. Although many became naturalized U.S. citizens and worked in the United States for decades, their aspirations included making a contribution to their homeland. According to Woo: "They had talent, they had ability, but in the end, what brought them here was their hearts" (Course 2001, 9).

Academics of that generation included Jay-Chung Chen, an aeronautics expert recruited from the Jet Propulsion Laboratory at the California Institute of Technology. Chih-Yung Chien was a top experimental physicist from Johns Hopkins University who had conducted his research on the world's largest high-energy accelerator at the European Organization for Nuclear Research. Shain-Dow Kung, a specialist in biotechnology and acting provost at the University of Maryland Biotechnology Institute, became the dean of science in 1991. Other recruits during the first decade included Leroy Chang, a world-renowned experimental physicist from International Business Machines (IBM), and fivefold national academy member in the United States and China. Another internationally noted HKUST scholar was Ping Ko, who came from the University of California, Berkeley, and was director of the microfabrication laboratory. Otto C. C. Lin, who was dean of the School of Engineering at Tsing Hua University and director of the world-famous Industrial Technology Research Institute (ITRI) in Taiwan, China, became HKUST's vice president for research and development. Other notable scientists included Eugene Wong, who had been recruited by the U.S. White House to be associate director of the Office of Science and Technology Policy and who came to HKUST from the chair of electrical engineering and computer science at the University of California, Berkeley, where he developed the theory that provides the statistical foundation for processing images and other multidimensional data.

The younger generation of recruits comprised those in their late 30s and early 40s, including Chan Yuk-Shee, who was the Justin Dart Professor of Finance at the University of Southern California and became the founding dean of the HKUST School of Business and Management. They were mandated to "establish a leading business school in Asia by the end of the century" (Course 2001; Kung 2002).

A striking theme among top recruits was the idea of making a new beginning with a vision that HKUST could become a world-class research university. The caliber of these scholars and scientists in turn attracted other senior academics, including many non-Chinese, from North America, Asia, and Europe. Peter Dobson, first HKUST's director of planning and coordination and later its associate vice president for academic affairs, was recruited from the University of Hawaii. Thomas Stelson was executive vice president of the Georgia Institute of Technology and became vice president for research and development. Gregory James came from the University of Exeter to become the director of the HKUST Language Center.

Recruitment is one of the most strategic aspects in the rapid establishment of internationally recognized universities. Although this recruitment requires finding already-established leaders in their fields, a good portion of these scholars may be close to retirement and will lead their departments in the new university for only a few years. Thus, their value may be more in attracting top younger scholars than in contributing over the long run at the new university. They could also become influential emeritus professors if they reside in the university's region and maintain close contact after retirement, which is less likely if they were originally recruited from overseas. Moreover, in any new recruitment exercise, a certain degree of attrition of top scholars is not unexpected, something that factor must be built into all recruitment plans.

Finally, although salaries may not be a singular attraction for some scholars, their salaries at the new university will be viewed as an indication of their status and can signal to other scholars in their home university that their departure is not one of downward mobility. In short, a new university must be prepared to provide attractive salaries to distinguished scholars while viewing their motive for joining the university as not merely financial.

Timing

Although salaries were clearly not the most essential attraction for the original group of leading HKUST scholars, the economic growth rate in Hong Kong at the time permitted academic salaries to approach levels compatible with those overseas, thus making relocation easier. Nevertheless, for academics based at U.S. universities, relocating often meant a transition from spacious houses to modest apartments. Although Hong Kong academic salary levels had generally been lower than their counterparts in U.S. universities, this situation began to change. The five-year period from 1988 to 1993 saw a doubling of salaries. By 1998, the increases were 2.7 times more than in 1988.

In the 1990s, academic salary scales were linked to those of the civil service and rose steadily, though academic salaries have since been unlinked from those of the civil service.[14] Although some government officials had opposed the rise in academic salaries, the approaching date of sovereignty retrocession had caused some concern about a possible brain drain. HKUST recruited 120 faculty members each year, averaging about 10 recruits per month, 80 percent of whom had received their PhDs in North America.

Timing contributed to HKUST's success in several other ways. It acted as a confidence booster to a society in transition from a colony to a new system within China. As stated earlier, many of HKUST's Chinese academics would probably not have accepted an offer to work at HKUST a decade earlier when it was not clear that the colonial status of Hong Kong would end. Other timely factors were the expansion of Hong Kong's degree enrollment from 8 percent to 16 percent of the relevant age group between 1989 and 1995 and the increasing availability of research funds from the newly established Hong Kong Research Grants Council.

Governance Structure

HKUST established itself as a new international university without assaulting the governing traditions of the United Kingdom in Hong Kong. The governance structure now consists of a court, council, and senate.[15] The court, established in May 1994, meets once per academic year for several hours, is an advisory body on general policy, and considers presidential and council reports. However, it plays no actual role in the governance of the university.[16]

The council is the supreme governing and executive body of the university. It is responsible for investments, contracts, property, appointments of presidents and vice presidents, budget, finances, and statutes; and it confers honorary degrees and academic awards. It consists of up to three public officers appointed by the chief executive of Hong Kong SAR, China; up to 18 external members who are not public officers or employees of the university; and 12 internal members of the university including the president, vice presidents, deans of schools, and academic members nominated by the senate. It is presided over by a lay chair (that is, a non-HKUST employee). The council may meet several times per year. However, an executive committee, known as the standing committee of the council, meets regularly. This body promotes the university's interests in local, regional, and international spheres, and some of its members volunteer to raise funds.

The senate sets academic policies. Members are employees and students, including the president; vice presidents; deans of schools; heads of academic departments, units, and centers; academic staff members elected by their peers; and student representatives. It has a maximum of 54 members, of whom 32 hold academic offices or department positions, while 19 are elected or co-opted from the academic staff and three are student representatives. Its work covers academic planning and development; management of facilities for residence, teaching, learning, and research (libraries, laboratories, and so forth); and provision of student welfare. Finally, boards of the four schools (science, engineering, business and management, and humanities and social science) and the newly named HKUST Fok Ying Tung Graduate School are responsible to the senate for teaching and other work of the schools.

The top governance layers of the government-funded universities of Hong Kong SAR, China, generally manage with some uniformity. They provide a certain amount of integrity with the elite leadership strata of Hong Kong SAR, China, as reflected in the membership of the court and council. This uniformity does not mean that government university relations are always smooth. For example, despite the University Grants Committee being a buffer between government and universities, the HKUST planning stage was not without controversy. The chair of the planning committee's view was that the University and Polytechnic Grants Committee (now the University Grants Committee) stifled its development by allocating places "equitably" rather than according to "needs and values" (Chung 2001, 155). However, in general the government has not interfered directly with the universities in Hong Kong SAR, China. This situation is reflected in Jamil Salmi (2009, 59) quoting Ruth Simmons: "Great universities are not only useful in their own time, but in preparing for future times. What allows a great university to do that is as little interference from the state as possible." However, the amount of interference by government can be interpreted in various ways. Although government interference may not be direct, it does have ways to steer the path of universities—making its interference more subtle. Chung Sze-yuen interpreted what he thought were limits placed on HKUST's postgraduate expansion, and a more recent University Grants Committee report supported the secretary of education's preference that HKUST and the Chinese University of Hong Kong consider a merger. In fact, the University Grants Committee's role in university development in general and in HKUST's development in particular cannot be overlooked. For example, the committee sees itself as key for proactively helping universities make Hong Kong SAR, China, Asia's world city and the education hub of the region, particularly with mainland China. However, the University Grants Committee has not been proactive in helping the universities fend off efforts by government to interfere in their development. Clearly, some debate exists about the committee's role. Its supposed proactive role extends into "strategic planning and policy development to advise and steer the higher education sector," which is to be done with incentives and other mechanisms that "assist institutions to perform at an internationally competitive level in their respective roles" (UGC 2010b). These mechanisms include the Teaching and Learning Quality Process Reviews, Research Assessment Exercise, and Management Reviews, which are mandated for HKUST and other institutions. HKUST submitted a Self-Evaluation Document in July 2002 and successfully completed the Teaching and Learning Quality Process Reviews in 2003. These were its second set of such reviews. It also successfully completed management reviews in 1998 and 2002. The Research Assessment Exercise, a mechanism borrowed from the United Kingdom, was still used in Hong Kong SAR, China, in 2006. Yet, the perceived value of these and related University Grants Committee exercises, by the administration of HKUST and other universities, has not been evident.

Research Funding and Donations

HKUST remains a young university, and its governance structure continues to evolve. In 2009, HKUST's second president, Paul Ching-Wu Chu, completed his term, and Tony Chan began his presidency. President Chu, a world-renowned scientist, took office during difficult times—when Hong Kong SAR, China, still suffered the effects of both the Asian economic crisis and the SARS (severe acute respiratory syndrome) crisis. He still managed to establish an Institute for Advanced Study, modeled after the one at Princeton University. The institute provides a center for noted scientists from around the world to visit, think, and conduct workshops.

The Institute for Advanced Study of HKUST champions collaborative projects across disciplines and institutions. It forges relationships with academic, business, community, and government leaders for helping to transform Hong Kong SAR, China, and the greater Chinese region into a global source of creative and intellectual power. Its visiting members included Aaron Ciechanover, Nobel Prize winner in chemistry in 2004. Eric Maskin, Nobel laureate in economics in 2007, visited on March 17, 2010. The Institute for Advanced Study also has a highly distinguished international advisory board, comprising 12 Nobel laureates. It is also recruiting 10 "star scholars" as permanent institute faculty members and will honor each with a named professorship (each with an endowment of HK$30 million [US$3.87 million]), which provides salary enhancement and additional research funding. Another 60 named fellowships (each with an endowment of HK$10 million [US$1.29 million]) are available for young and promising scholars who join the institute as postdoctoral fellows to work closely with the permanent institute faculty.

The research and development (R&D) budget for Hong Kong SAR, China, is only 0.7 percent of gross domestic product, placing it 50th in global rankings for this indicator. Thus, the amount of research funds available to HKUST might be considered as quite substantial, until compared with the counterpart universities from which the first generation of its leading scientists were recruited. Though modest by comparison, research funding available to HKUST has steadily increased except around the time of the Asian economic crisis. Donations for research by such groups as Hong Kong Telecom of about HK$10 million (US$1.3 million) and the donation by the Hong Kong Jockey Club of HK$130 million (US$17 million) for biotechnology were also helpful to the research profile of HKUST.

As of June 2008, the HK$350.9 million (US$4.5 million) research fund included Hong Kong SAR, China, private funds of HK$98.8 million (US$12.66 million; 28.2 percent); non–Hong Kong SAR, China, sources of HK$6.5 million (US$832,860; 1.9 percent); Research Grants Council funds of HK$125.3 million (US$16.05; 35.7 percent); University Grants Committee funds of HK$84.7 million (US$10.85 million; 24.1 percent); and other Hong Kong SAR, China, government funds (mostly from the Innovation and Technology Commission) of HK$35.5 million (US$4.55 million; 10.1 percent).[17] The total includes R&D projects administered by R&D corporations (HKUST R and D Corporation Ltd 2010). The high-impact areas of research are nanoscience and nanotechnology, electronics, wireless and information technology, environment and sustainable development, and management education and research. Aside from their scientific significance, these areas are viewed as adding value to the social and economic development of the region, including Hong Kong SAR, China, and the surrounding Pearl River Delta.

Donations have come to play an increasingly important role in the finance and development of higher education in Hong Kong SAR, China. Starting off as the only university in Hong Kong without an alumni sector, HKUST was keen to find ways to offset this condition and took advantage of the timely rise of Chinese philanthropy. The Hong Kong government facilitated the donation culture by providing matching grants to donations made to universities. Selected donations included Sino Group HK$20 million (US$2.56 million), Kerry Group HK$20 million (US$2.56 million), Shun Hing Group HK$10 million (US$1.28 million), Shui On Group HK$25 million (US$3.20 million), and Hang Lung Group HK$20 million (US$2.56 million).[18] By agreement, the donation amounts from the following donors were not disclosed: Hang Seng Bank, Hysan Trust Fund, and Li Wing Tat Family. IBM and JEOL (Japan Electron Optics Laboratory) also donated equipment. The Croucher Foundation made continuous donations to various projects of the university. All these donations were made during HKUST's early development stage. During its 10th anniversary, HKUST noted that it had received contributions from 18 foundations and 19 corporations, as well as seven individual and family donors. There has been a continuous stream of donations too extensive to list here.

Collaborations and Partnerships

HKUST's collaborations and partnerships have contributed to its success (Ji 2009). The university has taken specific measures to address one of its major goals, stated earlier in the chapter, to collaborate closely with business and industry in promoting technological innovation and economic development. When declared, this goal set HKUST apart from the other two leading research universities of the time. Its major innovation in this respect was to establish a wholly owned company known as the Research and Development Corporation (RDC), a unit that serves as the business arm of the university to commercialize research. RDC is the signatory for contracts and contract administration carried out by all university departments.

To further develop its collaborations and partnerships with the private and public sectors in Hong Kong SAR, China, and the region, RDC has established a number of subsidiaries and joint ventures and has extended its reach into the Pearl River Delta and beyond. It has increased its presence on mainland China, where it offers services that meet specific market requirements. For example, RDC develops collaborations with public and private sectors within the adjoining Pearl River Delta in Guangdong Province and elsewhere in China, including Beijing. The corporation has a partnership with Peking University and the Shenzhen municipal government in a tripartite cooperative institution that engages in production, study, and research. The institution helps to commercialize high-technology research products. HKUST also has a partnership in Beijing's financial district under a tripartite agreement to establish an International Financial Education and Training Center in Beijing with Beijing Street Holding Company, Ltd., and Beijing International Financial Center (Liu and Zweig 2010).

RDC works closely with the university's technology transfer office to market intellectual property that has been created by the university. In this way, it acts as a technology transfer point between HKUST and both public and private sectors. It handles licensing for commercial collaboration in biotechnology, computer engineering, information technology, and 10 other areas.

As part of RDC, the university also established an Entrepreneurship Center. Opened in 2000, the center seeks to encourage participation of university academic staff members and students in the commercialization of new technology. The Entrepreneurship Center provides them with workspace, business consultation services, and incubation facilities. It also helps introduce venture capitalists to academic staff members and students, resulting in more than 20 spin-off and seven start-up companies, one of which is listed on the Hong Kong Stock Exchange.

In July 2010, HKUST submitted a Knowledge Transfer Report to the University Grants Committee (HKUST 2010a), in which it proposed a five-year strategy to establish a knowledge transfer platform to strengthen entrepreneurship, generate funding for innovation, and create new business opportunities.

Conclusion

Universities are nested within regional civilizations, each of which provides unique conditions that can be drawn upon to establish outstanding research universities. HKUST has drawn upon both Chinese and Western civilizations for talent and innovation and has capitalized on advantageous conditions such as institutional autonomy and the provision of capital resources. Yet its success was ensured by a strategically proactive recruitment that yielded an academic faculty with global recognition, shared purpose, and relentless drive, which taken together supported HKUST's rapidly unprecedented rise within one decade into the ranks of the so-called world-class research universities.

Establishment and Planning

A planning committee for a new research university needs to know how to take advantage of the context within which the institution will be established, including an economy on the rise, industrial restructuring, a shifting emphasis in higher education toward more research, an existing local system of distinguished research universities, and the intensification of the global discourse of knowledge economics. A planning committee also must be skillful enough to establish a new international university without assaulting the existing governing traditions, in this case the British academic model of Hong Kong.

In short, the HKUST case emphasizes the centrality of a skillfully executed establishment phase. The caliber of the individuals who design and carry forth the planning during the preparatory phase has a profound influence on the initial trajectory of a research university and can make or break its takeoff period. Among the many key decisions made by a preparatory committee is the selection of a university leadership that can drive the recruitment of the top layer of academic talent. Clearly, there is no more crucial activity for the establishment of an internationally recognized research university than initial faculty recruitment.

Recruitment

Undoubtedly, access to top talent from around the world is a process that cannot be fully controlled. However, access on a personal level to defined networks of noted scientists and the ability to persuade academic leaders to trade a secure position at a top university for the opportunity to join a new enterprise in a country of their ethnic heritage are indispensible traits for a founding university president. In the case of HKUST, that recruitment process involved geographically expansive interviewing of prospective faculty, in one case conducting interviews in nine cities within seven days. Moreover, the HKUST case demonstrates that competitive salaries, though helpful, may be of only limited benefit to recruitment efforts. This issue holds true especially for recruitment of academics who can drive a university beyond its opening day and remain committed over time not only to maintain a high caliber of research, but also to build a purposeful engagement with the society and country where the university is situated. For HKUST, salary was not the main factor in persuading already-established top talent to move. Many recruits were already highly paid in U.S. universities, and relocation to HKUST meant a significant decrease in their living space, often affecting their family's routines and children's educations. Given the risks, distinguished scientists at top U.S. universities would have been unlikely to relocate to a new but unknown university if ethnic and emotional attachments to China had not been as much a factor as competitive salaries.

Sustainability

For any newly established university rapidly achieving success and status within the larger international network of research universities, the long-term aim is to sustain the gains of the initial developmental stage. As HKUST's vice president for research remarked, "eighteen years is not a long time" (Chin 2009). Therefore, the focus must remain on the areas of strength in terms of faculties and their programs. The areas identified by the founders continue to remain central to the institution. However, certain aspects of globalization have made universities, including HKUST, modify the type of emphasis on courses and specialized areas of research. For example, disciplines of study have maintained their integrity; but as discussed earlier, a strategic shift toward multidisciplinarity had to occur (Chin 2009). The need for depth remains, but the interactivity across fields on campus has increased. It is more widely recognized that the problems facing the region require solutions not focused on disciplinary boundaries. Whether it is gene-sequencing and community health policy, civil engineering and climate change, or life sciences and global communication, students increasingly need to look ahead and be prepared to solve problems across a spectrum of areas.

Models

Research universities are also sensitive to models. HKUST has remained cognizant of the Massachusetts Institute of Technology and Stanford University models. HKUST has already had to make modifications as the limitations of the original models arose. Although it experienced good timing and some luck, its focus remains the same: emphasize research, and hire the best scientists. Nevertheless, a shift has occurred. While the university can recruit top scientists from the outside initially, continuity cannot be sustained unless a certain indigenization takes hold in the next phase. The next generation of young scholars was more easily able to make Hong Kong SAR, China, a centerpiece of their academic lives. In short, the university went forward with the preparation of a generation of local scientists who will serve and become leaders for the surrounding region of south China as it develops in the decades to come.

Context: Institutions and Systems

Several sections of this chapter highlight how a new research university nests itself within a larger system of existing research universities. It can draw strength from other research universities as well as become a catalyst for those universities' reforms. Although this development requires a new university to identify with other research universities as part of a system, it also benefits the new institution to stand apart with enough vision and vitality to clearly project the institution's uniqueness. This balance can become upset from intrasystem recruitment during the establishment phase. Therefore, it is important for university leaders to reach an informal consensus on such matters. University heads in Hong Kong SAR, China, have channels for communication and meet periodically, not by government proclamation but as a group of university presidents with common interests. Registrars and other university officers at different levels also have informal networks of communication. For example, although each university is currently developing its new first-year general education curriculum and each is free to design and develop in its own way, informal opportunities exist to periodically share experiences and outcomes at forums or other academic events.

HKUST and other research universities in the Hong Kong SAR, China, system share basic characteristics at the institutional level that are common to research universities everywhere. However, these research universities share the challenge to justify their existence within a bustling Asian business center whose lifeline is global competition in business, trade, and commerce and whose institutional and academic conventions were largely born from colonial transplants. It was within that system that HKUST had to distinguish itself from the other colonial institutions of the time. It did so by establishing a highly entrepreneurial research-culture university without assaulting local governing traditions. It also anticipated the postcolonial context from the beginning.

Thus, this case provides knowledge about lessons for the way a new research university nests itself within a larger system of research universities. In each phase, from planning to establishment to daily operations, the new institution must enhance rather than tip the balance in the larger system. For HKUST to succeed, there needed to be an existing system of respected and well-established institutions that viewed the massive investment of resources in a new institution not as a loss for themselves but as a win-win situation for the system as a whole. This cooperation will not diminish the competitive discourse among the institutions in the system. If anything, it sharpens it. The new research university draws strength, stands apart, and becomes a catalyst for change. Such system change would have been inevitable, but weighty traditions in long-established universities can resist change without the needed catalyst.

Yet it is useful to point out certain systemwide conditions for the successful establishment and development of a new research university that were then present in Hong Kong and for which a new institution cannot be a catalyst. Academic ethics and a corruption-free environment were in place before HKUST joined the larger system and have been sustained since then.

In a small system of less than 10 universities, it is easier to form and present a coherent identity across borders. Sharing core commitments such as intellectual freedom, knowledge exchange, ethnic equality, and other factors, which all help wed institutions to a larger system, facilitates this collaboration. The University Grants Committee also plays a role here in articulating the differences in institutional roles within the larger system and reinforces these differences in the way it finances institutions.

Financing Research

If Hong Kong SAR, China, had not moved to innovations in competitive financing, there would be less vitality in the system and less of a platform for a new university to have a compelling presence within a larger system. Within that framework, there is also a built-in collaborative element. Competitive research grants are administered by the Research Grants Council of Hong Kong. These research grants, though not on a scale compatible with major universities in the United States, have generally led to effective outcomes in terms of research productivity. For example, in 2002, a decade into HKUST's development, a portion (less than 15 percent) of these grants was directly allocated to HKUST and other universities to support small-scale research projects. HKUST administered these grants through internal competition. However, the major portion (more than 80 percent) was allocated for competitive bids from individuals or groups of academic staff members from all universities. The remaining portion (about 5 percent) placed an emphasis on collaboration across institutions and disciplines—"allocated in response to bids from the institutions for major research facilities/equipment or library collections to support collaborative research involving two or more institutions, or group research activities that operate across disciplines and/or normal institutional boundaries" (UGC 2002b). HKUST has established collaborative projects at other universities within Hong Kong SAR, China. These projects cover a number of areas, including Chinese Medicine Research and Further Development (with the Chinese University of Hong Kong), the Institute of Molecular Technology for Drug Discovery and Synthesis (with the University of Hong Kong), the Centre for Marine Environmental Research and Innovation Technology (with the City University of Hong Kong), Developmental Genomics and Skeletal Research (with the University of Hong Kong), and Control of Pandemic and Inter-Pandemic Influenza (with the University of Hong Kong). Nevertheless, the depth of collaboration may be shallow in certain areas, because this scheme was a top-down initiative by the University Grants Committee.

The Research Grants Council of Hong Kong's competitive bidding occurs on the basis of evaluations by specialized academic referees in Hong Kong SAR, China, and overseas. Overseas assessment, though expensive on a large scale, is crucial because of a limited number of assessors in particular fields within Hong Kong SAR, China. Another factor distinguishing HKUST from other universities is that during the early phase of development, many of its scientists already had experience with major research grants from their previous academic appointments at U.S. universities.

In sum, the crucial factors learned from this case study illustrate that purpose must include a shared vision. HKUST's founding president summed up these crucial factors: (a) vision—shared vision, clear mission, zeal; (b) goals—regional preference, national positioning, global impact in selected specialties; (c) focus—selection of fields and specialties, focusing of resources; (d) governance—organization and system; (e) adaptation—internationalization without an assault on the dual traditions; (f) heart—brains, muscles, spirit, mind, strength; and (g) soul—faculty as the soul of the university, shared purpose, and relentless drive. In this formula, the goal is to become the preferred regional university, with national positioning and global impact in selected academic research specialties. The focus must be on the selection of fields and specialties for an efficient focusing of resources. Governance needs to support an organization and system that is innovative and unique, promotes a sense of ownership among academic staff, protects the academic research atmosphere, and is international without assaulting local or national traditions. Finally, the heart of a research university is always a faculty that is not only talented, but also has a shared purpose, proactive spirit, and relentless drive.

HKUST facilitated the creation of a robust scholarly community adjoining a globally emergent and reformist China. In this sense, HKUST identified a niche within the Hong Kong system—by establishing a new international university and projecting its vision far beyond that system and into mainland China—especially signified by the new Southern University of Science and Technology under planning in the adjacent Shenzhen Special Economic Zone.

HKUST identified a niche not only in the field of science and technology, but also in delivery of a research-focused university culture, and it encapsulated that niche into an institutional vision that stressed its entrepreneurial uniqueness. The central factor underlying its success was the substantial recruitment from two generations of overseas-based Chinese scholars. By providing them and other local and international faculty members with a unique historical opportunity and a scholarly work environment that was adequately resourced, HKUST sustained its creation of a robust scholarly community.

Hong Kong's two-pronged development strategy was resilient enough to provide HKUST with the autonomy to sustain its uniqueness even during economic recession. When a consolidation of HKUST with one of the other top two universities was considered, the initiative was unanimously opposed by HKUST's faculty and staff members, students, and alumni and was eventually buried. HKUST was able to successfully distinguish itself from other local institutions in a system largely financed by government that guarantees a high degree of autonomy for innovation.

Notes

1. In 1900, US$50 million was roughly equivalent to US$3 billion in 2000.

2. HKUST's first president, Woo Chia-wei, was influenced by his time as a post-doctoral fellow in physics at the University of California, San Diego, and 11 years later as its provost, when its Revelle College required science and technology students to take 40 percent of their coursework in the humanities and social sciences.

3. The government's later support for establishment of a cyberport, conceived in 1999 and modeled on Silicon Valley, failed miserably as the technology stock bubble began to deflate. The cyberport became viewed more as a high-end real estate development rather than a setting where technology companies would fuel the leap of Hong Kong SAR, China, into the 21st century.

4. Because of the Tiananmen Square event, some Chinese mainland academics studying overseas at the time were granted automatic residency in the United States, and a few of them later sought employment in the Hong Kong academe. Nevertheless, most of the first tier of senior academic leaders recruited by HKUST from the United States had originally studied in Taiwan, China.

5. These universities include Chinese University of Hong Kong, City University of Hong Kong, Hong Kong Baptist University, Hong Kong Polytechnic University, Hong Kong University of Science and Technology, Lingnan University, and the University of Hong Kong. The only exception is the recent decision to bestow university status to Shue Yan College, the first private university in Hong Kong. The Open University of Hong Kong is not included because it was initially financed by the government before moving toward a self-financing model.

6. The Chinese University of Hong Kong was also, to some extent, American in character because of its U.S. missionary heritage, four-year curriculum, and high proportion of academic staff with degrees from universities in the

United States. However, it was established when the colonial government was in a dominant position, whereas HKUST was established in the last years of the colonial government when its legitimacy was more open to question.

7. The data in a, b, c, and d are from the Academic Ranking of World Universities in Shanghai. The category rank for social science (e) results from the methodology of these Shanghai rankings in which the data distribution for the various indicators used is examined for any significant distorting effect and standard statistical techniques are used to adjust the indicator. See http://www.arwu .org/ and also http://www.arwu.org/FieldSOC2010.jsp.

8. President Paul Chin-Wu Chu led HKUST from the beginning of 2001 to August 2009.

9. Faculty and student numbers were to rise proportionately, but the third phase of the expansion plan did not take place, leaving faculty numbers below their planned expansion number.

10. See Joint Declaration of the Government of the United Kingdom of Great Britain and Northern Ireland and the Government of the People's Republic of China on the Question of Hong Kong, December 1984, Ministry of Foreign Affairs, China. http://www.fmprc.gov.cn/eng/ljzg/3566/t25956.htm.

11. The Hong Kong Jockey Club is the largest single taxpayer in Hong Kong SAR, China—HK$12,976 million (US$1,666 million) in 2008–09 or about 6.8 percent of all taxes collected by the government's Inland Revenue Department. (By 1997, "Royal" had been dropped from the club's name.) A unique feature of the club is its nonprofit business model whereby its surplus goes to charity. Over the past decade, the club has donated an average of HK$1 billion (US$0.13 billion) (rate effective January 1, 2008) every year to hundreds of charities and community projects, such as HKUST. The club ranks alongside organizations such as the Rockefeller Foundation as one of the largest charity donors in the world. It is also one of the largest employers in Hong Kong SAR, China, with about 5,300 full-time and 21,000 part-time staff members.

12. The only exception is for those students who major in the study of Chinese language and literature. The language of campus life moved from bilingual (English and Cantonese) to trilingual as the number of students from the Chinese mainland increased, along with the international rise in popularity of Mandarin.

13. It is useful to note that the total figure in the original staff planning scheme, without the faculty of humanities and social sciences, was 525, while the figure for all academic staff was only 483 as of 2009 (see table 3.2).

14. Since then, academic salaries have been reduced more than once because of market forces and the economic recessions.

15. Information on the governance structure of HKUST is drawn from the detailed regulations found in the university calendar and replicated on its website. http://www.ust.hk/.

16. It consists of one immediate and two honorary chairs, eight ex officio members, and up to 44 appointed members, plus a maximum of 100 honorary members. Currently appointed members include 40 business and community leaders appointed by the council or by the chancellor (chief executive of the government of Hong Kong SAR, China), in addition to four representatives of the university senate appointed by the council. Members hold office for three years from the date of their appointment and are eligible for reappointment.

17. These amounts were converted using the rate effective June 1, 2008.

18. These amounts were converted using the rate effective June 1, 2008.

References

Altbach, Philip G. 2003. "The Costs and Benefits of World-Class Universities." *International Higher Education* 33 (6): 5–8.

Altbach, Philip G., and Jorge Balán. 2007. *World Class Worldwide: Transforming Research Universities in Asia and Latin America*. Baltimore: Johns Hopkins University Press.

Chin, Roland. 2009. Personal interview, Hong Kong University of Science and Technology, Hong Kong SAR, China, October 28.

Chung, Sze-yuen. 2001. *Hong Kong's Journey to Reunification*. Hong Kong SAR, China: Chinese University of Hong Kong Press.

Course, Sally. 2001. *HKUST Soars: The First Decade*. Hong Kong SAR, China: Office of University Development and Public Affairs and the Publishing Technology Center, Hong Kong University of Science and Technology.

Ding, Xueliang. 2004. *On University Reform and Development*. Beijing: Peking University Press.

Flahavin, Paulette. 1991. *Building a University: The Story of the Hong Kong University of Science and Technology*. Hong Kong: Office of Public Affairs, Hong Kong University of Science and Technology.

HKUST (Hong Kong University of Science and Technology). 2010a. "Knowledge Transfer Annual Report 2009–10." Report to the University Grants Committee, HKUST, Hong Kong SAR, China. http://www.ugc.edu.hk/eng/doc/ugc/activity/kt/HKUST.pdf. Accessed November 10, 2010.

———. 2010b. "Mission and Vision." HKUST, Hong Kong SAR, China. http://www.ust.hk/eng/about/mission_vision.htm. Accessed August 23, 2010.

————. 2010c. "Our Mission." Postgraduate Programs, HKUST, Hong Kong SAR, China. http://publish.ust.hk/pgstudies/.

————. 2010d. "Rankings and Awards." HKUST, Hong Kong SAR, China. http://www.ust.hk/eng/about/ranking.htm. Accessed August 23, 2010.

————. 2010e. "Strategy." HKUST, Hong Kong SAR, China. http://www.ust.hk/strategy/e_2.html.

HKUST R and D Corporation Ltd. 2010. "Policy and Procedures." Hong Kong University of Science and Technology, Hong Kong SAR, China. http://rdc.ust.hk/eng/policy.html. Accessed June 10, 2011.

Ji, Shuoming. 2009. "Taking Aim at Hong Kong's Science and Technology: Fuse China with International Power." *International Chinese Weekly* (May 24): 24–31.

Kung, Shain-Dow. 2002. *My Ten Years at the Hong Kong University of Science and Technology*. Hong Kong SAR, China: Hong Kong Joint Publishing Company.

Liu, Amy, and David Zweig. 2010. "Training a New Generation of Mainland Students: The Role of Hong Kong." Paper prepared for submission to *Asian Survey*. http://www.cctr.ust.hk/about/pdf/David_CV_2010.pdf.

Postiglione, Gerard A. 2008. "Transformations in Transnational Higher Education." *Journal of Higher Education* 29 (October): 21–31.

————. 2009. "Community Colleges in China's Two Systems." In *Community College Models: Globalization and Higher Education Reform*, ed. Rosalind Latiner Raby and Edward J. Valeau, 157–71. Amsterdam: Springer.

Salmi, Jamil. 2009. *The Challenge of Establishing World-Class Universities*. Washington, DC: World Bank.

So, Alvin, and Ming K. Chan. 2002. *Crisis and Transformation in China's Hong Kong*. New York: M. E. Sharpe.

Times Higher Education Supplement. 2008. http://www.topuniversities.com/worlduniversityrankings/results/2008/overall_rankings/fullrankings/.

UGC (University Grants Committee). 1996. *Higher Education in Hong Kong: A Report by the University Grants Committee*. Hong Kong: UGC. http://www.ugc.hk/eng/ugc/publication/report/hervw/ugcreport.htm.

————. 1999. *Higher Education in Hong Kong: A Report by the University Grants Committee: Supplement*. Hong Kong: UGC. http://www.ugc.hk/eng/ugc/publication/report/hervw_s/content.htm.

————. 2000. *Facts and Figures*. Hong Kong SAR, China: UGC.

————. 2002a. *Higher Education in Hong Kong: Report of the University Grants Committee*, Report for UGC prepared by Stewart R. Sutherland. Hong Kong SAR, China: UGC. http://www.ugc.edu.hk/eng/ugc/publication/report/her/her.htm.

————. 2002b. "Overview." UGC, Hong Kong SAR, China. http://www.ugc .edu.hk/english/documents/figures/eng/overview2.html. Accessed November 10, 2010.

————. 2004a. "Hong Kong Higher Education: To Make a Difference, To Move with the Times." UGC, Hong Kong SAR, China. http://www.ugc.edu.hk/eng/ doc/ugc/publication/report/policy_document_e.pdf.

————. 2004b. "Integration Matters." UGC, Hong Kong SAR, China. http://www. ugc.edu.hk/eng/doc/ugc/publication/report/report_integration_matters_e. pdf.

————. 2008. "Role Statements of UGC-funded Institutions, Annex IV." UGC, Hong Kong SAR, China. http://www.ugc.edu.hk/english/documents/figures/ pdf/A4_Eng.pdf. Accessed August 23, 2010.

————. 2010a. "Statistics." UGC, Hong Kong SAR, China. http://cdcf.ugc.edu .hk/cdcf/statIndex.do. Accessed June 10, 2011.

————. 20010b. "UGC Policy." UGC, Hong Kong SAR, China. http://www.ugc .edu.hk/eng/ugc/policy/policy.htm.

Walker, Anthony. 1994. *Building the Future: The Controversial Construction of the Campus of the Hong Kong University of Science and Technology.* Hong Kong: Longman.

Wong, Yuk Shan. 2010. Personal interview, University of Hong Kong, Hong Kong SAR, China, December 21.

Woo, Chia-wei. 2006. *Jointly Creating the Hong Kong University of Science and Technology.* Hong Kong SAR, China: Commercial Press.

Zakaria, Fareed. 2009. *The Post-American World: And the Rise of the Rest.* London: Penguin.

CHAPTER 4

A World-Class Research University on the Periphery: The Pohang University of Science and Technology, the Republic of Korea

Byung Shik Rhee

Achieving world-class status requires a university to possess competitive advantages such as tradition, resources, and a supportive environment. This circumstance may explain why world-class universities are concentrated in developed countries, which possess a relatively long modern-university history, a nurturing environment of abundant resources, and entrenched academic freedom. Perhaps it should not be a surprise that every world-class university outside the United States, with only a few exceptions, is a public institution. The Republic of Korea is one of the few developing countries that has succeeded in developing world-renowned universities—Seoul National University, the Korea Advanced Institute of

Author's Note: The author thanks Seungpyo Hong for providing invaluable anecdotal information on POSTECH and for arranging meetings with university administrators; Sooji Kim, for her assistance in translating the earlier version of this manuscript; and Yuji Jeong, for collecting relevant university documents. Special thanks go to Philip G. Altbach, Jamil Salmi, and our distinguished research group for their helpful comments on the earlier version of this manuscript.

Science and Technology, and Pohang University of Science and Technology (POSTECH), among others. POSTECH deserves special attention.

POSTECH's uniqueness derives from its position as a private university that was able to achieve, over just the past two decades, world-class status. Significantly, it was able to overcome the serious geographical disadvantage, expressed in the typical "all roads lead to Seoul" preference for living in the capital, that normally limits a Korean university's capability of attracting the best scholars and students. This chapter will examine the way POSTECH achieved its current status over such a short period of time and the nature of the continuing challenges it faces. Three main questions will be addressed: First, what drove a private company, Pohang Iron and Steel Company (POSCO), to found POSTECH? Second, what characterizes POSTECH as a research university? Finally, what challenges must the university meet to maintain its position? The chapter concludes with a brief discussion of the implications for higher education stakeholders in developing countries.

POSTECH was established in 1986 by a private entity,[1] POSCO, currently the world's second-largest steel enterprise. POSTECH is a 267-acre (1.08–square kilometer) campus located in Pohang, a midsize coastal city of more than 500,000 inhabitants. Geographically, Pohang is situated in the southeast of the Korean peninsula, about 360 kilometers (224 miles) from Seoul, the capital. It is interesting that such a small, remote city would become the home of POSTECH. In Korea, where social, educational, and cultural infrastructures have long been centralized in the capital, the geographical proximity to Seoul has been considered critical for attracting high-quality academic staff members and students. There is an old Korean expression, "Send your kids to Seoul and your horses to Jeju Island."[2] No single university with any hope of becoming a prestigious research institution could be found outside Seoul. Nevertheless, POSTECH successfully settled in the local city, owing to the founder's visionary leadership, the unprecedented large-scale financial support from his company, and creative managerial strategies to attract talented scientists and students.

As its name suggests, POSTECH's broad fields of concentration are science and technology. POSTECH has four departments of science (Chemistry, Life Science, Mathematics, and Physics), six departments of engineering (Chemical Engineering, Computer Science and Engineering, Electronic and Electrical Engineering, Industrial and Management Engineering, Material Sciences and Engineering, and Mechanical Engineering), and, for general education, the Division of Humanities and

Social Sciences. The graduate school programs are similar to the undergraduate programs, yet also offer interdisciplinary programs in related academic fields. All instruction is given in English (beginning in 2010), except for general education, which continues to be taught in Korean.

POSTECH has kept enrollments small since its inception. The current student enrollment, in 2009 figures, is approximately 3,100, including 1,400 undergraduates and 1,700 graduates (50 percent of whom are PhD candidates). About 5,000 students have earned bachelor's degrees, about 6,000 master's degrees, and about 1,600 doctoral degrees from POSTECH. Because the university annually admits only about 300 qualified students, who are all Korean born and of Korean descent, undergraduate programs are highly competitive. POSTECH, however, has steadily increased the number of academic staff members and currently has 244 full-time professors, maintaining a low student-faculty ratio (6 to 1) comparable to those of highly regarded universities in developed countries.

POSTECH, moreover, is affluent in its financial resources. The university's endowment consists mostly of POSCO stock and, though fluctuating with the market, has now reached about US$2 billion.[3] The 2009 operating budget was approximately US$220 million; POSTECH's chief private competitor, boasting a 10-times larger enrollment, spent only twice as much in the same year. Thanks to POSTECH's financial health, students pay no tuition and live on campus surrounded by impressive buildings and advanced classroom and laboratory facilities.

POSTECH built its solid national and international reputation in just over two decades, by strategically focusing on science and technology, keeping the university small in size, and inviting internationally respected scientists. Since 1997, the university consistently has been among the top three on the domestic university rankings list; in 1998, it was judged Asia's best "science and technology university" by *AsiaWeek* (1999); and in 2010, it was ranked 28th in the World University Rankings by the Times Higher Education (2010). POSTECH is making a continuous effort to become a top-20 world university within the next 10 years.

The Korean System of Higher Education

The history of modern higher education in Korea is relatively brief. The oldest private university, Yonsei University, founded by a group of U.S. missionaries and medical doctors, celebrated its 125th anniversary in 2009. The national universities are even younger. The first public institution, Seoul National University, was established only 60 years ago. It was transformed into a comprehensive university by merging the Japanese-run Gyungsung Imperial College with other two-year public professional schools spread throughout the capital region. Although Korean higher learning had been under the influence of China for several centuries until the late 19th century and under the influence of Japan during the 1910–1945 colonial period, the contemporary Korean system of higher education mostly resembles its U.S. counterpart. This resemblance began when the U.S. Army military government at the end of World War II (and, not coincidentally, at the end of Japanese rule) laid the foundation of Korean education and contributed both financially and in the form of U.S. scholars who visited Korea to provide consultation to institutions on setting up curricula and overall institutional systems. As a result of the close relationship established between the United States and Korea, today one out of four professors in Korean universities has a U.S. degree, and such credentials particularly dominate the elite universities. Although the percentage is moderating, a large portion of Korean graduates still considers U.S. graduate schools their first choice for advanced study.

Despite its brief history, Korean higher education has substantially expanded in scope. Currently, 3.5 million undergraduate students are enrolled in about 400 colleges and universities. Roughly 80 percent of these students attend private institutions. This high share of private institutions is a distinctive characteristic of Korean higher education. Although private colleges and universities enroll more than four-fifths of undergraduate students, the government has only minimally subsidized these institutions. The lack of public funds to private institutions leads to a heavy reliance (about 70 percent, on average) on tuition and fees for revenue. Students of private universities typically pay two times more than their counterparts attending public institutions, where the central government is the main source of revenue (about 60 percent).

Over the past several decades, the types of higher education institutions have become more varied. Although Korea lacks classification schemes for institutions of higher education (such as that of the Carnegie Foundation for the Advancement of Teaching in the United States), Korean universities can be divided roughly into several categories by primary mission (that is, research and teaching) and coverage of disciplines. National universities, including Seoul National University and regional universities, are research universities that cover a comprehensive array of academic fields. The most prestigious, Seoul National University, currently has about 17,000 undergraduates and 1,500 full-time professors in 86 departments and expends approximately US$300 million every year (Seoul National University 2009). Private research universities such as Yonsei University and Korea University are comparable to Seoul National University in those respects. A few highly regarded but smaller research universities narrowly focus on science and technology, including the Korea Advanced Institute of Science and Technology and POSTECH. The former institution enrolls 4,000 undergraduates, employs about 400 full-time professors in 23 degree programs, and spends US$100 million yearly (KAIST 2009). The remaining universities are institutions that have the primary mission of teaching and that serve regional or vocational needs for higher education. This group includes colleges and universities of many kinds, such as industrial universities, universities of education, technical universities, open universities, and junior colleges.

Another distinctive characteristic of Korean higher education is the strong control the government traditionally has assumed. Although its influence has gradually eroded, the government still has a high stake in higher education even for private universities. As such, the government continues to lessen its direct intervention in or regulation on institutional management and instead exerts influence through such indirect measures as competition grants and performance funding. As a result of this new approach, high-performing universities have received more subsidies through various recent projects such as Brain Korea 21 (1999–2012) and World Class University project (2009–12).[4] Private research universities, including POSTECH, have significantly benefited from these government-initiated funding programs (Rhee 2007).

The Background of Building a New University

At the time of POSTECH's establishment, the education and research environments of Korean higher education institutions were, in fact, poor; that is, the idea of a research university in Korea was foreign. Until the late 1980s, academic atmospheres on university campuses were barely developed, specifically because of students' political demonstrations for democracy as well as the simple lack of institutional resources for quality education and research (Han 1983). For instance, even the Engineering College of Seoul National University, having an exceedingly high student-faculty ratio, failed to supply a sufficient number of computers essential for science and engineering education. Moreover, in 1985 the educational expense per student was as low as US$1,500, which was only about 10 to

20 percent of that in Japan (US$17,000) and the United States (US$8,000). Substantial governmental support for academic research, including the fields of science and technology, began only in the 1980s, as a result of the establishment of the Korea Science and Engineering Foundation in 1977 and the Korea Research Foundation in 1981 (Umakoshi 1997). Meanwhile, domestic private companies began either to buy into existing universities or to create new ones. For instance, Hyundai founded Ulsan Engineering College in 1970; in 1977, Woo Joong Kim, then president of Daewoo Corporation, contributed his assets to the takeover of Ajou Engineering College, turning it into a university in 1980; and finally, the LG Group founded the Yonam Institute of Digital Technology in 1981. The early 1970s to 1980s was an era in which private enterprise branched out into higher education and cultivated human resources in the fields of science and technology.

POSCO, established in 1973 with the help of a portion of the Japanese indemnity fund and the compensation for Japanese rule, accomplished an unexpected success with Japanese technical assistance. Thus, an anxious Japan avoided further technology transfer to Korea. POSCO, feeling that its own technology development was indispensable, eventually established the Research Institute of Industrial Science and Technology in 1987. POSTECH was established in the same year for the purpose of managing the research institute, as well as for providing advanced education for budding engineers and laying the groundwork for future technology development. Then, in 1986, the POSCO's chief executive officer, Tae Joon Park, articulated his vision of what POSTECH should pursue in his inaugural remarks:

I would reiterate that POSTECH's opening today not only is going to nurture national leaders with a clear national outlook, a creative intelligence, and a great humanity for the future society, as any traditional university would do, but also, as a leading institution, is going to pave the way for our nation's advancement in science and technology. For industrial advancement and global competitiveness, it is of the utmost importance to secure advanced technology. POSCO also is in urgent need of world-class talent and research capability, in order to further advanced technology development and become a leading company in the 1990s. To this end, POSCO will continue to increase investment in Research and Development; and certainly, we established this research-oriented university (POSTECH) in the belief that a close link between industry, an industrial research institute and a university will make our dream come true. (POSTECH 2007)

The idea of establishing the new research university met with much opposition at the time. Stakeholders in the government and in POSCO were skeptical about whether POSCO could continuously provide sufficient support until the university became financially independent. POSCO proved itself up to the task of providing POSTECH with sufficient and reliable financial support, thanks to its successful business operations. Still, from a financial stability aspect, it was an acute risk. As the plans for the establishment of POSTECH took shape, the local community proved resistant, as well, because it expected a comprehensive, large-enrollment university that could serve its higher education needs. At that time, Pohang, with a population of 200,000, was the only city in the country without a four-year university. However, POSTECH declared its aspiration to become a small-size research university exclusively concentrating on the science and technology fields. Despite these obstacles, and in keeping with Tae Joon Park's persistently strong leadership, POSTECH was established.

Early Development of POSTECH

From the time of its inception and foundation, POSTECH—as Tae Joon Park, the founder and chief executive officer intended—aimed to become a research university nurturing human resource competencies in the fields of science and technology, using the California Institute of Technology as its model. Park visited that university on his business trip to Los Angeles in the spring of 1985 when the establishment plan of POSTECH was being formulated, meeting the university's administrators to obtain advice. The visit to the California Institute of Technology apparently helped Park to specify and make concrete his ideas about POSTECH. He envisioned that the university should pursue the goal of becoming not a comprehensive university, but rather a small institution devoted to advanced research in science and technology. His specific requests to the university founding team reflect mostly the characteristics of a typical contemporary research university: a low student-faculty ratio, a greater proportion of graduate students to undergraduates, a low net education cost, student on-campus housing, and a high-quality campus environment. These features, as contained in the new university plan, represented a drastic departure from the Korean universities of the 1980s.

The leadership role that Tae Joon Park played at this stage was important but not sufficient for the establishment of a research university. The following innovative approaches undertaken by university administrators at various stages help explain the university's early success.

First, POSTECH filled all full-time faculty positions with PhD recipients, 60 to 70 percent of whom were renowned Korean scientists living abroad—PhD recipients in the science and engineering fields were rare in Korea at that time. These scientists voluntarily returned to Korea because they were dedicated to the cause of national development. Nevertheless, the university's offer certainly was enticing: an excellent research environment, a teaching load of only two or three courses per year, a sabbatical year every six years, a competitive salary that was among the highest within Korea, and faculty apartments near the campus. The unique two-step process of hiring professors in the early years of POSTECH is interesting: First, as mentioned, the university hired a small number of experienced Korean scientists living overseas who had established their international reputations; second, the university asked all of them to initiate a search for promising young scholars in their disciplines. Every year since then, the backbone professoriate has successfully attracted a large number of talented young scholars.

Regarding students at POSTECH, the undergraduate freshmen of the opening year were in the top 2 percent of their high school classes. The university had instituted a highly competitive admissions requirement,[5] and as extra enticement, all entering students were promised free tuition and provision of dormitory housing. Along with media promotions, the university reached out to the top high school students nationwide through a brochure, the hosting of a science camp on campus, and admissions conferences in major cities. Historically, such promotional activities simply were not practiced by universities, least of all by elite institutions—especially in the 1980s, when higher education was a supplier's market. After POSTECH's unexpected success in recruiting high-honors students in the first years, graduate students from prestigious universities considered it for their advanced research and academic careers. Graduate students were attracted not only because their tuition fees were waived and they were able to live free in well-appointed apartments on campus, but also because they had access to laboratories with the finest facilities and high-end computer systems, which no other universities had at that time.

At its inception, POSTECH did not adopt administrative procedures from other benchmarked universities, instead importing POSCO's own management techniques and systems, albeit selectively. Those advanced techniques and systems enabled efficient management of the university. POSTECH's overall administrative system and staff proved very supportive, unlike those of other national and private institutions that saddled faculty with bureaucratic red tape and decision-making procrastination.

The study of failure models also contributed to POSTECH's initial success. Officials from Seoul National University and Ajou University generously suggested approaches on founding a university—in fact, cautionary tales based on their experiences of failure. They emphasized that the academic plan must be formulated ahead of the facility plan. In fact, faculty recruitment strategies were formulated to avoid the less-than-positive results achieved by Ulsan University (located in Ulsan, an industrial city about 65 kilometers [40 miles] south of Pohang). Ulsan University's College of Engineering, founded by the Hyundai Group in 1970, had difficulties attracting science and engineering professors with doctorates and had to fill positions with those holding master degrees. In addition, it failed to attract a sufficient number of qualified students, which resulted in the admission of less-qualified students from the local community. Almost inevitably, and thus unintentionally, Ulsan University grew into a four-year comprehensive university, which was far from an institute of science and technology. POSTECH therefore ensured that all faculty positions were filled with doctoral-degree recipients, and it raised the admissions standard for first-year students to a higher level than that of Yonsei University and Korea University, which were and remain the top private universities in Korea.

Governance and Leadership

The University Corporation,[6] established by POSCO, holds final executive authority and is responsible for decisions on major academic, financial, and policy matters. Specifically, POSTECH's board of trustees within the corporation is similar to that typical of U.S. private universities; they both have a number of external figures deliberating and making decisions for the university. However, POSTECH's board is much smaller—for example, one-fifth the members of the California Institute of Technology's board of trustees—although the two universities are comparable in size of enrollment. For this reason, the chairman of the board happens to be relatively more influential than other members in the general management of the university. However, since the beginning, autonomous management of the university has been guaranteed. Thus, the chairperson entrusts management authority—such as the power to appoint faculty—to the president. This is unusual in Korean private universities, where the chairperson, who typically is the owner of the university or a member of the owner's family, is actively involved in institutional management. In many cases, as well, family members functioning as trustees or chief administrators intervene in decision making on important university affairs—such as faculty hiring and institutional financial management. Actions that sometimes amount to meddling for the purposes or benefits of these family members or the family overall have often led to disputes over faculty hiring or, even worse, financial corruption (for example, embezzlement of university funds). POSTECH, notwithstanding the chairman's powerful influence, has never reported any such incidents.

Institutional Management

Since its establishment, POSTECH has continually devised university development plans; most recently, a new vision and set of strategies—VISION 2020 for a World-Class University—was inaugurated. POSTECH's plan, accordingly, is to become a top-20 world-class research university by 2020. To achieve this goal, POSTECH has selected 11 performance indicators in five areas, the progress of these indicators is monitored, and the results are publicized annually on the Web. These ambitious performance goals clearly show not only POSTECH's aspiration, but also the performance gap that remains between it and top-class U.S. universities. POSTECH endeavors to reduce that gap using three main strategies: selectivity and focus of approach, research collaboration, and internationalization. Because POSTECH, a small university, cannot easily secure professors for every academic field, it strategically selects high-impact research areas and also encourages faculty members to work together through team-based projects with potential synergy. To strengthen research collaboration, POSTECH has implemented the split-appointment system, a joint faculty appointment by two or more departments, and actively encourages interdisciplinary research. The university also recognizes that internationalization is a must, if world-class status is to prove an attainable goal, and makes a tremendous effort to attract distinguished scholars from abroad.

Another distinctive characteristic of POSTECH's management is the president's authority to empower department chairs. In most Korean universities, department chairs are appointed by the pertinent individual departments and have only nominal authority to carry out routine departmental affairs for two years in rotation. However, at POSTECH, department chairs do not have a fixed term and also face the primary responsibility of hiring new faculty and assessing faculty performance in their own units. This is a very interesting development in institutional management because it goes against the Korean trend, which is centralization. By empowering the engaged middle level of management, POSTECH has been quite successful in recruiting and retaining qualified scientists.

Research and the University-Industry Link

Since its inception, POSTECH has endowed itself with highly competent scientists and has provided them with possibly the best research environment for generating high-impact research. Undoubtedly, even with its small faculty, POSTECH has been producing excellent research results. In 2008, POSTECH faculty members published 1,464 papers, both nationally and internationally, or an average of about six papers per faculty member—the highest level among Korean universities and a level comparable to that of major U.S. universities. In addition to the respectable number of published papers—and in view of its small enrollment and quality of papers—POSTECH appears in the world's top-20 universities per faculty citation index.

Among POSTECH's excellent research departments, the integrated Department of Chemistry and Life Science and the Department of Materials and Devices are particularly outstanding. In the former department, there are a number of best scientist award and science award recipients among the faculty members, in addition to those topping the field in Brain Korea 21 projects. Also, recently the Department of Life Science was selected for financial support from a government-funded program offering assistance to universities in their progress toward world-class university status. In the Department of Materials and Devices, which would require first-rate facilities in any university, POSTECH maintains a premier research environment that includes the establishment of a particle accelerator and the National Center for Nanomaterials Technology.

To continuously produce high-impact research outcomes, POSTECH has been reinforcing strategic resource allocation, collaborative research, and international research partnerships, as mentioned earlier. POSTECH has chosen to emphasize research fields in which faculty members can enjoy collaborative research synergy and also has invited international scholars to participate. The future appears bright regarding active international collaborative research. Notably, beginning in 2009 and continuing until 2014, POSTECH has conducted and will conduct additional high-end research in collaboration with 23 internationally distinguished scholars invited under the auspices of the World Class University project. Additionally, the university plans to strengthen international collaboration through cooperation with the Max Planck Institute in Germany and RIKEN, a natural sciences research institute running SPring-8 (a synchrotron radiation facility), in Japan.

As mentioned earlier, POSTECH's founding company, POSCO, considered industrial collaboration to be one of the university's main functions and, hence, established the Research Institute of Industrial Science and Technology (RIST) next to the main buildings on campus. Some risks are created by industry affiliation—the most significant of which is the compromising of research integrity because of a conflict of interest between faculty and a sponsoring company. Likewise, research potential could be curtailed by a perceived gap between requested research and research that faculty members would rather undertake. Indeed, some POSTECH faculty members working at RIST as adjunct researchers have been frustrated by this special conflict, which typically involves applied versus basic research. This situation is understandable, considering that POSCO in the 1980s needed applied science research to serve company-specific agendas and issues, while most faculty members had been trained—typically at U.S. research universities and research centers—for basic research.

This tension was notably acute during the university's first 10 years, when all newly hired faculty members were required to have a joint RIST and academic appointment. However, the conflict has eased steadily for two reasons. First, POSCO dropped the dual appointment policy and began to provide research funds directly to individual faculty members. Second, as POSCO's need for advanced technology and frontier knowledge to sustain its competitive advantage over global competitors grew, it began to perceive the greater benefits accruing from the POSTECH faculty's basic, not applied, research. However, this tension might still exist, but in a new form. Although the growth of public funding of research has provided POSTECH faculty members with more freedom to select research topics consonant with their interests, the sponsoring government agencies have put more emphasis on national strategic areas as well as research outputs that can be readily commercialized. Statistics show that, universitywide, applied research accounts for about 75 percent of the total public funding of university research and development (MEST 2009). This is almost precisely the proportion of POSTECH's public funding to its overall research funding. The university recently took in approximately US$98 million from public funding and about US$33 million from private sources (POSTECH 2009). As such, applied research is still a dominant form.

Whereas impartiality and communality have long characterized the international scientific community, a recent study shows that the majority of scientists in Korean universities appear to have a favorable attitude toward commercialization of research (Bak 2006). A nationalist perspective that considers such commercialization a legitimate means of promoting national interests might account for that view. The Korean government's continuous support of the commercial application of scientific research has encouraged Korean universities' active participation in the process. POSTECH, with the support of POSCO and government agencies, has long sought to boost the commercial value of its research, particularly by creating an administrative support system and running a business incubation center along with a venture capital operation.

The advanced system POSTECH developed in 2006, the Technology Utilization System, manages the interplay of research, patents, and knowledge transfer. Currently, 11 enterprises are under development in the POSTECH Venture Business Incubation Center. POSTECH has invested US$6.3 million in its venture companies. Moreover, during the past 20 years, 26 faculty members have started new businesses relating to the commercialization of their research. The estimated value of knowledge transfer for 2009 is about US$2 million, which is equivalent to about 3 percent per faculty member, the highest level in Korea.

Curriculum, Teaching and Learning, and Student Life

Extremely talented students constituting the top 1 percent of the Korean high school student body choose POSTECH. POSTECH students enjoy the challenges in their academic life, devoting exceptionally long hours to study during semesters. Reciprocally, they demand the university's support in achieving a ranking of the top 0.1 percent of Korean university graduates. POSTECH makes every effort to nurture the high science and technology competencies of its students. In the regular curriculum, the chief characteristics of POSTECH's undergraduate education are the high prevalence of small classes, the cross-curriculum expansion of English lectures, and the intensification of its math courses. As for the undergraduate program, small-size classes (those with enrollments of 20 students or fewer) constitute more than 60 percent of the total, and the low student-professor ratio provides students with abundant opportunities to interact with their professors and enhance their higher-order intellectual skills.

POSTECH also plans to intensify English education and to conduct all courses in English to mentor its students as global leaders. To those ends, POSTECH requires its students in their first two years to take intensive English courses conducted by native English-speaking instructors. Upon entering the university, freshmen must take a placement test for English. According to the results, they are required to register for a maximum of nine levels of English courses (the majority of students take six to seven courses). For acceptance into the final course, they must be able to write a paper in English. Students who successfully complete all the courses receive the POSTECH Certificate of English. Significantly, the university announced that beginning in 2010, all courses except for general education will be taught exclusively in English.

At the same time, mathematics education has been given greater emphasis. All freshmen are required to register for advanced mathematics courses. The intensification of math education reportedly is more closely related to POSTECH's philosophy of education rather than to the trend of lesser preparedness among high school graduates. In fact, according to the administrator in charge of academic affairs, the stress on math is intended to reinforce the basic education required for undergraduate engineering students and to contribute to an overall deeper level of graduate education. Such intensive math education in any case reflects the fierce competition among elite institutions, as POSTECH attempts to gain a head start in maintaining its hard-won reputation for excellence in education. Like the majority of research universities, however, POSTECH must confront the issue of faculty members' diminishing interest in undergraduate education. Although no easy solution to this particular problem exists (Bok 2006; Lewis 2006), POSTECH is attempting a typical "carrot and stick" approach. For example, financial incentives are extended to faculty members willing to develop a program to enhance students' active learning or creativity. The university also has introduced student course evaluations and made the results accessible to students. POSTECH faculty members' generally less-than-ardent interest in teaching does not necessarily mean poor education. Quite to the contrary, despite professors' lack of enthusiasm for teaching, a recent survey of both current undergraduate students and graduates showed that they were quite satisfied with the instructional quality in general at the university. However, they complained most about the lack of interaction with their professors outside the classroom. This situation is regrettable, because interaction with faculty members is known to be an important ingredient in students' university development (Pascarella and Terenzini 2005).

The Academic Profession

Although POSTECH has not had a Nobel Prize winner among its full-time faculty, 16 national scientist award recipients, 115 international academic award or medal recipients, and hundreds of domestic award recipients are testament to its excellence. Such a success in faculty hiring should be attributed to the pivotal role that individual departments play in hiring faculty. Now common at research universities in Korea, this practice was rarely attempted at the time POSTECH first adopted it. Although the department makes the hiring plan and initiates the process, several steps were set in place to prevent anyone from exerting undue or illegitimate influence on the hiring decision. A typical hiring process works as follows: (a) a search committee consisting of three to five tenured professors in a department, plus one external reviewer, reviews applicants' documents and recommends a sufficient number of candidates, typically five or more, for open talks and an interview; (b) the selected competing candidates are interviewed, followed by a departmental personnel committee's recommendation of the most-qualified candidate to a university personnel committee composed of eight tenured, cross-departmental professors plus the director of academic affairs; and (c) the university personnel committee members, all appointed by the president, conduct a final review.

Once hired as an assistant or associate professor, the successful candidate must meet the minimum requirements for promotion, which vary by department. In general, the minimum requirements for promotion to associate professor include teaching three or more courses with satisfactory student course evaluations, publishing at least four research articles (eight articles for promotion to full professor) in high-impact international journals, and conducting adequate professional activities within and outside of the university. Despite the high standards, most candidates have been able to pass the promotion review. Between 1997 and 2007, five assistant professors and one associate professor left the university because they could not meet the requirements. Moreover, as the requirements for promotion have been further tightened, professors have had to publish additional articles at higher-impact journals to stay at POSTECH and, indeed, to be internationally recognized. Lately, the university has made requirements even tougher, such as requiring all assistant professors to apply for and pass their tenure review[7] within seven years of their initial appointment. Those who fail their tenure review will have only a one-year grace period. It remains to be seen whether such stringent standards succeed in attracting young high-potential scholars or, in fact, discourage them from choosing POSTECH.

POSTECH, a fast-changing institution, has attempted a variety of its own self-imposed transformations over the past 20 years. One remarkable change relating to the academic profession is the introduction of a performance-based compensation system in 2000. With the new system, faculty salary is determined not by seniority but by a faculty member's accomplishments over the preceding three years in teaching, research, and public service. The university further refined the salary system so that the president could allocate incentives, according to six graded levels, to only two-thirds of eligible professors in consideration of their annual contributions to the university, the industry, and the national economy. POSTECH was one of the first champions of a performance-based salary system that is now widely instituted among private Korean universities, mainly to intensify competition among faculty members.

Internationalization

Internationalization has been the backbone of POSTECH's aspiration to become a world-class research university since its foundation. POSTECH envisaged itself as a university offering excellence in education and research to Korean students who, thus, would have no need to study abroad. To reach its goal, POSTECH developed a research network with top-class universities worldwide. In the early days, this approach was made possible by taking advantage of its faculty's personal connections with such universities as the University of California, Berkeley, and Carnegie Mellon University in the United States, Imperial College London and the University of Birmingham in the United Kingdom, Aachen University in Germany, and Université de Technologie de Compiègne in France. Since then, POSTECH has continued to strengthen international collaborative research with foreign partners in France, Germany, Japan, and the United States. In 1996, POSTECH established the Association of East Asian Research Universities with leading universities such as the University of Tokyo and Hong Kong University of Science and Technology, along with 14 other universities in East Asian countries. More recently, the headquarters of the Asia Pacific Center for Theoretical Physics, an international research center in the field of basic science, moved to the POSTECH campus in 2001, and POSTECH is promoting the establishment of a Korean research branch of the Max

Planck Institute. Moreover, POSTECH has established a strategic partnership with RIKEN—as mentioned earlier—a natural sciences research institute in Japan running SPring-8 (a synchrotron radiation facility), thereby further solidifying its basis for high-impact research.

POSTECH has also steadily expanded international student-exchange programs. Currently, the university has 71 sisterhood universities in 19 countries, about 387 POSTECH students have studied abroad short term (a semester or two), and 295 foreign students have come to POSTECH for short-term study. Since 2004, POSTECH has sent abroad an average of 90 students per year through the summer session program, which allows students to take summer school courses at top-class foreign universities. In addition, through the Association of East Asian Research Universities Student Camp and Cross Straits Symposium, an academic exchange program (involving POSTECH and Pusan National University in Korea and Kyushu University in Japan) is being offered to PhD candidates studying environment, energy, and materials. A total of 1,500 students, in 10 exchanges from 1999 to 2008, have participated in this program. Despite its active collaboration with foreign institutions, however, POSTECH has a disappointingly negligible number of full-time international students and scholars. As of 2009, the university had about 10 percent foreign professors, about 4 percent international students at the graduate level, and no students at the undergraduate level. These surprisingly low proportions of international scholars and students may be attributable to the university's location in a local city that lacks an international dimension.

Nonetheless, a series of recent public announcements clearly indicates that POSTECH takes internationalization seriously. In February 2010, the university told the media that it would invite 10 Nobel laureates or Fields medalists as full-time professors that year. Each invited scholar would be given US$1 million for salary and an additional US$4 million for research and living costs during a three-year stay at POSTECH. The total amount to be paid would be five times more than that paid to participating international scholars through the government-funded World Class University project. POSTECH is also collaborating with Pohang city to open a new international K–12 (kindergarten–12th grade) school near the campus. Additionally, POSTECH will soon declare itself a bilingual campus where both English and Korean are used as formal languages. In this plan, all undergraduate (except general education) and graduate courses will be taught exclusively in English. All academic seminars and meetings at which an international person is present will use English as the primary language. Moreover, every official document to be circulated throughout the university will be written in both Korean and English.

Finance

POSTECH's budget was increased from US$15 million, the level at the time of its foundation in 1987, to US$170 million in 2009. During the first five years, POSTECH's financial dependence on the University Corporation was 80 percent on average, but this amount was gradually reduced to about 30 percent in recent years. The reduced contribution from the corporation to POSTECH's revenue was made up in large part through increased research income, which rose to 40 percent during the same period. Despite these changes in the revenue composition, the university has kept the proportion of tuition and fees to total revenue below 10 percent. It is interesting to note, however, that for reasons such as the lack of a culture of philanthropy in Korean society and the relatively very small number of POSTECH alumni, donations account for less than 5 percent of the total revenue.

POSTECH has expanded research collaboration with companies other than POSCO and, at the same time, has actively participated in government-funded projects. Nevertheless, POSCO's research fund still accounts for the largest portion of research revenue, about 50 percent. The university's close tie with and financial intakes from POSCO, paradoxically, restrict the university's collaborations with other companies and, thereby, its ability to secure donations from other sources. For this reason, fund-raising campaigns thus far have not been successful. The university has barely raised US$4.3 million since 1995. Nevertheless, in terms of endowment, POSTECH might be the richest private institution in Korea, with US$2 billion worth of stocks as of 2009. The university has no domestic competitors in expenditure on instruction per student, about US$70,000, a level about five times higher than that of typical universities in Korea (MEST and KEDI 2009, 116).

Notwithstanding the government's significant controls, private universities in Korea have been only minimally subsidized. POSTECH is no exception. Until the mid-1990s, public funding channeled into the university hardly reached 3 percent of total revenue. Over the past decade (2000–10), however, POSTECH witnessed a significant expansion of public funding of research, student scholarships, and even operating budgets. In 2008, about 30 percent of research funds came from public sources, mainly through the Ministry of Education, Science and Technology.

The government also provided full scholarships to all enrolled students until graduation, on the condition that they maintain their grade point average above 3.3 (out of 4.3). This sudden largesse can be attributed mainly to a shift in the government's funding policies. Competitive funding programs—such as Brain Korea 21 (1999–2012) and World-Class University (2008–2012)—have played an important role in expanding public funding of private universities with excellent research capabilities. Performance-based funding, introduced in 2008 and still in effect, has allocated public funds to selected public and private higher education institutions based on a small number of government-selected performance indicators. In 2010, POSTECH received US$2 million of this money. Whereas the increased public funding has helped POSTECH keep pace with international competitors, it is not wholeheartedly welcomed by many faculty members, who fear that such subsidies are likely to lead to significant public sector intrusiveness (see the following section).

Government Support and Control

Whereas POSCO's role in the development of POSTECH is unparalleled, the Korean government also has played a significant role, both as a supporter and as a regulator. This situation is not unique to POSTECH. Government funds always come with strings attached to further a higher education policy agenda. Also, it has been common for the government to control private universities through policy, regulation, and various administrative tools.[8] During the past 20 years, POSTECH has increased its reliance on the government's financial support, which ominously has resulted in numerous changes in POSTECH's academic programs, research environment, and institutional management.

First, POSTECH's participation in Brain Korea 21 and the World Class University projects changed academic programs at the graduate level. The government required universities to consolidate graduate programs into larger interdisciplinary divisions (*hakbu*) to join the new projects. In compliance, POSTECH reorganized its six graduate school departments into three divisions, the Division of Molecular and Life Science, the Division of Electrical and Computer Engineering, and the Division of Mechanical and Industrial Engineering, as well as one school—the School of Systems Biosciences and Bioengineering. More recently, to participate in the World Class University project, POSTECH established new graduate-level interdisciplinary programs, including Integrative Biosciences and Biotechnology, the Division of Advanced Materials Science, and the

Division of IT Convergence Engineering. The government will subsidize the university for a total of US$83 million until 2012, if the participating programs perform as expected.

POSTECH's partnership with the government has also greatly enhanced its research environment. For instance, the third Pohang Light Source, completed in 1994, is an exemplary US$150 million research facility built near the POSTECH campus. The government contributed about US$60 million for its construction, and it has been run and managed by the Pohang Accelerator Laboratory (POSTECH's annex research center) as a national user facility (the operating budget of US$20.5 million is being met by the government). Recently, POSTECH made a request to the Ministry of Education, Science and Technology for a feasibility study regarding the establishment of a fourth Pohang Light Source. Approximately US$400 million has been earmarked, and a full operational plan is forthcoming in the near future. There is also the National Center for Nanomaterials Technology, a research facility founded under POSTECH's own supervision, which has been under construction on campus since 2004. The Ministry of Knowledge Economy has been providing financial support up to US$90 million for five years. In addition, the Pohang Institute of Intelligent Robotics (established in early 2000), the National Core Research Center, the Information Technology Research Center, the National Research Laboratory, and the National Defense Micro Electro Mechanical Systems (MEMS) Research Center are all being run with assistance from the government's budget.

More penetrating governmental effects on POSTECH can be found in institutional management, the area in which the university traditionally has been least likely to experience external intrusion. Over the past 10 years, the government has been increasing the university operating budget subsidy, as well as the research funding for private universities, to achieve its higher education policy goals. For instance, it is funding public and private universities subject to institutional performance indicators relating to postgraduate student employment, quality of education, financial aid, and educational expenditure per student. Through this funding scheme, POSTECH received about US$350,000 in 2008. The government also is funding universities that have instituted the admissions officer system, a new admissions process promoted by the current administration in which applicants are judged not only on academic achievements in college entrance exams and high school, but also, and more important, on their socioeconomic and cultural backgrounds and academic potentials. After receiving the pertinent financial support—in this case, about US$300,000—POSTECH duly selected all students for 2010 using this new admissions process and is expected to continue to do so while the inflow of financial support continues. Clearly, new funding programs such as these, which force POSTECH to accept government impositions regarding its goals and methods of student selection, might not be suitable or helpful for a private university to embrace.

In some respects, the government's financial support can be validated as a contributor to the growth of POSTECH into a research university. However, it is impossible to disregard the negative aspects of the government's contribution, which have restricted the university's autonomy by inducing participation in the government's chosen strategic fields of study or by interfering in university management. Whether these lasting changes, as corollaries of governmental interventions, will benefit POSTECH remains unclear. If the government relies overly on a regulatory role, the changes could well hold back the university's potential growth.

Changing Environment and Emerging Challenges

POSTECH's current strengths are the result of quality faculty members, talented and hardworking students, and an exceptional research environment. To achieve world-class status, the university, like other world-class universities, must invite even more talented scholars and students, regardless of their nation of origin, to provide top-rated support for research and teaching. POSTECH, however, may experience difficulties in many aspects because of intensifying competition among universities, a location that lacks an international dimension, a weak collaborative culture, insecure finances, and shortsighted internal management.

POSTECH is experiencing deepened competition not only because of the force of globalization, but also because of new research universities, competition among research universities, and the increased bargaining power of students in Korea (Peterson and Dill 1997). New public universities of science and technology recently were established in nearby cities, and domestically competing universities are rapidly growing and moving aggressively to hire faculty members, increasing the trend of faculty relocation to Seoul or other major cities. This battle for talent among the research universities is attributable, in part, to the increase in the government's competitive research grants such as Brain Korea 21 and the World Class University projects in Korea. Furthermore, if several U.S. universities with strong engineering programs enter Incheon City near Seoul as planned, the competition could be even greater. Although government support for higher education has not yet decreased in Korea, the increasing quantity of outstanding science and technology universities might cause dispersion of that support. This situation could create a new threat to POSTECH, which is located in a vulnerable city where social and cultural infrastructures and educational conditions are weak. Such circumstances will especially bring more challenging problems to POSTECH as it attempts to fortify and improve its position as a world-class university by attracting and hiring more foreign professors, students, and researchers.

To compete globally, POSTECH must produce high-impact research. As mentioned earlier, such research will be made feasible with the finding of new research fields of competitive advantage and the conducting of collaborative, synergy-rich research. POSTECH's advancement in research may be hampered by both its vulnerability to the influence of the government's power to set research agendas and its weak culture of collaboration among professors. Although the government has attempted to help POSTECH carry out international collaborative research, the scale of support is not sufficiently large, and the support tends in any case to center on the government's strategic fields of science and technology that characterize the relatively short-term perspective of applied research. As such, this support can possibly interfere with or even retard development of the field of basic science research at POSTECH. For many reasons, however, research collaboration among faculty members across disciplines is not taking place as desired. POSTECH hopes to establish a separate research space, similar to the Massachusetts Institute of Technology's media lab, where such collaborative research can occur.

Over the past few years at POSTECH, where only a few full-time international students and professors have been present at any one time, English has gained sufficient popularity to be adopted formally as the language of instruction. Although this is not uncommon in contemporary Korean universities, it shows a clear increasing trend in science and engineering education. For example, at Yonsei University, a private research university, one out of every two undergraduate courses, on average, is taught in English, whereas more than seven out of 10 courses offered in engineering programs are so conducted. In leading this trend, in 2010 POSTECH began teaching all courses, except general education courses, exclusively in English. An underlying rationale for increasing the number of courses taught in English is the idea that such a measure will attract more international students and scholars. This is doubtful. Students learn outside of class as well as in class. Students also learn from both their teachers and their peers. In this sense, then, the current emphasis on the use of a certain language for instruction is insufficient justification for international students to choose POSTECH and may also negatively affect Korean students' learning, in that few of them have the language skills necessary for participation in courses taught in English.

Securing adequate and reliable finances is another key element in POSTECH's quest to become a world-class university. The two main sources of POSTECH's current revenue—the founding company (POSCO) and the government—are insecure in the long term. The endowment itself consists of nothing but POSCO stock, which fluctuates with economic circumstances. For the first 10 years after POSTECH's founding, POSCO's tremendous support contributed to POSTECH's growth, but that support has decreased substantially since then. Although governmental support grew somewhat substantially in scale over the past decade, it cannot be regarded as stable for the long term, as the experience of other developed countries shows. For example, the U.S. government's support for higher education is largely influenced by economic circumstances and tends gradually to decrease (Gladieux, King, and Corrigan 2005). The recent promotion of incorporation of public universities in Korea can be seen as the government's effort to lessen its financial share in the support of higher education (Rhee 2007). Notwithstanding these circumstances, as mentioned earlier, the fact that POSTECH has an actual patron (POSCO) makes it more difficult to reach out to other potential sponsors and donors for institutional development assistance. Furthermore, a short, 20-year history and a small class of 300 undergraduates militate against the university's raising significant donations from alumni.

POSTECH's current share of revenue from student tuition (10 percent or less) along with its low tuition (about 50 percent of that of private competitors) may provide it with more than enough justification for a tuition increase. Nonetheless, raising tuition fees is not a good alternative, for multiple reasons. First, government policy discourages it.[9] Second, the university corporation, which is responsible for institutional finance, has a long-standing internal policy of keeping tuition fees below 10 percent of total revenue. Third, public competitors—Seoul National University and Korean Advanced Institute of Science and Technology—maintain their tuition at about 50 percent of the level of private institutions. Fourth, since its inception POSTECH has been well known and admired for its provision of full scholarships to its students, which is one of the compelling reasons why so many gifted high school students from low- and middle-income families select POSTECH as their first choice of university.

Finally, a tuition increase to the level of private competitors will bring in an additional US$6 million per year—only about 3 percent of total annual revenue. The costs would well exceed the financial gains of any such hike. Nevertheless, in the long run, a tuition increase must be seriously considered, for at least two reasons. First, national universities will soon be seen as incorporated. If so, tuition fees, if international experience is any indication, likely will rise significantly. Second, because POSTECH's student body is filled with an increasing number of students from wealthy families, POSTECH could adopt a policy similar to that of U.S. Ivy League universities, which provide significant financial assistance to students from low-income families while asking other students to pay more.

For POSTECH's first eight years, it was helmed by the visionary leader Dr. Hogil Kim, a world-renowned nuclear physicist. POSTECH's founder, Tae Joon Park, had endorsed Dr. Kim wholeheartedly and let him take full charge of university management. Under President Kim's leadership, a solid foundation was laid for POSTECH as a research university.[10] Since President Kim's passing, which was a great loss to POSTECH, the university unfortunately has experienced leadership difficulties. No new leaders selected since then have presided in office longer than four years, and vice-presidents and executive directors of administrative units have served for even shorter periods (two years, in general). Certainly, there is concern involving this short-term charge of executive and administrative affairs by internal faculty members who lack administrative experience and leadership skills, presenting potentially large obstacles in the path of the university's transformation into a world-class institution.

Conclusion

POSTECH is one of the few non-U.S. private universities that may attain top status. The university continues to aspire to move up in world rankings. Indeed, the university hopes to fill, with a bust of one of its own faculty members, a designated space at the center of campus for honoring the first Korean Nobel laureate in science. This case study attempts to analyze how a relatively new, small, private university in a non-English-speaking country could achieve world-class status amid the challenges that emerged in the course of its evolution. From the findings of this analysis, it is hoped that higher education stakeholders in developing countries may gain insights into the creation of world-class universities in their own nation. These findings show that top status is achieved through visionary leadership, the empowering of subordinates, a superior supporting environment, and partnership with the government. In addition, POSTECH must continue to deal with various kinds of emerging challenges for which there are no easy solutions.

To leap to a higher status, the enterprising POSTECH is about to experiment with the controversial but bold idea of using a nonnative language—English—as the primary tool for teaching science and engineering students. Whether this audacious attempt will succeed or fail, many lessons undoubtedly will be learned.

Notes

1. POSCO began as a public corporation and was privatized in 2000.

2. Jeju Island is an exotic vacation island off the southern coast of Korea.

3. For simplicity, current values and a flat exchange rate (1,000 to 1) between Korean won and U.S. dollars are used throughout this manuscript.

4. Brain Korea 21 began in 1999 and will last until 2012, providing financial support to graduate students in research projects. In the first stage, which ended in 2007, the government transferred US$1.3 billion to 564 research teams nationwide. The second stage, which began in 2008, has US$2 billion set aside to support 568 research teams from 74 universities. The World Class University project, which was initiated in 2008, is a higher education subsidy program of the Korean government that aims to create new academic programs in new growth-generating fields and to enhance international research and teaching collaboration by inviting distinguished scholars from around the world. The government will have invested US$825 million in the program between 2008 and 2012 (MEST 2008).

5. POSTECH recognized the significance to the success of any research university of attracting eminent faculty members and students. However, some individuals at the university were concerned that undergraduate applicant qualifications were set too high. President Hogil Kim, in an entertaining expression of his determination, replied: "Even if there is only one applicant, it is of no matter because then, the faculty can focus only on doing research" (POSTECH 2007, 98).

6. According to Korean law, a university is founded either by the government or by a university corporation. So, a private citizen or private entity must create a university corporation beforehand, and then a private university can be funded through the corporation.

7. The tenure system was introduced at POSTECH in 1998.

8. Although there is ongoing debate about whether Korean higher education policies reflect neoliberalism, it is fair to say that Korea is in transition from a

regulating nation to a consumer advocacy or steering nation in which the market shapes university behaviors (Reeves-Bracco et al. 1999; Rhee 2008).

9. According to the Higher Education Act as amended in early 2010, college tuition should be increased by no more than 1.5 times the recent three-year average consumer price inflation rate. The institutions that fail to abide by this guideline face administration or financial penalties, or both, imposed by the minister of education, science and technology.

10. Dr. Kim made it possible to design and construct the Pohang Light Source near the campus.

References

AsiaWeek. 1999. "Best Science and Technology Schools." http://www-cgi.cnn .com/ASIANOW/asiaweek/universities/scitech/2.html. Accessed August 3, 2009.

Bak, Hee-Je. 2006. "Commercialization of Science and Changing Normative Structure of the Scientific Community." *Korean Journal of Sociology* 40 (4): 19–47.

Bok, Derek. 2006. *Our Underachieving Colleges: A Candid Look at How Much Students Learn and Why They Should Be Learning More*. Princeton, NJ: Princeton University Press.

Gladieux, Lawrence E., Jacqueline E. King, and Melanie E. Corrigan. 2005. "The Federal Government and Higher Education." In *American Higher Education in the Twenty-First Century: Social, Political, and Economic Challenges*, ed. Philip G. Altbach, Robert O. Berdahl, and Patricia J. Gumport, 163–97. Baltimore: Johns Hopkins University Press.

Han, Zun-Sang. 1983. *The Sacrifice of Korean Higher Education*. Seoul: Moonumsa.

KAIST (Korean Advanced Institute of Science and Technology). 2009. "University statistics." KAIST, Daedeok, Republic of Korea. http://www.kaist.ac.kr. Accessed August 5, 2009.

Lewis, Harry R. 2006. *Excellence Without a Soul: How a Great University Forgot Education*. New York: Public Affairs.

(MEST) Ministry of Education, Science and Technology. 2008. *National Project Towards Building World Class Universities*. Seoul: MEST.

———. 2009. *Science and Technology Annual Report*. Seoul: MEST.

MEST and KEDI (Ministry of Education, Science and Technology and Korean Educational Development Institute). 2009. *2008 University Public Information Analysis Report* SM 2009–01. Seoul: KEDI.

Pascarella, Ernest T., and Patrick T. Terenzini, 2005. *How College Affects Students: A Third Decade of Research.* Vol. 2. San Francisco: Jossey-Bass.

Peterson, Marvin W., and David D. Dill. 1997. "Understanding the Competitive Environment of the Postsecondary Knowledge Industry." In *Planning and Management for a Changing Environment,* ed. M. W. Peterson, D. D. Dill, L. A. Mets, and Associates, 3–29. San Francisco: Jossey-Bass.

POSTECH (Pohang University of Science and Technology). 2007. *A History of Pohang University of Science and Technology: 1986–2006.* Pohang, Republic of Korea: Dong-in Forum.

———. 2009. "Annual Financial Report." POSTECH, Pohang, Republic of Korea. http://thome.postech.ac.kr/user/postech/es/2010/aif-1.pdf.

Reeves-Bracco, Kathy, Richard C. Richardson, Jr., Patrick M. Callan, and Joni E. Finney. 1999. "Policy Environments and System Design: Understanding State Governance Structures." *Review of Higher Education* 23 (1): 23–44.

Rhee, Byung S. 2007. "Incorporation of National Universities in Korea: Dynamic Forces, Key Features, and Challenges." *Asia Pacific Journal of Education* 27 (3): 341–57.

———. 2008. "Neoliberalism and Challenges of Korean Higher Education Policy. *Journal of Politics of Education* 15 (2): 7–25.

Seoul National University. 2009. "University statistics." Seoul National University, Seoul. http://www.academyinfo.go.kr/?process=schoolDisclose00&schoolCd =51012000&orgcode=1&sry_yy=2008&. Accessed August 5, 2009.

Times Higher Education. 2010. "The World University Rankings 2010." London. http://www.timeshighereducation.co.uk/world-university-rankings/2010-2011/top-200.html.

Umakoshi, Toru. 1997. *Establishment and Development of Modern Universities in Korea.* Seoul: Kyoyookbook.

CHAPTER 5

The National University of Singapore and the University of Malaya: Common Roots and Different Paths

Hena Mukherjee and Poh Kam Wong

In their characterization of world-class research universities, Jamil Salmi (2009) and Philip G. Altbach and Jorge Balán (2007) direct attention to universities' international standings as research institutions and their responsibility in creating new knowledge with science and technological innovation at its core. Globally, higher education is increasingly valued for its links to economic development and its major contributions to a country's gross domestic product (GDP) (Hatakenaka 2004), with recognition of its catalytic role in growing the knowledge economy and society.

The impact of universities' teaching, learning, and research activities related to the accelerated expansion of knowledge is tracked closely—leading to interinstitutional competition for human and financial resources within a worldwide framework. Policy makers and institution managers refer to globally acknowledged benchmarks that have been proven to strengthen universities—making them more competitive among their peers and more attractive to students, academic staff members, researchers,

employers, funding bodies, and industry. Universities in industrial economies appear to have the edge (for example, Harvard University, Stanford
University, and University of Cambridge) as seen in their research outputs
and outcomes and reflected in world university rankings, but newer universities in Asia (such as the University of Hong Kong and the National
University of Singapore) are holding their own.

   Governments of emerging economies also look to their higher education institutions to provide the fundamentals for their participation in the
growth of their knowledge economies, particularly in competitive innovation and research products. This chapter reviews the paths taken by two
universities—the National University of Singapore (Singapore) and the
University of Malaya (Malaysia)—that branched out from the same roots.
King Edward VII College of Medicine, established in Singapore in 1905,
merged with Raffles College in 1949 to become the University of Malaya,
in Singapore. Expansion of the university, coupled with independence
from the United Kingdom (Malaya in 1957 and Singapore in 1959) as
two separate countries, led to the creation of two branches in 1959, one
in Singapore and one in Kuala Lumpur. In 1962, following the decision
of the Singapore and Malayan governments (Malaysia was formed in
1963 with the addition of Sabah and Sarawak states in Borneo), the two
became autonomous national universities—the University of Singapore
and the University of Malaya—in their respective countries. The University
of Singapore merged with Nanyang University in 1980 to become the
National University of Singapore.

   Immediately following the separation and establishment of the two
universities in 1962, both universities made efforts to strengthen their
academic staffing base and consolidate their teaching programs. Both had
acquired reasonable reputations in the Southeast Asian region. The populations served in both countries are multiracial with the same racial mix
in different proportions (see table 5.1). The plurality of races is particularly significant in Malaysia where education policy is influenced by different opportunities for students and academic staff members, who
constitute the heart of higher education institutions.

   Several questions guide this analysis. What were the attributes favorable to institutional development in the national and institutional policy
contexts of the two institutions? What significant decisions have been
made regarding the selection of students and academic staff members,
and how are the best staff members attracted and retained? Do the universities' research activities have the assurance of stable and adequate
financial support? To what extent have strategies to internationalize the

Table 5.1   Population Distribution by Ethnic Groups in Singapore and Malaysia

percent

Ethnic group	Singapore (4.8 million inhabitants)	Malaysia (28.7 million inhabitants)
Bumiputras[a]	14	65
Chinese	77	26
Indians	8	8
Others	1	1

Sources: Singapore figures drawn from "Population Trends 2009," Singapore Department of Statistics website, http://www.singstat.gov.sg/pubn/popn/population2009.pdf. Malaysian figures drawn from "Population, Household and Living Quarters (2010)," Malaysia Department of Statistics website, http://www.statistics.gov.my/ccount12/click.php?id=1620.
a. Malays and indigenous groups in Sabah and Sarawak are called Bumiputras.

student body and academic staff been successful? Seeking answers to these questions leads to the final question: What lessons can be drawn from the experiences of the National University of Singapore (NUS) and the University of Malaya (UM) for sharing with the global academic community, particularly with colleagues in emerging economies aspiring to join the ranks of world-class research universities?

Postseparation Policy Environment

At an early stage, the Singapore government realized the universities' role in sustaining economic growth, and in the early 1970s, as the "labor-intensive strategy gradually gave way to a higher value technology-intensive strategy . . . a new tertiary education philosophy crystalized in Singapore" (Seah 1983, 14). As a result, being on the cutting edge of teaching and research has continued as a priority for NUS since 1962, with research excellence becoming an increasingly important mission since the late 1980s. In contrast, after 1970, UM's institutional goals reflected the New Economic Policy, an affirmative action plan for ethnic Malays and indigenous groups, put in place in the wake of disastrous 1969 ethnic riots that took the lives of hundreds of people on both sides of the racial divide. The civil disturbances, partly the result of dissatisfaction among the Malays with their progress in the education and economic sectors, brought about sweeping changes—leading to the New Economic Policy, with education perceived as a vital instrument for achieving its objectives.

The New Economic Policy was designed to achieve national integration and unity through a two-pronged strategy: (a) eradicating poverty by raising income levels and increasing employment opportunities for all Malaysians and (b) restructuring Malaysian society to correct economic imbalances so as to reduce and eventually eliminate the identification of race with economic function. It was expected to be in place for only 20 years but has continued under different labels—such as the National Development Policy and, most recently, the New Economic Model. A major outcome of the New Economic Policy was the imposition of ethnic quotas for student admission at a ratio of 55 to 45 for Bumiputras to non-Bumiputras, in line with their distribution in the Malaysian population. These quotas were in place until the meritocracy system was introduced in 2002, but the proportions have not varied much since then.

Apart from the student quota system, the New Economic Policy translated into more scholarships to Bumiputra students, a special foundation and matriculation programs to facilitate their entry into higher education institutions, the use of the Malay language in place of English in the entire education system by 1983, special preuniversity schools and colleges set up for rural Bumiputra children, and greater opportunities provided to Bumiputra students to study science. In UM and in government, the policy impact spiraled upward so that Bumiputra staff members, over time, secured almost all senior management, administrative, and academic positions.

As NUS kept pace with the demands of a growing economy that sought to become competitive internationally, with English continuing as the language of instruction and research, UM began to focus inward as proficiency in English declined in favor of the national language—Bahasa Malaysia—and the New Economic Policy's social goals took precedence. The erstwhile premier university was unable to compete successfully in strategic innovations and production with regional universities. Economic competition—from economies such as China; the Republic of Korea; and Taiwan, China—revealed that unless it could bring high, value-added technology to industry, Malaysia would be unable to hold its own. The time for resting on the advantage of low-cost labor had ended, particularly when China's cheap labor force entered the marketplace.

NUS developed in a political and economic environment where the political leadership had consistently and unequivocally emphasized that human capital development was the foremost goal for the country that was scarce in other natural resources. From NUS's inception, the national educational development policies (Low, Toh, and Soon 1991) were based squarely on meritocracy and the need for graduates who could enhance Singapore's growth as a hub for international financial services and trade.

As the Singapore economy increasingly shifted over the years from labor- and capital-intensive manufacturing activities toward knowledge-based activities, the role of NUS has progressively broadened to include a significant focus on research since the late 1980s and technology commercialization since the early 2000s (Wong, Ho, and Singh 2007). Moreover, the NUS mission also broadened from being a local tertiary labor developer to becoming a globally oriented university, competing for the best faculty and student talent from around the world and seeking to make a meaningful impact on the world through knowledge creation and diffusion. To provide NUS the flexibility it needed to transform its role in the Singapore economy, the Ministry of Education corporatized NUS in the mid-2000s.

In the mid-1990s, four watershed pieces of legislation were passed in Malaysia for the higher education subsector, providing a regulatory framework for the burgeoning private sector while placing strict parameters for public university management: (a) the National Council on Higher Education Act, 1996, to establish a council that formulates policy for the Malaysian higher education sector; (b) the Universities and University Colleges Act, 1971, amended in 1996 to enable corporatization of public universities and to modernize the management of public universities; (c) the National Higher Education Fund Board Act, 1997, to establish a higher education, student loan–funding agency; and (d) the National Accreditation Board Act, 1996. The latter legislation led to the Malaysian Qualifications Agency Act, 2007, which developed the Malaysian Qualifications Framework to unify and harmonize all Malaysian qualifications. Notwithstanding such efforts to reform the higher education system, the pro-Bumiputra affirmative action policy remained in force.

Between 2004 and 2009, the Times Higher Education–QS World University Rankings (THE-QS 2008, 2009) showed NUS among the world's top 20 (2004, 2005, and 2006) and top 30 (2008 and 2009), with UM moving progressively lower between 2004 and 2008 from 89th to 230th (180th in 2009). The much-advertised rankings by the media and perceived declining standards of UM led to public questioning in Malaysia, with calls for action. One of UM management's first actions, was to retool its institutional goals and processes. Without putting aside the long-term goals of the New Economic Policy, management developed new institutional goals in the 2000s, recognizing that the talent pool would need to be widened beyond the existing student quota levels and inward-focused staffing policies. The change to the policy of meritocracy for student admissions, based on results of recognized examinations in 2002, was a response to the issue of widening the net for talent. UM's mission included the goal of becoming "an internationally renowned institution of higher learning in research, innovation, publication and research" (UM 2008, 21). New priorities have brought additional challenges.

There has been widespread recognition that the implementation of affirmative action policies in Malaysia has hurt the higher education system, sapping Malaysia's economic competitiveness and driving some (mainly Chinese and Indians) to more meritocratic countries, such as Singapore. Meanwhile, the government has announced the New Economic Model, which would replace the New Economic Policy (NEAC 2010). With the aim of turning Malaysia into a high-income economy by 2020 with per capita income expected to move from US$7,000 to US$15,000–US$20,000, the New Economic Model plans to institute tough economic reform policies to increase the country's competitiveness. The authors of the New Economic Model identified "insufficient innovation and creativity" and "lack of appropriately skilled human capital" among the critical factors contributing to current sluggish economic growth (NEAC 2010, 22) and inability to participate in the knowledge economy.

Language Policy

Keeping native-language instruction available within the Singapore school system, the first postindependence prime minister, Lee Kuan Yew, laid special emphasis on English as a common language that both connected citizens of all ethnic backgrounds and tied Singapore to the world economy. Apart from the native language, at the secondary-school level students can opt to study French, German, or Japanese, and the Ministry of Education Language Centre provides free language education for most additional languages that schools do not cover. The range of languages at school level, with English as the language of instruction throughout the system, prepares NUS graduates well for international participation. The requirement for English proficiency is not up for debate in NUS, and this policy has served its international objectives well.

In Malaysia, the language of instruction in mainstream government schools changed from English to Bahasa Malaysia in 1971, with provision for primary schooling in Chinese (Mandarin) and Tamil. At the secondary level, only the Bahasa Malaysia track comes under government provision. Chinese school students opt to switch to this mainstream track or to proceed to private, generally well-run Chinese secondary schools (about

60 schools). There are no secondary-level Tamil schools. In all schools, English is taught as a subject, and not all teachers are adequately trained.

Political exigencies accelerated the implementation schedule of moving from English to Bahasa Malaysia, bringing implementation forward to the mid-1970s instead of 1983 (Chai 1977). Academic staff members and students were not equally proficient, and infrastructural support, such as textbooks and reference materials, was in English. Massive language-training programs were put in place accompanied by a scramble to translate English texts into Bahasa Malaysia and to write new textbooks.

The Malays benefited from the rapid change in language medium, particularly those from the rural areas. However, the short-term outcome of this policy, apart from improved grades among the Malay students, was the inability or unwillingness of many to deal with English. Opportunities were lost to function in English, which is currently the global language of research, publication, scientific discourse, and electronic communication and a tool for increasing mobility. Students regurgitated lecture notes, reluctant to refer to English-language texts, journals, and sources of reference. The focus on Bahasa Malaysia brought with it an interest in Malay language, culture, and history, and this trend would have occurred anyway, given academic expertise and patterns of financial support. Efforts to internationalize teaching and research have brought renewed focus to the tension between strengthening English and supporting Bahasa Malaysia, the national language and the language of the Malay race. Unless political measures support the widespread use of English, the engagement of young Malaysians in global knowledge creation will continue to be limited.

Meanwhile, the 60 or so independent Chinese secondary schools have received a dramatic surge of applicants taking their highly competitive entrance examination. A growing number of Malay and Indian parents register their children in Chinese schools, considering them qualitatively superior with good discipline. In addition, they are convinced that learning Mandarin might give their children a head start in employment with the strong Chinese business community. Most Malaysian private universities, NUS (since 1998), and about 100 overseas institutions accept the exit examination—the United Education Certificate—for entry. In response to appeals from Chinese education groups, the Malaysian government has agreed to review the certificate's conferral of eligibility for admission to public universities in stages, with a key criterion being attainment of Bahasa Malaysia qualifications (*The Sun* 2010, 3).

Financing

World-class research universities are characterized by stable and higher levels of financial support, compared with comprehensive universities that focus mainly on teaching rather than research. A history of strong government financial support, buttressed by an institution's own fund-raising success, tend to mark the financial experience of acclaimed research universities.

Whereas the Singapore government's financial commitment to education has stayed at about the same proportion since 1962—around 3 percent of its GDP—the proportion of public educational expenditure going to university education has climbed from 10.8 percent to 19.8 percent between 1962 and 2007. In absolute terms, this proportion amounts to approximately US$1.31 billion for 2007, indicating that all three universities have a strong base of government financial resources. The annual operating budget for NUS for 2008–09 reached US$1.55 billion with government grants constituting 58 percent of the operating budget, up from just US$287.72 million in 1990 (NUS 1990, 2009). In 2008, UM's total income was US$280 million, and about 68 percent of this income came from federal government grants (UM 2009). Miscellaneous fees constituted 11 percent, investment income 10 percent, amortization of the grant 5 percent, and 6 percent from other income (UM 2009, 298).

Although public expenditure for education in Malaysia has constituted around 25 percent of its budget for a period of time, the absolute amounts clearly are not comparable with those of Singapore. Although the high proportion shows strong government commitment to education, inefficiencies in institutional budget practices, as discussed later in this section, render fund use less than optimal. Furthermore, Malaysia's economy has not been in step with the expansion of country economies in the region. Table 5.2 shows an increase in GDP per capita income in current terms for Hong Kong SAR, China; Korea; Malaysia; and Singapore between 1970 and 2005, when Korea, behind Malaysia in 1970, more than tripled Malaysia's per capita income by 2005. Singapore's GDP per capita income was more than double that of Malaysia in 1970 and had stormed ahead to more than five times the amount by 2005. These figures translate into lower levels of financial resources available to all sectors.

A matter of concern for planners is that public expenditure for education in Malaysia does not exhibit consistent levels of allocations to the various subsectors. Between 1970 and 2006, overall public expenditure

Table 5.2   Gross Domestic Product Per Capita Income for Malaysia; the Republic of Korea; Hong Kong SAR, China; and Singapore, 1970 and 2005

Economy	GDP per capita, 1970 (current US$)	GDP per capita, 2005 (current US$)
Malaysia	394.1	5,141.6
Korea, Rep.	278.8	16,308.9
Singapore	913.8	26,892.9
Hong Kong SAR, China	959.2	25,592.8

Source: IMF 2009.

on education as a percentage of GDP in 1970 constituted 3.98 percent, climbing to a peak in 2002 of 7.66 percent, then falling to 4.67 percent in 2006. The impact is seen in the reduced allocations of public expenditure per tertiary student (as a percentage of per capita GDP) from 97.83 percent in 2002 to 59.72 percent in 2006 (IMF 2009). In the same year, annual student expenditure at NUS (US$6,300) was higher than at UM (US$4,053) even after taking into consideration the differential costs of living in Singapore and Malaysia. The cost of living was only 1.3 times higher than that of Malaysia in 2006 (IMD 2006). Decreasing allocations translate to less financial support for institutional development. This trend is also evident in research allocations that are not consistent over time.

UM student fees are highly subsidized; only US$0.94 million, or 3 percent of the 2008 operating budget, came from tuition fees. For NUS, in 2008 tuition income was 16.6 percent of its operating budget. A comparison of average annual fees for local and international undergraduate and graduate programs in both universities showed high subsidy levels for local students in UM, whereas NUS appeared to base its fees for local students more on the principle of cost recovery. Annual tuition subsidy per local student from the government of Malaysia for a bachelor's degree in economics is currently just under US$4,783. For medical students, while the annual student tuition fee is US$780, the government's annual tuition subsidy per student is US$9,856 (Fernandez-Chung 2010). In NUS, in 2009 the average annual local and international student tuition fees for an undergraduate humanities program were US$4,560 and US$6,840, respectively—according to the NUS Registrar's Office. Within a context of uncertain economic growth worldwide and the ever-increasing costs of higher education, current high subsidy levels may not be sustainable over the long term: better cost-sharing strategies need to be encouraged.

UM's fund-raising capacities are unable to offset the gap between government allocations and the levels required for meeting teaching expenditure requirements and international-level academic research. Strategies to increase and diversify income sources include the establishment of an endowment fund, as yet modest, which stood at almost US$124 million in 2008 (according to the UM Bursar's Office), increasing income from consultancy contracts (0.89 percent of annual income in 2008), and mounting of new market-oriented programs. Exacerbating the scarcity of resources in UM are the rigidities of the government financing modality, which is primarily a historical and negotiated incremental-cost approach (linked with inputs) in the distribution of funds among public universities. Agreed line items such as salary levels and fees leave the institution little flexibility, and UM submits monthly balance sheets to the Ministry of Finance to demonstrate expenditure carried out as agreed. This practice is in force despite the fact that the Modified Budgeting System, which operates as an output-oriented budget allocation, was introduced in 1997. An approach with a delay built into the process has the disadvantage of impairing both efficiency and institutional agility to respond swiftly to change.

Challenges Facing University Management and Administration

The decades since 1962 have brought about a sea change in the level of complexity confronting the management, administration, and overall organization of NUS and UM. University leadership has had to adjust to the now universally accepted understanding of the deep links between economic growth and education. Institutional managers and administrators, largely from a bureaucratic civil service background, have had to learn to be more entrepreneurial, to work with industry, and to collaborate in joint outputs and commercialization of products against a background of increasingly sophisticated and high-tech electronic tools. Management has had to become responsible for overseeing the updating and fine-tuning of curriculum, pedagogy, and assessment techniques to match growth and change areas. Economic growth, with its need for stimulating locally grown innovations along with the creation of new knowledge, propelled the institutions to shift from pursuing the primary role of teaching to pursuing both teaching and research. The policy shift to encompass a significant role in research has been implemented with greater resource intensity and outcomes in NUS than in UM.

The changing nature of the universities' functional goals ran parallel to equally challenging physical and logistical changes with new faculties, institutes, and centers and growing student and staff numbers. Additionally, both universities have had to develop policies for internationalizing academic and research staff members as well as students, keeping in mind the effect of such policies on programs, financial, and human resources.

The external tertiary education environment has been equally in flux. Emerging from a situation of monopoly, the two universities have had to develop competitive strategies for human and financial resources as other tertiary institutions were established. Singapore has three public universities, whereas Malaysia has 20. Both countries host a vast array of twinning programs and partnerships with international universities. Singapore has positioned itself as a regional hub by attracting leading foreign universities such as Institut Européen d'Administration des Affaires (INSEAD) and the University of Chicago to the city state. In Malaysia, a vibrant, private higher education segment has also grown with branches of five foreign universities—Curtin University of Technology, Monash University, and Swinburne University from Australia; and the University of Nottingham and Newcastle University from the United Kingdom.

What mechanisms did university management and leadership develop to deal with such extensive and deep changes, and what was the impact on institutional development? To what extent did the two universities possess or develop the nimbleness to adjust to these changes?

University Management and Governance

After Singapore separated from Malaysia, the Singapore campus of the University of Malaya was renamed Singapore University and was constituted as a public university under the Ministry of Education of Singapore. Like UM, Singapore University was structured as a statutory board, with the vice-chancellor appointed by the cabinet and the strategic direction of the university overseen by a university council with public- and private-sector members who were appointed by the government. In both Singapore University and UM, faculty and administrative staff members were treated as government employees and their salary structure pegged to that of the civil service system. Although this governance structure continued when Singapore University became the National University of Singapore, more autonomy was granted to the university administration over the years, culminating in the corporatization of the university in the mid-2000s. Concomitantly, there was a gradual shift in university administrative practices from those of the U.K. model to that of the U.S. model.

For example, the faculty-rank structure shifted from the British system of lecturers, senior lecturers, and other positions to the U.S. professorial ranking system, and the title of vice-chancellor was changed to president.

Between 1962 and the mid-1970s, policy setting and decision making in UM, as in NUS, were the functions of the University Council, which had representation from the private sector and government—the latter including the Ministry of Education and later the Ministry of Higher Education (established in 2004). The Minister of Higher Education appoints the vice-chancellor, and the vice-chancellor appoints the deans. The centralized system's inertia restrained UM's management from acting in its own best interests, foregoing the agility that autonomy brings to strong world-class universities. A central Ministry of Higher Education unit handles students' selection and their distribution across all departments. Government approval is required for new programs and clearance of course content in which 30 percent is new content. Hiring, firing, and salary decisions are not fully independent of the Ministry of Higher Education, making it difficult for management and university leadership to replace unproductive staff and reward productive staff. There have been some changes over the past decade. Campus activities, except for those that are political in nature, have enjoyed resurgence. In a reformist move in 2009 triggered by new leadership, there were open elections for deans' positions (taken up by only four faculty groups).

The New Economic Policy succeeded in reducing poverty and substantially addressed interethnic economic imbalances. Its implementation, however, has increased the cost of doing business, because of "rent-seeking, patronage . . . (engendering) pervasive corruption, which needs to be addressed earnestly" (NEAC 2010, 7). In a bid to gain confidence and improve transparency, accountability, and overall governance, the universities' administrative procedures such as criteria for staff promotion, and evaluations by internal and external academic assessors are now disclosed (since 2009) on each university's electronic network, moving from little or no informed discussion to a more open forum. Such practices have the potential for changing the management and academic culture of the university by moving away from decisions based on personal relationships to those based on agreed institutional goals and individual achievement.

Leadership
Between 1962 and the present, NUS leadership demonstrated the value of continuity in position, with only five vice-chancellors during the period—most of whom were respected scholars of international repute.

This experience contrasts with the 10 vice-chancellors for UM over the same period, only some of whom were recognized as top-notch scholars and two were nonacademic senior civil-service personnel. Many served for single tenures of three years, and at least two did not complete their first tenures. Few have had sufficient experience in steering a large, complex educational institution through a highly political environment. Many have, therefore, relied heavily on rigid government guidelines with scant regard for managerial, academic, and financial autonomy.

On the heels of the negative publicity brought about by poor global ranking of Malaysia's leading universities, government authorities provided new leadership to UM in 2008 by appointing a vice-chancellor with a proven performance record from a successful government-linked university. His program of institutional change reflects an attempt to bring about internal realignment with the policies and practices of successful international research universities, focusing on developing a culture of scholarship. He has a significant challenge, having to woo both administrative and academic staff to his reformist views.

Strategic Planning

In the early 1980s, NUS had followed the policy of capping the number of traditional courses to allow for growth in professional courses—such as engineering, architecture, construction, and real estate management. Prevailing government policies related to high-level labor requirements continued to influence university admissions in science and technology-based areas as did constant monitoring of market forces to reduce risks of graduate unemployment. In more recent years, in response to the changing needs of the economy, NUS has launched new schools such as the Lee Kuan Yew School of Public Policy and new multidisciplinary programs such as bioengineering. UM's strategic planning focused on the student-entry level; grounded in the New Economic Policy, distribution was based on 55 percent Bumiputra to 45 percent non-Bumiputra, and the goal was to increase the number of Bumiputra admissions in national priority areas of science, technology, and professional program admissions rather than capping enrollment in courses. The Ministry of Higher Education's targets of a 60 to 40 distribution between science and technology programs and the humanities programs provide a guideline.

Autonomy and Responsiveness to Change

In Singapore, after Parliament passed the bill to corporatize NUS in 2006, the greater autonomy conferred by the act enabled NUS to accelerate the process of organizational transformation that it had begun in the late 1990s to better meet the challenge of global competition. For example, although NUS had already begun to offer more competitive compensation packages to recruit faculty from overseas before 2006, corporatization gave the university, as a not-for-profit organization, greater flexibility in structuring offers, including providing generous start-up research grants and reduced teaching loads in initial years for top researchers. It also further increased NUS leadership and management flexibility in institutional practices such as market adjustment allowance for faculty in fields with high-market demand (for example, medical and finance) and recruiting of deans and department heads through international search committees.

The progressive increase in autonomy granted to NUS has enabled it to respond to new opportunities more proactively and more nimbly. In response to perceived needs, NUS could develop relatively quickly, for example, a wide range of new interdisciplinary educational programs such as nanotechnology and interactive digital media. To support diversity of educational approaches, NUS has launched a new medical school (in collaboration with Duke University, in the United States) based on the U.S. postgraduate and research-based medical school model, while continuing to expand the existing U.K.-style undergraduate medical school. As part of the campus expansion program, NUS is also developing a new residential college system, adapting elements of the residential college system of the United Kingdom's University of Cambridge and University of Oxford.

The Corporatization of Higher Education Act in Malaysia was passed in 1997. As in the case of NUS, the act would allow universities to manage themselves like corporate bodies, reducing bureaucratic red tape and delays in the decision-making process. Critical features included securing financial autonomy for higher education institutions; freedom to appoint university leaders, deans, and heads of institutes; and freedom to select students. However, the legislative framework that would have opened the door to university autonomy was never fully implemented. The official reason provided was that in the cash-strapped environment following the 1997 financial crisis, universities would find it impossible to function without government funding. UM lost the opportunity to manage itself and continued as an executor of government policy and decision making, drawing the comment that

> university autonomy has been systematically eroded in Malaysia. The University of Malaya, which enjoyed a certain autonomy during its early days, has now joined younger universities that are directly controlled or

strongly influenced by the government. Basic freedoms of university staff and students have been so effectively curbed. . . . It is not surprising, therefore, that the quality and standards of local universities have been deteriorating. (Ali 2009, 266)

The 1980s and 1990s ushered in a global technology explosion. Because of insufficient technological understanding, vision, resources, and know-how, UM—and, indeed, the government—did not act swiftly enough at systemic and institutional levels to implement measures to take advantage of new technology. The education management information system, for instance, is woefully inadequate—where it exists. At the institutional level, student and staff databases for UM, and from the Ministry of Education for the country as a whole, were available in electronic form only after 2002. This modernization was continued by the Ministry of Higher Education after its establishment in 2004 (Ministry of Higher Education 2005, 2006, 2007). There is greater recognition now that as research activities expand and become more sophisticated, high-level performance in computing and effective database management become indispensable building blocks of the research environment.

Secondary Schooling and Preparedness for Tertiary Education

In both Singapore and Malaysia, government-funded schools follow a centralized, common curriculum leading to common examinations. International testimony to the Singapore secondary education system is borne out by the country's repeated successful performance in TIMSS (Trends in International Mathematics and Science Study). For example, among children age 13, Singapore was ranked top in both mathematics and science in the TIMSS cycles of 1995 and 2003 and third and first, respectively, in the most recent cycle (Salmi 2009). Malaysia participated in the TIMSS eighth-grade assessment in 1999 (28 countries), 2003 (44 countries), and 2007 (49 countries). Although Malaysia's performance ranking improved from 1999 to 2003 (World Bank 2007, 48), average scores in mathematics and science in 2007 remained significantly behind those of Singapore (474 versus 593 and 471 versus 567, respectively) and other East Asian emerging economies.

School curriculum in Singapore is regularly reviewed and revised—the A-level curriculum in 2007 being a case in point—which broadens a student's choice of options for examinations. A new subject, knowledge and inquiry, was designed to expose students to the construction and nature of knowledge, creating the need to cut across disciplines. To gain acceptance into university, students must pass the knowledge and inquiry course or the general paper, which tests general knowledge. About 25 percent of the A-level cohort gains seats in one of Singapore's three universities.

A longitudinal study on the transition from school to work analyzed the experiences of students seven years after leaving school in Malaysia. It concluded that the public education system had "in large measure been responsible for a memory-based learning designed for the average student" (Nagaraj et al. 2009) rather than a system that stimulates and fosters creative thinking and excellence. Study findings indicated that the system fosters the fear of providing the wrong answer, promoting conformity and uniformity rather than fresh and creative thinking, with rote learning and memorization appearing to be the key factor for success in examinations (Wong 2004, 159–60). Rote learning, memorization, uniformity, and conformity foster risk aversion but not the development of creative thinkers (*The Economist* 2000). These findings do not augur well for tertiary-education entrants expected to fulfill Malaysia's plans for graduating future high-performing researchers.

Undergraduate, Graduate, and International Students

The primary significant constituents of world-class research universities are students and faculty members. Strong international research universities are known to be highly selective, admitting the best and brightest *students* nationally and internationally, growing their graduate numbers compared with the undergraduate enrollment, and hiring high-performing *faculty members* from a worldwide talent pool.

NUS has traditionally admitted students at the end of 12 years of schooling on the basis of A-level examination results. Although the requirements for qualification to various departments vary according to their popularity, the general trend is that of increased stringency over the years, particularly for courses that are high in demand—such as those in medicine, law, and business. Focusing on nurturing creativity, NUS adopted a more holistic approach in 2003 where attributes such as reasoning ability, critical thinking, and leadership potential are taken into consideration through the incorporation of scores in Scholastic Aptitude Test 1, which tests analytical and problem-solving skills, and bonus points are awarded in the admissions decision for participation in co-curricular activities. Departments are also allowed to reserve a certain percentage of places for candidates who excel in areas beyond academic grades.

The strong secondary school system yielded high school graduates who have met university admissions criteria, with enrollment in NUS growing steadily from 2,149 undergraduate and graduate students in 1962 to 29,761 in 2000 (NUS 1962, 2000). Despite increasing stringency in admissions criteria, the share of academically strong foreign students has also increased over the years, particularly from Malaysia, Indonesia, China, and India. Since 2000, the total student enrollment has been relatively stable, reaching 30,350 in 2008, and is expected to stay about the same in the near future. Although undergraduates dominated in the early years (about 95 percent of total enrollment in the period 1962–70), the proportion of graduate students has increased steadily over time, reaching more than 23 percent in 2008, with a long-term target of achieving one-third. The ratio of students to teaching faculty members climbed from 11 to 1 in 1980 to 18 to 1 in 2000, decreasing to 14 to 1 in 2008. The ratio of students to teaching and research staff members was 10 to 1 in 1990, decreasing to 8 to 1 in 2008, consistent with the university's objective of inducting students effectively into university-level learning and research.

The distribution of students among departments has changed over the years, reflecting the changing labor demands of the Singapore economy. Between 1970 and 2008, the share of student enrollment in engineering increased the most, from around 14 percent to around 27 percent at both the undergraduate and the graduate levels. However, medicine experienced a steadily declining enrollment share, from 27.0 percent to 5.6 percent for undergraduates and 47.0 percent to 8.0 percent for graduates. In the arts and social sciences, the proportion of undergraduates remained steady at around 20 percent over the same period, but their share of graduate enrollment had declined from 25 percent in 1970 to 10 percent in 2008.

Many program innovations were introduced over time to expose the students to industrial practices, research engagement, and international socialization. In 1999, a core curriculum program, modeled after that of Harvard University, was launched to provide a broad-based education emphasizing writing, critical thinking, and an appreciation of interdisciplinary connections. In July 2001, a new University Scholars Programme was started as a fusion of these two programs to provide greater curriculum flexibility to talented students wishing to pursue a more interdisciplinary program of study. In addition to innovative educational programs, NUS has invested heavily in teaching infrastructure and pedagogy. An advanced learning management system, the Integrated Virtual Learning Environment, supports ubiquitous e-learning; the system has been widely adopted across all departments and subsequently has been commercialized through a spin-off company.

Carefully planned international exchange programs may be seen as a combination of NUS goals of internationalization and experiential learning, leading to enhanced research outcomes in the long term. Distinctive programs give NUS an advantage. For example, a partnership program with the Massachusetts Institute of Technology was initiated in 1998 to enable top NUS graduate students in cutting-edge engineering and life science fields to take jointly conducted courses and to conduct research supervised by faculties from both universities. Besides the use of video-conferencing technology, NUS students in the program spent one semester to one year at the Massachusetts Institute of Technology. The program was so successful that it evolved from an NUS-degree-only program to a joint-degree program. In 2000, the new NUS Overseas College program was launched to allow NUS undergraduate students with entrepreneurial interests to work as interns in high-tech start-ups in Silicon Valley, California, for one year while taking entrepreneurship classes at Stanford University. The NUS Overseas College program has since been extended to partnerships in five other high-tech hubs: Philadelphia, with the University of Pennsylvania; Stockholm, with KTH (Royal Institute of Technology); Shanghai, with Fudan University; Bangalore, with the Indian Institute of Science; and Beijing, with Tsinghua University.

Malaysian students primarily have two modes of entry to public university education. The first is the Malaysian Higher School Certificate (local acronym STPM) based on a national, standardized examination taken at the end of 13 years of primary, secondary, and higher secondary education. The second is the one-year or two-year (for weaker students) matriculation program, developed and conducted by various institutions at the end of 11 years of schooling. The 2002 policy of admitting students based on merit, as measured by the results of STPM and matriculation examinations, raises important questions about the dual entry modes. All students admitted are required to have a minimum cumulative grade point average ranging from 2.5 to 3.0 out of 4.0, but the extent to which these very different schooling standards and assessments are equivalent is an issue that has not been openly debated. Although the different pathways increase access, they do not assure quality at entry.

As with NUS, expansion of enrollment at UM showed upward trends with 8,545 students in 1971, rising to 27,396 in 2009, with the attendant issues of students at weak entry–level performance, insufficient numbers of experienced staff members, and relevance of curriculum and instructional materials dogged by the language policy. Enrollment in UM in the 1960s and 1970s was heavily concentrated in the social sciences and humanities, in part because of the lower cost of establishing and developing these disciplines, the pull of employment opportunities in the postcolonial expanding state bureaucracy, and the increased admission of Bumiputras who crowded into subjects such as Islamic and Malay studies. By 2008, however, student enrollment in science, technology, and medical sciences was almost 40 percent—with humanities and social sciences at 60 percent—moving toward the Education Development Plan for Malaysia 2001–10 target of 60 percent for science and technology and 40 percent for humanities and social sciences (Ministry of Education 2001).

UM has made efforts to reinvigorate and globalize the curriculum using international benchmarks. Inputs from external assessors, industry liaison panels, employers, and students themselves are being included in curriculum design and review panels with support for improved student-learning habits. To attract students to research activities, the administration has introduced mechanisms (such as the compulsory Students Project) at the undergraduate level with research electives available. To improve teaching and learning quality, UM made efforts to improve student-to-staff ratios. Student-to-faculty ratio targets as set up by the Malaysian Qualifications Agency are 25 to 1 for arts, 15 to 1 for sciences, and 4 to 1 for clinical programs. Figures reported in 2010 indicate an overall ratio of 12 to 1, with 6 to 1 for arts and social sciences, 7 to 1 for science, 8 to 1 for engineering, and 2 to 1 for medicine. The numbers for academic staff members include tutors and part-time staff.

Graduate Enrollment

In 2002, two reform policies were put in place: graduate enrollment was to be increased to 50 percent, and foreign students were to be actively recruited. In 2008–09, graduate enrollment was 35 percent of total enrollment, and foreign student enrollment increased to 12.3 percent. The total number of UM master's and PhD students in 2008 was 33 percent of the total student population of 26,963, far from the 461 students, or less than 15 percent, in 1971. In 1971, arts doctoral students constituted about 34 percent of all PhD students, with engineering at 4 percent and science at 25 percent. By 2008, of the 2,246 doctoral students, arts students made up less than 10 percent of doctoral candidates, with engineering at above 9 percent, and science at almost 14 percent. Although absolute numbers have moved upward in science and engineering, in proportion to the total number enrolled in doctoral programs, UM's development of skills in strategic research areas has some way to go. Because undergraduate admissions policies do not focus on selecting the country's best students (although there are some efforts to be more selective), those students are also not represented among graduate research students, most of whom are UM first-degree graduates. Adopting the policy of internationalizing the student population is one way of expanding the talent pool, a policy taken up by both NUS and UM.

Internationalization of Students

In line with the national strategy to promote immigration of highly skilled foreign talents to supplement the limited supply of local labor, by the late 1990s NUS took on the broader objective of attracting foreign research talent to Singapore, while providing local students with international exposure. In addition, in the steps of Western countries such as the United States (Fiske 1997), the Singapore government recognized that education itself can be a major export industry. By the late 1990s, it had established a strategic program to turn the island economy into a leading educational hub in Asia—seeing itself as the "Boston of the East." Today, local schools and universities regularly advertise information on admissions, offering generous financial aid. Chinese and Indian students see the Singapore education system as an avenue out of the Malaysian system, where they perceive they are disadvantaged both in university selection and employment opportunities. The government has also set a goal of attracting 10 leading universities from around the world to establish campuses in Singapore (Olds 2007).

Foreign students continue to be attracted to Singapore's international reputation for research and scholarship, instructional and research facilities, English-language instruction, excellent living conditions in a cosmopolitan society, and access to strong financial support. In 2008, the proportion of international students in NUS was 34.6 percent of the total student population, constituting 22.3 percent of undergraduate students and 57.8 percent of graduate students. The four largest sources of foreign students in NUS have traditionally been China, India, Malaysia, and Indonesia, but student numbers from newer sources like Vietnam are rising rapidly as well.

In 2008, international students made up 12.3 percent of the total UM student body, composing 5 percent of undergraduate and 26 percent of graduate students. Malaysia's efforts to become a regional education hub have been strengthened with the Ministry of Higher Education's plan to increase the number of foreign undergraduate students annually at the rate of 5 percent and postgraduate students at 25 percent. The 10 countries with the largest number of students enrolled in 2008, in descending order, are the Islamic Republic of Iran, Indonesia, China, Iraq, the Republic of Yemen, Sudan, Saudi Arabia, Somalia, and Thailand. However, the value that foreign graduate students have added to research and innovation output has yet to be evaluated.

The number of international exchange students in NUS has also been increasing, with an annual average of 1,000 between 2005 and 2008. NUS aims to provide an overseas educational experience for more than half of its undergraduates. In 2009, UM hosted 991 international exchange students, while 1,008 students traveled abroad, with plans for 25 percent of each undergraduate cohort participating in programs abroad.

Development of Academic Faculty

With the strategic goal of making NUS a globally competitive university, the NUS senior administration had been steadily raising the bar over the years for academic faculty recruitment and retention, with the process greatly accelerated since the late 1990s. The key policy instruments include (a) progressively increasing salaries and compensation packages and making them more flexible and performance based to be more competitive internationally, especially for top talent; (b) increasing the level of research funding support and providing research facilities and infrastructure; (c) relentlessly raising the threshold for promotion and tenure; and (d) increasing the flexibility of faculty time allocation, including reducing the teaching workloads for faculty with excellent research performance records to devote more time to research. In extending the faculty tenure term from age 55 to age 65 for new hires, NUS has also been progressively raising the bar for tenure in the drive for excellence. In addition, NUS implemented a one-off exercise to selectively offer the tenure extension only to existing faculty that the university intends to retain, thus facilitating the transition to a higher level of excellence.

Improved Qualifications

The steadily improving quality of NUS faculty can be measured using a number of proxy indicators. First, the proportion of faculty with a PhD has increased substantially over the years; by 2005, 99 percent of the engineering faculty had a PhD versus only 50 percent in 1970, while for science, arts and social sciences, and business, the proportion with a PhD by 2003 was 88.7 percent, 80.2 percent, and 79.8 percent, respectively. For professional schools like medicine, design and architecture, and law, the increase was more gradual because of the nature of professional practice. Second, and more tellingly, the average research productivity and quality of NUS faculty have both increased considerably over the past two decades.

The question of sound leadership in research and teaching in UM has never been more relevant where research productivity, innovation, and commercialization are concerned. UM staff shows progressive improvement of doctoral-level qualifications, particularly in science and technology areas. In 1999, only 37 percent of staff had a PhD, rising to 61 percent in 2009, or 75 percent (which is the UM institutional target for proportion of PhD recipients) when equivalents are included. Additionally, UM has made a PhD degree a requirement from the lecturer level upward, while talented local or foreign postgraduate students, particularly in science- and technology-based programs, are seen as a potential source of faculty appointments.

Attracting and Retaining of Talent

World-class universities usually possess the characteristic of wooing and retaining strong faculty, irrespective of nationality or ethnicity. Although data for earlier years are not available, a comparison of NUS faculty composition between 1997 and 2005 shows a pattern of rapid increase of international staff for the categories of "faculty" and "research" staff. In 1997, 61 percent of NUS's 1,414 faculty members were Singaporeans, compared with 48 percent in 2005 (Wong, Ho, and Singh forthcoming). Other faculty members were from, in descending order, Malaysia, India, China, other Asian countries, the United States, Canada, and other countries. The high presence of faculty from Malaysia in NUS (10.8 percent in 2005, down from 12.8 percent in 1997) reflects a larger phenomenon of net talent loss from Malaysia to Singapore since their political separation. Indeed, because many Malaysians subsequently took citizenship in Singapore, the actual contribution of Malaysians to the NUS faculty was probably higher than these statistics suggest.

The situation has not gone unnoticed in Malaysia. In 2008, approximately 500,000 Malaysians were working abroad, half of whom had tertiary education. Identifying the weak education system as part of the overall depletion of skilled human resources, one must painfully conclude that "We are not developing talent and what we have is leaving. The human capital situation in Malaysia is reaching a critical stage. The rate of outward migration of skilled Malaysians is rising rapidly . . . ." (NEAC 2010, 6). The typical reasons ascribed to outward migration include better employment and business prospects, higher salaries, better working environments, and greater chances of promotion.

By 2008, NUS had been diversifying its international sources of faculty recruitment for at least a decade, as the global competition for talent intensified. In particular, between 1997 and 2005, the proportion of foreign faculty had risen to more than 50 percent. Whereas Malaysia continued to be the largest source country for NUS faculty, other sources—particularly India, China, and North America—contributed significantly increased numbers of both faculty and research staff in recent years. Faculty and research staff from China made up 4.5 percent and 32.2 percent, respectively, in 1997. In 2005, Chinese faculty members composed 6.9 percent of 1,765 members, while Chinese research staff members had a share of 42.4 percent of 1,087 research staff members (NUS 1998, 2005). The policy of broadening the base of well-qualified faculty members and researchers has stood NUS in good stead, both in the quantity and quality of research outputs and in the density of international collaboration networks.

Until recently, foreign staff numbers in Malaysian public universities were capped at 5 percent, but current Ministry of Higher Education policy encourages higher education institutions to increase foreign staff proportion to 15 percent by 2015. At UM, the effects of foreign staff recruitment are becoming more significant as numbers increase, intertwined with the effect of the New Economic Policy affirmative action practices. The emerging pattern of academic staff members hired by UM between 2001 and 2009 shows that (a) the majority continues to be Bumiputra; (b) the proportion of non-Bumiputra Malaysians constitutes one-third of total staff, with numbers dipping in 2009; (c) in general, the reduction in the proportion of local staff, particularly non-Bumiputra, across different categories, appears to be compensated by an increase in foreign staff at professorial and senior lecturer levels; and (d) the constant high proportion of Bumiputra lecturers between 2001 and 2009 suggests that as the first two levels of senior non-Bumiputra academic staff members retire and as foreign hires increase and existing senior lecturers and lecturers move upward through the system (on tenured civil service terms), the proportion of senior-level non-Bumiputra Malaysians will continue to decrease.

Efforts to increase the proportion of international faculty will continue for two major reasons: (a) the lack of local expertise in key research and teaching programs, particularly at the postgraduate level; and (b) the increased focus on research and hence the wider casting of recruiting nets in search of highly qualified researchers. Most foreign staff members (almost all of whom possess a PhD and work mainly in the sciences and engineering) are from South Asia, Southeast Asia, and the Middle East. UM has found it difficult to attract the best qualified and experienced international candidates, given its relatively low profile in research and publication and noncompetitive salary packages.

Salary Packages

Comparative data on staff salaries in NUS and UM from registrars' offices at both universities showed that NUS salary packages were far superior to those offered by UM, even after accounting for differences in the relative cost of living. The annual performance bonuses for faculty in NUS vary, ranging from nothing to more than two months of pay with possible cuts in base pay for poorly performing faculty. In UM, allowances are not subject to income tax, and foreign nationals receive similar salary and allowance levels as nationals, except for a housing allowance of US$469 for all levels. At the professional level, special incentive allowances are given to staff from the engineering, accounting, architecture, and surveying fields. NUS has similar incentive allowances that are annually adjusted to market rates. The high NUS salaries for local and foreign staff show awareness of the global competition for talent and the need to retain the most skilled individuals to keep abreast, if not ahead, of regional and global economic growth. NUS's human resource policy also includes an aggressive program to woo the diaspora. Malaysia's human resource policies, as demonstrated at UM's institutional level, may do well to emulate those Singapore models that might work. This process could happen sooner than expected because the prime minister has recently established and now chairs the Talent Corporation. This agency's major task is to woo and retain international talent, including from the Malaysian diaspora, by offering, among other things, "Remuneration packages (that will be) . . . internationally competitive" (*New Straits Times* 2010).

Evaluation of Staff Performance

In tandem with making its compensation more competitive internationally, NUS has progressively raised the bar for staff performance evaluations. In particular, criteria for tenure and promotion have been significantly raised in recent years, approaching those of leading universities in the world. In particular, it has increased the emphasis on assessment of the research impact of faculty as measured by citations in Science Citation Index (SCI) and Social Sciences Citation Index (SSCI) and publications in top-tier journals.

For UM, newly established targets have been set for staff performance evaluation that relates to publications ranked by the Institute for Scientific Information (ISI) publications, teaching hours and courses, supervision of doctoral and master's students, supervision of research students, success in obtaining research funds, minimum teaching performance scores (based on student evaluations), completion of consultancies, and satisfactory contribution to administrative work as required by faculty and departmental responsibilities. The strong focus on ISI articles is reportedly linked to the world-class research universities ranking criteria. Although the links among research, ISI articles, and promotion opportunities provide a strong motivational force for improvement in publications, the risk lies in overlooking a more measured approach toward building an analytical and innovative institutional culture of scholarship and research.

Development and Management of Research

NUS has steadily increased its budget for research and development (R&D), particularly in recent years. Concomitant with this increase in direct R&D expenditure has been an increased investment in R&D infrastructure. For example, NUS established links to international academic networks through a computer network (BITNET), becoming one of the first Asian countries to join this network. Subsequently, NUS was also among the first Asian universities to implement campuswide access to the Internet. In 1989, NUS linked up with one of only two supercomputers in Singapore, enhancing the university's role in the globalization of computing technology and skills. In 1991, NUS implemented NUSNET, a campuswide optical fiber network, and in May 1995, the library became the first in the region to launch a full-text electronic document management and retrieval system.

NUS was also among the first universities in Asia to implement a technology licensing and industry liaison office in the 1990s to manage the university's emerging intellectual property portfolio and industry R&D collaborations. This office had progressively established a system for managing invention disclosure and technology commercialization that is modeled after the best practices of leading universities in North America, including implementing standardized research collaborative agreements with external collaboration parties; assigning intellectual property ownership to the university; distributing licensing royalty income fairly among the individual faculty members, departments, and central administration to align interest in technology commercialization; and taking equity in lieu of royalty when an NUS technology is licensed to a spin-off founded by an NUS faculty member or student.

Driven by the rapid growth in research outputs and facilitated by the streamlined IP (Internet protocol) management support system, the number of research collaboration agreements, invention disclosures, and patents granted to NUS increased rapidly since the early 2000s, with a corresponding increase in technology licensing income. The number of external research collaboration agreements increased from 109 during 1995–97 to 394 during 2005–07. The number of patents granted by the U.S. patent office to NUS rose from 40 during 1990–99 to 204 during 2000–08, while the number of licensing agreements increased from 60 to 198 in the corresponding periods. Total licensing royalties also increased from S$335,000 (US$203,091.80 [currency converted January 1, 1999]) in 1996–99 to S$3.3 million (US$2.29 million [currency converted January 1, 2008]) during 2003–08 (see Wong, Ho, and Singh forthcoming for more details).

In the early 2000s, as part of the new vision articulated by the then-new vice-chancellor for NUS to become a "global knowledge enterprise," the university further expanded its technology commercialization support role by explicitly establishing NUS Enterprise, a new organizational division to promote technology commercialization and entrepreneurship on a holistic basis. Reporting directly to the vice-chancellor and president, NUS Enterprise not only absorbed the functions of the technology licensing and industry liaison office into an expanded Industry Liaison Office, but also incorporated a university-level Entrepreneurship Centre that integrated the functions of entrepreneurship education, entrepreneurship promotion and outreach, and incubation support for NUS spin-offs (see Wong, Ho, and Singh 2007). Since its inception in 2002, the NUS Enterprise Incubator has supported more than 70 university spin-offs by professors, students, and recent alumni. More than 10 such companies have received follow-on investment by external investors, and one company, tenCube, has recently been acquired by McAfee Inc. (see Wong, Ho, and Singh forthcoming).

In 1982, 0.05 percent of Malaysia's labor force or about 13 percent of its scientific workforce was engaged in R&D, comparing unfavorably to an average of 0.5 percent in newly industrialized countries, including Singapore (Singh 1989). The contrast continues with a total of only 500 per million personnel currently involved in R&D in Malaysia, compared with Singapore's 5,500 per million—second globally only to Sweden at 6,000 per million (NEAC 2010, 53, figure 13).

Over the past decade, UM has invested in and upgraded its research infrastructure toward the objective of supporting R&D projects to promote multidisciplinary approaches and increased productivity. Eight interdisciplinary research clusters, such as the biotechnology and bioproducts and the sustainability sciences groups, have been established. The Institute of Research Management and Monitoring organizes the promotion, management, coordination, and monitoring of activities of all research entities. Collaboration with industry is at a fledgling stage, with public universities looking forward to the recently unveiled Ministry of Higher Education–backed Strategic Enhancement Plan for University-Industry and Community Collaboration, which is expected to include small and medium enterprises.

Staffing at many levels continues to be a challenge: senior, international, and experienced research leaders are needed to provide direction and increase the productivity of outcomes, supported by teams of well-qualified junior staff members and graduate students and by well-trained technicians for the efficient management of laboratories and equipment. Equally critical is strong technical infrastructural support such as information and communications technologies facilities. Currently, the fastest bandwidth and cost of broadband connections in Malaysia (4Mbps [megabits per second] at US$76), compares most unfavorably with Singapore's 100Mbps at US$84.68. Within the region, the fastest bandwidth in Malaysia is five times slower and more than three times more expensive than the lowest bandwidth in Korea (NEAC 2010, 186).

Indicative of its growing emphasis on research in recent years, NUS had increased its research expenditures more than threefold in the past decade, from US$89.5 million in 1997 to US$321.0 million in 2007. Relative to the total operating expenses of the university, research spending has increased from about 12 percent in 2000 to more than 27 percent in 2007. Since corporatization, research funding allocation has become more performance driven and focused as NUS has positioned itself to excel in niche areas and to compete for external funding. Hence, the bulk of the research spending is in the engineering and medicine fields, with an increasing proportion going to the latter in line with the growing emphasis on biomedical sciences in Singapore's national R&D strategy in recent years (NUS 2000, 2002, 2008a, 2008b).

Research financing at UM has not been constant or steadily increasing over time, unlike at NUS. Government research allocations decreased from US$26.6 million in 2002 to US$8.1 million in 2004 to US$6 million in 2006 and then jumped to US$41.2 million in 2008 (UM 2010). The last figure includes additional resources provided for four universities designated as research universities in 2008. Sources of research funding were diverse. Apart from the Ministry of Education's annual grant, funding was received from departments in the Ministry of Science, Technology and Innovation (most awarded on a competitive basis); Toray Foundation of Japan (also competitive); and various private companies, local foundations, agencies, and foreign universities. Unaudited accounts for 2008 showed a healthy trend of research funds increasing from 7 percent of the annual budget allocation in 2006 to 22 percent in 2008 (UM 2008, 25).

Data on research expenditure were not available, and hence, research output levels were not reviewed. By designating funds for four research universities—including UM—the Ministry of Higher Education expects that concentrating resources in institutions with the most potential will pay better dividends than spreading them thinly over 20 public universities. A contribution of approximately US$31.2 million equivalent annually, on a noncompetitive basis, to each of the four research universities since 2008 is a welcomed, but marginal benefit when compared with NUS. Changing trends indicate that whereas the annual grant to research universities from the Ministry of Higher Education is a direct allocation, awards from other ministries (such as the Ministry of Science, Technology and Innovation), external funding sources, and intra-university funds to UM researchers are competitively won.

Performance Measures and Indicators of Success

The journey taken by universities toward excellence in research and teaching is marked by measures indicating how far they have traveled and how far they might be from their destinations. These measures include external university rankings; productivity: research output, international peer-reviewed publications, citations received, and average citations per publication; and international recognition of faculty as seen in invitational leadership positions and membership in professional organizations, invitational participation in select conferences and associations, and receipt of achievement awards.

Overall International Ranking

Acknowledging that ranking methodology is much debated, this chapter uses available data from recent exercises. In key academic fields (table 5.3), NUS has the highest rank in technology, followed by biomedicine, whereas for UM, biomedicine ranks highest, followed by social sciences. The gap between the two universities appears to be widest in the fields of science and technology.

SCI- and SSCI-Indexed Papers and Citations

Perhaps one of the more useful outcomes of world university ranking exercises is an increasing awareness by government and higher education officials of publications and citations, contributing to policy changes in some higher education institutions regarding faculty research output. Such publications serve as quantitative indicators of productivity and as an important avenue of knowledge transfer. On this measure, there is a significant gap between the research output of UM and other Malaysian research universities, on the one hand, and those of the leading Asian countries, on the other. Table 5.4 shows that SCI and SSCI indexed 3,440 papers produced by UM from January 1999 to February 2009, only about one-third of the output of the next closest university outside Malaysia, the Hong Kong University of Science and Technology, which published 10,400 papers over this period. NUS's publications output for the same

Table 5.3   Ranking of NUS and UM in the World University Rankings, 2004–09

	2004	2005	2006	2007	2008	2009
NUS						
Overall	18	22	19	33	30	30
Biomedicine	25	15	9	12	17	20
Science	35	34	22	25	31	27
Technology	9	9	8	10	11	14
Social sciences	10	13	11	20	18	20
Arts and humanities	17	56	22	21	30	23
UM						
Overall	89	169	192	246	230	180
Biomedicine	—	82	56	107	127	132
Science	—	—	95	124	197	244
Technology	—	—	—	166	179	201
Social sciences	—	83	49	119	137	167
Arts and humanities	—	45	—	233	190	178

Source: THE-QS World University Rankings, http://www.topuniversities.com/worlduniversityrankings/.
Note: — = not available. Rankings from 2007 are not strictly comparable to those in earlier years because of a change in methodology used by THE-QS.

period was double that of Hong Kong University of Science and Technology. The difference is all the greater when taking into account the size difference between the universities: Hong Kong University of Science and Technology has approximately 400 faculty members, compared to UM's 1,918 faculty members in 2008.

Malaysian universities also fall somewhat behind the others in number of citations, whether measured per paper or per faculty member. For the former, all three Malaysian universities received approximately four citations per paper, whereas most of the comparison universities received more than seven citations per paper (table 5.4). The number of SCI- and SSCI-indexed engineering publications by NUS increased 25 times from an average of 37 per year during 1981–83 to 941 per year during 2001–03, whereas those for medicine increased nearly tenfold (from 62 to 602), and economics and business 4.5 times (from 20 to 90). The quality of the publications, as measured by average citations per publication in the following three years, also increased significantly—from 1.45 to 5.66 for engineering, 3.16 to 11.33 for medicine, and 0.32 to 6.36 for economics and business.

Table 5.5 compares the research publication performance of NUS and UM in four major academic fields from 1981 to 2003. As shown, UM has fallen behind NUS not only in the *quantity* of international-refereed pub-

Table 5.4   Publications and Citations of Selected Malaysian Universities versus Other Leading Asian Universities, January 1999–February 2009

University	Economy	Number of papers	Number of citations	Number of citations per paper
Universiti Sains Malaysia	Malaysia	3,250	13,257	4.08
University of Malaya	Malaysia	3,439	14,316	4.16
Universiti Kebangsaan Malaysia	Malaysia	1,528	5,624	3.68
Hong Kong University of Science and Technology	Hong Kong SAR, China	10,402	96,281	9.26
University of Hong Kong	Hong Kong SAR, China	18,700	187,339	10.02
Seoul National University	Korea, Rep.	33,779	271,702	8.04
National Taiwan University	Taiwan, China	27,255	196,631	7.21
Tsinghua University	China	23,182	121,584	5.24
University of Tokyo	Japan	67,864	882,361	13.00
National University of Singapore	Singapore	28,602	236,388	8.26

Source: Wong, Ho, and Singh (forthcoming) compiled from Thomson Reuters ISI Essential Science Indicators.

Table 5.5   Publications and Citations of UM and NUS, 1981–2003

Year	Engineering fields		Medicine fields		Economics fields		Business and management fields	
	UM	NUS	UM	NUS	UM	NUS	UM	NUS
				Number of papers				
1981–83	9	111	132	186	11	51	2	8
1991–93	40	586	192	747	5	32	0	45
2001–03	146	2,823	324	1,808	6	123	6	148
			Average citation rate per publication					
1981–83	1.00	1.45	2.85	3.16	0.09	0.35	6.50	0.13
1991–93	1.40	2.54	4.43	6.24	0.40	2.47	—	3.69
2001–03	3.83	5.66	5.08	11.33	3.17	3.89	0.17	8.41

Source: Author's calculations based on Thomson Reuters, Web of Science.
Note: — = not available. Data are for SCI- and SSCI-indexed journals only; the citation rate is calculated as follows: The number of citations within five years of publication were collated (for example, the number of citations made in 1981–86 are collated for papers published in 1981, and so forth.). The total number of publications and citations for each of the three time periods (1981–83, 1991–93 and 2001–03) are then pooled, and according to this figure, the average citation rate per publication rate is calculated.

lications tracked by SCI and SSCI over the years in all four fields, but also in the *quality* of their publications as measured by the average number citations received in the five years after the date of the publications.

Although the debate continues within UM faculty on the use of ISI articles and citations as a qualitative indicator, Malaysian universities have recently developed their own policies in encouraging and supporting publications by their academic staff. The new strategy of UM management to improve the overall academic culture has specific requirements for promotions based on ISI publications and citations. The ISI publication requirements stretch to the admission of doctoral-level students: doctoral candidates should have at least two ISI-listed publications. Among the concerns is the status of UM's own 50 plus journals, some of which have been regularly published for three to four decades and have developed a clientele of their own. One wonders how this shift in focus will affect these journals and currently available resources.

One of the by-products of world university ranking exercises is the Ministry of Higher Education's own ranking system for Malaysian public universities—the Rating System for Malaysian Higher Education Institutions (SETARA, in Malay)—following an Academic Reputation Survey conducted in the previous year (Malaysian Qualifications Agency 2010). The results of the first SETARA exercise, involving seven of the more established universities, were published in 2008, and UM placed first in the country. In SETARA for 2009, the Malaysian Qualifications Agency reviewed undergraduate teaching and learning in public and private universities, including foreign branch campuses, in six tiers with Tier 6 as outstanding. None was in Tier 6; UM was one of 18 public and private higher education institutions in Tier 5 (Malaysian Qualifications Agency 2009). Given the current leadership and management and the spirit of competition among the four research universities in the country, UM will likely invest energy and resources in maintaining the lead position nationally.

Levels of Patenting

Despite its flaws, patenting can be used as a proxy measure of technological inventions that have potential economic value. In particular, the number of patents granted by the U.S. patent office is often used as an international benchmark indicator to ensure comparability across countries, given that the United States is the largest market in the world (Trajtenberg 2002). Whereas NUS has significantly increased its patenting output in the post-2000 period (from an average of four U.S.-issued patents per year during 1990–99 to an average of 22.7 patents per year during 2000–08), UM has had negligible patenting output since 1990 (two U.S. patents issued since 1990) (Wong, Ho, and Singh forthcoming).

Ming Yu Cheng (forthcoming) has argued that the low level of patenting by Malaysian universities may be in part an outcome of a government policy, which clearly delineated the research roles played by universities and public research institutes. The Fifth Malaysia Plan, implemented from 1986 to 1990, stipulated that universities would give greater emphasis to basic research (40 percent) relative to public research institutes (10 percent) (Cheng forthcoming). However, her assumption that a high emphasis on basic research does not generate research of commercial value is not valid, because many of the leading universities in the world, including the Massachusetts Institute of Technology and Stanford University, that are highly focused on basic research have also been prolific in generating patents. Likewise, the rapid rise in patenting among the leading Asian universities such as NUS and Tsinghua University over the past 10 years coincided with a growing emphasis on basic research. Rather than the basic versus applied distinction, it is the quality of the research and its strategic focus on economic significance (the so-called strategic basic research, or "Pasteur's quadrant") that matters.

International Reputation, Recognition, Award, and Collaborations

The recognition given by peers to institutions and to individual scholars and researchers is an important marker of quality, based on peer evaluation through invitations to join selected academic and professional societies, attendance at high-level academic and professional conferences, election to world bodies, and prestigious awards. For example, in 2007, the Lee Kuan Yew School of Public Policy became the first institution outside Europe and North America to join the prestigious Global Public Policy Network. In the same year, NUS President Shih Choon Fong received the Chief Executive Leadership Award by the Council for Advancement and Support of Education. NUS also became a founding member of the 10-member International Alliance of Research Universities in 2006. At the faculty level, an increasing number of joint-degree programs have been established between NUS and other leading universities (for example, University of California, Los Angeles; Karolinska Institutet; and Peking University), testifying to the growing standing of NUS in the international academic community.

Records show that in the past, UM's participation and performance in international academic activities have depended on individual staff pro-action rather than on common university practice. Over the past five years, as Malaysian universities have become more competitive, UM has acquitted itself well as an institution in international research and innovation events such as the International Exhibition of Inventions, Techniques and Products in Geneva. UM faculty members, such as those in the field of medicine, have become aggressive in seeking and achieving accreditation at unit level: in 2008, for example, the gastrointestinal endoscopy unit was designated as one of 16 world centers of excellence by the Organisation Mondiale d'Endoscopie Digestive.

UM continues to work to obtain international accreditation, key to worldwide recognition, for teaching programs such as its bachelor of dental surgery by the general Dental Council of the United Kingdom and other professional institutions. Joint PhD programs with universities of repute—such as the Imperial College London, the University of Melbourne, and the University of Sydney—are healthy signs of growing international recognition.

Lessons Learned

The comparison between NUS and UM is instructive. The Singapore case shows how strategic thinking directed toward national development and economic growth can become a driver for academic excellence, enabling a university from a newly industrialized economy to rapidly ascend into the league of leading global universities. For UM, this review of NUS's achievements highlights the latter's attention to continuity of leadership, a balanced national language policy that takes the global economic environment into account, investment in strategic planning, nurturing of students and investment in pedagogy, provision of consistent and more-than-adequate funding and qualified human resources, and establishment of a research and academic infrastructure that seamlessly spans local and international settings.

The decades that NUS has taken to progressively transform itself to move up the ladder of global excellence mirror the larger transformation of the Singapore economy from third world to first world (Lee 2000). As Singapore moves inexorably toward competing as a knowledge-based economy in the 21st century, NUS no longer aims to simply meet the educational needs of the local population, but has set its vision to become a "global knowledge enterprise" that not only excels globally in the traditional missions of research and teaching, but also takes on the "third mission" of becoming an "entrepreneurial" university that spawns successful high-tech spin-offs and generates economic wealth through technology commercialization (Etzkowitz et al. 2000; Wong, Ho, and Singh forthcoming). More important, the NUS story provides UM and other universities in emerging economies an exemplar of "development . . . as a process of integration *within* the world economy—rather than a process of parallel or separate development" (Lall and Urata 2003).

The challenge that faces UM is one faced by any institution or organization that needs to change its mission and priorities, affecting deep-rooted working principles, regulations, and financial management systems (Salmi 2009, 39–43). The history of UM demonstrates that national policies can severely constrain the institutional development of a public university. This situation can have significant long-term consequences that limit the university's capacity to pursue academic excellence and compete internationally, given that such institutional capacity takes many years to build. Equally, both NUS and UM show that leadership within institutions can leverage its understanding, experience, and knowledge in fashioning strategies to bring about positive institutional change.

Affirmative action policies have worked in UM as seen in increasing enrollments and upward mobility within academic ranks for the ethnic group perceived as the most disadvantaged. Whereas Malaysia's attention to social justice goals is important, providing information for institutions in plural societies, it also raises the issue of balancing social goals with that of institutional competitiveness and quality. If UM is able to implement its new generation policies of merit-based student admission and staff recruitment, training, and promotion—directed to the most able, irrespective of race or nationality—then it has the potential to forge ahead.

However, a serious impediment to UM's world-class aspirations is apparent in the low level of available financing, coupled with inefficient financial practices. The consistent, high-level financial resources of NUS allow it to offer the best instructional and research infrastructure, telecommunication, and living facilities that help to attract able graduate students and highly qualified local and international academicians and researchers. In the face of declining government funding and the need to respond to rapid change, UM must direct serious energy to accelerate its income generation and fund-raising capacity, while ensuring cost-effective management with synergy among services and functions of managerial, administrative, academic, technical, and support staff. The likelihood is that both university management and the government would want to sustain recent gains, using world and national rankings and internal incentive mechanisms as sources of motivation for laggards.

The transformation of a university to match a new vision and new targets is a courageous endeavor. It also requires the political will to stay the course over the long term, bringing together "national policies, institutional capabilities, and knowledge integration" (Mammo and Baskaran 2009, 141).

References

Ali, Syed Husin. 2009. "Death Knell to Varsity Autonomy." In *Multiethnic Malaysia: Past, Present and Future*, ed. Lim Teck Ghee, Alberto Gomes, and Azly Rahman, 265–70. Puchong, Malaysia: Vinlin.

Altbach, Philip G., and Jorge Balán, eds. 2007. *World Class Worldwide: Transforming Research Universities in Asia and Latin America*. Baltimore: Johns Hopkins University Press.

Chai, Hon-Chan. 1977. *Education and Nation-building in Plural Societies: The West Malaysian Experience*. Development Studies Centre, Monograph. 6. Canberra: Australian National University, National Centre for Development Studies.

Cheng, Ming Yu. Forthcoming. "University Technology Transfer and Commercialization: The Case of Multimedia University, Malaysia." In *University Technology Commercialization and Academic Entrepreneurship in Asia*, ed. P. K. Wong, Y. P. Ho, and A. Singh, chapter 12. Cheltenham, UK: Edward Elgar.

The Economist. 2000. "The Tiger and the Tech: Asia has gone Internet-mad and its star-struck governments talk of reinventing their economies. Do they have a chance?" February 3. http://www.economist.com/node/279308?story_id=E1_NSJPDR.

Etzkowitz, Henry, Andrew Webster, Christiane Gebhardt, and Branca Regina Cantisano Terra. 2000. "The Future of the University and the University of the Future: Evolution of Ivory Tower to Entrepreneurial Paradigm." *Research Policy* 29 (2): 313–30.

Fernandez-Chung, Rozilini M. 2010. "Access and Equity in Higher Education (Malaysia)." Paper presented at the Higher Education and Dynamic Asia Workshop, Asian Development Bank, Manila, June.

Fiske, Edward B. 1997. "Is U.S. Less Hospitable? Boom in Foreign Students Seems to Be Over." *International Herald Tribune,* February 11.

Hatakenaka, Sachi. 2004. "Internationalism in Higher Education: A Review." http://www.hepi.ac.uk/466-1127/Internationalism-in-Higher-Education--A-Review.html.

IMD (International Institute for Management Development). 2006. World Competitiveness Online database. IMD, Lausanne, Switzerland. https://www.worldcompetitiveness.com/OnLine/App/Index.htm.

IMF (International Monetary Fund). 2009. *World Economic Outlook: Crisis and Recovery.* Washington, DC: IMF.

Lall, Sanjaya, and Shujiro Urata, eds. 2003. *Competitiveness, FDI and Technological Activity in East Asia.* Cheltenham, UK: Edward Elgar.

Lee, Kuan Yew. 2000. *From Third World to First: The Singapore Story,* 1965–2000. London: Harper Collins.

Low, Linda, Toh Mun Heng, and Soon Teck Wong. 1991. *Economics of Education and Manpower Development: Issues and Policies in Singapore.* Singapore: McGraw Hill.

Malaysian Qualifications Agency. 2009. "SETARA: 2009 Rating System for Malaysian Higher Education Institutions." http://www.mqa.gov.my/.

———. 2010. SETARA: Rating System for Malaysian Higher Education Institutions. http://www.mqa.gov.my/.

Mammo, Muchie, and Angathevar Baskaran. 2009. "The National Technology System Framework: Sanjaya Lall's Contribution to Appreciation Theory." *International Journal of Institutions and Economics* 1 (1): 134–55.

Ministry of Education. 2001. *Malaysia Education Development Plan 2001–2010.* Kuala Lumpur: National Printing Press.

Ministry of Higher Education. 2005. *Annual Report, 2004.* Kuala Lumpur: National Printing Press.

————. 2006. *Annual Report, 2005*. Kuala Lumpur: National Printing Press.

————. 2007. *Annual Report, 2006*. Kuala Lumpur: National Printing Press.

Nagaraj, Shyamala, Chew Sing Buan, Lee Kiong Hock, and Rahimah Ahmad. 2009. *Education and Work: The World of Work*. Kuala Lumpur: University of Malaya Press.

NEAC (National Economic Advisory Council). 2010. *New Economic Model for Malaysia, part 1*. Kuala Lumpur: Malaysian National Press.

New Straits Times (Kuala Lumpur). 2010. "Competing for Talent." December 8.

NUS (National University of Singapore). 1962. *Annual Report 1961/62*. Singapore: NUS.

————. 1990. *Annual Report 1989/90*. Singapore: NUS.

————. 1998. *Annual Report 1997/98*. Singapore: NUS.

————. 2000. *Annual Report 2000*. Singapore: NUS.

————. 2002. *Research Report 2001/02*. Singapore: NUS.

————. 2005. *Annual Report 2005*. Singapore: NUS.

————. 2008a. *Annual Report 2008*. Singapore: NUS.

————. 2008b. *Research Report 2007/08*. Singapore: NUS.

————. 2009. *Annual Report 2008/09*. Singapore: NUS.

Olds, Kris. 2007. "Global Assemblage: Singapore, Foreign Universities, and the Construction of a Global Education Hub." *World Development* 35 (6): 959–75.

Salmi, Jamil. 2009. *The Challenge of Establishing World-Class Universities*. Washington, DC: World Bank.

Seah, Chee Meow. 1983. *Student Admission to Higher Education in Singapore*. Singapore: Regional Institute of Higher Education and Development.

Singh, Jasbir Sarjit. 1989. "Scientific Personnel, Research Environment, and Higher Education in Malaysia." In *Scientific Development and Higher Education: The Case of Newly Industrializing Nations*, ed. Philip G. Altbach, Charles H. Davis, Thomas O. Eisemon, Saravanan Gopinathan, H. Steve Hsieh, Sungho Lee, Pang Eng Fong, and Jasbir Sarjit Singh, 83–186. New York: Praeger.

The Sun, (Kuala Lumpur). 2010. "Government Ready to Recognize UEC." April 6.

THE-QS (Times Higher Education-QS). 2008. "World University Rankings." http://www.topuniversities.com/university-rankings/world-university-rankings/2008.

————. 2009. "World University Rankings." http://www.topuniversities.com/university-rankings/world-university-rankings/2009.

Trajtenberg, Manuel. 2002. "A Penny for Your Quotes: Patent Citations and the Value of Innovations." In *Patents, Citations, and Innovations: A Window on the Knowledge Economy*, ed. A. B. Jaffe and M. Trajtenberg, 25–50. Cambridge, MA: MIT Press.

UM (University of Malaya). 2008. *Annual Report 2007*. Kuala Lumpur: University of Malaya Press.

———. 2009. *Annual Report 2008*. Kuala Lumpur: University of Malaya Press.

———. 2010. "Information on Areas of Evaluation, Part B, Vol. 1, Main Report." Quality Management Enhancement Center, UM, Kuala Lumpur.

Wong, Joseph Kee-Kuok. 2004. "Are the Learning Styles of Asian International Students Culturally or Contextually Based?" *International Educational Journal* 4 (4): 154–66.

Wong, Poh Kam, Yuen Ping Ho, and Annette Singh. 2007. "Towards an Entrepreneurial University Model to Support Knowledge-Based Economic Development: The Case of the National University of Singapore." *World Development* 35 (6): 941–958.

———. Forthcoming. "Towards a Global Knowledge Enterprise: The Entrepreneurial University Model of National University of Singapore." In *University Technology Commercialization and Academic Entrepreneurship in Asia*, ed. Wong, P.K., Y.P. Ho, and A. Singh, chapter 7. Cheltenham, UK: Edward Elgar.

World Bank. 2007. *Malaysia and the Knowledge Economy: Building a World-Class University System*. Washington, DC: World Bank.

CHAPTER 6

Toward World-Class Status? The IIT System and IIT Bombay

Narayana Jayaram

In the realm of higher education in India, the Indian Institutes of Technology (IITs) have been islands of excellence. Started as an innovation in technology education outside the conventional university system, IITs have increased in number from the so-called original five established during the period 1950–63 to 16 in 2010. Degrees awarded by IITs are recognized and respected all over the world. The success that the IIT alumni have achieved in various walks of life and in a variety of professions has contributed immensely to the brand IIT.

Thus, it is not surprising that IITs consistently rank above other engineering colleges (more than 1,200 in number) under the university system in India. The first eight of the top 10 engineering colleges listed by an Outlook-GfK-Mode Survey, based on the perceptions of 300 stakeholders in six of India's metropolitan areas in June 2009, were IITs. The only Indian institutions to find a place in the Times Higher Education–QS World University Rankings for Engineering and IT Universities in 2008 were IITs: IIT Bombay (ranked 36th) and IIT Delhi (ranked 42nd). In the Shanghai Jiao Tong University's Academic Ranking of World Universities, one of the three Indian education institutions among the top 500 universities worldwide was IIT Kharagpur. Thus, if any institutions in India can aspire to world-class status—other than the Indian Institute of Science (Bangalore)—the original five are potential candidates.

However, the success of the IIT system seems to have brought it under massive strain: "Its autonomy is seriously eroded; its infrastructure is wearing thin; laboratories are getting outdated; faculty is depleting; and the competition for admission is pushing aspirants into an unhealthy grind," observes Shashi K. Gulhati (2007, book cover), a recently retired professor of 40-year standing at IIT Delhi. The IIT system appears to be at a critical juncture: it "can slide down the hill or gear up to climb new peaks" (Gulhati 2007, viii). What explains the success of the IIT system, and what challenges does it face in sustaining the excellence that it has fostered thus far? This chapter addresses these twin questions in three parts: The first part focuses on the IIT system in general, the second part presents a case study of IIT Bombay, and the third part reflects on the problems and prospects of sustaining IITs and replicating them.

The IIT System

Origin and Development
In March 1946, at the insistence of two Indian members—namely, Sir Ardeshir Dalal and Sir Jogendra Singh—the Viceroy's Executive Council set up a committee to create the direction for development of technical education for postwar India. The 22-member committee headed by Nalini Ranjan Sarkar submitted its interim report recommending the establishment of four technical institutes different from the run-of-the-mill engineering colleges: they were designed to provide the necessary dynamism and flexibility of organization in light of expanding knowledge and a changing society. Considering that the country was still under British rule, one finds it noteworthy that the model proposed by the Sarkar Committee was the Massachusetts Institute of Technology, rather than a British institution like the Imperial College London (Indiresan and Nigam 1993, 339).

The recommendations of the Sarkar Committee, though provisional, found favor with a visionary like Pandit Jawaharlal Nehru, the first prime minister of independent India. The first IIT was founded in May 1950 in Kharagpur, near Calcutta (since renamed Kolkata), and three more campuses were established: Bombay (since renamed Mumbai) in 1958, Madras (since renamed Chennai) in 1959, and Kanpur in 1959. By an act of Parliament (the 1961 Institutes of Technology Act), these institutes were designated as "institutions of national importance." The College of Engineering, established in New Delhi in 1961, was renamed IIT Delhi in 1963 (through an amendment to the 1961 act). The structure and functioning of these five pioneering IITs—Kharagpur, Bombay, Madras, Kanpur, and Delhi—as defined by the Institutes of Technology Act is called the IIT system.

Four of the original five IITs were established in collaboration with or with active assistance from international organizations or foreign governments: IIT Bombay, with the assistance of the United Nations Educational, Scientific and Cultural Organization and the former Soviet Union; IIT Madras, with the assistance of the Federal Republic of Germany; IIT Kanpur, under the Indo-American Program with the help of a consortium of nine U.S. universities; and IIT Delhi, with the support of the United Kingdom. Since 1973, when all international assistance and association ended, the institutes have been managing on their own with financial support from the government.

For three decades after the establishment of the original five IITs, no new IIT was established. Then, in response to student agitation in the northeastern state of Assam in the early 1990s, Prime Minister Rajiv Gandhi promised the establishment of an IIT in that state. Thus, in 1994, IIT Guwahati was founded. In 2001, the University of Roorkee (in the northern state of Uttarakhand)—which had originated as the Thomson College of Civil Engineering in 1854 and was renamed after independence—was incorporated into the IIT system, becoming IIT Roorkee. As a result, in 2001, there were seven institutes under the IIT system.

In October 2003, prime minister Atal Bihari Vajpayee announced plans to create more IITs "by upgrading existing academic institutions that have the necessary promise and potential" (Upadhyaya 2005). Established in November 2003, the S. K. Joshi Committee recommended the selection of five institutions that could be upgraded as IITs. In March 2008, the government of India identified eight states—Andhra Pradesh (Hyderabad), Bihar (Patna), Gujarat (Gandhinagar), Himachal Pradesh (Mandi), Madhya Pradesh (Indore), Orissa (Bhubaneswar), Punjab (Rupnagar), and Rajasthan—for establishment of new IITs and recommended the conversion of the Institute of Technology (Banaras Hindu University) into an IIT. Thus, as of March 2010, there were 16 institutes under the IIT system.

Two major reviews of the IIT system have been initiated by the Ministry of Human Resource Development. A committee chaired by Professor Y. Nayudamma performed the first review and submitted its report in 1986. This report became the guiding document for the second review by a committee chaired by Professor P. Rama Rao (the second review committee), which submitted its report in 2004 (Government of

India 2004). As is the case with all such government-appointed committees, the committee reports, each its own package of recommendations,
were accepted "in principle," but only the recommendations convenient
to the government were implemented. Beyond these two *systemic reviews*,
each of the original five IITs has undertaken *institutional reviews* on specific aspects—organization, curriculum, and other topics—for adapting
themselves to changing situations.

Organization of the IIT System

The president of India is known as the Visitor (the highest ceremonial
authority in the IIT system, comparable to the chancellor in state universities who serves ex officio as governor of the state) of all IITs and has
residual powers. Directly under the Visitor is the IIT Council, which
comprises the minister-in-charge of technical education in the government
of India; the chairpersons and directors of all IITs; the chairperson of the
University Grants Commission; the director general of the Council of
Scientific and Industrial Research; the chairperson of the Indian Institute
of Science; three members of Parliament; the joint secretary of the
Ministry of Human Resource Development; and three nominees each of
the government of India, the All India Council for Technical Education,
and the Visitor.

Under the IIT Council is the Board of Governors—the executive body
of each IIT—whose chairperson is nominated by the Visitor. Under the
Board of Governors is the director, who is the chief academic and executive officer of the IIT. Unlike at the universities, the director of an IIT is
not the chairperson of the Board of Governors, its managing body. This
situation, instead of circumscribing the freedom of the director, seems to
provide a cushion from the pressures of government and labor, as well as
breathing space for making important decisions (Indiresan and Nigam
1993, 349–50). Under the director are the deputy director, deans, and
department heads. The registrar is the chief administrative officer of the
IIT and oversees the day-to-day business operations. Under the department heads are the faculty members (professors, associate professors, and
assistant professors).

Although the IIT Council provides broad policy guidelines, the internal governance of each IIT rests with its Board of Governors and its
routine academic policies are decided by its senate. The senate comprises
all professors of an institute and a few student representatives; the director is its ex officio chairperson. The senate defines programs, approves
courses and curricula, prescribes evaluations and examinations, ratifies

results, and appoints committees to look into specific academic matters. To maintain educational standards, the senate periodically reviews the institute's teaching, research, and training activities. Unlike universities, IITs can respond to situations and implement changes without delay.

As "institutions of national importance," IITs function autonomously. They have been, by and large, free from political or governmental interference from either the center or the states in which they are located. Although the state governments in each region have their representation on the Board of Governors, they have no control over decision making at the institute level on matters like faculty recruitment or curriculum. It is remarkable that each IIT has had eminent persons drawn from spheres relevant to the system as chairpersons of its Board of Governors.

The institutes' top authority complains about the bureaucratic hurdles at the government level; faculty members complain about similar hurdles at the institute level. If one considers the enormous dependence of IITs on governmental funding, it is understandable that the government determines the quantum of grants that each IIT obtains and that the bureaucracy regulates the release of the grants. On both counts, IITs often face difficulty. Similarly, because the institutes receive grants from the public exchequer, they must observe strict accounting and auditing norms. On this issue, faculty members often face difficulty. Nevertheless, these bureaucratic hurdles are nothing compared with those faced by universities because of their humiliating dependence on state governments and the political interference to which they are subjected.

More important, student politics is kept under control in IITs. Student councils are singularly free from the influence of political parties; student agitations are almost unknown. Students respect the academic calendar, as do the faculty and the administration. Thus, functionally, the academic system is extraordinarily efficient. This situation is in marked contrast to the university system, where the academic calendar is perennially derailed by student agitations. Even reputable universities are not free from the bane of student politics and agitations in which political parties take an active interest.

Student Enrollment

Admission to IITs is extremely competitive. Candidates seeking admission to the four-year bachelor of technology program and the five-year integrated bachelor of technology and master of technology program appear for an all-India annual examination—the IIT–Joint Entrance Examination—that is known for its rigor and transparency. Admission to postgraduate programs involves various entrance examinations: the Graduate Aptitude Test in Engineering for master of technology, doctor of philosophy (PhD), and some master of science programs, as well as joint admission to master of science programs; and the Joint Management Entrance Test for management studies. Admission to master of philosophy and PhD programs is primarily based on a personal interview, although candidates may also need to appear for written tests.

The IIT–Joint Entrance Examination is a flagship entrance examination conducted by an IIT chosen in rotation. A science-oriented examination that tests the candidate's knowledge of chemistry, mathematics, and physics, it is open only to candidates who have completed their higher secondary schooling (12 years) and have scored not less than 60 percent in the qualifying examination conducted by a recognized education board. The number of candidates appearing for this examination has steadily increased over the years: in the examination held in April 2010, nearly 450,000 candidates appeared for about 7,400 seats. With the average number of candidates vying for a seat being very high, this examination has been a "significantly effective filter" (Government of India 2004, 3).[1] Candidates obtaining higher ranks obviously have greater choice of the institute and the program of study.

It is argued that the format of the IIT–Joint Entrance Examination, tough though it may be, "cannot differentiate between the naturally brilliant grasshopper and the slog-your-butt-off ant" (Deb 2004, 48). Because this differentiation is "fundamental to the IIT system," the fact that the examination has become tougher by the year is viewed as "the principal threat the JEE [Joint Entrance Examination]—and the people who set the JEE papers—face today" (Deb 2004, 48). To improve their chances of success (however small these chances may be) at an extremely demanding examination, most IIT aspirants enroll in coaching classes that prepare candidates for the IIT–Joint Entrance Examination. It is well known that, the middle-class aspiration ("the IIT dream") being what it is, students devote four or five years of their life to this entrance examination, "turning the JEE into more a test of endurance than of intelligence or talent for science" (Deb 2004, 53).

However, at any given time 16,000 undergraduate and 12,000 postgraduate students study in the seven IITs. These numbers are in addition to the number of research scholars (MPhil and PhD). In 2002–03, IITs produced 2,274 graduates, 3,675 postgraduates (including dual degrees), and 444 PhD recipients. The faculty-to-student ratio in IITs is between 1 to 6 and 1 to 8—a great luxury by Indian university standards.

Protective Discrimination

Since its inception, the IIT system has decided admission by meritocracy, with merit determined through the IIT–Joint Entrance Examination. However, since 1973, IITs have followed the policy of protective discrimination (a type of affirmative action): 15 percent of the seats are reserved for candidates belonging to the traditionally excluded indigent caste groups listed under a schedule (scheduled castes) and 7.5 percent for those belonging to tribes that have remained outside the mainstream society listed under a schedule (scheduled tribes). Since 2008, the scheme of reservation has been extended to other underprivileged classes up to 27 percent. Thus, in all, 49.5 percent of the seats are reserved.

Furthermore, to enable candidates from the scheduled castes and scheduled tribes (but not other underprivileged classes) to compete for admission with the general category candidates, IITs grant them a handicap: they may score 5 percentage points (55 percent) less than the general category candidates (60 percent) in the qualifying examination (namely, the higher secondary school). Similarly, the cutoff mark for qualifying in the IIT–Joint Entrance Examination is significantly low: it is two-thirds of the mark of the last student admitted in the general category. Also, the upper age limit for appearing for this examination, which is 25 years for the general category students, is relaxed to 30 years for the scheduled castes and scheduled tribes.

The reservation policy as followed in the IIT system is significantly different from that of other public-funded education institutions. From among the scheduled castes and scheduled tribes candidates who do not meet the relaxed criterion (of lower cutoff marks), a select number are offered a preparatory course (comprising English, physics, chemistry, and mathematics) at the particular IIT. After one year of study, those candidates who are able to score a grade higher than the prescribed cutoff mark at the end-of-semester examination are allowed to continue with regular classes. However, there is no relaxation in the criteria for passing the examinations or graduating a course.

The reservation of seats has been a contentious issue in the IIT system. According to P. V. Indiresan and N. C. Nigam (both former directors of IIT), it has "brought into the IIT system a significant number of academically deficient students who have considerable difficulty in coping with the system in spite of remedial measures" (Indiresan and Nigam 1993, 357–58). About 50 percent of "the reserved seats remain vacant as [scheduled castes and scheduled tribes] candidates are unable to secure the threshold marks," and of those admitted, about 25 percent drop out of the program because of their inability to cope with its demands (Indiresan and Nigam 1993, 358). Not surprisingly, the extension of the reservation strategy to other underprivileged classes resulted in violent protests (even in IITs, which are otherwise free of protests). According to Indiresan and Nigam (1993, 358), "reservation and attendant problems have brought political interference in the functioning of IITs" (see also Gulhati 2007, 34–35).

Faculty Matters

The core caliber of the IIT system lies in the stature and competence of its faculty. Over decades, the system has attracted bright scholars and committed teachers to its faculty, which has contributed much to building and sustaining the IIT brand. However, the total number of faculty members has not increased much. As of 2003, the seven IITs had a total of 2,375 faculty members, which was 27 percent less than their total sanctioned number (Government of India 2004, 49). The procedure for faculty selection at IITs is, no doubt, stringent as compared to that in engineering colleges in the university system. Most faculty members have a PhD degree, which is a prerequisite for all regular faculty appointments. However, many bright scholars would readily find more remunerative and highly prestigious jobs outside the IIT system, both in India and abroad.

Moreover, the faculty members appointed in the early years of the system have retired. The second review committee noted with concern that "more than 80 Professors have retired since 2000–01," which accounted for a drop of 7 percent (Government of India 2004, 49). New recruitment at the entry level (that is, assistant professor) may fill the gap, but does not bring the needed experience. The inverted pyramid structure (with more professors, compared to assistant professors) is a matter of concern: the number of professors (1,041) and associate professors (562) is about 2.5 to 2.9 times that of the number of assistant professors (636) (Government of India 2004). Although this may indicate a greater fraction, it is not a good sign for an ongoing system, because superannuation of senior faculty will create a void that cannot be easily filled.

The age profile of the faculty is more or less similar across the seven IITs: professors, 51–56 years; associate professors, 40–49 years; and assistant professors, 33–34 years. More worrisome are the fact that "the number of faculty members below the age of 35 years is a low fraction of the total faculty strength" (Government of India 2004, 51) and the fact that most professors in IITs at Chennai, Delhi, Kharagpur, and Roorkee were eligible to retire by 2010, a significant proportion of them taking advantage of this option. The second review committee recommended the upward revision of the age of superannuation from 62 years to 65 years, a modification that has since been implemented. In fact, if an institute finds the need for a superannuated faculty member, that member's services may be continued up to age 70. This modification has brought some relief to the system.

Nevertheless, the shortage of qualified faculty members is daunting: it ranges from a minimum of 10 percent in IIT Bombay to a maximum of 60 percent in IIT Guwahati. The faculty shortage in the other five IITs ranges between 14 and 37 percent. If established IITs in Chennai, Delhi, and Mumbai find it difficult to recruit qualified faculty members, one can imagine the fate of the eight new IITs. If one goes by the experience of 15-year-old IIT Guwahati, it will take decades before the new IITs can recruit even 50 percent of their faculty. This situation is ominous for the IIT system.

To enlarge the pool of candidates for faculty positions, the Ministry of Human Resource Development has decided to permit the appointment of non-PhD recipients as "lecturers" (a fourth-tier academic cadre) and to reserve 10 percent of the posts to this cadre. Although this approach is supposed to be an "enabling clause" for IITs, the move is widely criticized as being retrograde because it would dilute their lofty standards. It is not that PhD candidates are lacking; unlike in the early years of IITs when they received very few applicants with a PhD, they now get 40–50 applicants with a PhD for each post. As a dean at IIT Bombay said, "we are extremely choosy about who we pick" (see Mukul and Chhapla 2009, 19).

Until recently, according to government norms for public-funded institutions, IITs could appoint only Indian nationals as faculty members. This requirement ruled out the possibility of appointing even illustrious alumni, if those alumni had changed citizenship after emigration to a foreign country. However, the norms have been amended, and "foreign nationals" can now be appointed under contract for up to five years. There is also a proposal to shortlist a pool of international faculty members for short-term teaching assignments.

Surprisingly, the mobility of the faculty members across IITs seems to be difficult. A faculty member wanting to switch institutes must go through the same induction process, as if she or he were an outsider candidate. Movement for limited periods or on a permanent basis should be a possibility; such movements bring fresh blood into the system and enrich the academic environment of an institute. Such movement could also address critical shortages in particular departments and strengthen specific fields of technology.

That bright young people do not opt for teaching positions is a general problem of higher education in India. For a long period, in relative terms, the pay package of IIT faculty members was only marginally better than that in the university system, and was ridiculously low compared with that of a fresh IIT graduate in the private sector (see Pushkarna 2009, 16). Dissatisfied with the package, the faculty of IIT Bombay, in an unprecedented move, struck work for a day on August 24, 2009 (Chhapla 2009b). The government has since decided to implement the Govardhan Mehta Pay Review Committee recommendations in this regard.

The second review committee had emphasized the need for an urgent review of pay packages for IIT faculty members. It recommended augmenting emoluments through a "professional allowance." In a market economy, compensation rules the scarce commodity of qualified and competent teachers. This climate is particularly prevalent in the IITs considering the demand for the best faculty worldwide. Perhaps what is needed most urgently is a performance-linked emoluments system besides the standardized minimum pay package for the faculty.

IIT faculty members enjoy full academic autonomy. They can update curricula to keep pace with the latest developments and embark on challenging research projects.

Over decades, by Indian standards at least, the original five IITs have built up enviable infrastructure—libraries, laboratories, and allied facilities—that provides the best learning environment for their students and research facilities for their faculty. However, faculty productivity does not appear to be commensurate. In 2002–03, on average, every IIT faculty member produced 2.70 students (0.96 graduates, 1.55 postgraduates, and 0.19 doctoral students) and 1.4 research publications, generated Rs 830,000[2] per annum through consultancy and sponsored research, and managed 10.5 enrolled students (Government of India 2004, 27). The second review committee also found that "at an aggregate level, engineering departments have produced a higher number of publications than science departments, research centers and departments of humanities/management" (Government of India 2004, 67). As in any system, the academic productivity of the faculty is uneven, and averages do not present the realistic picture. Hence, in thinking of performance-linked emoluments, one must give appropriate consideration to teaching, research, and extension activities engaged in by the faculty.

Academic Programs

The four-year bachelor of technology is the most common first degree offered by IITs. Some IITs also offer dual degrees (bachelor of technology and master of technology, five-year) and integrated master of science (five-year) degrees. The academic calendar follows the semester system. In the first two semesters, all bachelor of technology and dual-degree students undergo a common course structure (covering basics in physics, chemistry, electronics, and mechanics). In some IITs, a single department-theme-based course is also offered. Meritorious students have the option to change departments at the end of the first year, but such change is not common.

From the second year (third semester) onward, students branch out into respective departments. Nevertheless, they must take some compulsory advanced courses from other departments to broaden their knowledge base. At the end of the third year, students undertake a summer project at an industry or an academic institute. In the final year of their study, should they so choose, students are placed in industries and organizations through the institute's placement cell.

Among the postgraduate programs (two-year) offered by the IIT system, master of technology is the most common, followed by master of science. Some IITs offer master of business administration, but admission to this program is restricted to engineers and postgraduates in science. Some IITs offer specialized programs: master of design, master in medical science and technology, master of city planning, postgraduate diploma in information technology, postgraduate diploma in intellectual property law, postgraduate diploma in maritime operation and management, and others. All IITs offer PhD degrees and some masters of philosophy as research-based advanced degrees. It is noteworthy that IITs together account for more than 60 percent of all PhD degrees in engineering awarded in India.

The IIT system follows the credit system for performance evaluation of students, with proportional weighting of courses based on their importance in the program. A continuous assessment system has been consistently followed, with due emphasis on tutorials. The main learning takes place in the libraries, laboratories, and computer centers. Student evaluation of teaching (both curriculum and teachers) is an established norm.

English is the medium of instruction at IITs. Even those who pass the IIT–Joint Entrance Examination and are admitted to the system must improve their English-language skills if they hope to perform better in their studies. As noted earlier, the scheduled castes and scheduled tribes candidates—who are admitted as a special category (for the "preparatory course")—must pass an examination in the English language. Of course, the politicians who are opposed to English as a colonial hangover have been critical of the IITs' stand on the use of English. Yet, these critics have hardly been able to make the same changes they have made in the state universities.

Finance and Resources

Although autonomous, IITs are primarily public-funded institutions. Compared with the universities, IITs receive disproportionately high grants: "While the total government funding to most other engineering colleges is around Rs 100–200 million per year, the amount varies between Rs 900 and 1,300 million per year for each IIT" (Wikipedia 2008). Nevertheless, the total budget of the IIT system is nowhere near that of the model (the Massachusetts Institute of Technology) to which it aspired. However, with the donations received from their alumni and the industry, some IITs have been able to develop a sound endowment, the interest from which helps fund many developmental activities. Furthermore, unlike public-funded universities, IITs generate additional resources. Thus, for every rupee that the government spends, IITs generate an additional Rs 0.24 through sponsored research and consultancy and make a net addition of Rs 0.16 to the endowment. Recovery of funds from student fees is only Rs 0.06 (Government of India 2004, 29).

With the large public grants that they receive, IITs subsidize undergraduate student fees by approximately 80 percent, and they provide scholarships to all master of technology students and PhD scholars to encourage students to higher studies. The cost borne by undergraduate students, including boarding and meal expenses, is around Rs 50,000 per annum, whereas an institute's direct expenditure on students is Rs 72,000.

Brain Drain

If one considers the heavy investment by the government in the IIT system, the annual expenditure that the government incurs for IITs, and the fact that study at IITs is subsidized very heavily, the migration of IIT alumni abroad—*brain drain*—has attracted critical attention. The second review committee estimated that, as of March 2003, about 30 percent of the alumni (about 133,245) were working abroad. According to another estimate, since 1953, nearly 25,000 "IITians" have settled in the United States (Friedman 2006, 127–28).

Some have argued that such brain drain was inevitable because of the mismatch between the orientation of the IIT system and the nature of industrialization under a state-regulated economy. As Thomas L. Friedman (2006, 127) notes, "up until the mid-1990s India could not provide good jobs for most of those talented engineers." Furthermore, the remittances by the expatriate IITians were a major source of foreign exchange, especially during the period of substantial trade deficit.

However, since the 1990s, there has been a turnaround, resulting from globalization as well as from changes in the country's industrial policy: government is now encouraging entrepreneurs among the IIT graduates, there has been a steady flow of foreign investment, the manufacturing industry and the service sector have gotten a boost, and technical jobs have been outsourced from North America and Western Europe. All of these changes have created opportunities in India for the aspiring IIT graduates. Not only has the percentage of IIT graduates going abroad declined (from a high of 70 to a low of 30), but the country also has become attractive to those who had migrated earlier (Wikipedia 2008, endnote 62).

As "institutions of national importance," IITs are truly all-India in character regarding the composition of their faculty members and students. Over the course of their five-decade existence, each of the original five IITs has developed a name and identity of its own. The prospect of more recently established IITs developing as did the original five is an important question, especially if one considers that the IIT system is at a critical juncture. To reflect on this question, the chapter will now turn to a case study of the success story of IIT Bombay.

IIT Bombay: A Case Study

The Indian Institute of Technology–Bombay, popularly known as IIT Bombay, is the second-oldest IIT. It was established in 1958 with the assistance of the United Nations Educational, Scientific, and Cultural Organization (UNESCO), using the contribution of the government of the USSR. Until 1973, the institute received substantial assistance in the form of equipment and technical expertise: all 59 experts and 14 technicians from reputed institutions in the USSR helped the institute in its formative years. UNESCO also offered 27 fellowships for training Indian faculty members in the USSR. Under the bilateral agreement of 1965, the government of the USSR provided additional assistance. The government of India underwrote all other expenses, including the cost of the building projects and recurring expenses.

The institute began its first academic session on July 25, 1958, in a rented building in Bombay with 100 students selected from more than 3,400 applicants for the bachelor of technology programs. As buildings were completed on the sprawling 550-acre Powai campus in the northern suburb, the institute shifted from its temporary home to this present idyllic location. By the time IIT Bombay celebrated its golden jubilee in 2008, the campus had its entire infrastructure in place and had become a landmark on Mumbai's map. With more than 6,000 people (students, professors, and auxiliary staff members) living on the Powai campus, IIT Bombay has the ambience of a mini-township.

The institute's emblem in Sanskrit proclaims *"Gyanam Paramam Dhyeyam"* (knowledge is the ultimate goal) as its motto. The vision of the institute is "to be the fountainhead of new ideas and of innovators in technology and science," and its mission "is to create an ambience in which new ideas, research and scholarship flourish and from which the leaders and innovators of tomorrow emerge" (IIT Bombay 2009d, 2). The institute's curriculum reflects its hope that its graduates will be the leaders of tomorrow. In addition to offering professional courses, IIT Bombay strongly emphasizes acquiring a thorough grounding in the basic sciences of physics, chemistry, and mathematics and an exposure to subjects like philosophy and social sciences. The emphasis on basic sciences is expected to address, at least to some extent, the fear of rapid obsolescence of technology. The emphasis on the humanities and social sciences is intended to help students engage more positively with the society in which they live. Apart from providing facilities for higher education, training, and research in various fields of engineering and technology, the institute has been contributing to India's advancement of science and technology in the country and its industrial development and economic growth.

Today, IIT Bombay is recognized as one of the few centers of academic excellence in the country; UNESCO has declared it the first knowledge heritage site (IIT Bombay 2008, 1). IIT Bombay alumni have achieved success in different fields and various capacities—as world-class engineers, managers and technocrats, consultants and advisers, faculty and researchers, and entrepreneurs—both within the country and abroad. Notwithstanding the different methodologies adopted for institutional ranking, IIT Bombay is rated one of the best technical institutes in the world: it ranked 36th in the Times Higher Education–QS World University Rankings for Engineering and IT Universities and 174th among 200 top higher educational institutions in the world in 2008, missing a slot in the top 100 because of low scoring on two indicators—international faculty members and international students (Mukul 2009, 13).

It is no wonder that, during the past five years, IIT Bombay has emerged as the most-favored destination for students among all IITs: 52, 46, 50, 54, and 69 of the top-ranked IIT–Joint Entrance Examination test takers (the elite among the engineering aspirants in the country) have opted for this institute in the years 2005, 2006, 2007, 2008, and 2009, respectively. Overall, 178 (35.6 percent) of the top 500 candidates, the single-largest group, opted for IIT Bombay in 2009 (Chhapla 2009a). The institute's location in the country's financial and entertainment capital, its reputation for academic rigor and quality of campus life, and its record placement figures have all contributed to its growing attraction.

Academic Organization

Under the aegis of the IIT Council, IIT Bombay is governed by a Board of Governors with a chairperson nominated by the Visitor. The board consists of the director; four experts in the field of education, science, or engineering nominated by the council; two professors nominated by the senate; and one technologist or industrialist of repute each nominated by the governments of the states of Goa, Gujarat, Karnataka, and Maharashtra. The registrar is the secretary to the board. Since 2000, the board is assisted by an advisory committee consisting of eminent experts in the fields relevant to the institute and its distinguished alumni. The second review committee found this mechanism to positively contribute to the institute and hence recommended it for other IITs, as well (Government of India 2004, 42).

On all academic matters, the senate is supreme: it has the authority and responsibility to maintain standards of education, instruction, and examination for the various programs of study and for all other academic matters generally. All professors of IIT Bombay are members of the senate, and the director is its chairperson. The director is assisted by a deputy director. There is an orderly division of labor between the academic and allied functions: there are seven functional deans, each with a well-defined authority and sphere of responsibility. The registrar is responsible for the overall administration of the institute, and she or he is assisted by five administrative officers (and support staff members) who are assigned specific areas of administration. The Academic Office, under the dean of academic programs, facilitates and coordinates academic work, especially the teaching and evaluation of students. It is also the repository of grades and academic records of all students, and it provides administrative support to the senate.

The Academic Office closely interacts with the office of the Dean of Student Affairs, which looks after the nonacademic problems of students and coordinates their various cocurricular activities.

IIT Bombay offers a wide variety of programs and courses of study in engineering (its main competency), design, pure sciences, management, humanities, and social sciences organized under 14 discipline-specific departments, 10 multidisciplinary centers, and three schools of excellence. Given the autonomy that the institute enjoys, these programs and courses are flexible so that they can respond to the challenge of change. The institute emphasizes teaching and learning basics, and the pedagogy and evaluation are geared to it. Annually, more than 1,000 students pass through the institute with different degrees.

A special feature of IIT Bombay's academic organization is the Continuing Education Programme. The courses offered under this banner include short- and long-term courses on topics of interest to the industry and research; in-house courses run exclusively for a specific company or organization (either at its site or at the institute); long-term certificate courses on selected topics; and postgraduate-level evening courses for professionals. Selected courses are offered to a large number of participants across the country through video broadcast of lectures supported by course handbooks. The use of Web and satellite transmission for virtual classroom transaction is an innovation that spreads advanced technological knowledge to people who cannot otherwise access it.

Making concessions for individual idiosyncrasies, for which professors are well known, the institute has been fortunate to obtain able leadership. Unlike at state universities where the vice-chancellor's position is now a political appointment and is based on extra-academic considerations, the directors of IIT Bombay have been professors of stature and achievement. By and large, there is no interference from the government or politicians. However, the institute must reckon with Shiv Sena, a Hindu right-wing nativistic political party that controls the unions of the support staff.

Student Enrollment

As noted earlier, over the years, IIT Bombay has attracted the best among the candidates successful at the IIT–Joint Entrance Examination for its undergraduate programs. Similarly, the postgraduate programs attract the best among the candidates passing the Graduate Aptitude Test in Engineering, the Joint Admission, and other admissions procedures. However, because a master of technology and a PhD are not priorities for bachelor of technology graduates, the caliber of students at this level is not high, and the standard of education is accordingly pegged down. The annual intake of students has steadily increased: from 1,135 in 1998–99 to 1,754 in 2008–09 (that is, an increase of 54.54 percent). The increase in intake for the undergraduate program (including a dual-degree program and the preparatory course) is most striking: from 319 in 1998–99 to 652 in 2008–09 (that is, an increase of 107.07 percent). The enrollment in various programs is as follows: bachelor of technology, dual degree, and preparatory, 652; master of science and master of science and PhD, 162; master of philosophy, 12; master of design 49; master of management, 86; master of technology, 596; and PhD, 197.[3]

In 2007–08, there were 5,507 students, of which 2,313 (42 percent) were undergraduates and 3,194 (58 percent) postgraduates. It is envisaged that in 2014–15, this number will be 8,250 (that is, an increase of 49.81 percent): 2,750 (33.33 percent) undergraduates and 5,500 (66.67 percent) postgraduates. Enrollment increase at the first degree level in 2008–09 is explained in part by the implementation of the first phase of reservation (9 percent) of the quota of seats for other underprivileged classes (27 percent); the remaining two phases 9 percent each) will be implemented in 2009–10 and 2010–11.

The Faculty

"Recruiting and retaining high quality for the Institute has always been a challenge. The situation has become acute with the new reservation policy of the Government of India for admission of students at all levels," observes former director Professor Ashok Misra (IIT Bombay 2008, 12). In 2007–08, there were 433 full-time and 31 adjunct faculty members. The professorate at the institute is top-heavy: about 50 percent are professors and 25 percent each are associate professors and assistant professors. There is a faculty shortage of about 10 percent. The average age of professors, associate professors, and assistant professors is 51, 42, and 36, respectively (Government of India 2004, 51). The age profile of the faculty tends to be younger in IIT Bombay as compared to other IITs.

The breakdown of faculty members by discipline is engineering (61 percent); science (26 percent); and humanities, social sciences, and management (13 percent). About 44 percent of the faculty members have at least one degree from the IIT system (see Government of India 2004, 5). Almost all faculty members have a PhD degree; it is noteworthy that 158 (36.49 percent) of them obtained their PhD degree from universities abroad and 74 (17.09 percent) from IIT Bombay itself. The rate of degrees earned from the institute by institute faculty, which is not detrimental by itself, would be higher if one considers that many other faculty members may have at least one degree from the institute.

Unlike at universities, IIT Bombay (as do other IITs) follows the practice of posting rolling advertisements on its website. Applications are solicited throughout the year, and the selection procedure is initiated when the institute has a critical mass of applications for consideration or if there is an urgent need for appointment in a given department, center, or school. Even so, the institute's procedures are more rigidly defined as compared to the system prevalent even in the Indian Institute of Science.

Research and Development

Unlike faculty members at most engineering colleges whose primary activity is teaching and evaluation, faculty members at IIT Bombay undertake research and consultancy projects sponsored by government organizations and private industrial establishments.[4] They have undertaken such projects for the government's Department of Science and Technology, Department of Electronics, Department of Space, Aeronautical Development Agency, Department of Atomic Energy, and Oil and Natural Gas Commission. Some research projects are funded by international agencies. There are also collaborative and consultancy projects with many industries, including some from abroad. On average, in any given year faculty members are engaged in about 400–500 sponsored projects.

Sponsored research projects demand innovativeness, active teamwork, and the creation of state-of-the-art research facilities. These projects enhance interaction between the institute and industry, something at which Indian higher education has been notoriously weak. Sponsored research and consultancy also are a source of additional revenue. IIT Bombay has drawn up clear norms for revenue sharing from the commercialization of its own intellectual property.

The Industrial Research and Consultancy Centre at IIT Bombay coordinates sponsored research and consultancy projects, providing necessary liaison with industry and other sponsors of research. Under the auspices of this center, the academic departments, centers, and schools have set up experimental facilities for aerodynamics, biotechnology, low temperature physics, microelectronics, microprocessor applications, remote sensing, robotics, telematics, and other areas. Painstakingly built over the decades, these state-of-the-art laboratories and facilities are an immense source of pride for the institute. The Computer Aided Design Centre caters to design activity in chemical engineering and metallurgical engineering. In addition to this main computer center, many other research groups at IIT Bombay have computing facilities that are accessed by the faculty for special computational work. The Central Library,[5] central workshop, and the printing press complement the necessary infrastructure for quality research work.

To attract candidates with research potential, the institute offers research fellowships (for graduate and postgraduate degree holders with or without experience) and summer internships (for prefinal-year graduate and postgraduate students). Awardees work on research projects and could be considered for admission into postgraduate or doctoral programs subject to fulfilling the institute's admission requirements. Faculty members and students are provided with liberal financial assistance to participate in international conferences. IIT Bombay has instituted several awards for outstanding faculty achievements in research and development.

From Education to Entrepreneurship

It is the institutional mission of IIT Bombay to encourage and promote entrepreneurship. In 1999, the institute adopted the concept of business incubation. It now hosts the Society for Innovation and Entrepreneurship, which provides "an environment to translate knowledge and innovation into creation of successful entrepreneurs" (IIT Bombay 2009a, 1). In April 2009, to showcase the institute's research and innovations, its Industrial Research and Consultancy Centre held an event called TechConnect (IIT Bombay 2009b). A large number of products from the institute's research laboratories and Society for Innovation and Entrepreneurship were put on display. It is noteworthy that IIT Bombay now holds more than 80 patents in varied streams of engineering (IIT Bombay 2009b) and it has filed 53 more parent applications (IIT Bombay 2009d, 10–11).

Alumni

The alumni of IIT Bombay are its precious assets. Their website (http://www.iitbombay.org) was one of the earliest alumni sites for an Indian educational institution. They have two official organizations: IIT Bombay Heritage Fund and IIT Bombay Alumni Association. The IIT Bombay Heritage Fund is registered as a public charitable organization under Section 501(c)(3) of the U.S. Internal Revenue Code, and its mission is to fund and promote education and research among students, faculty, and alumni of IIT Bombay. It has raised more than US$20 million and helped fund the new schools on campus—Kanwal Rekhi School of Information Technology and the Shailesh J. Mehta School of Management.[6] The IIT

Bombay Alumni Association is registered under Section 25 of the Indian Companies Act (1956), and its mission is to strengthen the connections between alumni, assist them in different ways, and nourish their ties to the alma mater. The association has played a key role in building the alumni network and supporting the local chapters all over the world. The IIT Bombay Heritage Fund and Alumni Association together maintain the alumni directory and website so that alumni can stay in touch with one another and with their alma mater.

International Relations

IIT Bombay's relations with institutions and organizations abroad have grown over the decades. To coordinate and oversee international programs, the institute now has an International Relations Office and a dean for international relations. This office also works with the Ministry of Human Resource Development and Ministry of External Affairs on all matters pertaining to IIT Bombay's memoranda of understanding with overseas institutions and organizations.

The institute is a member of LAOTSE (Links to Asia by Organizing Traineeship and Student Exchange), an international network of universities in Europe and Asia, under which it exchanges students and senior scholars with universities in other countries. Among the institute's recent international collaborative initiatives are the joint PhD program with Monash University (Australia) and research in nanoscience and technology with the University of Cambridge (United Kingdom). Given its elaborate and tough admission procedures, the institute has been unable to attract foreign students.

Finance and Resource Mobilization

IIT Bombay operates one of the largest budgets for educational institutions in the country: its balance sheet for 2007–08 shows a sum of more than Rs 5,743 million. Its income was about Rs 1,544 million, of which about Rs 1,074 million (69.56 percent) came from the government. In absolute terms, the increase in funding during the past two decades appears to be steep, but one also must consider the decline in the rupee value during the period. More than 48 percent of its income, or more than 69 percent of receipts from the government, is spent on pay and allowance and retirement benefits for faculty and staff members. Much of the institute's development expenditure is paid for by monies generated from sponsored research projects and consultancy receipts. In 2007–08, Rs 731 million was generated from research projects (10 percent increase from the previous year); 180 new projects brought as much as Rs 440 million. Similarly, Rs 167 million was generated from consultancy (20 percent increase from the previous year). Alumni and corporate donations and endowments were previously addressed.

Overall, IIT Bombay is less dependent on the government than are the universities, whose dependence on governmental support is as high as 85–90 percent. Nevertheless, to succeed in its quest for becoming a world-class institution, the institute must overcome its dependence on governmental support. This requirement appears to be particularly important if one considers the increasing governmental (and political) interference in the IIT system, something that was unheard of in the first few decades of its development. On this count, IIT Bombay has a long way to go.

Conclusion: Whither the IIT System?

Over the past five decades, the IIT system has established a brand, and its alumni have been its proud brand ambassadors. Beginning with the autonomous model that was evolved to foster excellence in technology, education policy makers marked a break with the moribund state university system. This autonomy has been well used by IITs to respond to the challenges of change and to approximate the best in technology education in the world. The IIT system is highly competitive, and only the best candidates are selected. Even with the government's sustained campaign for implementing the protective discrimination policy and expanding its scope in the name of social justice, the IIT system has upheld quality and meritocracy still prevails.

Quality teaching has been the IIT system's forte: although emphasis is placed on basic sciences, IIT courses cover cutting-edge fields in technology and engineering. The system has been choosy in recruiting faculty members, and the faculty-student ratio in the original five institutes is considered a luxury by Indian standards. IIT Bombay's continuing education program has contributed to the improvement of the quality of engineering education in the country. Although an adjunct to teaching, the system has developed enormous capacity for research and development, especially in applied technology. The state-of-the-art facilities— laboratories, libraries, and computational centers—at the original five institutes are the best in the country. The concept of business incubation adopted by IIT Bombay to promote entrepreneurship among the students has yielded positive results.

Comparative assessment of diverse institutions, in terms of either quantitative indicators or qualitative markers, is difficult and often invidious. Much depends on who is comparing which institutions and for what purpose. Comparing IITs with engineering colleges and universities in India (see table 6.1) would surely reveal IITs to be islands of excellence, far beyond the reach or imagination of the universities. This situation is remarkable, if one considers the odds at which excellence in education must be pursued in India, where there is tremendous pressure for

Table 6.1   IITs and State Universities: A Study in Contrasts

IITs	State universities
IITs are established by an act of Parliament; president of India is the Visitor of all IITs.	Universities are established by an act of a state legislature; governor of the state is the chancellor of the universities within the state.
IIT Council is an overarching policy-making body for all IITs—"the IIT system."	Some states have a common legislative framework for their universities; there is no overarching policy-making body.
Academic ambit is covered by the All India Council for Technical Education.	Academic ambit is covered by the University Grants Commission.
As the academic and executive head, the director (an academic appointee) is not the chairperson of the managing body—the Governing Board.	As the academic and executive head, the vice-chancellor (primarily a political appointee) is the chairperson of the managing body—the Syndicate or Executive Council.
IITs are financially dependent on the central government, but generate funds through projects, consultancy, and alumni support.	Universities are humiliatingly dependent on state government funding and hardly generate any funding of their own.
IITs enjoy greater functional autonomy.	Universities have very little functional autonomy; the state's directives override.
The government does not interfere in an institute's decision-making process. Politicians do not interfere.	Government interference occurs in a university's decision-making process. Political interference occurs in both policy matters and day-to-day affairs.
IITs are limited in number; there is planned and regulated expansion (at least in the first five decades).	Universities are large in number; expansion is unplanned.
Faculty recruitment and student admission are all-India in scope; outlook is cosmopolitan.	Faculty recruitment and student admission are largely restricted to state or even region within it; outlook is parochial.
Focus is on technology and its application with a strong foundation in basic sciences.	There are many focuses, especially on the practice of engineering in engineering colleges.

(continued next page)

Table 6.1   *(continued)*

IITs	*State universities*
Although teaching is the forte, research is encouraged; faculty members do considerable research.	Teaching, to the exclusion of research, is the norm.
Flexible structure and process exist: IITs respond to changing situations and implement changes without delay.	Rigid structure and process exist: universities are unable to respond to changes when required.
Faculty have functional autonomy in teaching and evaluation.	Faculty members teach and evaluate approved courses on a standard format.
Common all-India entrance test is needed for admission: IIT-Joint Entrance Examination is required.	Admissions are based on previous academic credentials: no entrance test is required.
Meritocracy prevails, even with the government's protective discrimination policy.	Mediocrity rules.
Favorable faculty-student ratio exists.	Large classes and unfavorable faculty-student ratio exist.
English is the exclusive medium of instruction and evaluation.	Vernacular is the main medium of instruction; even where English is the medium of instruction, students have the option to write the examination in the vernacular.
Student activism is kept under control; no political patronage of student groups occurs; academic calendar is followed.	Student activism is unchecked; active political participation occurs in student politics; academic calendar is periodically derailed by agitations.
Continuous process evaluation is carried out by the teacher; credit-based grading is used.	Year- and semester-end product evaluation takes place; external evaluation is used.
Student evaluation of courses and teachers is an established norm.	Student evaluation of courses and teachers hardly exists.
Credentials are recognized worldwide.	Credentials are not respected even within the country.
Proud alumni are a well-organized asset and are a resource for mobilization and as brand ambassadors.	The idea of an alumni organization does not exist.

Source: Author.
Note: The comparisons are based on general observations.

massification, mediocrity, and general debasement of academic standards. Any talk of excellence will be dubbed as elitist and as against the principles of social justice. However, if one compares IITs with high-ranking, world-class universities—including the Massachusetts Institute of Technology, the model on which IITs were based—IITs have a long way to go. Approximating that model calls for a huge investment of resources, unwavering dedication, and consistent hard work. At the same time, the strain toward decline is worrisome. Perhaps the extra effort made by the IIT system may only help it stay where it is.

The IIT system faces both external and internal challenges. "A university needs to have three basic freedoms: freedom to decide what to teach, whom to teach, and who will teach. It is the corrosion of these freedoms that we are witnessing today," bemoaned former IIT directors, Indiresan and Nigam, in the early 1990s (1993, 359). The corrosion to which they referred involved the reservation of seats for the scheduled castes and scheduled tribes candidates and the attendant political interference that it brought into the functioning of IITs. This problem has been exacerbated with the extension of the reservation strategy to other underprivileged classes in 2008, even as the experience of reservation of seats for scheduled castes and scheduled tribes highlighted its negative effect on both IITs and the students accepted under the reservation quota. The government sought to address the critics by increasing the number of seats, which only added pressure on the system.

It is here that the functional autonomy of IITs is seriously compromised. Their continued dependence on governmental funds is an open invitation for greater political interference. Recent governmental decisions—concerning the creation of a lecturer's position in IITs, the relaxation of PhD qualification for this position, the starting of new IITs without adequate preparation, the pay packages for the faculty, and other options—suggest that the government has begun treating IITs as regional universities if not as its own departments. The increasing proclivity of politicians to interfere in the IIT system seems to be related to the decline in their pride about the system.

IITs face significant challenges internally, as well. These include the difficulties faced in recruitment of faculty members, the inability to determine suitable pay packages and allied benefits, and the lack of a performance-based reward system. More important, IITs have not adequately addressed the need for revisiting the system's objectives. They have succeeded in producing the best engineering and technology graduates in large numbers, but they need to move beyond this mission; research and extension cannot be mere appendages in education. In international comparisons, IITs fall short in research output, publications, and citation indexes. Fine-tuning their teaching and research programs to the developmental needs of a predominantly rural economy is another gray area, especially because IITs receive huge public funding.

Furthermore, in spite of existing for more than five decades, the IIT system has not fostered interinstitutional interaction. Synergy among IITs could improve the quality of their teaching and research programs. As of now, such interaction is extremely limited; interinstitutional mobility of faculty is uncommon. If one considers the sudden expansion of the system, the importance of such synergy and faculty mobility can hardly be exaggerated.

The stringency of IIT entrance procedures is criticized for diverting educational efforts from higher secondary schools to coaching classes. Coaching classes are expensive; not all students can afford to invest money, energy, and time on coaching. Furthermore, coaching classes favor the better-off sections of society. Often, candidates who fail the IIT–Joint Entrance Examination face depression and other psychological problems, as do their families. But, IITs can ill afford to dilute their standards; the IIT system cannot be blamed for the deficiencies of secondary school education. Dubbing meritocracy—the lynchpin of the IIT system—as elitism is an invitation to mediocrity.

The challenges, both external and internal, faced by the IIT system reduce optimism about the ability of existing IITs to realize their dream of world-class status or the ability of new IITs to replicate the achievements of the original five. One fears that the fledgling IITs will hardly take off, and even if they do, it will be several decades before they reach a modicum of what the original five achieved during the quarter century of their existence.

Notes

1. The 2005 profile of the successful candidates, which has changed only marginally over time, is as follows: 72 percent come from cities, 40 percent are 18 years old, 40 percent pass the examination in the second attempt, 32 percent score more than 90 percent in their class-10 examination, 53 percent come from CBSE (Central Board of Secondary Examination)-affiliated schools, 45 percent have fathers in public or government service, and 60 percent have parents who are both graduates. Interestingly, 45 percent of these candidates took the examination in just five cities: Delhi, Hyderabad, Jaipur, Kota, and Kanpur (Gulhati 2007, 34–35).

2. In March 2010, US$1 = Rs 46.24.

3. The statistical information cited in this section is from the Annual Reports of IIT Bombay and particularly the Director's Report in the Annual Report for 2007–08 (IIT Bombay 2008).

4. The Second Review Committee (Government of India 2004, 7) records the important role that IIT Bombay has played in the development of (a) technologies for India's Light Combat Aircraft, Tejas; (b) aeroservoelasticity analysis software (not commercially available anywhere in the world); and (c) computational fluid dynamics packages.

5. The Central Library at IIT Bombay has a net collection of 408,805 volumes and an institutional repository; it serves a membership of 7,753. It procures more than 1,100 periodicals, 12,000 full-text electronics journals, and 12 databases. It is the first university library in the country to support online submission of theses and dissertations; on the institute's Intranet, the library now has a full-text database of 4,467 items submitted since 1999–2000.

6. Alumni donations (from India and abroad) to IIT Bombay in 2007–08 amounted to Rs 55 million. The institute received corporate donations of Rs 70.7 million. At a conference held in New York to mark the golden jubilee of IIT Bombay, its alumni in the United States committed to donate US$7 million (see IIT Bombay 2009c). Some of the donations are for specific purposes, such as establishment of chairs. The Class of 1982 donated Rs 1.03 million to set up the New Faculty Joining Bonus fund. With the funds made available by Raj Mashurwala (a 1972 graduate), the Suman Mashurwala Advanced Microengineering Lab was inaugurated in April 2007 (IIT Bombay 2008, 11–12). India's first Nanomanufacturing Lab, inaugurated in November 2007, is a gift from the IIT Bombay Heritage Fund.

References

Chhapla, Hemali. 2009a. "IIT-B: The New Favourite Among JEE Top 100, Delhi, Chennai Next." *Times of India* (Mumbai), June 25.

———. 2009b. "IIT Profs Ask for Their Dues." *Times of India* (Mumbai), August 25.

Deb, Sandipan. 2004. *The IITians: The Story of a Remarkable Indian Institution and How Its Alumni Are Reshaping the World.* New Delhi: Viking/Penguin Books India.

Friedman, Thomas L. 2006. *The World Is Flat: The Globalized World in the Twenty-First Century.* London: Penguin Books.

Government of India. 2004. *Indian Institutes of Technology: Report of the Review Committee, 2004.* New Delhi: Ministry of Human Resource Development. http://www.iitk.ac.in/infocell/Commrev/Committee/I.pdf. Accessed August 16, 2008.

Gulhati, Shashi K. 2007. *The IITs: Slumping or Soaring.* New Delhi: Macmillan India.

IIT Bombay (Indian Institute of Technology–Bombay). 2008. "The Director's Report." In *IIT Bombay Annual Report, 2007–08*, ed. IIT Bombay, 1–22. Mumbai: IIT Bombay.

———. 2009a. "Our Vision." Society for Innovation and Entrepreneurship, IIT Bombay, Mumbai. http://www.sineiitb.org/. Accessed August 8, 2009.

———. 2009b. "TechConnect 2009: IIT Bombay Showcases Its Innovations." IIT Bombay, Mumbai. http://www.iitb.ac.in/News_09/TechConnect09.html. Accessed August 8, 2009.

———. 2009c. "IIT Bombay Alumni." http://www.alumni.iitb.ac.in/. Accessed August 8, 2009.

———. 2009d. "R&D Spectrum." IIT Bombay, Mumbai. http://www.ircc.iitb.ac .in/webnew/R&DSpectrum/index.html. Accessed August 8, 2009.

Indiresan, P. V., and N. C. Nigam. 1993. "The Indian Institutes of Technology: Excellence in Peril." In *Higher Education Reform in India: Experience and Perspectives*, ed. Suma Chitnis and Philip G. Altbach, 334–63. New Delhi: Sage Publications India.

Mukul, Akshaya. 2009. "Delhi, Mum IITs Zoom on *Times* List: Fail to Breach Top 100 Mark Only on Two Indicators—International Staff and Students." *Times of India* (Mumbai), July 10.

Mukul, Akshaya, and Hemali Chhapla. 2009. "Non-PhDs Can Be IIT Lecturers." *Times of India* (Mumbai), August 28.

Pushkarna, Neha. 2009. "For Them IIT No Green Pasture." *Times of India* (Mumbai), September 2.

Upadhyaya, Yogesh K. 2005. "The Making of New IITs." rediff.com. http://www .rediff.com/money/2005/mar/23iit.htm. Accessed March 23, 2005.

Wikipedia. 2008. "Indian Institutes of Technology." Wikipedia.org. http://en .wikipedia.org/wiki/Indian_Institutes_of_Technology. Accessed August 16, 2008.

CHAPTER 7

The Rise, Fall, and Reemergence of the University of Ibadan, Nigeria

Peter Materu, Pai Obanya, and Petra Righetti

African universities of the 1948 generation (preindependence era)—
University of Ibadan, Nigeria; University of Khartoum, Sudan; University
of Ghana in Legon, Ghana; Makerere University, Uganda; and University
Cheikh Anta Diop of Dakar, Senegal—were affiliated with partner universities in the colonizing countries, such as France, Portugal, and the
United Kingdom. Through these affiliations, the institutions automatically became part of the French, Portuguese, U.K., or other systems of
quality assurance through their partner universities. This type of close
administrative and curricular alliances provided African countries with
educational qualifications comparable to the academic standards, culture,
and character of European universities of that time.

Upon independence, the increased power of state authority over
higher education altered the autonomy of the institutions. National government priorities included increased access, tuition-free education, and
measures to control political dissent, which was often seen as originating
in the universities.

Between 1985 and 2002, the number of tertiary students in Sub-
Saharan Africa increased 3.6 times (from 800,000 to about 3 million), on
average by about 15 percent yearly. The public's demand for tertiary
education is shaped in part by overall trends in population growth and, in

part, by trends in access at the lower educational levels. The youth population in Sub-Saharan Africa already constitutes more than four times its 1950 level. With broadening access to lower levels of education, pressures to access tertiary education are expected to intensify. Meanwhile, the education system inherited from the colonial past did not adapt to the countries' social and economic transformation, remaining rooted in traditional, hierarchical academics meant for the elites.

Private provision of higher education has been expanding in response to the increasing demand for access. The fastest-growing private institutions are the nonuniversity tertiary ones, and they generally feature programs that emphasize social sciences, economics and business, and law because of their lower start-up costs. They undertake little research and tend to respond to student interest rather than labor-market demand.

The expansion in enrollments has taken a harsh toll on public resources. Expenditure per student decreased from US$6,800 in 1980 to US$1,200 in 2002, recently averaging US$981 in 33 low-income countries in Sub-Saharan Africa. The decline in unit costs has affected the quality of education programs. Tertiary institutions are finding it increasingly difficult to recruit and retain teaching staff, lecture halls are overcrowded, equipment is outdated, and few postgraduate programs exist. These factors were exacerbated by the economic and political crises that rocked the region in the past 40 to 50 years. The consequence of this environment is the inability of universities in most of Africa (with the possible exception of South Africa) to keep pace with global developments in the management of universities as well as in curricula, teaching, and research.

African leaders recognize that the continent's development depends on its ability to fit into today's knowledge economy. Finding a place for Africa in this era of globalization is also based largely on Africa's ability to be a viable contributor to the global pool of knowledge. Because universities are the major center points for knowledge generation (through research), knowledge transmission (through teaching), and knowledge application (through engagement with the wider society), commitment is strong for African universities to take appropriate steps to revive their vision for world standards.

Nigeria, as the largest and most populous country in Africa (140 million people), reflects the general education patterns and challenges throughout the region. Nigeria is a vast country, defined by an ethnically and religiously diverse population. The provision of education addresses these aspects through the concurrent responsibility of the federal, state, and local governments. Each level of government provides services that benefit its respective constituency. Thus, the federal budget for education addresses four national interests: (a) produce highly specialized skills for a national labor market, (b) establish training standards and credentials that permit a national labor market to emerge for learned professions, (c) increase understanding and tolerance across major ethnic divisions, and (d) promote a sense of national identity (World Bank 2006).

The system is hindered by its complicated constitutional and legal framework. In particular, the division of responsibilities among the three tiers of government (together controlling 50 percent of resources) complicates accountability. Within the federal system, the division of responsibilities between the federal Ministry of Education and its parastatals is not always clear, suggesting duplication and inefficiency. At the federal level, institutional roles and responsibilities sometimes appear to overlap or are out-of-date with recent developments. Underlying these problems is the inadequate capacity for planning and policy analysis and a lack of reliable statistical data, including enrollment data, financial data, and population projections (World Bank 2006).

This chapter focuses on one of Africa's 1948-generation institutions, the University of Ibadan in Nigeria. This three-part discussion examines (a) the close link between the political, economic, and social evolution of the Nigerian state in the past 60 or so years and the fortunes of the university; (b) attempts by the university to revitalize itself; and (c) necessary interventions at the system and the institutional levels to move the revitalization process forward and place the institution on the path to world-class status.

The advent of world rankings of universities in the past half decade (2005–10) has ignited in Nigerian educational institutions the desire to compete and benchmark their institutions. Even though the value and parameters of rankings can be contested, the fact that no Nigerian university has ever been featured among the top institutions was a wake-up call, both within the universities and in the wider society. Nigerians have since begun to benchmark their universities against those of South Africa, which have occupied the top of the ranking table on the African continent.

Within the country itself, the struggle by the older universities to rank among the top 100 institutions in Africa can be seen and felt. The most highly ranked Nigerian institution in each year's ranking readily acquires the title of "best university in the country." The University of Ibadan, often referred to as the nation's "premier university" and "the first and the best," has thus far not earned this title. To the contending universities, this is evidence that the first has not remained the best.

Influence of Nigeria's Political, Economic, and Social Trends on the Evolution of the University

A statement by a historian at the University of Ibadan has often been quoted: "The history of the University of Ibadan is, in a sense, inseparable from the history of Nigeria after the Second World War" (Adewoye 2000, 16).

From a historical perspective, the evolution of the University of Ibadan fits neatly into three distinct phases: the University of London years (1945–62), the era of the nascent national university (1962–66), and the turbulent years (1966–99). Each phase represents some form of landmark in Nigeria's political and socioeconomic evolution and has had a major impact on the development of the University of Ibadan.

The University of London Years: 1945–62

This phase in Nigeria's sociopolitical and economic development ran from the end of World War II (1945) through the process of political independence (1960) to the attainment of full university status (1962). This period was characterized by formation of Nigerian political parties (1951) and the institutionalization of a three-region political structure in the north, east, and west (1952). The next steps brought self-government for the regions in 1957 and 1958 and, eventually, independence in 1960.

Both the federal and the regional governments expanded public services during this period, pushing for *nigerianization* policies to bring national cohesion and encourage an influx of nationals into public services. This period brought a growing political momentum for self-rule and decolonization in Africa. Great Britain saw the development of higher education as essential for preparing colonies for emergence into self-ruled states with appropriate human resources to run political and economic affairs.

To cultivate an elite of leaders and civil servants, the British colonial government set up two commissions in 1943. The Asquith Commission looked into the "principles which should guide the promotion of higher education, learning and research and the development of universities in the colonies" (Adewoye 2000, 16). The Elliot Commission was expected to report on the organization and facilities of existing centers of higher education in British West Africa and to make recommendations regarding future university development in that area. The commissions' reports led to the upgrading of existing postsecondary institutions in different parts of the British Empire. In Nigeria, Yaba Higher College, which had existed since 1934 for training an intermediate-level indigenous workforce, was upgraded and moved to the city of Ibadan to become Nigeria's first university college, formally inaugurated in November 1948.

Like its counterparts (Makerere University in Uganda and University of Ghana in Legon, Ghana) that were established at about the same time, the University of Ibadan was affiliated with the University of London and was, for all intents and purposes, an external campus and a replica of the latter. This designation was in keeping with the recommendations of both the Asquith and the Elliot commissions that "these should aspire from the outset to academic standards equal to those of universities and university colleges in Britain" (Montani 1979).

Staff (academic, technical, and administrative) recruitment and advancement followed strictly British standards. Student recruitment was stiffly competitive. Courses were limited to the classical British areas of arts (classics, English, history, and geography); science (mathematics, botany, chemistry, physics, and zoology); agriculture (introduced in 1949); and medicine (only preclinical courses in the early years).

There were, however, two major departures from the typical London standard. The first was the expansive campus with full municipal services and full residential facilities for senior staff members and students. These elements were to raise serious challenges for the university at a later date. The second point of departure from London standards was the introduction of "concessional entry" for students without the standard British university qualification of General Certificate of Education at an advanced level—obtained after seven years of secondary education. Students who came in through concessional entrance examinations had to complete a preliminary academic year successfully before full admission to a degree program.

The University of London tag, the preponderance of London-type lecturers and professors, the London-dictated and London-controlled curricula, and the highly competitive and elitist student admissions procedures combined to enhance the prestige of the university all over the then-British commonwealth.

Other contributing factors to the early academic prestige of Ibadan are worth mentioning. First, the authorities consciously attempted to attract high-caliber academic, technical, and administrative staff. This effort included special encouragement to promising Nigerian young professionals and academics. Second, staff composition was truly international, contributing to the rich academic and social culture of the university. In these early years, the staff had only a handful of Nigerian academics,

mainly those inherited from the Yaba Higher College that was the predecessor of Ibadan. These nationals constituted less than 10 percent of the
total number of academic staff members. Third, physical and pedagogical
facilities were of high standards. Fourth, student numbers were relatively
small, which translated to manageable teacher-student ratios. Ultimately,
Ibadan built a culture of research into its academic life from the beginning. In the words of Mellanby (1958, 104), "the provision of teaching for
our students and the prosecution of original research by our staff were
our most important duties."

From about 1951 (when it produced the first set of Ibadan graduates
of the University of London) to the advent of independence in 1960,
the university was able to generate a pod of Nigerian graduates with the
capacity to take up public services across a wide spectrum—education,
administration, diplomatic services, medicine, agriculture, broadcasting,
police, and other areas. A record number of Ibadan-London graduates also
undertook graduate courses overseas and later joined the academic staff
of the university. Thus, the wider Nigerian society felt the effect of Ibadan
from the first decade of its existence. The university's recognition was
further supported by the significant contribution of a number of graduates to the emerging African literature in English.

These literary pioneers have remained sources of pride to the nation—
Chinua Achebe, Wole Soyinka (1986 Nobel laureate for literature), John
Pepper Clark, Chukwuemeka Ike, and others. This period also witnessed
the emergence of Ibadan-trained Nigerian scholars who later became
world-acclaimed academics in various disciplines—J. F. Ade Ajayi (history), Akin Mabogunje (geography), Ayo Bamgbose (linguistics), and
C. Agodi Onwumechili (physics), among many others.

During this period, Ibadan also pioneered research and teaching of
African history under the leadership of Kenneth Dike, who later became
the first Nigerian academic head of the institution. The product of these
efforts—the Ibadan History Series—became instantly recognized as
the most accurate interpretation of Africa's past. Ibadan was able, through
the African history initiative, to build links with other universities in
Africa and with world centers of study and documentation on Africa.
Ibadan also became a force to which researchers on African history of
diverse origins gravitated.

The university's research and publications on African history later
exerted a transformational effect on school curricula at the preuniversity
level. Progressively, the study of Africa took precedence over the study of
other regions (especially the study of British Empire history) at the

secondary-school level. Similar spillover effects also occurred with the emergence of African literature in English at the secondary level, which was fueled by creative writing from Ibadan graduates, with contributions from other sources.

Ibadan was not, however, without its critics during these early years. The Nigerian elite class and some of the political parties were unhappy with the narrow range of courses offered by the university. Links to European standards were seen as detrimental to the specific workforce needs for Nigeria's nation building, ethnic diversity, identity, and socioeconomic priorities. Many qualified young men and women (secondary school graduates) were excluded from higher education because of the highly competitive admissions requirements and began migration to Fourah Bay College in Sierra Leone and to the University of Ghana in Legon. The university did not remain unresponsive to these criticisms. Its practical responses and the fallouts will be discussed in later sections.

The Nascent National University: 1962–66

This phase coincided with the era of great expectations in Nigeria, as well as in the rest of the world. The words of the British prime minister, Harold Macmillan, resonated powerfully in Nigeria as he spoke of the birth of independent nations in Africa and the strong appearance of Africa on the global scene.

Nigeria's fervor for political independence and organization was reflected in the new governance structures established by the three constituent regions of the federation (east, west, and north). The produce marketing boards (cocoa, rubber, palm oil, cotton, and groundnuts) were yielding enough revenue to sustain government activities. Healthy competition among the regions led to notable improvements in the provision of infrastructure, education, health, and agricultural extension services.

By 1959, however, the first ideological conflicts began to manifest themselves. The struggle for political control at the federal level led to an election-related crisis. Tribalism came strongly to the forefront of national discourse, and competition among the three regions took on a hostile tone. Tribalism also became a serious consideration in deciding who should occupy which position in the emerging bureaucracy and in most decision-making positions. By 1964–65, disputed federal elections and national census results compounded the situation. The political situation deteriorated rapidly; the first military coup occurred in January 1966 and a second one just six months later—both of them bloody and with strong tribal coloration. The eastern region declared independence and named itself the Republic of Biafra, a decision that was unacceptable to the federal government. A civil war followed that lasted three years (1967–70), which will be discussed in more detail in the next section.

Regarding social reform, these years witnessed a conscious attempt by the governments of the Nigerian federation to meet huge social demands for education. Free primary education was successfully established in the western region in January 1955. The eastern region, less capable of implementing such reform, had to rely on local communities to support improvements in education. The northern region, although not formally declaring a free-education policy, still took steps to expand access to education by opening more government schools, offering subventions to nongovernment providers, and strengthening school supervision.

The period also witnessed vigorous postsecondary scholarship schemes at both regional and federal levels. These programs were aimed at training Nigerian personnel for public service and led to the creation of special institutions for the upgrading of junior administrative staff (for example, the Institute of Administration at Zaria) of regional and local governments. At the same time, similar initiatives were taking place in the fields of agriculture, education, public works, and health. However, the greatest area of concentration for the scholarship boards was university-type studies in Nigeria and outside the country.

In April 1959, the federal government of Nigeria constituted the Ashby Commission to investigate and report Nigeria's workforce needs for a period of 20 years, 1960–80 (Ashby 1959). The commission recommended expanding and improving primary and secondary education, upgrading the University College of Ibadan to a full-fledged university, and establishing universities at Nsukka (1960), Ile-Ife (1962), and Zaria (1962). It also recommended establishing a University Commission in Nigeria so that universities could maintain uniform academic standards. The postsecondary school system was to produce the postindependence high-level workforce needs of Nigeria (Fabunmi 2005).

The University of Nigeria, Nsukka, was in several respects revolutionary regarding university education in Nigeria. It introduced professional degree programs in such disciplines as law, education, management, mass communication, home economics, engineering, and architecture—most of which were nonuniversity courses in the conventional British system that Ibadan had inherited. Courses in the social sciences (sociology, political science, and psychology) were also introduced, while agriculture was taught with a variety of specializations—plant and soil science, animal production, agricultural economics, and others. In its second year

(1961), Nsukka admitted more than a thousand new students, some five times the number usually admitted by Ibadan.

Ibadan's response to these developments took a variety of forms. There was a programmed transition from university college status (that is, a dependent college of London) to that of an autonomous institution, with authentic Ibadan programs beginning from the 1962/63 academic year. New faculties of education and the social sciences were established, as well as the introduction of French in the faculty of arts, while new departments were created in the faculty of agriculture (forestry, agronomy, animal science, soil science, agricultural biology, and agricultural economics). Student intake was expanded, and new student hostels (designed to take two students per room) were built.

The university also took significant steps toward nigerianization. The first Nigerian head of the institution (Kenneth Dike) was appointed in 1958, as principal, and became the vice-chancellor with Ibadan's transformation to full-university status in 1962. More Nigerians were appointed to professorial chairs in such fields as history, political science, agriculture, medicine, and the natural sciences. Nigerian professors also began to occupy headship and deanship positions in larger numbers.

This phase of the university's development witnessed great intellectual ferment. Ibadan became home to major international conferences and collaborative research endeavors. A postgraduate training program took root under collaborative arrangements with universities in other parts of the world. The wider society felt the effect of the university in a number of ways. The Department of Extra Mural Studies organized academic and professional courses for all levels of education across the country. The Institute of Education helped professionalize teaching in the schools through its associateship (nongraduate) and postgraduate diploma in education programs.

Ibadan also became the "mother" to Nigeria's newer universities in Ile-Ife, Nsukka, and Zaria. The first vice-chancellors of these universities, who later achieved international recognition, developed their research and expertise at Ibadan. Many professors at these universities came from Ibadan, as did many younger members of their academic staffs, a good number of whom had been postdoctoral fellows in Ibadan.

Ibadan's relatively high global reputation during this phase of its development can be explained by the following factors. First, the period represented a consolidation of the solid foundation of the earlier years—the international caliber and composition of staff, the relatively good standard of facilities, the competitive nature of student intake, and other aspects.

Second, a broadening of academic links was under way with foreign institutions and foundations (mainly the Ford, Rockefeller, and Nuffield foundations) that funded programs and facilities and promoted staff development initiatives. Third, staff development was taken seriously, as steps were taken to ensure that academic staff members remained abreast of developments in their disciplines through attendance at conferences, research and travel grants, and sabbatical leave attachment with internationally acclaimed centers of excellence.

Ultimately though, the university was deeply affected by the violent socio-political changes developing in the country, which began with disputes over elections and a national census and led to two successive military coups and, finally, a civil war. The institutional level experienced a progressive politicization of the governing council of the university—a phenomenon that threatened institutional autonomy. The tribal dimension of this politicization later manifested itself in the polarization of staff members and even students along ethnic lines.

The Turbulent Years: 1967–99

Ibadan's turbulent years coincided with a period of grave challenges to the building of the Nigerian nation. The period was characterized by the civil war of 1967–70 and its aftermath of prolonged military rule with a civil interregnum (1979–83), often referred to as Nigeria's "Second Republic." The political turbulence in the nation had pronounced effects on the university.

The civil war years: 1967–70. The civil war years were a period of deep-seated political upheavals in Nigeria and of complete stoppage of all developmental activities. The University of Ibadan underwent an exodus of academic and other staff members of Igbo origin, in the same manner in which hundreds of thousands of Igbos had escaped from all other parts of Nigeria to their home regions. This impact was further worsened by the departure of a large number of non-Nigerian staff members because of the security threat. The vice-chancellor resigned, and the institution had to be managed by the university librarian as acting vice-chancellor. Importation of books and equipment was almost impossible, while government funding dwindled because of the pursuit of war efforts. In spite of all these events, courses were held and degrees awarded. Academic links with external sources were not broken, while staff development efforts continued.

One explanation for the maintenance of academic activities and a relative sense of stability at the university was the continued support (academic and financial) from the university's external partners, who continued to inject funds into the institution to support research, indigenous staff development, the secondment of academics (from Europe, North America, and the Middle East), and the provision of physical facilities (a university postgraduate library, a Faculty of Education building, and new departments of Nursing and Forestry). Moreover, the acting vice-chancellor had belonged to the original Ibadan-London school (as did most of the senior academics in the institution). These factors helped to ensure that well-established academic traditions and links with foreign institutions were maintained, in spite of the civil disruptions of those years.

The immediate postwar years: 1970–79. These years began with a phase tagged in Nigeria as "reconciliation and reconstruction" that ran from 1970 to mid-1975, marked by the reign of General Yakubu Gowon. During this time, some concerted efforts were made to direct Nigeria's overall socioeconomic development, with particular emphasis on the development of education. It also marked the first period of direct confrontation between universities and the military authorities. Finally, it marked the beginning of Ibadan's decline in quality and prestige.

Free primary education was introduced in 1975, while a National Policy on Education was published in 1977, along with an implementation blueprint and a national implementation secretariat (Federal Ministry of Education 1977). A new university (the sixth in the country, originally called Midwest Institute of Technology and now the University of Benin) was established in 1972. In the same year, Ibadan established a campus in the middle region of Nigeria, which became a full-fledged university in 1975, the year in which the number of universities grew exponentially. Through a military decree, the federal government took over the state-owned (regional) universities in Nsukka, Zaria, and Benin City. The same decree also converted university colleges (campuses of existing universities) in Calabar, Jos, Maiduguri, and Port Harcourt into full-fledged universities and created new ones in Ilorin and Sokoto.

From the government's viewpoint, it was important to have a fair geographical distribution of universities. However, the approach lacked a sustainable strategy to allocate resources to run and manage these institutions. For Ibadan, the move presented three major threats. First, experienced staff moved from Ibadan to more attractive contracts at these new universities. Second, government subvention drastically declined, as it was stretched across a greater number of universities. The military regime devised ways of distributing available resources to universities that were patently unfavorable to Ibadan with its large staff strength and aging facilities. Third, the emergence of other universities in the country entailed greater competition and thus the need for the University of Ibadan to expand into new programs and attract a broader range of students, overstretching its resources.

The impact of Ibadan's policy choices throughout the decades had evident repercussions in this period. The university began in 1948 as a fully residential institution and had to take on municipal services (access roads, residential accommodations for staff, water, and electricity) that were then not readily available in the city of Ibadan. Over time and with increases in student and staff numbers, these services became too costly and difficult to maintain. New programs had been added throughout the years to respond to increasing demand and shifts in interests. Initially, the new programs were financed by government and external assistance. Thus, Ibadan was able to build a research library; introduce programs in nursing and forestry; modernize its science laboratories; and erect modern buildings for the social sciences, agriculture, and education. Arrangements with external bodies were also largely responsible for sustaining the university's staff development programs. This progress came to a halt with the political unrest caused by civil war and military rule.

Disputes over university autonomy and academic freedom characterized the 1970s, when the University of Ibadan came under military dictatorship. The appointment of the vice-chancellors had hitherto been the sole responsibility of the Governing Councils of Universities. However, with Decree No. 23 of 1975, when the federal government took over the regional universities, the power to appoint and remove vice-chancellors was vested in the head of state or the federal military government. A joint committee of the senate and council sent names of three eligible candidates to the head of state (the "Visitor" to the institution), who exercised the right to appoint any of the three. The choice has not often been based on academic stature and managerial competence. The senate of the University of Ibadan also experienced an erosion of its statutory powers by 1978 as pressure was increased from the federal Ministry of Education to reduce the number of students failing (Ekundayo and Adedokun 2009, 63).

Faculty members who went on strike in 1972–73 against the expropriation of a number of institutional rights were fired on the spot. The government sacked Marxist-oriented lecturers from Nigerian higher institutions in 1978. These lecturers had raised the level of intellectual discourse on campuses and had contributed to a rising climate of critical appraisal of the military regime by the wider Nigerian society. Government saw this group as instigators of an academic staff strike that rocked the nation in 1977–78 and ordered their dismissal. Radical scholarship in the country and in Ibadan began a steady decline from this period onward, while the university began to lose its ground as a hub of knowledge sharing and debate.

The quota system, otherwise known as "federal character," is another way the autonomy of the university was eroded. The quota system, included in the 1979 constitution, aimed to rectify the recruitment imbalances that, in the past, had made one ethnic group or state the majority of personnel in federal parastatals (universities included). The system was also intended to ensure equity and fairness in the admissions process. With the quota system, the university was under obligation to admit students not entirely on merit but on the quota per state as stipulated by the government (Ekundayo and Adedokun 2009).

Thus, as a result of poor strategy, competition for limited funds from government sources, increasing government encroachment on university autonomy, and rising capital maintenance demand, Ibadan's financial-coping capacity withered severely. All these issues were happening when the government had decreed free tuition in universities. Nigeria had also at that time become a petroleum-producing country and a strong member of the Organization of the Petroleum Exporting Countries (OPEC) and therefore was ineligible for external financial assistance. The country was, in fact, financially buoyant (though not economically so) during this period, and yet this phase marked the steady fall of the University of Ibadan in its national and international prestige.

The second republic: 1979–83. This period of Nigeria's brief return to civil rule was marked by high and dashed hopes. People were relieved to see military rule come to an end but were unimpressed by the return to wasteful spending and corruption. Revenue from petroleum was already on the downward trend in the last year of military rule (1978–79), and government had imposed a number of austerity measures, which were soon overturned by the civilian administration. There was massive importation of rice and related abuses of import licenses. The civilian-supervised elections of 1983 were believed to have been massively rigged. Another fiasco occurred with the conduct of a national census, and the economic downturn worsened. All these conditions prepared the grounds for yet another military coup that took place on December 31, 1983.

The short-lived civilian regime, however, tinkered with the education system. The 1977 National Policy on Education was revised in 1981, the major change being an encouragement for private sector participation in education. This policy immediately led to the mushrooming of private universities, established without any strict regulatory guidelines.

The civilian government also pursued a policy of "fair geographical spread of universities" and in the process established federal universities of technology in Akure, Minna, Owerri, and Yola—a continuation of unplanned and unstrategized expansion. As usual, this development led to a further erosion of the staff strength of Ibadan, as it lost a number of experienced academics and administrators to the new universities. Ibadan extended its programs to include three new faculties: technology, law, and pharmacy. In the early 1980s, the courses taught by the three new faculties were already well established in some other universities in the country. These are all capital-intensive programs, and gaining international-level staff for them was not easy. Despite critical resource constraints, expansion continued with the creation of new departments within existing faculties, especially in arts, education, the social sciences, agriculture and forestry, and natural sciences. The extent to which advances in development in the respective disciplines guided this process is not clear. What is clear is that the process further overstretched the resources of the university and also constituted a heavy threat to standards.

By 1983, the end of the Second Republic, Ibadan still maintained the image of Nigeria's premier university and had the largest concentration of researchers, academic journals, and research output in the country. However, the decline that had set in during the earlier phase had increased—especially as the provision of human, financial, and technical facilities had become clearly unsustainable.

The second era of military rule: 1983–99. This period from December 31, 1983, to September 30, 1999, was a very trying one for the Nigerian state, covering four military regimes. The period witnessed a national International Monetary Fund–dictated structural adjustment program accompanied by massive devaluation of the national currency—the naira. In an import-dependent economy, devaluation resulted in high increases in the costs of goods, while people's real income fell drastically.

Mismanagement of the economy had been a feature of Nigerian life since independence, but it intensified during the military years as dictatorial rule meant the complete erosion of transparency and accountability in public affairs. By the mid-1980s, massive wasteful spending by government, the introduction of many white-elephant government initiatives, the creation of a multiplicity of parastatals for every government department, the bloating of the staff strength of government ministries, and the swelling of the executive arm of government all combined to fuel corruption on a phenomenally large scale.

On the education scene, the major development was the proliferation of universities and other tertiary institutions. In 1962, only two of the five existing universities belonged to the federal government, while the other three were regional universities. By 1976, the federal government had taken over all universities and created more to bring the total number to 13. The number has continued to increase since then.

The civilian government in 1979 allowed the states to own universities. Most of the states saw this capacity as a sovereignty symbol and rushed to establish their own universities. The private universities that mushroomed during the 1979–83 civilian regimes were closed down when the military returned to rule. The federal government took over more of the old regional universities (University of Uyo in Akwa Ibom State, Abubakar Tafawa Balewa University in Bauchi State, and Nnamdi Azikiwe University in Anambra State). It also established specialized universities of agriculture in Makurdi (Benue State), Abeokuta (Ogun State), and Umudike (Abia State) and even went on to transform the military academy into a university.

The policy of proliferation succeeded only in stifling higher education in the country. Government interference in running universities reached its apogee, while haphazard funding became the norm. Universities began to outdo one another in currying government favor. Academic pursuits became severely constrained, limited to face-to-face teaching. Intellectual ferment became a forgotten phenomenon, because free discourse cannot thrive under a military dictatorship.

Again, the University of Ibadan bore the brunt of this highly unfavorable political and socioeconomic climate. In the days of structural adjustment, the university was unable to shift from a monopoly to a competitive strategy as other institutions were born. The pull of management and administration between political interests, inept appointees, and stagnating bureaucracy led to the exodus of faculty and the disrepair of facilities and equipment. Scholars from different disciplines moved in large numbers to Europe and to South Africa and the United States. What was left of the university's non-Nigerian staff also left the country.

This period thus ended with Ibadan drained of its senior academics, its facilities depleted, its flawed policies still yielding large student numbers and a bourgeoning administrative structure, its subvention from government barely covering only staff salaries, its external links severed, and its research output in deep decline.

Attempts at Revitalizing the University

The previous sections have highlighted how the state, under different political regimes and at distinct historical conjunctures, can form a mechanism for either social change or social control. The university becomes a site for power struggle in the domain of intellectual freedom and knowledge production, reflecting the political and social environment of the country.

Nigeria is currently characterized by 10 years of uninterrupted civil rule—a way of saying that the country has returned to the path of political stability. This new state of affairs has also influenced efforts since 2000 at giving the University of Ibadan a renewed lease on academic life.

This section summarizes the institutional choices and trends that characterized the development of the University of Ibadan in the past decade and the way it has been shaping its policies to build academic excellence.

Autonomy and Accountability

As part of the ongoing restoration and democratization efforts in Nigerian public institutions, the government policy on university autonomy was introduced in 2000, followed by a new law to establish a permanent legal basis for these changes in 2002. The Academic Staff Union of Universities sponsored the Universities Autonomy Act of 2003, which makes new provisions for the autonomy, management, and reorganization of the universities in Nigeria. Major features of the bill include the restoration of the powers of the council on administrative matters and those of the senate on academic matters, as well as the participation of students in aspects of university governance (Onyeonoru 2008). The new policy framework gave university councils the responsibility of setting institutional policies, hiring new management, and forwarding institutional budgets to government; provided institutions control over their own student admissions; limited the role of the National Universities Commission to quality assurance and system coordination; placed curbs on the right of employees to strike; and legally unlinked universities from the public service—thereby ending their adherence to government civil service policies with regard to employment, remuneration, and benefits. This was a major step forward to empower the institutions on academic matters such as curriculum, quality assurance, staff development, and information access. It is unclear, however, if this legal framework was accompanied by requisite changes in the composition of university councils and senates. A typical university council in Nigeria today has about 55 percent of its membership from within the institution, 25 percent from government, and 30 percent from various other places including the private sector. The chair of the council is appointed by the head of state, whereas the other members are appointed by the minister responsible for higher education (Saint and Lao 2009). Then just a year later, a bill on university autonomy passed, which partially undermined university autonomy by placing key academic powers in the hands of the National Universities Commission, including determining course content, the academic calendar, and so forth. The bill also vested large arbitrary powers in the Visitor, including the power to determine the composition and tenure of governing councils. The powers of the vice-chancellor were also magnified to include the power to hire and fire, coupled with the power of the senate to discipline students and the power of the council to discipline staff (Pereira 2007, 173).

One of the major constraints on institutional autonomy still exists: financial decision making. The federal government maintains a policy of no tuition fees in federal universities; in 2002, it issued an order *forbidding* the charging of tuition fees at all 24 federal universities as these universities were contemplating charging tuition fees as a cost-recovery strategy. Such policies impede flexibility in identifying options for financial sustainability of academic programs and staff and also make it harder for Ibadan to compete with the array of state and privately owned institutions that are allowed to charge fees (a count in 2009 recognized 26 state institutions and 34 private universities).

Other measures limiting the power of the institution represent pressure by the government to control the disbursement of internally generated revenues and to set percentages on the origin of revenues (more discussion on these aspects is in the section titled "Financing."

The University of Ibadan also needs to address the assurance of a diversified staff and student environment that is at least somewhat representative of the ethnic and religious diversity of the country. This diversification entails some distance from the concept of academic freedom in selecting, teaching, and examining students, because of the need to use some form of affirmative action.

Strategic Planning

Instability and power struggles of the past 50 years have caused fragmentation and discontinuity in the university's institutional vision and strategy. More long-term strategies began in 1975, in search of social relevance (1975–80), prioritization of expansion (1980–85), and, more recently, a focus on revision and restrictions on budgets (1985–90). A number of strategies were developed afterward without a focused strategic planning process. A strategic plan to internationalize the University of Ibadan was produced in March 2008 for the 2009–14 period, in realization of the competitive environment presented by the growing number of private institutions and by the international outlook and standards that institutions are required to follow.

The strategic plan for 2009–14 provides the road map for achieving the vision of a world-class institution with academic excellence geared toward meeting societal needs (University of Ibadan 2009b, 7). The then vice-chancellor of the University of Ibadan, Olufemi A. Bamiro, emphasized the importance of linking the work and aspirations of the university to national economic priorities:

> Technological innovations and the development of entrepreneurial capacity are pre-requisite to the success of modern economies. Universities have a central role to play in this regard. The University of Ibadan must provide leadership to achieve the desired science-and-technology-led development of Nigeria by fostering among others government-industry-university partnerships. (University of Ibadan 2009b, ix)

In this framework, the university has identified 12 strategic issues that will drive the overall strategic plan. Some priority issues relevant to this chapter are mentioned in table 7.1 and include establishing an effective and efficient governance structure and management process; developing an environment that is conducive to teaching and learning and that promotes the development of excellence and innovation; and having globally competitive and locally relevant programs geared toward producing knowledgeable, entrepreneurial, and responsible individuals.

Undergraduate, Graduate, and International Students

The university has been able, in past years, to consistently lower the marginal intake of students, while focusing on increasing the number of graduate students (37 percent of students were at the graduate level in 2009). The plan is to progressively transform Ibadan into a research-focused university with a graduate-to-undergraduate student ratio of 60 to 40. Increases in graduate outputs from the University in recent years seem to confirm this direction (figure 7.1).

Research output in the university has not been adequately documented, and the nearest proxy available for it is the number of potential researchers (that is, doctoral graduates) produced. As table 7.2 shows, the percentage of PhD recipients—relative to the total number of postgraduate qualifications awarded—has not been impressive.

Table 7.1   Selected Strategic Issues and Objectives of the University of Ibadan, 2009–14 Plan

Strategic issue	Objective
Management and governance	Reform structure to reduce delays and duplications of functions.
	Build capacity for effective and efficient management of University resources.
	Develop effective communication strategy for dissemination of information for timely feedback.
Teaching and learning	Create an atmosphere of teamwork and interdisciplinary effort in teaching, research, and service.
	Foster a culture of excellence and innovation in curriculum design, content development, and delivery.
	Institute a reward system that recognizes teaching and learning as key elements in the dissemination of knowledge; develop and implement an electronic learning policy.
	Exploit the benefits of University-industry links in the learning process.
Research, development, and innovation	Establish and develop an effective research management culture that ensures sustainable funding of pure and applied innovative research.
	Promote interdisciplinary research that will affect societal needs.
	Promote commercialization of research results.
	Promote research and documentation of indigenous knowledge systems.
Human resource development	Institute a reward system that attracts and retains high-quality staff.
	Promote excellence in staff recruitment and service delivery that emphasizes merit and performance.
	Motivate members of the University community to adopt a positive attitude to their responsibility, including jobs, learning, and research.
	Expand opportunities for staff members and students to acquire national and international experience.
	Strengthen commitment to equality, diversity, and equity in staff recruitment and development.
Community service and partnership	Engage alumni in lifelong relationship with the University.
	Expand and enhance the University's interactions with governments, the private sector, civil society, and the local and international communities.
Finance	Develop a mechanism to ensure that the University has adequate resources to achieve its vision, mission, and objectives.
	Improve efficiencies in management of University finances.
	Develop and implement a risk management and financial control framework for safeguarding of assets and mitigation of risks.
	Institute a mechanism for improved budgeting for all activities of the University.

(continued next page)

Table 7.1   *(continued)*

Strategic issue	Objective
Program development	Create demand- and needs-driven core academic and other relevant programs that are globally competitive.
	Review programs and curricula to promote interdisciplinary and skills development.
	Incorporate like skills training and strategic leadership development into program and curricula.
	Integrate information and communication technologies and open distance learning delivery platform and practices into learning situation.
Internationalization	Be a university whose teaching and research are driven by modern and global trends.
	Mainstream services and perspectives into the global academic agenda.
	Develop strong relationships with international communities in Nigeria.

Source: University of Ibadan 2009b.

Figure 7.1   Enrollments in First Degrees and Postgraduate Degrees at the University of Ibadan, 1948–2009

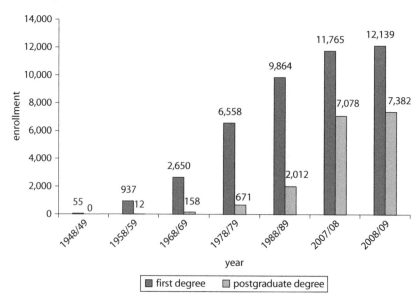

Source: University of Ibadan 2009b.
Note: The figure does not show graduates from all programs.

Table 7.2   Potential Researchers (PhD recipients) Produced over a 10-Year Period, University of Ibadan, 1999–2008

Year	Bachelor diploma	One-year master	MPhil	PhD	Total	% of PhD
1999	126	670	12	70	878	8
2000	180	2,539	29	227	2,975	7.6
2001	13	943	18	156	1,130	13.8
2002	4,061	0	18	0	4,079	0
2003	349	3,355	36	311	4,051	7.6
2004	204	2,203	41	226	2,674	8.5
2005	362	2,271	34	209	2,876	7.3
2006	216	2,132	47	182	2,577	7.1
2007	185	2,220	36	162	2,603	6.2
2008	462	2,852	41	204	3,559	5.7
Total	6,158	19,185	312	1,747	27,402	6.4

Source: University of Ibadan 2008.

Yet efforts have been made to improve the capacity and relevance of both students and staff members in research and to promote links to industry with the establishment of the Centre for Entrepreneurship and Innovations for private sector collaborations, the Student Leadership Development Programme, and the Multidisciplinary Central Research Laboratory. To inform performance-based policies, the university's strategy includes an attempt at better documenting the status of publications and research findings by faculty.

In regard to geographical composition of the students, 12,863 of the students (68 percent) are indigenes of the southwestern geopolitical zone of Nigeria, where the University of Ibadan is located. The situation was better, though not quite satisfactory, a decade and a half earlier. According to available reports, there were 307 foreign students out of a total enrollment of 12,132 (2.5 percent) in 1983/84. In 1984/85, 316 out of 13,862 students (2.3 percent) were foreign nationals, with Cameroon, Ghana, and India accounting for the bulk. Indigenes of Nigeria's southwest accounted for 37 percent of the student body in 1983/84 and 38 percent in 1984/85. Data on staff strength in the years before 1998/99 are not easily available.

Internationalization

Throughout the years, the University of Ibadan was able to maintain partnerships with several universities, donor agencies, and development organizations around the world. As of October 2009, Ibadan had links with 111 institutions around the world (see figure 7.2). These partnerships have been in the form of exchanges of staff members and students, collaborative research, development of internationalized curricula, increasing joint internships, and other policies.

The University of Ibadan, with the assistance of the John D. and Catherine T. MacArthur Foundation, has also established a Digital Learning Centre. In line with the vision of the University, the center has been developed to help provide a solution for access to higher education in Nigeria. To date, well over 15,000 students have been enrolled through the Distance Learning Centre. Further efforts to connect to global knowledge and networks have been made with the establishment of access to electronic journals and databases, at the Kenneth Dike Library, and the upgrade of the medical library to a world-class medical library with electronic learning facilities.

To lead the efforts toward internationalization, the university has also established the Office of International Programmes. Its mission is to enrich global awareness among staff members and students, expand the international composition of the University of Ibadan, promote a reputable international presence, and showcase the University of Ibadan's role as a leading institution in Africa. To accomplish the mission, the center engages in coordinating and supporting international academic programs, generating and disseminating information on international opportunities, promoting and sustaining international partnerships, and advocating the internationalization of facilities and programs (University of Ibadan 2010).

Figure 7.2   Number of Collaborations per Region or Agency

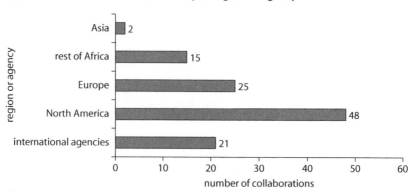

Source: University of Ibadan 2009b.

Development of Academic Faculty

According to the latest figures (University of Ibadan 2009a), Ibadan had 1,197 academic staff members in 2008. With a total student enrollment of 18,843 in 2007/08, this figure translates into a student–to–staff member ratio of 16 to 1—a figure that varies among fields of study, as illustrated in table 7.3.

The hierarchical order of the university academic staff (figure 7.3) shows a relatively high proportion of senior-level academics who should be able to lead research teams (professors 19 percent, readers 5 percent, and senior lecturers 24 percent—a total of 48 percent). For supervising postgraduate work, staff in the Lecturer I category would also qualify. Thus, some 72 percent of the academic staff members of the university should be in a position to teach, counsel, and direct postgraduate students (that is, they possess PhD degrees).

A daunting challenge for Ibadan is the size of its nonacademic staff. The university has reported some rebalancing in this regard over the years. Thus, the number of nonacademic staff members fell from 4,988 in 1988/89 to 3,263 in 2007/08. During the same period, the figure for academic staff members rose from 1,135 to 1,197. Although there are still three nonacademic staff members to one academic staff member, these efforts are evidence of a new approach to improving efficiency in the allocation and use of resources.

What also remains a challenge is the international composition of academic staff. For example, 1,193 of the academic staff members of 1,197 are resident Nigerians, meaning that only four are non-Nigerians. This situation shows the difficulty in attracting and retaining talent. Even among Nigerians, the university has to compete with the private sector

Table 7.3   Student-to-Teacher Ratio at the University of Ibadan, 2007/08

Faculty members	Academic staff members	Students	Student–to–staff member ratio
Arts	129	2,405	18:1
Social sciences	101	2,991	27:1
Law	25	510	20:1
Science	175	2,687	15:1
Technology	78	1,427	18:1
Agriculture	115	1,909	17:1
Education	116	3,011	26:1

Source: University of Ibadan 2008.

Figure 7.3   Academic Staff at the University of Ibadan

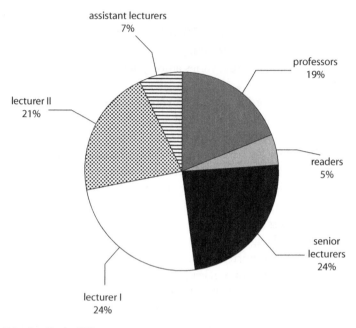

Source: University of Ibadan 2008.

for the best graduates. The field of academics is no longer seen as an attractive career, because compensation is not competitive enough.

Financing

Available data show that public funding for education in Nigeria increased from 2.8 percent of gross domestic product in 1999 to 9.5 percent in 2002, falling again to about 6 percent in the next three years before rising again to 9.4 percent in 2006 (Bamiro and Olugbenga 2010). This proportion is significantly higher than the averages for Sub-Saharan Africa and for the world, which currently stand at 4.5 and 4.3 percent, respectively. Conversely, fluctuations in fund flows challenge the capacity of the university to maintain consistency in its quality and provision of services.

Income Generation

The major sources of income for Ibadan and other federal institutions are government and proprietor allocations, the Education Trust Fund, students' fees and levies, endowments, grants, and internally generated revenues.

Federal government budget allocation to higher education institutions is in the form of personnel costs, goods and nonpersonnel services, and capital projects. All federal universities receive the bulk of their financing (on average, about 90 percent) from the federal government through the National Universities Commission (Hartnett 2000). Latest financial statistics for Ibadan show that the average funding by government is 85 percent, average funding from student charges 1 percent, donations 1 percent, and internally generated revenues 12 percent—with the potential to increase to more than 18 percent (University of Ibadan 2009b).

University spending always outstripped the available budget for the university until 2005/06 when, for the first time in recent years, expenditures were less than the budget (see figure 7.4). This welcome change demonstrates the efforts being undertaken to implement the strategic objective of an efficient, accountable, and sustainable financial management system (University of Ibadan 2009b).

Analysis of the various allocations to universities showed that, on average, allocation to personnel costs accounted for 84.7 percent of the total allocation, goods and nonpersonnel services accounted for 4.6 percent, and capital projects took 10.7 percent. Federal universities' budgeting processes and expenditures must adhere to the budgeting and expenditure formula stipulated by the National Universities Commission as follows: 60 percent for total academic expenditure, 39 percent for administrative

Figure 7.4   Budget and Total Expenditures for the University of Ibadan, 2000/09

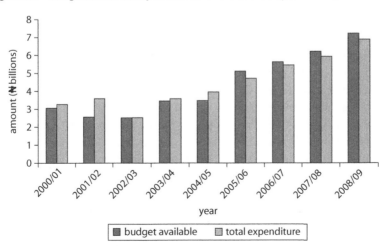

Source: Bamiro and Olugbenga 2010.
Note: Approximate exchange rate: US$1 = ₦150.

Figure 7.5   Expenditure Patterns over the Past 10 Years

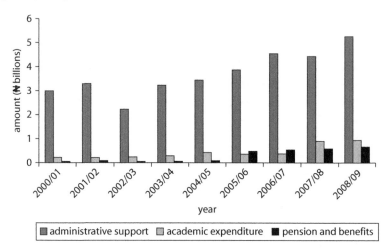

Source: University of Ibadan 2009b.

support, and 1 percent for pension and benefits (Hartnett 2000) (see figure 7.5).

Regarding student fees and levies, the University of Ibadan, as a federal institution, is not allowed to charge tuition fees for undergraduate programs. Federal institutions of higher learning are allowed only limited charges and levies for providing services such as accommodation in residence halls, sports, limited contributions toward the costs of municipal services (water and electricity), laboratory consumables in science-based programs, and other items. Attempts by the university to increase levies have been met with stiff opposition by students.

The government, through the National Universities Commission, mandates that all federal universities generate 10 percent of their total yearly funds internally through various revenue diversification means. This policy has led to diverse initiatives by the university with conflicting effects on the performance of their core research and academic functions. In internally generated revenue, the University of Ibadan obtained approximately ₦200 million in 2006 with distribution among sources shown in figure 7.6. This amount resulted in approximately 4.5 percent of the total allocation by the federal government of ₦4.4 billion during the year. Fees charged for postgraduate programs accounted for the highest source of internally generated revenue. Federal institutions are allowed to charge tuition fees for postgraduate programs.

Figure 7.6   Major Sources of Revenue for the University of Ibadan, July 2005–June 2006

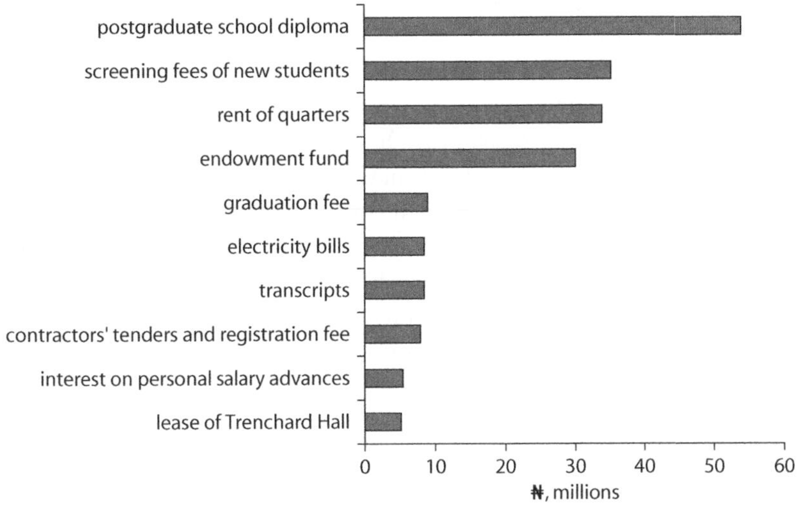

Source: Bamiro and Olugbenga 2010.
Note: Data are for internally generated revenues.

Endowments

Traditional sources of income for the University of Ibadan are endowments, gifts, and donations. Endowments include professional chairs, student scholarships, donations toward programs of interest to the donors, and other forms. Campaigns to raise endowment funds in Nigerian universities date as far back as the 1950s when the University College of Ibadan started an endowment drive. From 1988 to 1994, the university generated approximately ₦22.02 million from endowments and grants (Center for Comparative and Global Studies in Education 2001). The university endowment fund for the execution of selected projects constitutes ₦30 million and is being managed by committed alumni of the university. Alumni and corporate bodies have been the major sources of investable funds.

Grants from funding agencies have also been an important contribution to the University of Ibadan. For example, since 2000 the John D. and Catherine T. MacArthur Foundation has supported the university in the key areas of staff and infrastructure development of information and communications technology. Another contributor is the Petroleum Technology Development Fund, which established professional chairs related to capacity building in the oil and gas industry in six universities including Ibadan. Ibadan receives between ₦14 million and ₦20 million, annually, so far totaling ₦60 million under this fund (Bamiro and Olugbenga 2010, 62).

Expenditure Patterns

The university's annual expenditure has consistently outstripped what is regarded as the budget needed to function optimally, as figure 7.7 shows. The total expenditure on overhead at the University of Ibadan during the 2005–06 session was ₦417.7 million while the total allocation for overhead by the federal government was ₦197.7 million. The university still maintains a policy of providing municipal services (electricity, water, and so forth), which take up the majority of resources (Bamiro and Olugbenga 2010, xiv).

Financial Management

At a country level, efforts to institute a uniform accounting system took momentum in recent years with the creation of a manual of recommended accounting practices for all Nigerian universities. The uniform accounting system was to be complemented with the computerization of the management information service, with data on staff members, students, and

Figure 7.7   Major Sources of Income and Required Estimated Budget for University of Ibadan

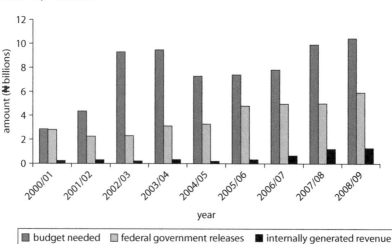

Source: University of Ibadan 2009b.

funds in the university system. Having this data available is critical for improved financial allocations as well as management of information (Pereira 2007, 177).

The University of Ibadan's strategy for 2009–14 highlights a number of bold and progressive activities to manage the sustainability and consistency of financial resources. The university plans to strengthen links with foundations, develop a strategy to encourage the university's philanthropists to endow prizes and fund research projects, encourage an alumni association, develop and implement a mechanism to increase internally generated revenue, and empower the Board of the Advancement Center and the Endowment Board with specific roles to raise funds.

Other measures include the developing postgraduate programs, charging economic rent on housing, eliminating subsidies on power and municipal services to university tenants, and developing a consultancy policy. Internally generated revenue will be a larger source by developing contract courses with government and private sector organizations, creating short summer courses and programs for overseas students, establishing an open university guest house in Lagos and Abuja, and forming incubator ventures and a joint venture in science and agriculture (University of Ibadan 2009b, 75).

Priorities also include strengthening financial processes and controls to eliminate waste and bureaucratic bottlenecks; implementing a policy to decentralize the bursary and audit units; developing a culture for financial planning and financial discipline at department, faculty, institute, and college levels; and carrying out a full-cost recovery policy, whereby every activity should be self-financing.

The university is performing remarkable efforts to manage and generate resources. The challenges endure as long as it is dependent on the government to cover recurrent and capital costs for facilities, programs, and services. Issues of financing also involve attaining the strategic vision of excellence in research and teaching and world recognition.

Conclusion

The conditions under which a university operates are a critical factor to the success or failure of its drive for excellence. The University of Ibadan demonstrates this notion and emphasizes the centrality of the national environment to the development of an institution.

The intricate constitutional and legal frameworks and the three tiers of government in Nigeria complicate accountability, the division of responsibilities, and the capacity for planning and implementation. These factors cause duplication, inefficiency, and mismanagement—not just in education but also in the general economy and in society. The complexity of the system further complicates policy development and planning, given the lack of comprehensive and easily accessible data regarding financial resources as well as population projections (World Bank 2006). Inevitably, these conditions affect the capacity of the University of Ibadan to plan and to create an innovative and flexible environment to attract the best students and staff members.

The lack of a diversified private sector and of a dynamic labor market that has a demand for the leading-edge research, technology transfer, and high-level graduates originating from universities makes it difficult for any institution to generate and maintain academic excellence. Though still nascent, Nigeria's private sector has been growing at an impressive rate (particularly in the telecommunications sector), and the country has one of the most dynamic labor markets on the continent. This potential strength could be tapped to accelerate growth.

Strategically, the country needs to keep focusing on diversifying the economy and promoting the private sector, aiming to increase productivity and expand employment. It is encouraging to see that the government is beginning to take critical steps to establish and improve necessary infrastructure—such as the Internet backbone, electricity, water, roads, and housing—to compete globally.

The international image of the country also depends on the capacity of the government to project stability and opportunity. Measures in this realm would support attracting talent from abroad (including Nigerians in the diaspora) and also international scholars and students to the country's universities. The efforts already under way to transform the country's image are noteworthy and need to be intensified.

On policy issues, the government needs to develop a consistent national policy on higher education, through a participatory approach with key stakeholders. It must play a balancing role between ensuring that institutions have a high degree of autonomy and ensuring that they remain accountable to their students and the community. For this approach to work well, the government should consider institutionalization of a benchmarking mechanism to allow an institution (and the entire higher education system) to assess its progress at different points in time and to benchmark itself against other comparator institutions and systems.

Establishing a performance-based financing environment grounded on a solid monitoring and evaluation mechanism is highly desirable. This system will entail a revision of the way financing is allocated and an increase of the autonomy granted to universities to govern, manage, and generate funding. Granting more autonomy to universities allows flexibility in hiring the best staff members and students and incentivizes universities to link up with industry to remain relevant and establish new sources of revenue.

Ultimately, the drive for excellence must be led by the University of Ibadan itself. Lessons from other universities around the world have shown that global recognition is shaped by an institution's shared purpose, consistent strategy, and long-term outlook. Fundamentally, a strong leadership can make the institution an attractive center for research and teaching.

As mentioned by Jamil Salmi (2009, 7) in a recent publication, the attributes of world-class universities comprise

> three complementary sets of factors at play among most top universities, namely (a) a high concentration of talent (faculty and students), (b) abundant resources to offer a rich learning environment and to conduct advanced research, and (c) favorable governance features that encourage strategic vision, innovation, and flexibility, and that enable institutions to make decisions and to manage resources without being encumbered by bureaucracy.

Achieving excellence in these three components will still take time for the university, but the process has already begun. It is moving into new ways of generating revenues, strengthening links to the private sector, and cutting subsidies to housing and utilities. The university is also developing mechanisms for financial management and accountability, which will raise efficiency and transparency.

Regarding governance, more steps must be taken toward greater institutional autonomy. A new law under consideration that increases autonomy to universities sets the platform for a range of new policies to better manage and drive the vision of the university. With an advanced system and an enabling legal framework, the university will be better positioned to define and manage its own development trajectory and venture into strategic partnerships with global beacons of excellence (universities, research centers, think tanks, and so forth) to share knowledge and exchange staff members, students, and researchers.

The University of Ibadan's vision to transform itself into a leading regional knowledge hub and to upgrade its international status is also a step in the right direction. Its strength, integrity, and sphere of responsibility not only are nested into Nigeria's development strategy, but also are relevant to the entire region.

References

Adewoye, Omoniyi. 2000. "Higher Education in Nigeria: The Birth of an Idea." In *Ibadan University at 50 (1948–1999): Nigeria's Premier University in Perspective*, ed. B. A. Mojuetan, 7–22. Ibadan, Nigeria: Ibadan University Press.

Ashby, Eric. 1959. *Investment in Education*. Report of a Commission on Postsecondary Education in Nigeria. Lagos: Government Printer.

Bamiro, Olufemi A., and S. A. Olugbenga. 2010. *Sustainable Financing of Higher Education in Nigeria: A Conceptual Framework:* Ibadan, Nigeria: Ibadan University Press.

Center for Comparative and Global Studies in Education. 2001. "Higher Education Finance and Cost-Sharing in Nigeria." University of Buffalo, Buffalo, NY. http://gse.buffalo.edu/org/inthigheredfinance/files/Country_Profiles/Africa/Nigeria.pdf.

Ekundayo, Haastrup T., and M. O. Adedokun. 2009. "The Unresolved Issue of University Autonomy and Academic Freedom in Nigerian Universities." *Humanity and Social Sciences Journal* 4 (1): 61–67.

Fabunmi, Martins. 2005. "Historical Analysis of Educational Policy in Nigeria: Implications for Educational Planning and Policy." *International Journal of African and African-American Studies* 7 (2): 1–7.

Federal Ministry of Education. 1977. *National Policy on Education*. Lagos: Federal Ministry of Education.

Hartnett, Teresa. 2000. "Financing and Trends and Expenditure Patterns in Nigerian Federal Universities: An Update." Background study for the Nigerian University System Innovation Project, World Bank, Washington, DC.

Mellanby, Kenneth. 1958. *The Birth of Nigeria's University*. London: Methuen.

Motani, Nizar A. 1979. "Makerere College 1922–1940: A Study in Colonial Rule and Educational Retardation." *African Affairs* 78 (312): 357–69.

Onyeonoru, Ifeanyi. 2008. "Governance: University Autonomy and Cost Recovery Policies—Union Contestation and Sustainable University System." United Nations Educational, Scientific, and Cultural Organization, Paris. http://portal.unesco.org/education/en/ev.php-URL_ID=36322&URL_DO=DO_TOPIC&URL_SECTION=201.html.

Pereira, Charmaine. 2007. *Gender in the Making of the Nigerian University System.* Oxford, U.K.: James Currey.

Saint, William S., and Christine V. Lao. 2009. "Legal Frameworks for Tertiary Education in Sub-Saharan Africa: The Quest for Institutional Responsiveness." Working Paper 175, Africa Human Development Series, World Bank, Washington, DC.

Salmi, Jamil. 2009. *The Challenge of Establishing World-Class Universities.* Washington, DC: World Bank.

University of Ibadan. 2008. *University of Ibadan Digest of Statistics* 4 (1).

———. 2009a. *Pocket Statistics.* Ibadan, Nigeria: Planning Unit, Office of the Vice Chancellor, University of Ibadan.

———. 2009b. *Promoting Excellence in Teaching, Research, and Community Service.* Ibadan, Nigeria: University of Ibadan.

———. 2010. "Office of International Programmes." University of Ibadan, Ibadan, Nigeria. http://www.oip.ui.edu.ng/.

World Bank. 2006. "Nigeria Science and Technology Education at Post-basic Levels (STEPB): Review of S&T Education in Federally Funded Institutions." Education Sector Review Report 37973, World Bank, Washington, DC.

CHAPTER 8

Private and Public Pathways to World-Class Research Universities: The Case of Chile

Andrés Bernasconi

Outside the United States, almost all world-class research universities—as defined by international rankings—are public institutions. There are good reasons for this pattern: achieving world-class status requires time and money, and most private universities worldwide are younger than public universities and are devoid of public subsidies.

Chile presents the distinguishing characteristic that of its two top-ranked universities, one is public and the other private. Tellingly, both were founded in the 19th century and both receive public subsidies. The University of Chile (Universidad de Chile or UCH) and the Pontifical Catholic University of Chile (Pontificia Universidad Católica de Chile or PUC) not only are located in the same city, but also compete for the best students and the greatest share of research funding. Unlike most cases in this book, these two institutions are not new universities. Their original characteristic is the embrace of a research mission, beginning in the 1960s, that has blossomed in the past two decades.

This chapter describes, however, not only what these universities have in common, but also how they differ. The aim is to illustrate the possible diverse paths to creating a world-class university. Although much comparative literature on elite universities contrasts cases in different countries, this study of two neighboring universities will examine variation, while keeping in mind that much is common in culture, policy environment, and national history.

UCH, founded in 1842, is Chile's oldest university and the largest and most prestigious in the public sector. It enrolls more than 25,000 students in 69 undergraduate programs and close to 5,000 in more than 100 graduate programs, 31 of which are doctorates. UCH conferred 95 doctoral degrees in 2007. Faculty members number more than 3,300, but only 34 percent are employed full time. Among full-time faculty members, 42 percent have doctoral degrees (CRUCH 2007). UCH produced more than 5,400 publications indexed by the Institute for Scientific Information (ISI) from 2004 to 2008, representing some 30 percent of Chile's total and the highest research output of any Chilean university.[1] It is ranked 462nd in the Academic Ranking of World Universities of the Shanghai Jiao Tong University and 320th in the Times Higher Education rankings, 2008 editions. Its campuses and teaching hospital are located in the capital city of Santiago and offer a comprehensive range of programs in all fields of study, organized in 14 *facultades* (schools)[2] and four interdisciplinary institutes.

PUC, founded in 1888, with headquarters a few blocks from UCH, competes with the latter for first place on the scale of prestige for universities in Chile. PUC is also internationally ranked (241st in the Times Higher Education list), and the magnitude of its research endeavor puts it second nationally after UCH, with close to 3,700 mainstream publications in the past five years.[3] Its student and faculty bodies are smaller: some 19,000 students in 41 undergraduate programs and a faculty of 2,700. Graduate students number 2,800 across 63 programs, including 23 doctorates, and 72 PhD degrees were earned in 2007. Three out of four professors hold a graduate degree, and half of the professoriate works full time at PUC. Among this group, 45 percent are PhD recipients (CRUCH 2007). This university is structured in 18 facultades covering all fields of knowledge. It also has a teaching hospital.

In the first section of this chapter, the discussion of changes in the political economy of Chilean higher education will set the historical context for the cases of the two universities under analysis, and basic statistics will be presented and explained. Then, the experiences of UCH and PUC will be discussed in sequence, from the point of view of their governance structures and administrative processes, financing, key academic dimensions, and development plans. The focus will be on the progress of UCH and PUC to date, the obstacles ahead for achieving world-class research distinction, and the way the universities are overcoming these obstacles. The last section will discuss the challenges each institution must surmount and the conclusions that can be drawn from the two cases, with respect to the process of building world-class research universities in middle-income countries.

Chile's Political Economy of Higher Education

The Early Years: Nation Building and Professional Training

Chile began its process of separation from the colonial rule of Spain in the same year the University of Berlin was founded. Yet, when UCH was established in 1842, the inspiration was not Prussia, but a unique mixture of the French Imperial University (1806), the Institute of France, and the universities of the 18th-century Scottish Enlightenment. From the French Imperial University, UCH took its role as superintendent of the national educational system and, later, its preoccupation with training professionals for the service of the nation. The new university's facultades, centers of scholarship (without students), resembled the academies of the Institute of France. From the Scottish universities, Andrés Bello, founder of UCH, took the emphasis on the practical, useful knowledge absent from the Oxbridge model (Serrano 1994, 69–78). In 1927, the Chilean government took away from UCH the function of educational superintendent and replaced it with a mandate to carry out scientific research. Yet, the first centers for scientific research became institutionalized in UCH only in the 1950s and 1960s (Mellafe, Rebolledo, and Cárdenas 1992, 163–66, 221–24).

The history of PUC, the second university founded in Chile, is no different from that of UCH with respect to its emphasis on teaching and its late arrival to research. Although PUC emerged in 1888 as a conservative reaction to liberalism and secularization in Chilean politics and society, it shared with the public university this "Napoleonic" tradition, which saw the essential mission of the university in the training of professionals.

First Steps of a Research Mission

By the late 1960s, the eight public and private Chilean universities, fully funded by the state, were devoted almost exclusively to teaching undergraduate courses leading to professional degrees—in line with the Latin

American tradition, also illustrated in this book by the case of Mexico—albeit enrolling just 7 percent of the country's 20-to-24 age cohort in 1967 (Brunner 1986, 17). Although universities engaged more than 80 percent of the nation's incipient research and development personnel, only one doctoral program existed in Chile in 1965—at UCH. By 1967, only 5 percent of the faculty members at this university held a doctoral degree and two-thirds of its professors were part time (Brunner 1986, 25, 27, 30). The readiness for research appeared even more embryonic in the rest of the Chilean university system.

Research as part of the direction for the university's mission took center stage during the university reform movement. This movement was a process of intense discussion about the nature of the university and its role in Chilean society and about experimentation with new forms of organization and governance, much in the spirit of the 1968 events on U.S. campuses and in the streets of Paris (Hunneus 1988). University reform brought unprecedented transformation. Enrollments soared to more than 146,000 students in 1973 up from 55,000 in 1967 (Brunner 1986, 32). Institutional governance and structure were reorganized: rectors and deans began to be elected by the faculty, and representation for students and administrative personnel was introduced in governing bodies. The chair system of European descent was replaced with the departments typical of the U.S. model.

Public funding doubled from 1969 to 1973 (Arriagada 1989, 130–31), mostly to pay for increased numbers of full-time faculty members who were expected to carry out research, leaving behind the paradigm of the "professionalist" teaching university. In reality, though, given the scarcity of trained researchers, scientific output did not experience an upsurge as a result. The political polarization that followed the election of (Socialist) President Salvador Allende in 1970 soon enveloped the universities, each becoming a sort of concentrated microcosm of the nation's political and social conflicts.

The Military Rule and Its Legacies

All this effervescence came to an end with the 1973 military coup. The regime led by General Augusto Pinochet (1973–90) intervened in the eight universities through military rectors, who assumed all governance functions previously distributed among various officials and governance bodies. Academic units with active or suspected involvement in leftist politics, especially in the social sciences, were purged and diminished. Governance reforms were abolished. Public spending in higher education decreased from 2.11 percent of gross domestic product in 1972 to 0.47 percent in 1988, while enrollments fell 26 percent from 1973 to 1989. UCH was the hardest hit: its state funding decreased by 30 percent from 1974 to 1980, whereas PUC, closer to the government, was largely spared budget cuts during this period. In 1981, UCH's numerous regional colleges were transformed into 14 small, independent public universities (Arriagada 1989, 27–33).

To make up for the budgetary shortfall, universities slashed payroll spending by 24 percent from 1981 to 1988 (Lehmann 1990, 72), increased tuition, and sought other outside sources of funding. Self-financing in Chilean universities grew from an average of 8 percent to 27 percent from 1973 to 1980 (Brunner 1986, 47) and rose to 41 percent by 1987 (Lehmann 1990, 54). A public student-loan fund was set up in 1981 to assist students in meeting the higher tuition payments required by institutions. This fund and the budget for research projects were the only items of public expenditure in higher education to increase during military rule. Indeed, funding for FONDECYT (Fondo Nacional de Desarrollo Científico y Tecnólogico, or the National Fund for Scientific and Technological Development), Chile's national research fund, grew by a factor of 18 from 1982 to 1989 (Arriagada 1989, 117). In the period between 1979 and Chile's return to democracy in 1990, government support for research and development grew 30 percent, numbers of scientific publications indexed by the ISI doubled, and the number of faculty members with master's or doctoral degrees tripled (Bernasconi 2007).

For greater access to higher education without additional cost to the government, the creation of new private universities and postsecondary vocational and technical institutions was authorized in 1981. These institutions were intended to survive without access to public subsidization, and, so far, they remain in that condition. Democratic rule was reestablished in Chile in 1991, but the general architecture of the higher education system, as defined by the military regime, has remained largely unchanged.

The Current Makeup of Higher Education

In Chile today, with 61 universities, total enrollments number 510,000, plus some 260,000 students in 135 nonuniversity postsecondary institutions. Together, these numbers represent a gross enrollment rate of close to 40 percent of the traditional age cohort. The private sector constitutes 93 percent of institutions and 75 percent of enrollments. In the university segment, 66 percent of the students are enrolled in private universities.

Funding has also been privatized, with nonpublic sources accounting for about 15 percent of the total national expenditures in higher education (OECD 2009, 225). These figures place Chile among the world's leaders in the extent of private participation and private funding in tertiary education. Tuition levels in Chile for private and public higher education are the highest in the world, as a proportion of per capita income, with only private universities in the United States being more expensive under this indicator (OECD 2009, 228).

Public expenditures in higher education in Chile are quite low by international comparative standards: 0.3 percent of gross domestic product (GDP), whereas the average for 2004 was 1.3 percent for the countries of the Organisation for Economic Co-operation and Development (OECD). The shortfall in government funding is made up by the contribution of private sources, chiefly tuition payments in public and private universities alike. As a result, Chile's overall expenditures in higher education, from public and private sources, represent 2 percent of the country's GDP—higher than the OECD's average of 1.4 percent—where private funding accounts for 85 percent of the total contribution to higher education funding (OECD 2009, 225).

The funding structure of universities reflects these figures: on average, for the 25 universities subsidized by the government, subsidies allocated directly from the government's budget represent just 17 percent of income (OECD 2009, 229). The rest is research funding and capital investment funds—also from the government, but competitively allocated—tuition revenues, donations, consulting fees, continuing education, and the like.

As indicated previously, research funding was spared from the budgetary cuts of the military period and has continued to thrive since 1990, and with it, the indicators of output conventionally associated with science. Expenditures in research and development climbed from 0.51 percent of GDP in 1990 to 0.67 percent in 2007. The number of personnel working in science and technology has tripled since 1990, reaching more than 30,500 in 2004, as well as the number of publications produced by universities that were indexed by ISI, reaching more than 3,500 in 2007. The number of doctorates granted has multiplied by 10 since 1990, with 287 earned in 2007.

Although public funding of higher education in Chile continues to be low in the international comparative perspective, it has increased overall by a factor of four since 1990. Yet, most of this growth in subsidization targeted the support of particular functions and goals. In effect, although base funding (that is, unconditional block grants) has approximately doubled in the past two decades, student aid has more than quadrupled, and funding for research has multiplied by almost seven in the same period (Ministry of Education 2010). This pattern of governmental support has affected university priorities, which have gravitated toward the growing of undergraduate enrollments (to increase tuition revenues), the provision of technical assistance and consulting services, and the development of research capabilities to tap into those sources of public revenues.

The Paradigm of the Research University

UCH and PUC are the best universities in Chile and among the finest in Latin America—in terms of prestige, quality of students, research accomplishments of faculty members, and success of graduates. They invariably hold leading positions in the rankings of Chilean universities and by a wide margin. Students with the best scores in the national test for admission to universities overwhelmingly choose UCH or PUC over any other. Combined, these top two universities publish more than half of all ISI-indexed papers generated by researchers in Chile, and their share of competitively assigned funding for research hovers around 60 percent of the nation's total. More than 60 percent of Chilean presidents studied at UCH, and its graduates, together with those of PUC, represent more than half of the business and political elite of the country.

Yet neither UCH nor PUC is a research university (Bernasconi 2007)—if the definition is a university with research as a core mission and function (Altbach 2007) that enables it to sustain large enrollments in graduate programs, nourished in part by international students, especially at the doctoral level and (in keeping with more recent global trends and expectations) serving as a basis for a significant technology transfer role that infuses the local economy with gains in productivity and competitiveness. This is not to say that research is not relevant at UCH and PUC or that the generation of economically valuable knowledge is absent from their preoccupations. On the contrary, both universities have in the past three decades developed substantial research capacities and achieved significant results and are now seeking to reinforce their scientific profiles and become more relevant to the economy.

However, as the summary data presented in table 8.1 attest, the main function of these universities continues to be teaching at the undergraduate level: graduate enrollments represent just 15 percent of total enrollments at UCH and a lower figure at PUC, and neither university awarded

Table 8.1   Basic Data Concerning the University of Chile and Pontifical Catholic University of Chile, 1992–2007

	1992		1998		2007	
	UCH	PUC	UCH	PUC	UCH	PUC
Student enrollment						
Total	18,617	12,660	24,259	17,170	30,702	22,035
Graduates	1,247	482	2,184	1,163	4,569	2,806
% of total	7	4	9	7	15	13
Foreign students (1990)	373	108	—	—	1,400	1,257
% of total	2	1	—	—	5	6
PhD recipients	9	7	51	16	95	72
Faculty members					*2008*	
Total	5,230	1,818	3,106	2,088	3,354	2,732
Full time	2,164	753	1,336	813	1,154	1,371
% of total	41	41	43	39	34	50
With PhD	381	424	398	553	758	—
% of total	7	23	13	26	23	—
Full time with PhD	266	294	273	346	489	623
% of full time	12	39	20	43	42	45
Research						
ISI-indexed publications	536	60	728	310	1,123	739
FONDECYT projects	201	121	213	182	295	234
Funding	*1991*					
Total revenues (US$, millions)[a]	172	164	280	281	520	453
State-based funding (US$, millions)[a]	70	33	56	42	56	51
% of total revenue	40	20	20	15	11	11
Sales of goods and services						
(US$, millions)[a]	49	98	142	197	320	346
% of total revenue	29	60	51	70	62	76

Sources: CRUCH 1992, 1998, and 2007, with the exceptions of data on foreign students for 2007, which were obtained from the websites of UCH (http://www.uchile.cl/) and PUC (http://www.uc.cl/); the numbers of ISI-indexed publications, which were obtained from Thomson Reuters (formerly ISI) Web of Knowledge; the number of FONDECYT projects (including grants in all FONDECYT instruments), which were obtained from FONDECYT's database, http://ri.conicyt.cl/575/channel.html; and data on faculty credentials for PUC, for which the 2007 *Anuario Estadístico* (CRUCH 2007) could not be used because in it PUC included the number of professors with a PhD and the number of professors who are medical doctors and have a medical specialization. Instead, for comparability with UCH, data for 2008 were obtained at PUC's website, from a source where professors with a PhD and medical doctors are reported separately.

Note: — = not available.

[a] For purposes of comparison, all figures on funding for 1991 and 1998 were first expressed in Chilean pesos (CH$) for the year 2007, and then, along with the data for 2007, converted into US$ at the exchange rate of CH$530 to US$1.00, current as of March 2010.

more than 100 doctoral degrees in 2007 (see table 8.1). Furthermore, a majority of full-time faculty members at both institutions do not yet hold a doctoral degree. Moreover, the composition of the faculty in terms of its dedication to the university also departs from what is expected from research universities: Half of the faculty members at PUC and two-thirds at UCH are part-time adjuncts, figures similar to that of 42 percent at the main campus of the Monterrey Institute of Technology—the other Latin American case in this book (see chapter 9), reported by Francisco Marmolejo.

Notwithstanding variations in the idea of a research university, table 8.1 provides evidence of steep progress of research involvement in the last two decades. More full-time faculty members with a PhD were present in both institutions—not only in absolute numbers, which doubled, but also in the total numbers of faculty members. Mainstream scientific publications and research grants show similar patterns of growth, as do the numbers of graduate students as a proportion of total enrollments, which have doubled in UCH and tripled in PUC from 1992 to 2007.

Given the funding, these developments have taken place as both universities tripled their revenues (corrected for inflation) since 1991, mainly in the form of self-generated income as opposed to direct government subsidies, which have slightly increased for PUC and actually diminished for UCH. Indeed, both institutions rely on state transfers for just over 10 percent of their budgets, whereas tuition fees, technical assistance, consulting fees, and income from university-owned businesses represent more than 60 percent of UCH's revenues and 75 percent of those of PUC. The remainder—that is, not direct transfers from the government or operational revenue captured from private sources—is composed mostly of research grants and other funds competitively allocated by the government, based on development projects and investment plans presented by the universities. The fall in the amount of public funding for UCH and its rise for PUC are a result of the formula used by the government to allocate these resources. This funding formula rewards universities with the highest proportions of full-time faculty members with a PhD and publications over total faculty members, a measure in which PUC has been leading UCH for two decades. UCH compensates by its greater success in securing competitively allocated funding for research, doctoral programs, and capital investment projects. As these competitive funds have grown, they more than make up for the lost base funding.

In sum, although UCH and PUC cannot yet be considered research universities if measured against top research universities in the United States and other advanced countries, they have for the past two decades been making steady and deliberate progress toward that institutional profile and have done so amid conditions of funding where competition for both private and public funds is an essential strategy.

The University of Chile

UCH, throughout its history and currently, represents one of the most respected institutions of any kind in Chile:

> It organized and supported education at all levels, was the center of the country's intellectual life, introduced scientific knowledge, helped establish the professions, and formed one of the region's more enlightened and successful ruling classes. [E]ven today, the UCH sits at the system's pinnacle . . . and is still regarded as the national university within a system widely heralded as the model for Latin America. Indeed, the UCH is routinely included in any informed listing of the region's best universities. (Levy and Bernasconi 1998, 464)

After the 1950s, UCH added to its role of training professionals a research mission, turning to the United States for assistance—the Ford and Rockefeller foundations and the University of California being key partners at the time—and, in the 1960s, began building a professional cadre of full-time academics with advanced degrees and its own graduate programs (Levy and Bernasconi 1998, 464–67).

The 1968 reform brought to the university shared governance by faculty members, students, and administrators; the replacement of professorial chairs by a departmental organization within the units and programs; a strong emphasis on redressing the structures of injustice embedded in Chilean society by education, research, and extension; and a great expansion of enrollments, from 27,000 in 1967 to almost 66,000 in 1973 (Brunner 1986, 31–40).

During the period of military rule (1973–90), shared governance was eliminated; academic units in the social sciences, humanities, and the arts were closed and their personnel dismissed; and enrollments shrank to 48,800 by 1980 (Brunner 1986, 49). The higher education reform of 1981 severed from UCH all of its regional branches, which were turned to small, independent regional universities. By the time democracy returned in 1990, UCH had 18,000 students, and the share of public funding in its budget had dropped to 37 percent. Tuition revenues, introduced in the early 1980s, were intended to make up the difference.

The restoration of democratic rule made it possible for faculty members to elect deans and a new rector, to normalize the governance of the institution, and to recover the academic momentum of earlier decades. However, consequences of the strain of previous years lingered, together with structural difficulties, making it difficult to adapt to changing environmental conditions.

Governance and Administration

Unlike all other public universities in Chile, UCH does not have a board of directors. The highest governing body is the university senate, the assembly of the rector, and 36 elected members of the university: 27 faculty members, seven students, and two administrative staff members—chosen by their peers. The senate's role is to define policy and set the strategic development plan of the university. Its functions include budget approval, sanctioning of university policy and regulations, creation or elimination of programs and academic units, and approval of indebtedness and sale of real estate.

Executive power at UCH is vested in the rector, the University Council, and the deans of the faculties. Members of the University Council are the rector, the provost, the deans, and two external councilors appointed by the president of Chile. For a public university, the weak presence of the government in the governance of UCH may appear striking, but from another perspective, it more or less corresponds to the equally feeble incidence of state involvement in university finances. In addition to its deliberative role in the regular conduct of the university, the council is also responsible for submitting to the University Senate the matters for senate consideration. The crucial role of the University Council in defining the budget creates a sort of institutionalized conflict of interest, which can only be checked by a tacit entente between deans in which historical funding allocations to faculties are not challenged. This pact deprives the university's administration of its most potent tool and often leads to deadlock.

The rector and the deans are elected by the professoriate. Faculties are variously composed of departments, centers, and schools. Department chairs are also elected, whereas the other heads of academic units are appointed by the dean. Deans govern with the assistance of a faculty council.

Administratively, UCH is an autonomous, public corporation. Its general statute is approved by an act of Congress, but within the limits of that statute and the general guidelines applicable to all units of the public administration, it is allowed to establish its own bylaws and organize itself freely. Unlike public universities elsewhere, state universities in Chile independently set tuition levels, define numbers and conditions for admission of students, create or eliminate programs, open or close campuses, and buy and sell real estate. Faculty members are civil servants, but are not subject to the regular civil-service personnel regime. Instead, the university defines for them a special labor regime. In contrast, administrative staff members are regulated by the general rules of the civil service.

Decentralization to the faculties is quite high at UCH; its members often conceptualize UCH as a federation of faculties. This feature, present since the inception of the university, is sustained by the fact that elected deans are accountable to the voting faculty, and not to the rector, and was reinforced by the drop in public funding, which forced academic units to generate their own revenue bases. As a consequence, the central administration often lacks sufficient political and financial clout to steer the university toward strategic goals.

University officials constantly decry the burden that public administration rules and procedures place on the ability of UCH to compete with private universities. Unlike private universities, it cannot, unless authorized by an act of Congress, offer monetary incentives for the voluntary retirement of its personnel, even if capable of such funding. Firing nonacademic staff members requires a trial-like inquiry into the alleged breach of duty or misconduct, a process with an uncertain result that can take months or years—so much so that hardly any boss bothers trying to remove ineffective workers. As a result, the administrative staff is bloated with unnecessary positions and carries the resulting financial burden. Additionally, numerous contracts and decisions of the authority require previous control of legality by the national comptroller's office. This is time consuming, deviates resources to bureaucratic maneuvering with no added value, and hampers UCH's reaction in the face of opportunities. Also, the university cannot incur debt for a term longer than the remaining period in office of the sitting president of Chile, unless authorized by an act of Congress. This rule is applicable to all entities in the public sector, meant to curb the temptation of a given administration to contract indebtedness that would need to be paid off by the next administration. It is a sound public finance rule, but is quite deleterious to the university, which must plan, at best, on four-year loans—the duration of a presidential period.

Finances

A dire legacy of the period of military rule was the inability of UCH to adjust salaries for inflation, and there had been hardly any investment in infrastructure. Pent-up expectations and demands from the academic community unraveled and had to be handled primarily through debt, given that the economic conditions of the university had not changed much after 1990. Continuous budget deficits caused indebtedness to triple from 1990 to 1997, reaching a point where servicing the debt was suffocating any attempt by the university to undertake strategic initiatives.

In 1998–99, the decision was reached to let nonperforming business units, such as the university press and bookstores, go bankrupt. Budgets for cultural extension in the performing arts were cut, and their units were required to break even financially. But these centrally defined measures were powerless to cut through the main engines of deficit—namely, salaries in the academic units. Therefore, a new budgeting model for UCH had to be agreed upon between the rector's management team and the deans, which sought to control the deficit, but at the cost of increasing decentralization. In effect, in 2004 faculties increased their share of the undergraduate student tuition revenues to 80 percent, from previous levels ranging from 33 to 55 percent, and were required to balance their budgets with these monies—plus the revenues from graduate tuition, research, and technical assistance. Deans were permitted to determine both enrollments and tuition levels—that is, quantity and price.

Faculties also receive the bulk of the public funding allocated to UCH, on the basis of historical distribution criteria. Efforts in the past decade to alter the allocation formula to recognize performance indicators have met with the resistance of the deans in the University Council and have failed.

Therefore, currently most university funding is either generated by the faculties or transferred from the central administration to the faculties, each of which has its own internal allocation mechanism. The capacity of the rector to use funding as a leverage to move the university toward corporate goals is thus greatly diminished. The rector cannot prevail over the deans, and changes can be attempted only after a great deal of persuasion and negotiation has taken place, if at all.

Financial decentralization has worked well for faculties capable of raising private funds, such as engineering, economics and business, and medicine. Also relatively better off are the faculties of basic science, with reliable access to the continuously growing public research grants and programs. The losers in this scheme of self-financing are the humanities, the social sciences, and the arts—with fewer opportunities in the market-place—and scholarly modes of production not fully validated by the nation's scientific establishment steeped in the habits and norms of the natural and exact disciplines. This problem goes beyond UCH: higher education in its entirety in Chile exhibits lagging development in the humanities, the social sciences, and the arts. In the market-dominant environment of the political economy of higher education in Chile, an injection of public funds appears to be the only solution to this problem. The second-best scenario would be for large universities such as UCH, which concentrates most of its potential in the humanities, the social sciences, and the arts, to redirect their discretionary resources to these fields. However, discretionary resources are scarce at UCH and are difficult to deploy in that manner for the governance reasons previously outlined.

Strategic Positioning and Goals

The university sees itself as a national leader but understands that global-ization, the knowledge society, and increasing competition with the pri-vate higher education sector demand from it greater attention to issues of management as they influence effectiveness and efficiency (UCH 2007, 12). In addition, in its latest accreditation report on UCH (2004), the National Accreditation Commission stressed as one of the challenges in the university's development the degree of heterogeneity across its academic units. Although some of these units are research-intensive cen-ters of creation and dissemination of new knowledge, others have made little progress beyond a basic teaching function served mostly by adjunct faculty members. Unchecked decentralization was suggested as a con-tributor to this state of affairs. The National Accreditation Commission also called into practice a better definition of specific development goals and indicators, as well as more instruments for monitoring and control. This lack of monitoring was observed by the National Accreditation Commission to reduce the efficiency and effectiveness of educational processes at UCH.

In turn, a self-study report, which served as a basis for accreditation, identified UCH's main strengths: (a) its strategic orientations in 1999, (b) the quality of its academic core, (c) the quality and increasing numbers of its undergraduate students, (d) the growing presence of accredited graduate programs (especially at the doctoral level), and (e) the rigorous processes of faculty evaluation and promotion. The report also identified the following major weaknesses: (a) outdated infrastructure and insufficient equipment to respond to the growth of the institution, (b) the aging of faculty members,[4] (c) public administration rules that prevent the university from responding with agility to external opportunities, (d) weak management information systems and indicators, (e) institutional funding that is unrelated to strategic priorities and is instead allocated internally according to purely historical criteria, and (f) a generalized lack of responsiveness by the academic community to the competitive conditions under which this university must operate. In short, the greater challenges to the development of the university appeared, from these accreditation results, to cluster around matters of governance, management, and funding rather than academics.

Shortly thereafter, UCH promulgated its 2006–10 strategic plan. The plan seeks to reinforce UCH's position as a national leader in education, with programs characterized by ideological pluralism and tightly aligned with the needs of Chile. Better selection, readiness assessment, and follow-up mechanisms for students are sought, as well as improved alumni relations. The university aspires to curb attrition and improve time-to-graduation indicators. A greater transition to graduate studies is also an objective, as are more English-language training, increased opportunities for general education, and more intensive use of information technologies. For graduate-level education, the goals are to expand the number of programs, especially doctorates, and make the programs a destination of choice for Latin Americans; to create pathways for continuing education opportunities; to foster nurturing relations with the business sector; to strengthen academic cadres; and to multiply opportunities for international exchange of students. In the area of research, UCH intends to increase research in the social sciences and the humanities, where it is less developed, and to pay greater attention to applied research and technological development, also a relatively less successful dimension of its performance to date. Adding young academic talent is a strategy, as is promoting interdisciplinary centers, projects, and programs.

A fundamental initiative to advance in the fulfillment of these goals has been the Plan of Institutional Improvement, an agreement between the government and UCH that will fund the measures the university must undertake to secure two essential management goals:

- The reform of the university's central administration structure so that the rector, the vice rectors, and other central officials are freed from management duties and can concentrate instead on policy making and monitoring, while management responsibilities are transferred to the campuses

• The introduction of a world-class information management system to run and monitor all activities and resources of the university, at all levels, in real time, and in an integrated platform

Academic Affairs

UCH recruits some of the best students in Chile, second only to PUC: 33 percent of the 2,000 applicants with the best scores in the national university entrance test choose to study at UCH. Surveys of business executives and human resources managers routinely place graduates of this university among those most sought by employers. UCH also employs some of the most talented faculty members in the country, especially in its professional schools and science departments. More than 40 percent of scholarships for doctoral studies in Chile are awarded to students in doctoral programs at UCH. The library system boasts 49 libraries, with some 3 million volumes and access to an electronic collection of more than 18,000 journals.

Yet the university is critical of the state of its educational programs. In its accreditation self-study report, UCH points to the lack of flexibility of study plans, exaggerated professional specialization to the detriment of a sound general education, extreme decentralization of curriculum design and delivery in dozens of schools with little common content and standards across curricula, and uneven quality of teaching. There appears to be little room for the exposure of students to multidisciplinary approaches, novel participatory methodologies, and use of information technologies in education. Hard data on retention, progression, performance of students and faculty members, and employability of graduates are fragmentary at best.

On the basis of this diagnosis, UCH has embarked upon a reform of its undergraduate education programs aimed at strengthening general studies, making professors more accountable for their teaching, increasing the use of technology to support the modernization of teaching methodologies, and fostering opportunities for continuing education after the first degree. All these issues will require improving the scope, timeliness, and reliability of the data on educational processes.

Research is strong in the natural and exact sciences and in some of the professional schools, such as engineering and medicine. UCH estimates that only about 340 of its full-time equivalent faculty members were actively involved in research in 2004 (UCH 2004, 127). Research foci are driven by the interests of individual researchers and their ability to attract external funding much more than by institutional priorities and budgets. As a result, the institution has little leverage to steer research toward the improvement of teaching, or toward technology transfer, or in any other strategic direction. This situation may also explain the paucity of science-based technology development at UCH, as measured by patents: only 14 national and international patents were granted to it prior to 2004. Since 2005, however, applications have seen a steep increase: before 2004, only 22 requests were presented, but from 2005 to 2008, there were 90 applications (UCH 2008, 24). However, applied research in the form of consulting and technical assistance to the government and industry is much more significant, representing a sizable portion of the operational revenue of UCH.

The presence of international students and faculty members is still weak at the university, as is generally the case throughout the country. Although UCH receives yearly about 1,400 international students, most of these are undergraduates coming for short study-abroad periods, while about 200 of the university's Chilean students travel annually to study overseas.

The Pontifical Catholic University of Chile

PUC was founded by the Archbishop of Santiago in 1888. The guiding inspiration of the new university was to educate professionals within the moral tradition of the Roman Catholic Church. Using funding provided by donors, PUC created its first study programs—law and mathematics—and soon added architecture and engineering.

In the 1920s, PUC was recognized by law as a "collaborator in the educational mission of the state" and granted a modest amount of public funding. State financial support for it was unstable for decades, becoming steadier in the 1950s and then reaching more than 80 percent of its revenues by 1970 (Levy 1986, 79–80).

PUC's teaching hospital began operating in the 1940s, and a decade later, the university was a pioneer in the development of television technology in Chile (Krebs, Muñoz, and Valdivieso 1994). Today, both the Health Care Network and the Channel 13 TVUC station are major affiliated enterprises of the university, responsible for a substantial part of its nonoperational revenues.

The university reform of 1968 gave new impetus to democratization of governance through participation of faculty members and students and to academic functions other than teaching. Numerous interdisciplinary centers and disciplinary institutes were created; a fund to finance research projects was instituted; and faculty numbers doubled from 1967 to 1970. In 1973, however, as happened at other universities, Chile's de facto government appointed a new rector for PUC, and the experiments in democratization and unbridled scholarship ended. Although PUC thereafter suffered its share of political intervention, the military government's attitude toward it is generally regarded as having been benign, compared to the treatment received by the other universities. The tenure of the retired admiral who served as rector was long and relatively independent of the government. The protection of PUC by the Catholic Church was certainly a factor, as were the influence of PUC faculty members and graduates in the military government, their support of PUC, and the largely oppositional role played by the institution's faculty members and students during the Socialist government of President Allende (1970–73).

In the mid-1980s the government and the Vatican agreed to the appointment of a civilian rector from within PUC. The new rector, who remained in office for 15 years, led the university along a path of self-sustained growth and development, which continues to this day. Although university leaders everywhere expected that the end of the Pinochet regime would give way to a reversal of its privatizing policies, PUC planned for a scenario of continuity of the funding scheme for higher education, introduced with the reforms of 1981. Moreover, the university's authorities saw in PUC's financial independence a form of protection against state intervention and a matter of loyalty to its Catholic roots and inspiration. The university's strategy was to plan for a zero-government-subsidy scenario, which required a sharp increase in tuition; between 1987 and 1992, tuition was raised 40 percent in real terms (Koljatic 1999, 350). However, because tuition-based resources would be insufficient, the university also required a policy of diversification of funding sources, incentives for faculties to raise their own revenues, efficiency gains in administrative and academic units, and better use of existing infrastructure through the expansion of undergraduate enrollments (Bernasconi 2005, 253). The teaching hospital was expanded and transformed into a profitable business unit, and the management of the TV station was professionalized and also approached as a profit center for the university. The size of the administrative staff was reduced by 20 percent, while the number and quality of the academic personnel were increased. These changes were made within the context of a strong policy of decentralization, meant to transfer decision making and operational responsibility from the central administration to the deans and—in the cases of its various ancillary units— like the hospital, the TV station, and the DUOC Professional Institute—to its executives (Koljatic 1999, 354; Bernasconi 2005, 257).

Today, PUC consistently ranks first in national rankings of universities published by media outlets. Globally, it places 1st in Chile, 4th in Latin America, and 241st worldwide in the Times Higher Education ranking, 2008 version. PUC enrolls about two-thirds of the top 100 students in the national university entrance test and more than half of the top 1,000 students. PUC produces one-quarter of Chile's scientific research. Seven of the research journals published by it are indexed by ISI (UCH has only three journals indexed). The number of articles published by PUC per year has grown from negligible in the early 1990s to more than 700 in 2007. In terms of articles published, doctorates conferred, and research grants obtained, PUC places second nationally, after UCH, but with a comfortable lead over third place.

As with UCH, all these positive developments have taken place as the university has come to rely increasingly on private sources of funding. Direct transfers from the government funded 95 percent of PUC's budget in 1973. By the mid-1980s, that source had dropped to 70 percent of revenues. In 1992, it represented 20 percent of income, and represents 11 percent today. However, between 1992 and 2007 total revenues experienced a threefold increase, as a result of PUC's success in harnessing private monies.

Becoming an internationally visible research university is an explicit strategic goal for PUC. It has selected 2038—its 150th anniversary—as the year when that goal will be achieved. In the following sections, the university's progress to date and remaining challenges toward world-class status are considered.

Governance and Administration

As a pontifical university, PUC's ultimate authority in matters of mission and legal structure is vested in the Roman Catholic Church, both at the Vatican level and the local (diocesan) level. The highest official is the great chancellor, ex officio the archbishop of Santiago. The rector, since 1968 a layperson, is appointed by the pope from a nonbinding and reserved list of candidates prepared by the archbishop of Santiago, based on the recommendation of a university search committee. Most members of the search committee are elected by votes of all the full and associate professors, and the great chancellor appoints the rest.

As with other Catholic universities in Chile, PUC does not have a board of trustees. The highest collegiate body is the Superior Council, composed of the rector and his leadership team, the deans, four academic members appointed by a group of two representatives per faculty unit, and two students representing the student government.

At PUC, faculty members' governance rights are expressed more strongly in their participation in faculty-level governing bodies than in the election of authorities. Faculty councils are elected by professors. Direct election of officials by faculty members takes place only at the departmental level. Deans are not elected, but chosen by search committees consisting of faculty-unit notables plus one representative of the rector.

The nonelectoral legitimacy of deans is relevant in the context of the decentralization model under which PUC operates. Deans are appointed with an eye to their management abilities and not only to their academic standing or popularity among their colleagues. Deans have ample autonomy to run their faculties, as long as they stay within centrally approved faculty budgets (Koljatic 1999, 354). The central administration defines general university policy; manages central funds for the support of research and the promotion of innovative teaching; creates and maintains cross-faculty and interdisciplinary centers and projects; ensures the observation of common standards across the university in matters such as the creation of new degree programs, quality of infrastructure, and information technology; and conducts the university's integrated planning and budgetary process, which will be explained further (Koljatic 1999, 354–55).

Finances

Just like UCH in the late 1990s, PUC faced a financial misalignment caused by the drop in public subsidization and the bloated and inefficient academic and administrative staffs. However, the crisis at PUC peaked 10 years earlier and was dealt with more radically than at UCH. As a private institution, PUC had more legal room to cut personnel, it faced less political interference to raising tuition, and it had the option of refinancing debt with long-term loans.

During the 1990s, PUC was also quite successful in creating a reliable revenue base from its affiliated enterprises, chiefly the TV channel and the medical centers, which together accounted for more than 60 percent of the total revenues of the university toward the end of that decade (Bernasconi 2005, 255). The business conglomerate associated with PUC now includes as major units—in addition to the health services networks and the TV station—several real estate ventures to exploit the university's valuable real estate assets and DICTUC (Dirección de Investigaciones Científicas y Tecnológicas de la Pontificia Universidad Católica de Chile), an engineering consulting, training, and testing firm created in the mid-1990s that has included significant activity (such as a business incubator) only in the past four years. In 2005, the holding company Empresas UC, was created to control and direct all for-profit entities affiliated with PUC. The idea was to separate the administration of these business ventures from the academic side of the university—while keeping the former accountable to the top leadership of the university, which is represented in the boards of the holding company and its various business units.

Budget allocations to faculties are based on PUC's five-year plans, and they take the form of yearly contracts between the central administration and the faculties. The faculties commit to certain projects and actions to advance the strategic goals of the institution, and the central administration commits the necessary funding. In addition, the continuity budget considers essential the salaries of personnel already hired and the budget for self-generated income, which is built upon the revenues faculties make from graduate and continuing education, overheads of research projects, and consulting and technical assistance.

Faculties retain for their own expenses only the self-generated income they produce, minus a 10 percent overhead to the central administration. Except for this self-generated income, all revenue in PUC is collected by the central administration and distributed to the faculties upon negotiated budgets. That is, undergraduate tuition fees, transfers from the public sector, and earnings of the central business units are allocated among the faculties without a priori distribution quotas. This funding structure gives the central administration at PUC, compared to that of UCH, considerably more budget leverage to project its plans and strategies. If a faculty needs incremental funding for new project initiatives, it must either persuade the central administration that those initiatives advance the university's development plan more than do others and thus merit central support, or get the additional funds from its self-generated income.

Strategic Positioning and Goals

The university's Catholic identity and mission to serve both Chile and the Catholic Church figure prominently in its strategic plan and other guiding statements. Its most recent plan, covering the 2005–10 period, considers this loyalty the bedrock of its tradition and future development.

Among the institution's strengths, the university notes the relatively long tenure of its rectors (just 10 in more than 120 years), which allows for long-term planning and follow through; the responsibility it has shown in managing its resources, especially in times of crisis; its capacity to innovate both in academic programs and in organizational features; and an institutional culture comparatively free from the politicization typical of universities in Latin America.

With its prestige, PUC seeks to transcend the confines of the Chilean higher education system and to project its influence throughout Latin America and the world, by transforming itself onto an internationally recognized research university over a period of two decades. This vision will require, according to the university's plan, efforts to renew curricula and program offerings; stronger research and doctoral programs; more intense internationalization; more influential outreach, community service, and public policy engagement; and development of academic and administrative staffs.

In the area of research and graduate programs, PUC realizes that its performance is uneven across faculties and that it needs to install or reinforce internationally competitive research groups in the social sciences, as it has done in the natural and exact sciences. For instance, although faculty members with a PhD constitute three-quarters or more of the full-time equivalent professoriate in the faculties of chemistry, physics, biology, and mathematics, they represent between one-half or one-third or even fewer of the academic staff members in the faculties of social science, business and economics, literature, education, law, communications, architecture, and the arts. The numbers of research grants, doctoral students, and publications are likewise higher in the natural and exact disciplines and in the applied sciences and technology.

The dimension of internationalization should, as envisioned in PUC's strategic plan, lead it to become the premier center for graduate studies in Latin America. This plan entails not only more exchange of students and faculty members and larger numbers of international hires, but also the establishment of global community standards in each discipline or profession by means, for instance, of international accreditation.

Finally, to make progress in all of these strategically relevant fronts, the university understands the key role of its professoriate, administrators, and staff members and the need to plan for financial sustainability through a diversified revenue structure and an efficient and effective use of those resources. PUC proposes to improve its methods for personnel recruitment, promotion, retention, compensation, development, evaluation, and retirement to ensure that it can select and keep the best talent. PUC not only stresses the importance of information technology for efficiency gains and confirms its adherence to a model of decentralized management, but also is better attuned to each faculty's strategic development plan, which is aligned to that of the institution.

Academic Affairs

In every dimension of development underlined in PUC's strategic plan, progress has occurred in the past few years. For instance, in the area of faculty development the university recently introduced a bold reform of its faculty regulations, which tightens requirements for faculty selection and promotion and makes evaluation more demanding, while giving the central administration more influence over these processes. Among the most significant changes in the new regulations is the requirement of all regular professors to perform both research and teaching, whereas faculty members who only teach, do research, or operate another single academic function are placed in the adjunct track. Achievements in both teaching and research are now conditions for promotion, although in the past either one sufficed. The doctorate, equivalent terminal degree, or internationally benchmarked equivalent competencies (for the arts, for instance) are now required for appointment in all regular ranks, although in the past a master's degree was enough for promotion to full professor.

Regarding internationalization, the university has been making steady progress in international accreditation of some of its programs. The business school is accredited by the Association to Advance Collegiate Schools of Business; engineering is accredited by the Accreditation Board for Engineering and Technology; architecture is accredited by the Royal Institute of British Architects; medicine is accredited under the Association of American Medical Colleges; and journalism is accredited by Accrediting Council on Education in Journalism and Mass Communications.

Research support at PUC has two basic challenges. The first challenge, for the natural and exact sciences, is to complement their successful basic science production with more business sector interaction to foster science-based innovation of economic relevance. The second challenge, for the humanities and the social sciences, is to establish them firmly in research, transcending the characteristic of professionalist schools to focus solely on knowledge accumulation and transmission. To support the research and development agenda, the university has organized business boards with its officials and executives representing the technology interests of industries (rather than individual firms) such as wineries, paper mills, fruit growers, mining companies, and energy companies. The idea is to provide a forum for business executives to discuss their production problems with the university, which will provide research-based solutions. For the social sciences and the humanities, in turn, the main strategy is to strengthen the research credentials and capacity of the faculty, a process that the new faculty regulations, detailed previously, should be able to support.

Conclusions

Chile's higher education system is an outlier in Latin America, in terms of funding structure and degree of privatization. Within this context, UCH and PUC are doing remarkably well in indicators of efficacy and efficiency—such as papers per researcher, public spending per student, and enrollment and graduation rates—compared with other top Latin American universities in Argentina, Brazil, and Mexico (see, for instance, data on scientific output of the Monterrey Institute of Technology, in chapter 9 of this book). Yet, the next stage of development of these two universities will demand greater government support and strategic involvement. For UCH, internal reforms are also a likely condition for takeoff, as will be explained further.

The University of Chile: The Road Ahead

Some of UCH's challenges emerge from public policy and will need government action if they are to be overcome. Such is the case with the paltry funding UCH receives from the state—insufficient by any measure to sustain a modern-day research institution—as clearly stated in a recent report on Chilean higher education issued by the Organisation for Economic Co-operation and Development.[5] A similar case involves administrative limitations and controls over the university, which drain from it the agility needed to respond to the demands and opportunities of a predominantly market environment.

But there are also obstacles within UCH, stemming chiefly from the heterogeneity across its 18 faculties and institutes in every dimension constituting the essence of a research university: faculty research credentials, fund-raising capacity, management skills, supportive governance, disposition to innovate, and links with the world outside. This variety in profiles and performance is the negative aspect of decentralization, otherwise a sound and possibly the only tenable strategy to manage a large and complex organization. But decentralization without checks and balances is a free-for-all approach, and in the case of UCH, the central administration—regardless of the legitimacy and capacity of the rectors and their teams—lacks effective instruments to steer the university toward its strategic goals. UCH is not completely devoid of such tools, because corrective measures are possible. But the tools available seem too blunt and politically costly to use regularly. For instance, the rector can order the reorganization of an academic unit and intervene in it. Under this exceptional regime, UCH can terminate the appointments of the faculty members affiliated with those units and can require them to reapply and submit to academic evaluation if they want their former jobs back. This process has been deployed twice in the past 10 years, first in the Faculty of Social Sciences and currently in the Institute of Public Affairs. However, such cataclysmic interventions obviously are not for the fainthearted or for the everyday management of a university.

The government, through regulation and funding, could become an ally for UCH in its transformation process. Revitalization programs for the humanities and the social sciences—which would inject about US$20 million within five years to UCH and would be subject to the accomplishment of predefined milestones and the meeting of agreed-upon productivity targets—are an encouraging example of this approach. Another model is the performance contract that will fund, with about US$7 million, the administrative reform of UCH, as described previously. On the regulation side, program accreditation has helped the university to clearly, publicly, and legitimately identify its problems and has put pressure on academic units to act upon these problems, shaking off from academe a mood of complacency that tends to befall those who perceive themselves as leaders.

These measures are promising but, unfortunately, are not sufficient. As UCH officials see their status—especially compared to PUC—in terms of funding, there appears to be little benefit to being a public university and great bureaucratic costs. In general, the government has shown little willingness to involve itself more heavily in the affairs of public universities, even in the face of rather open invitations by their rectors, who understand that a little loss of autonomy in exchange for leverage to promote change is not a poor bargain. The government is at fault here more than the university, which brings the analysis back to the issue of political economy of Chilean higher education with which this chapter opened. The fact that so much good has been accomplished within such a limited public investment is remarkable, but participating in the elite levels of universities internationally will require much more state participation.

The Pontifical Catholic University of Chile: The Road Ahead

PUC is one of a handful of private universities in Latin America to have successfully evolved a research profile. Other cases include a few Catholic universities located in the more prosperous states of Brazil and the Universidad de los Andes in Bogota, Colombia.

Yet PUC is no stranger to the kind of interinstitutional heterogeneity found also at UCH, as the 2004 accreditation report of PUC noted. Although some faculties have made significant progress toward the habits of academic work typical of a research university, other faculties continue to maintain a more traditional teaching profile.

These imbalances are shared by PUC with all universities in Chile. What sets PUC apart from the others is its successful negotiation of Chile's higher education environment and its resolution, satisfactory from its point of view, of the most fundamental issues of governance, administration, and financial sustainability that plague the development of the rest of Chile's universities, UCH among them. PUC has no pending issues with its owner, the Catholic Church, whereas public universities constantly bicker about the lack of guidance and support they receive from their owner, the state. PUC is not burdened by crippling debt (in fact, its annual debt obligations are one-sixth of those of UCH) and is more concerned with developing new sources of funding for growth than with balancing its budget. The governance and management structure of PUC provides a workable balance between faculty autonomy and central policy making and institutional steering. When centrifugal inertia has been required for equilibrium to be restored, PUC has been able to provide it, to which the 2008 adjustments in the Faculty Code attest.

Much of what PUC has been doing for the past 10 or 15 years can be articulated in the five process categories developed by Burton Clark to account for common features in innovative universities, first in Europe (Clark 1998) and later in other settings (Clark 2004).[6] In effect, the university has diversified its funding base to make up for the decrease in government support, tapping heavily into revenue from private sources other than tuition.

PUC has strengthened the influence of its "steering core" while maintaining an essentially decentralized structure. It has done so by keeping the ability of the center to direct funds to corporate priorities (which may come from the proposal of deans to advance from their faculties some strategic objective of the university) and by guarding the role of the center in maintaining consistent standards across faculties in the development of a professoriate appropriate to the university's strategic goals.

A "developmental periphery" (Clark 1998, 138–39) has emerged of business units grouped in Empresas UC and of research and development centers and technology transfer offices both in the faculties (DICTUC, in engineering) and in the central administration. The "stimulated heartland" of Clark (1998, 141–42) is not, in this case, composed of new faculties and departments that follow the entrepreneurial lead of new interdisciplinary centers and institutes, but instead involves the traditional academic units that turned entrepreneurial about 20 years ago when they were allowed to keep the revenues from their graduate and continuing education, consulting and technical assistance, and research overheads.

Finally, a culture of development through private resources is clearly institutionalized at PUC, as the result of a policy inaugurated in the mid-1980s of not expecting government funding to keep up with the growth of the university. Indeed, public-based funding for a private, religiously affiliated university is an anomaly in an international comparative perspective. Notwithstanding PUC's enormous contribution to the public good, it is not inconceivable that the government may choose to prefer concentrating its support on public universities in the future.

In its current state, PUC is well poised to achieve its goal of turning itself into an internationally recognized research university within the next 20 years, if it follows through with policies already deployed. Additional funding from the government would undoubtedly quicken the pace, but PUC seems to be hedging the odds of its development on the growing need of local industry to turn to knowledge to remain competitive.

The University of Chile and the Pontifical Catholic University of Chile: Common Patterns

Neither of these two universities has yet become a research university, if measured against the world-class standards of the most research-intensive universities in developed countries. However, UCH and PUC certainly qualify as research-oriented universities given their enormous progress in the past few decades to transcend a role centered only in teaching for professions, typical of the Latin American university. In this regard, they coincide and also concur in their aspirations to become internationally visible, research-intensive organizations, although the time frame and pathway to that goal are more clearly laid out at PUC. Compared to the rest of Chile's universities, and if one assumes that the country can support only two universities of their kind, it is these two institutions that today appear better able to eventually make the cut.

At both UCH and PUC, sectors of internationally connected excellence in research combine with schools traditionally centered in teaching of professions. Clusters of well-paid, full-time PhD recipients active in mainstream science production and technology transfer are found alongside groups of part-time instructors in other faculties who are active in the professions but removed from scholarship and do not make their living from their university salary. Research first began in the natural and exact sciences in the 1960s and then followed in the humanities. The social sciences, the arts, and the professions lagged by a full generation or two. However, scientists have the history, motivation, political leverage, and expertise to make public funding of research as well as university rules and policies work to their advantage. This situation gives rise to internal tensions between researchers and professional educators, in which the former—better placed and more active in university policy making—tend to prevail.

Scientific activity at UCH and PUC is driven much more by the research agenda of their scholars than by any strategic steering from the top. A better interaction between research and teaching and between basic and applied science does figure prominently in the agendas of UCH and PUC. Yet, examples of such synergies—such as PUC's new requirement that faculty promotion be decided on grounds of both teaching and research performance—remain more the exception than the rule.

Both universities lack a governance role for stakeholders, possibly a weakness from the perspective of forging enduring relationships with the communities they serve. However, there is an ample relationship with stakeholders at the level of the faculties, schools, centers, and programs— perhaps more tidily planned and organized at PUC. Additionally, the Catholic Church is a relevant stakeholder for that university. Although neither faculty members nor students there are required to be Catholic, top administrators are recruited from the faithful; even beyond that, they tend to coalesce into a rather culturally homogeneous cadre of likeminded people, limiting diversity at the top.

The distribution of power in both institutions can be characterized as bottom heavy, in the sense that most decisions are made at the level of the faculty unit and not at the institution's central level, let alone in the national government.[7] Yet, PUC is comparatively stronger at the center, in part a result of the cultural legacy of 80 years of Catholic Church–style authority and in part as an effect of the nonelectoral origin of the authorities. The rector at the university is ultimately an agent of the Church, not a delegate of the academic community, although he can enjoy the benefit of faculty support. The deans are appointed to help run the institution as well as to lead their faculties, whereas elected deans at UCH are responsible only for their faculties. The flip side of greater centralization in PUC is that if the rector leads in the wrong direction, the whole university suffers, whereas at UCH, it is more likely that some faculties will thrive while others will wane.

The government is largely absent from the strategic steering of universities in Chile. Public universities resent this state of abandonment and wait for the government to indicate what it expects from its universities. But the government is not revealing much, aside from stressing the importance to the Chilean economy of knowledge-based innovation and advanced human capital and supporting these declarations with money for research and development and for scholarships for graduate studies. This laissez-faire attitude, however, has the advantage of keeping universities free of unwelcome government mandates but, alas, not free of bureaucratic regulations. These regulations are particularly unfair because they apply to UCH (a public entity) and not to PUC (a private entity), regardless of the level of public funding each receives. One negative consequence of UCH's public sector constraints on its financial well-being is the life tenure of its nonacademic staff members. Although two decades ago PUC could shed any nonessential personnel it could no longer afford, UCH is burdened with such a group indefinitely. The numbers are revealing: UCH, slightly larger than PUC in number of students and faculty members, has an administrative staff 2.4 times larger than PUC's, not counting in both cases the nonacademic employees of hospitals and medical centers.

These differences between the two universities delineate the competitive conditions they face in their quest to develop as research-intensive universities. PUC's competitive conditions look more favorable. It has reached a steady state in crucial matters of organization, management, and finance, whereas UCH has not. UCH is still looking for the right balance between center and periphery, developing the relevant information systems to show what is occurring across the university, and demanding from the government what it terms a "new deal" of increased subsidization in exchange for serving the requirements of the government.

Notwithstanding numerous similarities between these two universities as they strive to become research-centered universities, together with several differences noted previously, one key difference stands out that derives from the nature of each institution: UCH has chosen the state as its strategic partner, whereas PUC opted for the private sector. This is not to say that UCH has no use for industry or for tuition-paying students or that

PUC can do away with public research funding. These current resources will not likely be taken away from them. The question concerns the arrival of the extra help needed to break the threshold of international distinction. UCH expects and demands that assistance will come from the public sector and mobilizes its political clout to make that happen. PUC, in turn, perhaps hopes that the government will step up to the task and lobbies just as intensely as UCH to make this happen, but at the same time cultivates its ties to industry.

In chapter 9 of this book, Francisco Marmolejo analyzes the "Mexican style" research university. It is likely that the two Chilean universities in this chapter will also evolve identities as research universities embedded in their local traditions and environments. In the Latin American tradition, research universities "Chilean style" will continue to heed the particular needs of professional training, with its sizable cadre of part-time instructors, along with knowledge production for its own sake. It is unlikely that research will trump teaching as the major function, but both UCH and PUC can aspire to embody an education process enhanced by faculty involvement in research. Graduate enrollments will continue to grow, but for many years they will not represent a majority of enrollments. Even with increased public-funding support, UCH and PUC will maintain a heavy reliance on private revenues and the extensive autonomy they enjoy today.

Notes

1. For more information on UCH's ISI-indexed publications, see Thomson Reuters Web of Knowledge.

2. In the Latin American tradition, derived from continental Europe, a *facultad* is the largest academic unit of which the university is composed. In the United States, it corresponds roughly to a school or college, centered on a profession or a discipline or group of epistemically germane disciplines.

3. For more information on PUC's ISI-indexed publications, see Thomson Reuters' Web of Knowledge.

4. The average age of faculty members at UCH is 48 years, compared to a national average for universities of 44.5 years, according to the SIES (Sistema de Información de la Educación Superior, or Higher Education Information System) database of the Ministry of Education of Chile (2008), http://www .sies.cl/.

5. In its report, the OECD recommends doubling public funding to higher education, not counting public investment and research and development, also well below OECD benchmarks (OECD 2009).

6. Indeed, PUC is one of the cases analyzed by Clark in his second book on entrepreneurial universities (Clark 2004, 110–21).

7. The ample autonomy of Chile's universities—private and public—to conduct their affairs is seldom found elsewhere. For contrast, see chapter 7 in this book.

References

Altbach, Philip G. 2007. "Empires of Knowledge and Development." In *World Class Worldwide: Transforming Research Universities in Asia and Latin America*, ed. Philip G. Altbach and Jorge Balán, 1–28. Baltimore: Johns Hopkins University Press.

Arriagada, Patricio. 1989. *Financiamiento de la educación superior en Chile 1960– 1988*. Santiago: FLACSO.

Bernasconi, Andrés. 2005. "University Entrepreneurship in a Developing Country: The Case of the P. Universidad Católica de Chile: 1985–2000." *Higher Education* 50 (2): 247–74.

———. 2007. "Are There Research Universities in Chile?" In *World Class Worldwide: Transforming Research Universities in Asia and Latin America*, ed. Philip G. Altbach and Jorge Balán, 234–59. Baltimore: Johns Hopkins University Press.

Brunner, José Joaquín. 1986. *Informe sobre la educación superior en Chile*. Santiago: FLACSO.

Clark, Burton R. 1998. *Creating Entrepreneurial Universities: Organizational Pathways of Transformation*. Oxford: Pergamon.

———. 2004. *Sustaining Change in Universities: Continuities in Case Studies and Concepts*. Maidenhead, U.K.: Open University Press.

CRUCH (Consejo de Rectores de las Universidades Chilenas). 1992. *Anuario Estadístico*. Santiago: CRUCH.

———. 1998. *Anuario Estadístico*. Santiago: CRUCH.

———. 2007. *Anuario Estadístico*. Santiago: CRUCH.

Hunneus, Carlos. 1988. *La Reforma Universitaria veinte años después*. Santiago: Corporación de Promoción Universitaria.

Koljatic, Matko. 1999. "Utilidades, orientación al mercado y descentralización: 'Nuevas' ideas para la administración universitaria en Latinoamérica." *Estudios Públicos* 73: 335–58.

Krebs, Ricardo, M. Angélica Muñoz, and Patricio Valdivieso. 1994. *Historia de la Pontificia Universidad Católica de Chile 1888–1988*. Santiago: Ediciones Universidad Católica de Chile.

Lehmann, Carla. 1990. "Antecedentes y tendencias en el sistema de financiamiento de la educación superior chilena." In *Financiamiento de la Educación Superior: Antecedentes y desafíos,* ed. Carla Lehmann, 31–78. Santiago: Centro de Estudios Públicos.

Levy, Daniel C. 1986. *Higher Education and the State in Latin America: Private Challenges to Public Dominance.* Chicago: University of Chicago Press.

Levy, Daniel C., and Andrés Bernasconi. 1998. "University of Chile." In *International Dictionary of University Histories,* ed. Carol Summerfield and Mary Elizabeth Devine, 464–67. Chicago: Fitzroy Dearborn.

Mellafe, Rolando, Antonia Rebolledo, and Mario Cárdenas. 1992. *Historia de la Universidad de Chile.* Santiago: Ediciones de la Universidad de Chile.

Ministry of Education, Chile. 2010. "Compendio Estadístico." Ministry of Education, Santiago. http://www.divesup.cl/index.php?option=com_content&view=article&id=94&Itemid=58.

OECD (Organization for Economic Cooperation and Development). 2009. *Tertiary Education in Chile: Reviews of National Policies for Education.* Paris: OECD.

Serrano, Sol. 1994. *Universidad y Nación: Chile en el siglo XIX.* Santiago: Editorial Universitaria.

UCH (Universidad de Chile). 2004. *Proyecto Piloto de Acreditación Institucional: Informe de la Universidad de Chile.* Santiago: Universidad de Chile.

———. 2007. *Plan de Mejoramiento Institucional.* Santiago: Universidad de Chile.

———. 2008. *Anuario 2008.* Santiago: Universidad de Chile.

CHAPTER 9

The Long Road toward Excellence in Mexico: The Monterrey Institute of Technology

Francisco Marmolejo

Following a trend common in other countries, in its recent history Mexico has aspired to develop some of its higher education institutions to the level of research-oriented peer universities of excellence. From a public sector standpoint, major efforts have been devoted to this pursuit by the National Autonomous University of Mexico[1] (Universidad Nacional Autónoma de México, or UNAM), while a private institution—the Technological Institute of Higher Education Studies of Monterrey (Instituto Tecnológico y de Estudios Superiores de Monterrey, or ITESM)[2]—has embarked on a similar yet distinct path of its own. Because many scholars have studied UNAM,[3] whereas ITESM has been less researched, this chapter attempts to contribute to a better understanding of ITESM, with special emphasis on its main campus located in the city of Monterrey.

In recent years, ITESM has developed a respectable reputation, both in Mexico and abroad, as a successful, high-quality institution. ITESM was founded in 1943 in the city of Monterrey, the capital of the northern state of Nuevo León. In recent years, it has expanded nationally through branch campuses established in most states of Mexico and internationally through remote cities in other countries, although it concentrates most of its research capabilities at its flagship campus in Monterrey. ITESM constitutes a good case for analysis considering its unique history, distinct characteristics, and officially expressed aspiration to become a top research university "*a la Mexicana.*" Using the model developed by Jamil Salmi (2009)—in which he identifies a number of features as being prevalent among world-class research universities—this chapter analyzes the main characteristics of ITESM to argue that, although ITESM is an institution in which many key operational components are concordant with these features, its overall research development is still small and is comparatively limited in scope. Most important among the features that Salmi identifies are the institution's ability to attract talent, its access to resources, and its governance model.

Many scholars argue that because of its unique history and evolution, ITESM is somewhat atypical of the structure of higher education in Mexico (Gacel-Ávila 2005; Ortega 1997; Rhoades et al. 2004). ITESM is sometimes criticized for its work, emphasis, and educational model; sometimes admired for its success on many fronts; sometimes associated with a hidden agenda of the Mexican business elite; and sometimes ignored in the development and implementation of educational policies in Mexico. Nevertheless, ITESM is also recognized as an important higher education institution in Latin America and sometimes acclaimed as the best institution in Mexico (Elizondo 2000; Gómez 1997).

Regarding research, it was not until 1996 that ITESM leadership officially declared its intention for ITESM to become a research university. Consequently, ITESM's race to excellence in research is still relatively new, and it has concentrated mostly on the Monterrey city campus. Certainly, as is analyzed in this chapter, the flagship campus of ITESM has embarked on a path to achieve the status of world-class research university but has yet to reach that goal.

A Brief Historical and Contextual Analysis of the System

In Mexico, public and private higher education subsectors have important differences, which should be analyzed to contextualize the history and role of ITESM. The Mexican higher education system is relatively young despite the fact that the Real y Pontificia Universidad de México, which is regarded as the first predecessor of UNAM, was established in 1553. UNAM adopted its current status as national and autonomous in 1929. Some years later, especially in the 1940s and 1950s, public state universities began to be established in various states of Mexico. In general, these institutions followed the academic and organizational model of UNAM, which consisted of traditional, professionally oriented academic programs, offered mostly at the undergraduate level and taught mostly by part-time teachers; the election of a rector and deans from among the faculty members; and the recruitment of both full- and part-time faculty members from among recent graduates and local professionals. In general, the governance model adopted by public universities in the country included an assembly-based authority—the University Council—composed of faculty members, students, and deans. The rapid proliferation of public universities was seen by some sectors—especially the influential Roman Catholic Church and the business organizations—as unbalanced or inadequate for the needs of their constituents. These sectors exercised pressure on the government that eventually led to the authorization to establish a few private universities, including ITESM in 1943.

The funding model for public institutions in most states was—and remains to this day—based on public subsidies that cover most of the operational costs. Public institutions, in general, charge very little—sometimes merely symbolic—tuition and fees to students regardless of their economic situation. In contrast, the operations of private universities such as ITESM are funded primarily by tuition and student fees, in addition to sales of services, private tax deductible donations, and even, in some cases, proceeds from the organization of lotteries. Private universities are not generally entitled to public funding, although a few exceptions are made in the case of competitively based financial support for certain specific research or consulting services, or where indirect participation is permitted in funded projects in partnership with public institutions.

During the second half of the 20th century, higher education in Mexico experienced tremendous growth. National enrollment in higher education rose from 30,000 in 1950 to almost 3 million in 2008. The demand was created by rapid population growth (from 25 million in 1950 to 103 million in 2005) and by rapid urbanization during that time. This demand was addressed by massive growth in the offering of academic programs, the expansion of enrollment in public universities, and the establishment of new types of postsecondary institutions. At the same time, especially in the 1990s, many private universities were established because of a relaxed authorization policy from government authorities more concerned with reducing demographic pressures on public higher education than with ensuring the quality of academic programs.

During the 1990s, the main emphasis of public higher education institutions was teaching, with a limited effort made on research. In addition, private universities in general were—and still are—dedicated mainly to the teaching of academic programs, especially low-cost programs requiring limited investment in laboratories and research infrastructure. Quality-assurance mechanisms applicable to both public and private universities were not in place until relatively recently. It was not until the final years of the 20th century and the first decade of the 21st century that a visible process of institutional differentiation emerged.

Today, most large, public flagship universities and a select number of advanced private universities place increased emphasis on research. At the same time—because a national framework for external peer-review-based accreditation of academic programs, applicable to both public and private institutions, has been progressively solidifying and gaining public acceptance (Malo and Fortes 2004)—institutions tend to differentiate themselves by having their programs accredited.

A variety of factors, including more refined government policies, national government decentralization, and institutional diversification, among others, have played a role in this recent developmental process (Brunner et al. 2006), which must be analyzed in the context of the overall evolution of Mexican society (Rubio 2006). The higher education system as a whole also has been influenced by the opening of the Mexican economy and society to the world, which has led to an increased awareness of international practices (Maldonado-Maldonado 2003) and more frequent contact with international research and academic networks.

In summary, the landscape of higher education in Mexico has changed rapidly in recent years in terms of its size, complexity, and diversification. In 2008, the entire national system comprised 2,442 higher education institutions, of which 843 were public and the remaining 1,599 were private. In those institutions, there were 2,814,871 students, of which 65.7 percent were enrolled in public institutions and 34.3 percent were enrolled in private institutions (Tuirán 2008). The growth of the system is impressive, considering that 60 years previously national enrollment in higher education totaled only about 30,000 students in just a few institutions, including ITESM, which had only about 200 students.

The Foundation and History of ITESM

In the analysis of the reasons for the creation and further development of ITESM, it becomes clear why the institution emerged in the state of

Nuevo León. Located in the northeastern part of Mexico, bordering the U.S. state of Texas, the state of Nuevo León is the major hub for trade between Mexico and the United States. Its capital city, Monterrey, is known as the financial capital of Mexico. In general, the most important regional competitiveness indexes consistently rank the state of Nuevo León as the second-most competitive in the country after the federal district (OECD 2009), and the third-largest state economy in Mexico.

Industrial activity in the state has been transitioning in recent years from a low-value-added manufacturing base toward a more sophisticated high-value-added base.[4] Also, living conditions in Nuevo León exceed average national levels.[5]

Nuevo León has a well-known entrepreneurial culture that spans generations. Its geographic location and the metropolitan character of the population are important factors explaining the economic development of the area, the entrepreneurial attitude of its business community, and the international approach of both the regional economy and the universities in Nuevo León (Mora, Marmolejo, and Pavlakovich 2006). Such factors played a major role in the foundation and further development of ITESM.

The state is served by 43 higher education institutions. The public Autonomous University of Nuevo León is the largest (third in the country with more than 120,000 students), followed by ITESM.

Founding of ITESM
The rapid industrialization of Nuevo León, in the early 1940s, required the availability of properly trained professionals and technicians and the consequent expansion of higher education institutions and their academic offerings. In consideration of the incipient development of public higher education institutions, a group of industrialists led by a prominent entrepreneur from the city of Monterrey, Eugenio Garza Sada, decided to establish a university that could respond directly to their needs.

Founded in 1943, ITESM is the fourth-oldest private university in Mexico. The founders of ITESM recognized that there was a shortage in the availability of engineers and middle managers for the region's companies (Elizondo 2003) and that the model of public universities being established at that time would not be adequate for their needs. A graduate of the Massachusetts Institute of Technology, Sada wanted to establish ITESM as a high-quality, private university in Mexico to prepare within the country "the type of professional required to build a modern Mexican society and economy" (Elizondo 2000). ITESM was officially established in 1943 as a private, nonprofit educational institution, independent of and unrelated to any political party or religious group.

ITESM began operations with 227 students and 14 faculty members in two undergraduate schools: industrial engineering and accounting (in addition to a high school). Similar private institutions already established in Mexico had emerged for different reasons: the Autonomous University of Guadalajara resulted from the confrontation between two antagonistic political groups in the state of Jalisco, the La Salle University was founded at the request of a Catholic religious group, and the University of the Americas was founded as a U.S.-style college in Mexico City. The only institution established in direct response to demands from the business sector was ITESM, in Monterrey. Although many important milestones exist in the history of ITESM (see annex 9A), some are more significant, especially in relation to ITESM's research aims, as explained further.

Establishing the ITESM Lottery, 1947

ITESM's initial operations were not without difficulties. Although initial funding was provided by a group of businesses supporting the newly created university, it became clear that to become a long-term sustainable initiative, ITESM would require other sources of support because of its lack of access to public funds. The founders of ITESM took advantage of a legal mechanism allowing nonprofit organizations to conduct lotteries— supervised by the federal government—with the purpose of supporting social causes. The ITESM lottery (currently known as *Sorteo Tec*) eventually became one of the most important sources of funds for the institution's growth. Currently, ITESM conducts three editions of its national lottery annually, in which it awards prizes totaling US$23 million per year. Each edition of the lottery has 450,000 tickets that, when sold, provide ITESM with gross revenues of US$29 million per edition, or US$97 million per year. Sorteo Tec provides resources for the awarding of scholarships and, more recently, for the establishment of endowed chairs, which have become key to supporting the research activities of the university.

Granting of U.S. Accreditation, 1950

In an environment in which laws and regulations for private universities were not clearly defined, the leadership of ITESM decided just a few years after its foundation to pursue accreditation in the U.S. system of higher education as a way to further legitimize its academic offerings. Obtaining accreditation in the United States was intended not only to gain international recognition, but also to mitigate the risk of potential changes in national regulations, which could jeopardize the institution. Because of geographic proximity, the Southern Association of Colleges and Schools—which accredits educational institutions in 11 U.S. states, including Texas—was approached with this unusual request. The process concluded in 1950, making ITESM the first institution outside the United States to obtain accreditation from any U.S. regional accrediting agency. Accreditation by the U.S. association not only gave ITESM a recognition of quality by a foreign educational entity, but also immersed the institution into a culture of peer-review evaluation and institutional effectiveness, which was uncommon at that time in Mexican higher education. This accreditation played an important role in further developments in the history and accomplishments of ITESM.

Granting of Special Autonomous Status from the Mexican Government, 1952

Worries about potential unexpected changes in government regulations dissipated nine years after ITESM's founding, when its leadership successfully negotiated with the federal government for the granting of a special status of Escuela Libre Universitaria (Free University School), which was formalized through a special presidential decree. This decree allowed ITESM to obtain the equivalent of an autonomous status because it gave the institution the authority to offer academic programs and award degrees under a special treatment from the Ministry of Education. Achieving the status of Free University School—attained by only a few other institutions in Mexico—gave ITESM enough flexibility to modify academic programs and to adapt to new educational and organizational models without the restrictions of other private institutions subject to standard government regulations.

Expansion to Other Cities, 1967

A few years after ITESM's founding, members of the business communities from other regions of Mexico, many of them ITESM graduates, began asking the authorities of the university to open branch campuses outside the city of Monterrey. In 1967, ITESM opened another campus—in the Pacific coastal city of Guaymas, Sonora. This campus was the beginning of a period of massive expansion to other Mexican cities, which was, in all cases, based on the concept of establishing a local board dedicated to obtaining funds for infrastructure and operational expenditures. ITESM assumed responsibility for establishing the campus's academic model and administering the institution. The model of shared responsibilities—the local business community responsible for funding and ITESM responsible for academic provision and management—proved a success in the opening of branch campuses, although maintaining the quality of academic programs presented a significant challenge. As of 2010, the ITESM system was composed of a vast network of 33 campuses and 25 sites established across Mexico, serving practically the entire country.

Offering of Doctoral Degrees, 1968

Twenty-five years after its founding, ITESM began offering its first doctoral degree: chemistry, with a specialty in organic chemistry. This ability to offer doctoral degrees was the first explicit effort by ITESM in its pursuit to become a research university. It opened up a new domain for ITESM, but also created challenges. This accomplishment was a result of a gradual consolidation of well-prepared faculty members who had begun offering a master's degree with a specialty in organic chemistry in 1961. The process for establishing a core faculty body under the umbrella of an academic department was later used as a basis for the creation of similar graduate programs at ITESM.

Formalization of ITESM as a System, 1986

The progressive and somewhat uncontrolled growth of ITESM branch campuses across the country, beginning in 1967, required ITESM authorities to better organize the institution's functioning. This organization led to the decision by ITESM's board to formalize the creation of a system with a rector general and a series of regional vice-presidencies.

Institutional Decision to Include Research as Part of Its Core Mission, 1996

Although research had been conducted at ITESM since the early years, it was not seen as central to the core functions of the university, especially because the institution had no access to public funding for research. However, the earlier creation of doctoral programs at the ITESM main campus created tensions between the functions of teaching and research that needed to be resolved if the institution wanted to retain well-qualified faculty members and graduate students interested in conducting research. Not until 1996, during the review of its strategic plan, did the institution decide to emphasize research as part of its core activities. This was a necessary step for ITESM to further consolidate its presence and prestige, both in the Mexican higher education landscape and abroad. It was made clear, however, that the major emphasis would be on applied research relevant to Mexico's development. This institutional decision would allow ITESM to seek access to research funding from companies and, occasionally, from the government. The decision also led ITESM as a system to begin a process of internal and informal differentiation, because not every ITESM campus would be capable of or interested in formally engaging in the research enterprise. Ten years later, only eight of the 33 campuses have been officially declared research oriented, and the remaining campuses are not expected to engage in research activities (Enriquez 2007).

Creation of Monterrey Tech Virtual University, 1997

In the early 1990s, the Southern Association of Colleges and Schools officially challenged the accreditation of ITESM, because of the fact that not all campuses had the same quality standards. Particularly, the association noted that a large number of faculty members lacked appropriate graduate credentials, a problem especially prevalent in ITESM branch campuses. Unable to resolve the problem by simply substituting faculty members, and facing the risk of losing its U.S. accreditation, ITESM authorities decided to massively upgrade the credentials of their faculty members—mostly by offering them distance-education graduate programs. This upgrade required heavily investing in infrastructure to offer distance-education-based graduate programs for faculty members located outside of Monterrey. At the same time, ITESM established partnerships with a variety of institutions, including the University of Texas at Austin and Carnegie Mellon University, both in the United States. These partnerships allowed faculty members from those institutions to teach master's degree and doctoral courses to ITESM faculty members from their own campuses using satellite videoconferencing. All investment in infrastructure and payment of instructors was covered by ITESM, and ITESM faculty members participating as students had to commit to working for the institution for at least the same amount of time in which they were students. At the same time, ITESM selected a large cadre of faculty members and funded them to study doctoral-degree programs at various universities, primarily in the United States. As a result, in a relatively short period of time ITESM complied with the accreditation requirements established by the Southern Association of Colleges and Schools, at the same time that it developed the expertise to teach distance-education-based programs. The newly acquired know-how was used to create the Virtual University (Cruz Limón 2001), which currently offers professional development and formal degree-seeking courses to more than 80,000 students annually at 1,270 sites in Mexico and 160 sites in 10 countries in Latin America (ITESM 2009c) using cutting-edge technology and standardized pedagogical methods.

Differentiation at ITESM between the Flagship Campus and the System

Located in the city of Monterrey, the flagship campus has the largest academic and research infrastructure of ITESM's 33-campus nationwide system. It also is the only campus with a School of Medicine. Although not officially recognized as such, the Monterrey campus is the focus of ITESM's attempts to raise its research profile, as reflected by the disproportionate devotion of resources and institutional efforts relative to the branch campuses.

At the system level, ITESM enrolled 96,649 in the academic year 2009/10, of which 25,705 attended the Monterrey campus, representing 27 percent of the total systemwide enrollment. The Monterrey campus has by far the largest enrollment within the system, followed by the campuses of Mexico City, the state of Mexico, and Guadalajara, respectively. Enrollment at the ITESM-Monterrey campus is distributed as follows: 17 percent in high school, 68 percent in undergraduate programs, and 14 percent in graduate programs. Part of the strategy aimed at strengthening the research capabilities of ITESM, specifically at the Monterrey campus, is evident when one compares the number of graduate students over time: from 2003 to 2009, overall enrollment at that campus grew 5.3 percent (in comparison to only 3.2 percent in the whole ITESM system). However, its high school enrollment decreased 13.8 percent, its undergraduate enrollment increased 4.5 percent, and its graduate enrollment had a spectacular increase of 50.4 percent in the same period (ITESM 2004a, 2010).

A similar pattern can be seen with ITESM's professoriate; in 2009, a total of 927 full-time faculty members represented a larger proportion of the total 2,102 faculty members at the Monterrey campus (44 percent) in comparison with that of the whole system (33 percent). In parallel, from 2003 to 2009, the number of full-time professors increased by 24 percent at the Monterrey campus, whereas the system as a whole experienced a decline of almost 2 percent. The Monterrey campus employs 32 percent of the total number of full-time faculty members in the ITESM system, whereas it employs only 20 percent of the total number of part-time faculty members (ITESM 2004a, 2010).

As expected, students at the ITESM-Monterrey campus have the greatest range of options in terms of academic programs. Of the 54 different undergraduate degrees offered systemwide, the Monterrey campus offers 43, distributed as follows: mechatronics and information technology (8); processes and manufacturing engineering (5); biotechnology, chemistry, and food sciences (6); architecture and civil engineering (2); biomedicine and health sciences (6); communications, literature, and media (3); international relations and political sciences (2); digital animation and design (2); economics and law (3); business (4); and accounting and finances (2). One important feature of ITESM is that 36 of the 43 undergraduate programs can be studied either in accordance with the traditional style of professionally oriented undergraduate studies prevalent in Mexico or in accordance with an internationally liberal arts–oriented curriculum, more similar to the type of bachelor's degree offered by U.S. institutions.

At the system level, ITESM offers 26 specialties, 46 master's degree programs, and 10 doctoral degree programs. Of those, the ITESM-Monterrey campus offers 15 specialties (2 in business, 12 in medicine, and 1 in engineering and architecture); 41 master's degree programs (2 in architecture, 6 in social sciences and humanities, 2 in communications and journalism, 2 in law, 4 in education, 14 in business administration, 1 in health, and 10 in information technology and electronics); and 7 doctoral degree programs in humanistic studies, public policy, social sciences, educational innovation, engineering sciences, administrative sciences, and information technology and communications.

In addition, in nine of its master's programs and one of its doctoral programs, the ITESM-Monterrey campus has double-degree agreements in place with a variety of peer institutions, mainly in the United States but also in Australia, Belgium, Canada, and France.

An important factor in strengthening the research profile of ITESM in general has been the financial and time-release support the institution has offered its faculty members to upgrade their academic credentials. In 2008, 11.1 percent of ITESM faculty members at the system level were also enrolled as students in a master's or doctoral program. The number of faculty members in training is smaller at the ITESM-Monterrey campus (5.6 percent) than the overall numbers at the system level, mainly because the flagship campus has been more successful in attracting faculty members who already have the appropriate credentials, whereas the other campuses must rely more on their own faculty members to achieve similar goals, by supporting the faculty members' pursuit of graduate education. This support is frequently accomplished by enrolling faculty members in

ITESM's own programs, either in a traditional classroom setting or through its Virtual University. In both cases, in consideration of the accreditation standards established initially by the Southern Association of Colleges and Schools and more recently by the Mexican accrediting agencies, a great majority of ITESM's faculty members hold an advanced degree. The proportion of faculty members with advanced degrees at ITESM is much higher than the average in the Mexican higher education system overall. At the ITESM-Monterrey campus in 2008, 95.7 percent of undergraduate courses were taught by faculty members holding a doctorate or master's degree, and 83.5 percent of graduate courses were taught by faculty members holding a doctorate degree (ITESM 2010).

Accreditation at ITESM and Support of Its Research

The accreditation system in Mexico is relatively recent. For many years, private institutions were required only to have official authorization awarded by the Ministry of Education, and subsequently to obtain further specific authorization for the offering of each academic program. As previously indicated, ITESM obtained a special status from the federal government in 1952 that allowed the institution greater flexibility in the development and subsequent authorization of its academic programs. In addition, since 1950 ITESM has pursued and obtained institutional accreditation in the United States from the Southern Association of Colleges and Schools. Such accreditation was reaffirmed for a further 10 years in 2008. ITESM is one of only seven higher education institutions outside the United States with accreditation granted by the association, of which four are in Mexico, although ITESM is the only one outside the United States accredited to offer four or more doctoral degree programs (SACS 2009).

The criteria for eligibility and consequent accreditation by the Southern Association of Colleges and Schools have helped ITESM over the years to develop an organizational culture and practices permeated by the concepts of self-evaluation, quality assurance, and institutional effectiveness. The experience gained during the accreditation process also forced the institution to develop innovative solutions to challenges related to meeting the association's standards, illustrated most clearly by ITESM's massive project of upgrading faculty credentials to retain its institutional accreditation.

The experience gained in accreditation not only helped ITESM during its internal process of development, but also had a consequent effect on other higher education institutions in Mexico because it helped engage the Mexican Federation of Private Universities in developing and implementing a Mexican-style institutional accreditation system in 1996. ITESM was among the first institutions to obtain this federation's accreditation in 1997, and ITESM's accreditation was reaffirmed in 2009 for a further 10 years.

Also, in response to the recent importance assumed by the Mexican Council for the Accreditation of Higher Education—established in 2000 as an umbrella accrediting agency in charge of developing standards and granting authorization to 26 independent, discipline-based accrediting agencies—ITESM has attained or is in the process of attaining accreditation for all eligible academic programs. In addition, some of its academic programs being offered in the Monterrey city campus have been granted accreditation by foreign agencies in a manner similar to the institutional accreditation granted by the Southern Association of Colleges and Schools. Such is the case of accreditations obtained by ITESM from the Association to Advance Collegiate Schools of Business for programs in business, from the Accreditation Board for Engineering and Technology for programs in engineering, and from the Latin American Council for Accreditation of Education in Journalism for programs in journalism.

Finally, at the graduate level, an important indicator of the quality of academic offerings in Mexico is a program's inclusion by the National Science and Technology Council in the National Program for Quality Graduate Programs, which is attained after an extensive and strict peer-based quality review. This recognition becomes especially important because students enrolled in programs included in this national program are eligible to receive a full, publicly funded scholarship from the National Science and Technology Council covering their tuition and cost of living. As of 2009, ITESM as a system had 40 of its 56 graduate programs included in the national program. Regarding its doctoral offerings, ITESM-Monterrey campus has had four of its seven programs included in this prestigious roster (CONACYT 2009a).

Fostering or Hindering the Research Enterprise?

Traditionally, research in higher education institutions is organized through a central office reporting either to the president of the institution or to the vice president for academic programs. That is not precisely the case at the ITESM-Monterrey campus, where paradoxically such a function does not even exist formally within the organizational structure.

The organizational structure of ITESM has been greatly influenced by the business orientation of its founders (Enriquez 2007). Such an approach is reflected in having a relatively simple, flat, and flexible hierarchical structure uncommon to a typical higher education institution.

At the system level, the highest executive authority of the institution is the rector general, who is appointed by the Board of Trustees. Internally, the management of the institution is distributed in four regional rectories. The largest of the four regions, in terms of enrollment, is the region in which the flagship campus of Monterrey city is located. On each campus, the highest executive authority is vested in the campus rector (officially known as director general), who reports to the corresponding regional rector. A campus rector usually has four staff offices in charge of academic affairs, business services and outreach, social and student development, and high school programs. In the case of the ITESM-Monterrey campus, the deans of the four schools report to the rector, and each of their sections is organized into academic divisions and graduate schools. Within each of the deanships, a variety of research centers are located.

General research policies and procedures are managed at the system level through the office of the vice rector for academic development and research, to which an Office of Graduate Programs and Research reports. The location of the ITESM system headquarters at the ITESM-Monterrey campus facilitates communication and synergy from the campus to the central office, but at the same time is perceived as a disadvantage at other campuses interested in pursuing research, such as those in Guadalajara and Mexico City.

ITESM's authorities insist on the importance of having a flexible organizational structure (ITESM 2010). However, such flexibility is reflected in the fact that such structure is frequently changed, according to perceived emerging needs and opportunities. Although it could be argued that flexibility is an important institutional strength, at the same time it could also be seen as a weakness. Because the corresponding higher executive authority appoints all individuals in leadership positions, one can observe entire units at the campus or system level suddenly being transferred, merged, expanded, or shut down. Consequently, academic or administrative executives of the institution are subject to constant changes in roles and location.

Governance

Salmi (2009, 28) indicates that one of the three main features of a world-class research university is the existence of a governance model "that encourages strategic vision, innovation, and flexibility." In this regard, the governance model at ITESM seems to follow Salmi's characterization. Long-term stability in the governing leadership of the institution has been crucial in the development of ITESM. Since its founding more than 60 years ago, ITESM has had only three board presidents and only three rectors. The current outgoing rector, Rafael Rangel-Sostmann, a main architect of ITESM's rise as a leading institution, has been in place since 1985.

ITESM follows a governance model in which external stakeholders are organized on a Board of Trustees and assume the key authority and appoint the key administrators. In contrast, most public higher education institutions in Mexico have a governance model with limited involvement from outside individuals and with high-level decision-making roles of faculty members and students.

ITESM's Board of Trustees has the authority to designate the rector general of the institution through its Executive Council and to approve the general budget, the offering of academic programs, and the awarding of degrees. Membership on the board is approved by the voting members. The board is currently composed of 49 individuals, most of them well-known businesspeople and benefactors of the institution.

Within the institution, each regional rector and the three system vice-rectors are appointed by the Executive Council of the board on the basis of a proposal made by the rector general of the ITESM system. The rector general also designates the rector for each of the campuses in consultation with the respective regional rector. Deans of schools are appointed by the respective rector at the campus level.

Regarding faculty governance, in each of the regional rectories there is an Academic Senate comprising the regional rector, who presides; a rector for each of the campuses; and professors serving in the capacity of "senators," elected by peers according to the rule of one senator for every 30 full- and half-time faculty members. The Academic Senate is responsible for defining academic policies and regulations regarding academic programs, admissions, equivalencies of studies, evaluation of students, sanctioning of students, awarding of degrees, academic requirements for professorships, sabbaticals, and recognitions for outstanding students and faculty members (ITESM 2004b). In addition, each campus has a Faculty Assembly that serves as a forum for consultation and submission of academic initiatives to be considered by the regional Academic Senate.

At the student level, ITESM's Federation of Students serves as a forum for the representation of students. However, it does not formally participate in the governance of the institution.

Finances

ITESM's financial model represents an inspiring case—a private institution that, officially, does not receive direct funding from the government. ITESM's funding base comes mostly from tuition and fees paid by students, revenues generated by a massive lottery, contract services, and donations from private individuals and companies. Physical infrastructure among the different campuses has been constructed and maintained, mainly as a result of capital campaigns targeting local donors and resources obtained from the national lotteries. The director general at the campus level is responsible for ensuring that the finances of the campus stay sound.

ITESM is an expensive institution that draws from the middle- and upper-level brackets of Mexican society. A highly sophisticated and well-managed financial system allows it to offer need-based scholarships and loans to a large number of its own students.

Although ITESM's highly publicized financial independence from the government is overemphasized, in practice the institution has managed in a number of ways to gain access to government funds originally designed for public institutions, although these funds are not as significant as the core funding obtained from traditional sources. Unfortunately, limited public information about the institution's finances prompts speculation about the level of financial stability of ITESM and the real support that it receives from government.

Recognizing that the issue of public funding is highly sensitive, ITESM's leadership has gradually been able to successfully lobby government agencies to extend some of their programs—originally designed for public institutions—in favor of ITESM. For instance, all students enrolled in graduate academic programs that are positively evaluated by the National Science and Technology Council receive a public scholarship covering living expenses and full tuition and fees, which is directly transferred to the institution. The scholarship program originally was designed for high-quality graduate programs offered in public institutions, but when ITESM subjected its program to the same strict evaluation as performed by the council, the council had no choice but to offer the same benefit to ITESM students. It would be very difficult for ITESM graduate programs approved by the National Science and Technology Council to survive without the indirect public support, because enrollment would be reduced dramatically without it.

Another indirect fiscal benefit to ITESM lies in tax policy. Like other nonprofit institutions and all public universities, ITESM does not pay revenue taxes, even in the case of the lottery, and is allowed to receive tax-deductible donations from private donors and companies.

An additional source of public financing comes from the sale of consulting services to government entities at various levels. For example, ITESM frequently conducts the periodic competitiveness and strategic-planning studies of state and municipal governments.

Finally, ITESM can compete for science and technology innovation funds made available in recent years by government agencies at federal and state levels. It also has indirect access to some small grant programs for international student exchanges.

Becoming a Research University: Why, Who, and How?

The research policy and related programs established by ITESM's leadership and implemented at the campus level have resulted in a more significant presence of the institution in the research arena. The flagship campus in Monterrey has in particular attained a more prominent international stature in research circles related to its fields of expertise.

The ITESM research model constitutes a unique approach to research by concentrating its efforts in a more focused and narrowed scope and by supporting research mostly through private funds. This approach has resulted in a series of intended consequences in terms of external effects, internal allocation of resources, and creation of interdisciplinary research groups, as well as an important increase in scientific production. At the same time, this approach has been associated with some unintended consequences, such as the marginalization of research topics not considered priorities by the institution, a further stratification of campuses within the system, and, in some respects, the reduced freedom for faculty members in their independent pursuit of research topics. The long-term effect of this research approach remains to be seen.

For the first 30 years of its existence, ITESM did not consider research an important component of its activities. This attitude was, in a way, concordant with events happening in public higher education. Finally, in 1970 the Mexican government recognized the need to support research by creating the National Science and Technology Council. However, because only public universities were eligible to use that council's funds to conduct research, ventures into research by the great majority of private universities, including ITESM, were marginal.

Thereafter, in 1985, while conducting a periodic review of ITESM's mission, its leadership concurred that the aspirations of becoming an institution of international stature and greater relevance in the national context would require a deeper involvement in research. Accordingly, ITESM's 1985–95 mission explicitly considered the importance of research (Enriquez 2007). Still, at that time the inclusion of research in the institutional mission was mostly an aspiration. Subsequent reviews of ITESM's institutional mission in 1996 and 2005 further reaffirmed and clarified the meaning of this institutional commitment to research. In the 2005 review of ITESM's mission—which established the long-term plan for the institution's direction until 2015—the rhetoric about the emphasis on research became associated with concrete institutional strategies aimed at supporting it.

This aspiration is not exempt from internal challenges and perceived inequalities, because not every ITESM campus considers the research aspiration viable. Authorities argue that efforts are made to compensate for intra-institutional differences and capabilities (ITESM 2009a), and in fact, the gap between the ITESM-Monterrey campus and the rest of the ITESM system seems to be gradually narrowing. Nevertheless, in practice, substantial differences remain. In such a diverse educational system as that of ITESM, with a few large campuses and many small ones, the pursuit of excellence in research creates intra-institutional stratification. ITESM's decentralized developmental and financial model, as well as the decision-making process established by the central administration, makes it difficult for small campuses to engage in research, whereas the larger campuses find this aspiration more legitimate, suitable, and achievable. As an example, campuses such as those in the cities of San Luis Potosí and Saltillo each have only one faculty member recognized by the selective National Roster of Researchers[6] (1.5 percent of all full-time faculty members), whereas the Monterrey campus has 122 members in the National Roster of Researchers (13 percent). This intra-institutional differentiation is exacerbated by the fact that the criteria for the institutional support of research consider that the support should be directly linked to officially defined research priorities and that it should show the potential to become self-sufficient or externally funded.

The ITESM research strategy has the following components: (a) making ITESM competitive in attracting researchers; (b) conducting research only in areas identified as institutional priorities; (c) supporting the creation of centers and institutes; (d) financially supporting a series of research-endowed chairs; (e) linking the work of researchers to specific metrics of success including long-term sustainability, patents, scientific publications, and so forth; and (f) connecting research to the development of new companies and industrial applications. These various elements of the overall strategy are explained later.

Attracting and Retaining Talented Researchers

Concordant with Salmi (2009), ITESM has made significant efforts to attract and retain faculty members with adequate credentials. At the Monterrey campus, faculty members with an interest in research will be added to the roster. A good indicator of this goal is provided by the membership of faculty members in the previously mentioned National Roster of Researchers.[7]

As expected, the ITESM-Monterrey campus has been the most successful at having faculty members who belong to the National Roster of Researchers. At the beginning of the 2009 academic year, 122 faculty members representing 13 percent of the total full-time faculty body were members of the National Roster of Researchers.[8] The campus with the next-highest number of members is the Mexico City campus with 36, followed by the state of Mexico campus with 33, and the Guadalajara campus with only 9 (ITESM 2009b). By far, the ITESM system has the highest number of faculty members belonging to the National Roster of Researchers of any private university in Mexico. However, in comparison with public universities, ITESM still lags significantly. For instance, the Autonomous University of Nuevo León, also located in the city of Monterrey, had in the same period 373 researchers who were members of the National Roster of Researchers (UANL 2009), more than three times the number at the ITESM-Monterrey campus.

Conducting Research in Areas Identified as Institutional Priorities

The ITESM authorities have decided to orient their research work toward the following areas: biotechnology and food sciences, health, manufacturing and design, mechatronics, nanotechnology, information and communications technology, sustainable development, entrepreneurship, government, social sciences, humanities, regional development, social development, and education. As a focus on those areas, a series of research centers have been created and linked to identified needs and areas of opportunity existing at the local level and based on the research capabilities of ITESM.

At the ITESM-Monterrey campus, 21 research centers are in operation (see table 9.1). The strategy of focusing only on a few selected areas has both positive and negative implications. On the one hand, the strategy helps the institution to focus its resources; on the other hand, the strategy concurrently limits creativity and innovation in other areas.

Research-Endowed Chairs

A very effective strategy has been the awarding of financial support for researchers doing work in the institution's priority areas. From its own funds, ITESM created the endowed chairs (*Cátedra*) program as a way to foster the creation of research groups supported with seed money. Each Cátedra is approved by a special committee on the basis of a proposal submitted by a group of researchers. Once approved, the Cátedra receives seed funds for a total amount of US$150,000 over five years, during which time additional external funding of equivalent or higher value should be pursued. Each Cátedra is evaluated on an annual basis as a requirement for renewal. Although several Cátedras have been cancelled for not accomplishing expected goals, most have been able to obtain additional funds either from companies or from national or international foundations. It is noticeable that the amount allocated to a Cátedra is significantly lower than the amount usually assigned to a similar type of endowed chair at the

Table 9.1   ITESM: Research Centers, Endowed Chairs, and Produced Patents, 2009

Priority area	ITESM-Monterrey campus			Other ITESM campuses		
	Research centers	Endowed chairs	Patents[a]	Research centers	Endowed chairs	Patents[a]
Biotechnology and food	1	11	4	0	1	0
Health	1	7	1	0	0	0
Manufacturing and design	2	20	31	15	38	0
Information and communications technology	4	23	3	0	7	1
Sustainable development	3	6	0	0	0	0
Business	3	25	1	9	21	0
Government	7	35	0	0	44	0
Education	0	4	0	1	0	0
TOTAL	21	131	40	25	111	1

Source: ITESM 2009a.
a. Includes patents published and awarded from 1998 to 2009.

international level. For instance, in the United States, US$1 million is considered standard for an endowed chair, and is usually allocated to one individual and for a longer period of time relative to ITESM's program. In contrast, ITESM's program has had less financial support, and the funds are allocated to a group of researchers rather than to an individual and are granted for a shorter period of time. Today, ITESM authorities view the Cátedras as the most important stimulator of research productivity, because previous attempts were not as effective. As in other cases, the flagship campus of ITESM has the largest share of Cátedras within the system. At the beginning of academic year 2009, the Monterrey campus had 131 of the 242 Cátedras established in the system.

Establishing Metrics for Research Productivity

Concordant with ITESM's institutional culture and the primary narrowed interest in applied science and technology, a series of specific indicators of research productivity was established and has been constantly monitored. Information by campus, area of research priority, or researcher is available through a public searchable online database. At ITESM, the data show that the overall research productivity of its researchers has significantly increased from 2004 to 2008 at the ITESM-Monterrey campus as well as at the system level (see table 9.2), although numbers remain relatively low in comparison with international standards. For instance, in 2008 faculty members at the ITESM-Monterrey campus published 193 indexed articles equivalent to 0.22 papers per full-time faculty member. However, in some areas the growth has been spectacular, as in the publishing of patents. By 2009, researchers from the ITESM-Monterrey campus had 40 patents published and awarded (see table 9.1). Most of the patents were awarded in the area of manufacturing and design, although more promising and lucrative patents were awarded in the areas of biotechnology and health. A good example of the disparities existing in research infrastructure and productivity among the ITESM campuses is the fact that only one patent has been published and awarded outside of the Monterrey campus. The growth in productivity at the ITESM-Monterrey campus is a direct result of the Cátedras, which included specific metrics of success in terms of patents and long-term financial self-sustainability.

Connecting Research with the Development
of New Companies or Applications

The overall research strategy of ITESM is complemented by a parallel program aimed at connecting the institution more effectively with the

Table 9.2   ITESM: Selected Indicators of Scientific Production, 2004–08

	ITESM system		Monterrey campus		Monterrey campus versus the ITESM system	
					2004	2008
Indicator	2004	2008	2004	2008	(%)	(%)
Articles in indexed journals	239	328	162	193	68	59
Articles in proceedings	626	516	524	291	84	56
Books (authoring and coauthoring)	47	109	30	39	64	36
Chapters in books	86	205	62	104	72	51
Newspaper editorials	173	412	139	129	80	31
Peer-reviewed articles	49	92	27	49	55	53
Dissemination of information articles	137	117	113	65	82	56
Invited lecturers	530	502	450	215	85	43
Paper presentations	341	679	246	377	72	56
Technical reports	212	138	178	89	84	64
Organizers of conferences	98	151	82	71	84	47
Members of program committees	59	54	51	29	86	54
Reviewers of conference/journal	109	200	101	121	93	61
Participation in editorial committees	47	47	40	22	85	47
Journal editors	17	27	12	6	71	22
Theses	331	337	285	173	86	51

Source: Author's calculations based on ITESM research database, http://www.itesm.edu/wps/portal?WCM_GLOBAL_CONTEXT=/wps/wcm/connect/ITESMv2/Tecnol%C3%B3gico+de+Monterrey/Investigaci%C3%B3n/.

business sector by fostering a more efficient transfer of knowledge from researchers to companies and vice versa. ITESM's leadership has devoted significant efforts to establishing a vast network of business incubators (helping the start-up of new high-tech, intermediate technology and of socially oriented microcompanies), business accelerators (supporting small and medium-size companies to help them explore new international markets), and technological parks (hosting companies at specialized facilities). In addition, a Technological Transfer and Intellectual Property Center based at ITESM-Guadalajara provides guidance to researchers from all campuses and companies. Results have been spectacular if one considers that in 2009, the ITESM system had 87 business incubators, 14 business accelerators, and 11 technological parks in operation.

The Academic Model of ITESM: Panacea or Predicament?

ITESM has focused most of its work not only on its renewed interest in research, but also on the further development of a standardized teaching-learning model (the ITESM educational model) that has gradually been implemented at all campuses and in all academic programs and their respective courses. By the end of the 2008/09 academic cycle, 74 percent of the courses at the ITESM-Monterrey campus were being taught in accordance with this educational model (ITESM 2009a).

Briefly, the ITESM educational model is based on the assumptions that graduates must be competitive on the global stage, must be strongly formed in terms of ethical values, must be highly committed to social responsibility, must be able to work in a multicultural environment, and must have an entrepreneurial spirit. It also assumes that students must be prepared to become leaders in their communities. The model considers professors as facilitators and guides of the more active and self-managed learning style of these students. It relies heavily on the use of information technology and tends to be highly standardized across all ITESM campuses.

The strategy of ITESM's educational model's strategy is based on three pillars: (a) standardization of the syllabus across the system, which helps the institution develop at a faster rate and use common pedagogical materials to support all courses of similar content—taking advantage of the combined expertise of faculty members and of economies of scale; (b) standardization of a technological platform developed in-house and used systemwide to support the teaching-learning process; and (c) a mandatory massive awareness and training program for all faculty members in the use of the technological platform for the development of materials, teaching of content, and learning assessment. Such an extensive standardization of ways and means of teaching has allowed ITESM to make rapid advances in implementing its educational model.

ITESM as an Elitist Institution

In terms of tuition, ITESM is an expensive institution that only a small proportion of Mexican families can afford. ITESM is among the top three most-expensive institutions in Mexico. Although no public information is available regarding the socioeconomic status of the families of ITESM students, it is widely accepted in Mexico that the majority of ITESM students belong to families with higher socioeconomic status and arrive, in most cases, from costly private high schools. This situation poses an important challenge to an institution that, according to its academic model, intends to prepare students with both a world-class sense of competitiveness and a local consciousness and awareness of social responsibility.

ITESM has made important efforts to become more affordable to students with limited financial resources. In fact, 35 percent of undergraduate students and 53 percent of graduate students at ITESM have some type of scholarship or loan provided to them from its own funds (ITESM 2009a). Nevertheless, a generalized public perception remains that ITESM is elitist and tends to distance graduates from the problems faced by the majority of the population. Efforts to reduce this negative perception seem to be in place, but it may take a number of years to change these long-standing perceptions.

At the same time, ITESM has taken advantage of certain legal education regulations in Mexico, adapting them to support the goals of its academic model in matters related to fostering more social awareness in its students. Such is the case of the mandatory performance of 480 hours of social service, which, under federal law, is a requirement for all undergraduate students in Mexico. A distortion of this regulation, typical in Mexican higher education, has been either to confound this program with an opportunity for professional training or to have participating students serve as cheap labor for office work. Recognizing that one public perception about ITESM students and graduates is their detachment from real problems being faced by the community, the ITESM academic model insists on the need to make students socially responsible and to cultivate in them a sense of solidarity with underserved sectors of the population. This set of factors led ITESM leadership to establish an internal regulation to ensure that all students from all academic programs dedicate at least 50 percent of these mandatory social-service hours to activities expressly designed to contribute to social causes and to gain awareness of social issues. However, there is still substantial room for improvement in this area.

International Dimensions at ITESM

ITESM has gained a solid reputation as an internationally oriented institution. Many of the strategies envisioned by experts in the field of international education are already present at ITESM. These strategies include the acquisition of complete fluency in at least a second language for all students, the inclusion of an international dimension in the curriculum of all academic programs, the attraction of international students and scholars, the sending of a large number of students and scholars abroad, the offering of dual-degree options for students, the development of international teams for research, and the performance of research with an international dimension. In all these areas, ITESM has made important advances.

As expected, the flagship Monterrey campus is the campus most involved in the internationalization strategy of the institution. For instance, in the case of international student mobility, 11 percent of the ITESM-Monterrey campus students were studying abroad in 2008, while the campus hosted international students equivalent to a significant 8 percent of its total enrollment. At the graduate level, 6 percent of the ITESM-Monterrey campus students went abroad in 2008, and 15 percent of its graduate enrollment was composed of international students. Regarding faculty mobility, during the same period 24 percent of the ITESM-Monterrey campus faculty members went abroad while the campus hosted international faculty members equivalent to 12 percent of its total faculty roster (ITESM 2009a).

In addition, ITESM has developed a variety of dual-degree and mutual credit–recognition programs with international peer institutions. It also has more than 400 international memoranda of understanding in place and maintains formal international offices in numerous countries. In summary, ITESM has a relatively comprehensive approach in its international strategy, which has helped substantially to raise its international reputation.

Conclusion

As shown in this examination of ITESM, the university has taken a number of steps toward becoming a world-class research university, at least on its Monterrey campus. Overall, the greatest challenge for ITESM is how to reconcile the desire to become a world-class research university, which is evident in the flagship campus, with the distant realities faced by the small campuses.

In general, ITESM partially exhibits the features outlined by Salmi (2009) in his description of a world-class university. These include the capacity to attract a high concentration of talented faculty members and students, the availability of abundant resources, and the presence of a visionary governance model.

Much of ITESM's progress has been due to the uniqueness and agility of its academic and organizational model, which has permitted the institution to advance at a much more rapid pace than would be possible at other, more traditional universities. Undoubtedly, such an academic and organizational model has resulted historically from its unique governance approach. At the same time, such uniqueness has caused ITESM to become somewhat isolated from the rest of the Mexican higher education system.

Regarding the availability of financial resources, the case of ITESM is significantly different from the one found in many countries, where the desire to have world-class research universities is supported by a strong commitment from the government. In contrast, ITESM's growth has been financed mostly by charging high tuition to students, relying on contributions from donors, and maintaining a lucrative lottery. Such an approach, although successful in sustaining the development of the institution, may not be enough to support higher levels of investment in the research infrastructure necessary to sustain the status of a world-class research university. Attempts by the ITESM leadership to obtain additional resources from the government are always limited by the fact that ITESM is not a public institution and by the general perception prevalent in Mexico that ITESM is an elitist institution serving primarily the better-off sector of society.

If one considers the limited availability of resources devoted to supporting the research ambitions of ITESM, its research model—which focuses on a relatively restricted number of areas of specialization and mostly on areas of applied research—has initially yielded some promising results. However, this limited set of priorities could become the principal liability to the further progress of the institution toward its long-term goal of research excellence by limiting the institution's flexibility.

As expected, ITESM has shown a strong capacity to attract talented faculty members and students to its flagship campus, whereas the results have been more mixed systemwide. This trend is reflected in both the membership of faculty in the National Roster of Researchers and ITESM's level of internationalization. The institution's Monterrey campus will continue to benefit from its geographic position, especially if it can further build working partnerships with other institutions of higher education in the region, especially the public Autonomous University of Nuevo León. Nevertheless, there is no question that ITESM plays, and will continue to play, a very prominent role in higher education in Mexico. ITESM's flagship campus also will likely continue to strive toward international recognition as a competent research university. The path for development adopted over the years by ITESM makes a unique case that must continue to be studied—to draw significant lessons that could be useful in other regional contexts. The solution "a la Mexicana" adopted by ITESM constitutes a relevant subject for further analysis.

Annex 9A   ITESM: A Brief History

Year	Event
1943	ITESM is founded in the city of Monterrey.
1947	The Monterrey campus is inaugurated. Eight graduates receive the first degrees in chemical engineering. The ITESM lottery is begun.
1950	ITESM is accredited in the United States by the Southern Association of Colleges and Schools.
1952	ITESM is granted special status at Escuela Libre Universitaria by the Presidential Decree published on July 24, 1952.
1963	The first graduate degree is awarded, with the specialty in chemical sciences. ITESM begins using computers and television-based instructional programs.
1967	The first campus outside of Monterrey is inaugurated in the city of Guaymas, Sonora.
1968	ITESM begins offering its first doctoral degree, in chemistry with specialty in organic chemistry.
1978	ITESM inaugurates its School of Medicine in the city of Monterrey.
1986	The mission statement is defined as preparing professionals with the highest levels of excellence in their respective areas of specialty. New general bylaws are adopted allowing for the official creation of the ITESM system as a multicampus system with a new organizational structure.
1986	ITESM is connected to BITNET, the international communications network among universities. The telecommunications satellite network is inaugurated.
1996	ITESM defines its 2005 mission: to prepare professionals committed to the development of their communities while internationally competitive in their respective fields of study. ITESM also defines in its mission the goal of conducting research and extension relevant to the development of the country.
1997	The Virtual University is established. ITESM begins offering distance-education-based programs in Mexico and Latin America. A redesign of its teaching-learning model is established.
1998	The social service of students in all academic programs becomes mandatory to benefit the community.
2004	The Mexican Council of Accreditation of Higher Education recognizes ITESM as the institution of higher education with the most academic programs either accredited or recognized as being quality programs by accrediting agencies in Mexico.
2005	A new ITESM vision is defined for the 2005–15 period, as well as the corresponding mission and strategies.

Source: Adapted from ITESM website, http://www.itesm.edu/wps/portal?WCM_GLOBAL_CONTEXT=/ITESMv2/ Tecnol%C3%B3gico+de+Monterrey/Con%C3%B3cenos/Qu%C3%A9+es+el+Tecnol%C3%B3gico+de+Monterrey/ Historia.

Notes

1. Undoubtedly, the best-known case of a Mexican research-oriented university of excellence is that of UNAM, which is self-defined as the highest house of studies of Mexico. UNAM, because of its history, scope, and size, is the largest university in the country—by all relevant indicators—and arguably the most

important one. Its prominence is reflected by its inclusion among the top universities in the world in widely known rankings such as those of Shanghai Jiao Tong University's Academic Ranking of World Universities and the Times Higher Education.

2. Although its official name is Instituto Tecnológico y de Estudios Superiores de Monterrey (ITESM), it is most widely known in Spanish as Tecnológico de Monterrey and in English as Monterrey Institute of Technology or just Monterrey Tech. For the purposes of this chapter, it will be referred as ITESM.

3. The case of UNAM has been analyzed by several authors who have reviewed different aspects of its role in shaping life, politics, and society in contemporary Mexico (Camp 1984); the limitations and constraints of its academic model (Malo 2007); its unique governance and structure (Ordorika 2003); and the challenges faced by this mega-university of 280,000 students. In contrast, ITESM's history and characteristics have been studied only on a limited basis.

4. The Technology Achievement Index of the state was measured by the United Nations as 0.476, still below that registered by the United States (0.733) but also higher than average for Mexico (0.389). This composite index focuses on how well the country or a region as a whole is participating in the creation and use of technology (Desai et al. 2002).

5. A good example is that state income per capita (US$15,437 in 2008) exceeds the national average by 87 percent and that life expectancy (75 years for men and 79 for women) also exceeds average national levels. In fact, the state has the second-lowest level of poverty in Mexico, one of the least-marginalized populations in the country, and a better income distribution than most of Mexico, as measured by the Gini coefficient (OECD 2009).

6. For a detailed description of the National Roster of Researchers, see footnote 7.

7. This program was created in 1984 by the Mexican government originally with the goal of compensating for the low salaries at public universities as a way to retain qualified researchers. Over the years, membership in the National Roster of Researchers has come to symbolize the quality and prestige of the scientific contributions of the researcher. A member receives not only prestige and recognition by peers, but also additional tax-free income given by the government directly to the researcher (CONACYT 2009b). However, this program funds only researchers working in public institutions, a fact that puts ITESM at a disadvantage when it attempts to attract or retain talented researchers. This situation has led ITESM's authorities to establish a policy under which its researchers can apply to the National Roster of Researchers for membership; but once the recognition is awarded, the monetary compensation owed to the researcher is paid by ITESM from its own funds.

8. Members of the National Roster of Researchers at the ITESM-Monterrey campus were distributed as follows: 27 candidates; 72 national researchers at level 1; 18 at level 2; and 5 at level 3 (the most prestigious level for active researchers).

References

Brunner, José. J., Paulo Santiago, Carmen Garcia Guadilla, Johann Gerlach, and Léa Velho. 2006. *OECD Thematic Review of Tertiary Education: Mexico Country Note.* Paris: Organisation for Economic Co-operation and Development.

Camp, Roderic A. 1984. *The Making of a Government: Political Leaders in Modern Mexico.* Tucson, AZ: University of Arizona Press.

CONACYT (National Science and Technology Council). 2009a. *Programa Nacional de Posgrados de Calidad: Posgrados vigentes 2009.* Mexico City: Consejo Nacional de Ciencia y Tecnología. http://www.conacyt.mx/Calidad/ Listado_PNPC_2009.pdf. Accessed September 20, 2009.

———. 2009b. *Sistema Nacional de Investigadores—SNI.* Mexico: Consejo Nacional de Ciencia y Tecnología. http://www.conacyt.gob.mx/SNI/Index_ SNI.html. Accessed September 28, 2009.

Cruz Limón, Carlos. 2001. "The Virtual University: Customized Education in a Nutshell." In *Technology Enhanced Learning: Opportunities for Change,* ed. Paul S. Goodman, 183–201. Mahwah, NJ: Lawrence Erlbaum Associates.

Desai, Meghnad, Sakiko Fukuda-Parr, Claes Johansson, and Francisco Sagasti. 2002. "Measuring the Technology Achievement of Nations and the Capacity to Participate in the Network Age." *Journal of Human Development* 3 (1): 95–122. http://unpan1.un.org/intradoc/groups/public/documents/APCITY/ UNPAN014340.pdf.

Elizondo, Ricardo. 2000. *Setenta veces siete.* Monterrey, Mexico: Ediciones Castillo.

———. 2003. *Cauce y corriente: Sesenta Aniversario.* Monterrey, Mexico: Instituto Tecnológico y de Estudios Superiores de Monterrey.

Enriquez, Juan C. 2007. "In the Pursuit of Becoming a Research University." PhD dissertation, University of Arizona, Tucson.

Gacel-Ávila, Jocelyne. 2005. "Internationalization of Higher Education in Mexico." In *Higher Education in Latin America: The International Dimension,* ed. Hans de Wit, Isabel Christina Jaramillo, Jocelyne Gacel-Ávila, and Jane Knight, 239–80. Washington, DC: World Bank.

Gómez J, Horacio. 1997. *Desde Adentro.* Monterrey, Mexico: CNCA/CND.

ITESM (Instituto Tecnológico y de Estudios Superiores de Monterrey). 2004a. *Informe Anual 2003.* Monterrey, Mexico: ITESM.

————. 2004b. *Reglamento Interno de la Facultad.* Mexico City: ITESM Campus Ciudad de México.

————. 2009a. *Informe Anual 2008.* Monterrey, Mexico: ITESM.

————. 2009b. "SNIs por Campus." ITESM, Monterrey, Mexico. http://www .itesm.edu/wps/portal?WCM_GLOBAL_CONTEXT=/ITESMv2/Tecnol% C3%B3gico+de+Monterrey/Investigaci%C3%B3n/Investigadores/ SNIs+por+campus. Accessed September 28, 2009.

————. 2009c. "Universidad Virtual: Quienes somos?" ITESM, Monterrey, Mexico. http://www.ruv.itesm.mx/portal/principal/qs/. Accessed September 15, 2009.

————. 2010. *Informe Anual 2009.* Monterrey, Mexico: ITESM.

Maldonado-Maldonado, Alma. 2003. "Investigación sobre organismos internacionales a partir de 1990 en México." In *La investigación educativa en México. 'Sujetos, actores y procesos de formación,' formación para la investigación. Los académicos en México, actores y organizaciones,* ed. Patricia Ducoing, 363–412. Mexico City: COMIE-SEP-CESU.

Malo, Salvador. 2007. "The Role of Research Universities in Mexico: A Change of Paradigm." In *World Class Worldwide: Transforming Research Universities in Asia and Latin America,* ed. Philip G. Altbach and Jorge Balán, 216–33. Baltimore: Johns Hopkins University Press.

Malo, Salvador, and Mauricio Fortes. 2004. "An Assessment of Peer Review Evaluation of Academic Programmes in Mexico." *Tertiary Education and Management* 10: 307–17.

Mora, José G., Francisco Marmolejo, and Vera Pavlakovich. 2006. *Supporting the Contribution of Higher Education Institutions to Regional Development: Nuevo León Peer Review Report.* Paris: Organisation for Economic Co-operation and Development.

OECD (Organisation for Economic Co-operation and Development). 2009. *OECD Reviews of Regional Innovation: 15 Mexican States.* Paris: OECD.

Ordorika, Imanol. 2003. *Power and Politics in University Governance: Organization and Change at the Universidad Nacional Autónoma de Mexico.* New York: RoutledgeFalmer.

Ortega, Sylvia. 1997. "Mexico." In *Transforming Higher Education: Views from Leaders Around the World,* ed. Madeleine Green, 173–93. Washington: Oryx Press, American Council on Education.

Rhoades, Gary, Alma Maldonado-Maldonado, Imanol Ordorika, and Martín Velazquez. 2004. "Imagining Alternatives to Global, Corporate, New Economy Academic Capitalism." *Policy Futures in Education* 2 (2): 316–29.

Rubio, Julio. 2006. *La política educativa y la educación superior en México. 1995– 2006: Un balance.* Mexico City: Fondo de Cultura Económica.

SACS (Southern Association of Colleges and Schools). 2009. "Extraterritorial Accreditation." SACS, Decatur, GA. http://www.sacscoc.org/ Accessed September 28, 2009.

Salmi, Jamil. 2009. *The Challenge of Establishing World-Class Universities.* Washington, DC: The World Bank.

Tuirán, Rodolfo. 2008. *La educación superior en México: Perspectivas para su desarrollo y financiamiento.* Proceedings, Segundo Foro Parlamentario de Consulta sobre Educación Media Superior, Superior, Ciencia, Tecnología e Innovación. Mexico City: SEP.

UANL (Autonomous University of Nuevo León). 2009. "Profesores/Investigadores de la UANL pertenecientes al Sistema Nacional de Investigadores 2009." http://www.uanl.mx/investigacion/investigadores/archivos/sni_2009.pdf. Accessed September 28, 2009.

CHAPTER 10

Establishing a New Research University: The Higher School of Economics, the Russian Federation

Isak Froumin

A number of different university rankings have been established in the Russian Federation. If one looks at the top 10 institutions (among 1,600 Russian universities) in these rankings, the lists are almost identical. Moreover, they do not change over time, with one exception. One university that did not exist 20 years ago now appears in the top 10 in all rankings—the Higher School of Economics (HSE). How could a small school established in 1992 (the year of the lowest Russian gross domestic product [GDP] per capita in many years) become a member of the elite group of the best Russian universities?

Another question arises regarding new publications by HSE professors in international journals and at their presentations at major international conferences. How could a group of economists and sociologists trained in a Soviet-style Marxian political economy and in such an exotic discipline as "scientific communism," under tight ideological control,

Author's Note: The author expresses his gratitude to the founders of HSE—Evgeny Yasin and Yaroslav Kuzminov—for their interviews and comments and to professors Martin Carnoy and Maria Yudkevich for their advice.

manage to enter a global arena of socioeconomic research? This accomplishment is even more surprising because the notion of a research university was exotic in the Soviet Union. Almost all research was concentrated at the Academy of Sciences. How did HSE fight the stereotypes and develop a culture that made research and teaching equally important for professors?

Where Does HSE Stand Today?

At present, HSE is the largest socioeconomic research and education center in eastern Europe. It operates in four Russian cities: Moscow, Nizhny Novgorod, Perm, and Saint Petersburg. It has 20 faculties (which include 120 departments), more than 120 continuing education programs (including master of business administration, doctor of business administration, and electronic master of business administration), and 21 research institutes. It has a team of 1,500 faculty members and 500 research staff members. HSE has more than 16,000 full-time students and 21,000 students in continuing education programs. Today it offers courses in almost all humanities, social sciences, economics, computer science, and mathematics. The university's reputation is confirmed by the fact that the average score of the national university entrance exam at HSE was the third highest in Russia in 2009.

Innovative curricular and pedagogical features of HSE include extended fundamental teaching of mathematics, philosophy, economics, sociology, and law; a system of research and development laboratories to help students develop the practical skills needed for productive research and analytical work; use of anticorruption technologies, including monitoring of students' work on the basis of written tests, and an antiplagiarism system.

HSE has developed strong links with leading European universities, including Humboldt University and Erasmus University, among others. In partnership with these universities, HSE offers 12 dual-degree bachelor's, master's, and PhD programs (with an annual enrollment of 350 students). It also offers a number of joint courses with foreign universities (often taught through video or Internet conferences). HSE has student exchange programs with more than 30 foreign universities (mostly in Western Europe). Together with the London School of Economics and Political Science, HSE has established the International College of Economics and Finance. This college awards two diplomas at the undergraduate and graduate levels: one by HSE and one by the London School of Economics and Political Science. However, the scale of internationalization is too small to allow HSE to participate effectively in the global exchange of talents and ideas.

HSE contributed to the development of Russia's new socioeconomic science almost from scratch. Today, university researchers and students carry out more than 200 research and analytical projects a year, worth over Rub 850 million. In research and development costs per faculty member (US$21,900), HSE is not only eight times ahead of the average Russian university (US$2,800), but also ranks higher than central and eastern European universities, almost matching the average level of German universities (US$25,000).

In 2007, HSE researchers published as many as 300 monographs and textbooks and 2,000 academic papers. HSE also leads Russian universities and research centers in international academic publications on socioeconomic studies. However, compared to leading foreign universities, the number of articles published by HSE researchers in international peer-reviewed journals is relatively small. The majority of professors still look at the national community of scholars as their target audience.

Academic research at HSE focuses primarily on the theoretical foundations underpinning effective modernization of the Russian economy and society, building on contemporary institutional economics and economic sociology. This focus helps HSE keep its strong position in Russia and receive additional funding from the government and private sector.

University researchers provided critical input into policy development in different areas: modernizing education and health care, advancing public administration and civil service reform, boosting competitiveness of Russia's economy and advancing the tools for a dynamic industry policy, reviewing prospects for effective policy making in innovations, improving government statistics (since 2002), and other issues.

Background to the Establishment of a New University

To understand the driving forces of the emergence of a new university, one must consider the history of HSE in the context of changes in social sciences and economics in Russia and in the Russian system of higher education. Three aspects highlight the story of the development of the university. One is the entry of a new participant into a crowded and competitive higher education market. Another is the transformation of a small school into a large university with strong ambitions to become a world-class research university. The third is the development of an organizational identity.

HSE systematically adopted and developed the main characteristics of the "emerging global model of the research university" in the specific Russian context (Altbach and Balán 2007; Froumin and Salmi 2007; Mohrman, Ma, and Baker 2008).

Following the research on newcomers in different markets (Geroski, Gilbert, and Jacquemin 1990; Pehrsson 2009) and on competition between universities (Del Rey 2001; Clark 2004), the chapter discusses the barriers to entry into higher education markets as a tool for understanding the strategic behavior of HSE.

For data collection, 20 interviews were conducted with the members of the current university management team and those who founded the university. The HSE institutional research unit provided the data about enrollment, graduation, and research activities. This unit also provided the results of different surveys conducted among students, professors, and alumni over the past 15 years.

For the reconstruction of the market niches and strategic choices, statistics data and interviews were used. The interviewees included leaders from other universities (HSE competitors) and former and recent officials from the Russian Ministry of Education.

In addition, the analysis of media sources was used to reconstruct the transformation of HSE's self-image and its central mission within the changing environment.

Building New Social Sciences and Economics

In the late 1980s, the Soviet Union found itself in the emerging market economy with a lack of intellectual tools to understand this transition. This situation became even more striking in the early 1990s; 1992 was the first year of independence for the Russian Federation. Drastic political and economic reforms needed sound research support. There was little capacity for forecasts and reviews of outcomes of ambitious socioeconomic development projects. With the exception of a couple of small groups of scholars in the Russian Academy of Science, nobody was familiar with modern economics as a science.

Setting for HSE

The roots of this situation start in the intellectual history of the Soviet Union. In the beginning of the 20th century (and even in the first postrevolutionary years), Russia produced quite a few bright scholars in humanities and social sciences. These scholars became the first target of the Bolsheviks. Some of them were executed or imprisoned; some were exiled abroad. The so-called iron curtain was erected between the Soviet economics and social sciences and the international mainstream. Thus, the Soviet academia had invented its own scholarship in these fields. Some of these areas of research (mainly the area related to construction of mathematical models) were of a high world-class level (it is not incidental that a Soviet scholar, Leonid V. Kantorovich, won the Nobel Prize in economics). But most areas either were dogmatic and ideological in their nature or reflected the reality of the planned state economy in the totalitarian state (Makasheva 2007). This science did not require internationally created knowledge.

Perestroika gave birth to new areas in social sciences, some of which had not existed before. Ironically, the first learning materials for teaching modern political science were published in 1989 in an official journal called *Moscow University Journal of Scientific Communism*. Often the modernization of social sciences was limited to simply renaming the Soviet textbooks. According to observers,

> The rapid change in benchmarks and the ideological (and sometimes political) pressure for the fastest possible assimilation of the Western standards in economic science led to schism and disorientation within the academic community. (Avtonomov et al. 2002, 4)

In 1992, a new Russian government led by Egor Gaidar conducted large-scale privatization and other economic reforms. Members of the government understood that the existing research and educational institutions were not capable of addressing these issues. Institutions, such as Moscow State University, resisted the changes; they became strongholds of political and economic conservatism. It became clear that reforms of existing universities would lead to huge political costs. A decision was then made to develop new Russian economic science by establishing a new university where advanced research would be combined with training of specialists in modern economics.

Therefore, the new organization was defined as an actor in the area of social sciences and economics, shaped as a competitor to existing relevant institutes rather than as a partner in solidarity with them. It was a process of imitation (of foreign science) and a negative reflection of the past and the recent practices of the existing Russian universities. At the same time, government requirements forcibly and clearly expressed to the new institute (HSE) must be examined. The positive identity was largely defined by the direct order of the state. The HSE case demonstrates that the government had a vision and directed this young university to provide theoretical support and human capacity during the transition period. The government influenced a particular direction of the new university's research and development activities. In the early 1990s, the government was not interested in basic research, but in knowledge support for ongoing social and economic reforms. This demand shaped the research profile of the university, making the research at HSE more applied and policy oriented.

Building an Educational Institute's Identity

Where did HSE receive its teaching model? Whereas the development of HSE's identity in research was done from scratch, a similar process in teaching was far more complicated given a common belief that Soviet higher education was of high quality and should form a model for young universities.

In 1992, Russia experienced one of the most difficult periods in its economic history, and thus, it was the worst year to establish a research university. The education system (all public at that time) suffered dramatically. Consolidated public expenditures on education dropped to 3.57 percent of GDP—the lowest level between 1980 and 1998 (Gokhberg, Mindeli, and Rosovetskaya 2002, 51). Public expenditures on higher education declined 39 percent in 1992 (Morgan, Kniazev, and Kulikova 2004). As a result, salaries of university professors became much lower than those in other sectors. The universities did not have access to public funding even to cover utility costs (Boldov et al. 2002). The state tried to reduce the number of places for new students in the existing universities. The relevant number of students in higher education in Soviet Russia was 219 students per 10,000 people in 1980. The third year of perestroika (1989) initiated the significant decline of this figure to 192. The lowest level was reached in 1993—171 (Bezglasnaya 2001).

Partly in response to the economic difficulties and as an element of movement to a capitalist economy, a new law on education (1992) made it possible to establish private higher education institutions (Shishikin 2007). By 2000, their numbers had increased to 358 from only 78 in 1994 (Klyachko 2002). Simultaneously, public universities earned the legal right to charge "additional" tuition fees to students. As a result, Russian public universities found themselves with two distinctive groups of students: those who were paying tuition fees and those who received their education free (budget-funded places). The number of fee-paying students in Russian public universities grew from 1.9 percent of the total student body to 45.0 percent in 2000 (Bezglasnaya 2001). Universities realized that they had to enter market competition to survive (Kolesnikov, Kucher, and Turchenko 2005). It was a critical moment in the marketization and commodification of the higher education system in Russia (Canaan and Shumar 2008). Mainly as the result of skyrocketing fee-based enrollments, Russia experienced a rapid growth in enrollments from the end of the 1990s up to 327 students per 10,000 people in 2000 (Gokhberg, Mindeli, and Rosovetskaya 2002, 12).

The overall growth in enrollment was particularly impressive in social and economic disciplines. In 1992, 33 (public only) higher education institutions specialized in economics and law. Their number expanded to 69 during the 2000/01 academic year (Gokhberg, Mindeli, and Rosovetskaya 2002, 16). The growth in the number of students in these areas was even more impressive—from 39,400 first-year students in the 1992/93 academic year to 151,300 in 2000/01 (Gokhberg, Mindeli, and Rosovetskaya 2002, 26). These figures provide a context for the establishment of this new university (HSE). Although this time was the most economically difficult in recent Russian history, it was a period of growing demand for higher education. For the first time, universities obtained access to both public and private finance. HSE could directly compete with the existing universities, as they also entered a period of substantial changes.

The Russian government lacked a clear strategy for higher education reform. This climate affected the behavior of the Russian universities. The mid-1990s were described as a time of structural adaptation of the Russian universities to the changing environment (Morgan, Kniazev, and Kulikova 2004). Most universities chose to survive and wait until better times returned (Titova 2008). HSE did not have this option because it needed to find resources to survive. As opposed to a proactive strategy, to a certain degree, HSE *reacted* rather than set goals. Thus, the identity of the new university did not emerge through a detailed strategy developed in advance, either by the government or by HSE itself. The government established HSE and forgot about its existence. The university was evolving mainly through competition with other universities as the entire higher education system adapted to constantly changing conditions. The following section examines how competition for leadership in the higher education market shaped HSE's identity as a research university.

HSE Establishment and Its Transformation through Competition

One can divide the history of HSE into two stages. During the first stage (from 1992 to the end of the 1990s), it created its own position in Russian higher education. Within the second stage (since the beginning of the 2000s), HSE discovered itself as an international actor and began to transform itself into a global research university.

HSE Competitive Advantages and Weaknesses

The situation around HSE's establishment explains both competitive advantages and limitations in actions undertaken by the university during its short history. HSE was founded by the Russian government as a single-discipline higher education institution under the Ministry of Economy. The government's resolution set the mission of HSE quite clearly: to train a national cadre for the emerging market economy and to provide technical assistance to the Ministry of Economy. The prime minister at that time, Egor Gaidar, supported this decision.

The establishment of HSE under the jurisdiction of the Ministry of Economy became its unquestionable advantage. At that time, an overwhelming majority of universities reported (and still report) to the Ministry of Education. They are forced to focus on centrally determined educational standards more than HSE. The powerful Ministry of Economy provided political protection to the innovations of "its" university. It allowed HSE to develop its curricula, bearing in mind worldwide best practices rather than the average standards of the Ministry of Education. Proximity to the Ministry of Economy also provided a unique place for many students. The Ministry of Economy began actively using HSE as a testing ground for discussing new ideas, which improved the prestige of the young university and helped update its curricula in accordance with new tasks and trends.

A rather high budget allocation per student, set by the government decision on the establishment of the university, became another HSE advantage. Until 1992, such a high per capita norm was used only for a small group of highly reputable traditional universities. Therefore, setting such a rate meant the recognition of the high status of the young university. In the early 1990s, however, this rate did not address the issue of HSE financing, as government funding of the entire higher education system was reduced.

Important advantages of the newly established university included the lack of institutional inertia and the possibility of putting together a team of modern and innovation-oriented teachers. These advantages resulted in international support for establishing HSE, because the early 1990s constituted a period of intensive foreign support of modernization processes in Russia. Although bulwarks of classical Soviet education were hesitant about the cooperation with "suspicious" Western institutions. HSE made the most of the substantial resources of the European Union programs. In 1997, HSE launched an external program of the London School of Economics and Political Science with the support of international and national sponsors. Today, this assistance looks rather small scale, but at that time it provided significant resources and support for university development and for launching of coordinated programs with leading international universities. Foreign grants made initial investments in human capital possible, especially helping contract negotiations with the first 25 staff members. The acquisition of a modern HSE library and the first purchase of computers occurred under these projects.

At the same time, when making its first steps, HSE ran into serious challenges compared to its competitors. A major impediment involved HSE's physical infrastructure; the government did not provide the necessary buildings. Underdevelopment of the infrastructure was and is still a major competitive weakness of HSE. The young university had to open its doors to students without a long preparatory period or adequate educational materials in the Russian language. But this weakness was converted into an advantage when in due course the university managed to provide the most advanced textbooks and educational technologies. Some Western textbooks were translated, and a number of new textbooks were written by HSE professors. The approach to the library creation was an example of intelligent strategy. HSE could not have a library larger than the libraries of its competitors. Thus, it decided to have the best digital library in the country and succeeded. At the same time, Moscow State University invested millions of dollars into a new library building that does not really reflect modern ideas of information support for learning. Priority given to digital resources helped HSE modernize not just a library, but also the learning process as a whole.

Energetic planning, considered an advantage, was also a weakness. The university did not have enough teachers for all training courses. Yet over time, this weakness became an advantage because to fill the gap, the university invited famous practitioners and foreign professors, which significantly improved its prestige. An interesting point here is to compare HSE with another university established in the same period—the Russian State University for the Humanities. To a great extent, their roots are similar; both universities were founded during a period of change and increasing need for modern social knowledge and humanities. However, the Russian State University for the Humanities was not a new university; it absorbed two existing schools and to a great extent became a hostage of its institutional culture. These competitive advantages and weaknesses underpinned the university strategies in a competitive struggle in various markets.

Strategies of Market Entry and Competition for Leadership

Theories defining the entry of new players to the market state conceptualize an accurate determination of niche, quantity, and price as a primary success factor. Initially, the management team of the new university was purely academic; it did not have basic marketing competencies. In defining its market strategy, HSE relied on a sensitivity to changes. Its success was defined by the fact that its competitors had the same level of marketing skills with a lot of self-assurance and snobbism.

Defining the niches to enter the market. Initially, HSE relied more on the will of the government. In the summer of 1992, the Ministry of Economy intended to launch a master's degree program in economics and retrain talented students from advanced universities.

It immediately became clear that to sustain this program, a bachelor's degree program in economics was also needed. So on September 1, 1993, both the bachelor's and the master's degree programs were launched for first-year students. This practice strengthened the initial self-identification of HSE as a single-subject institution.

HSE, led by its ambitions, looked to famous universities with a long history—for example, Moscow State University, whose economics faculty provided cadres for a Soviet elite. The decision was made not to directly compete with such universities but rather to focus on different subjects. In higher education, brand and tradition play such an important role that it is difficult to imagine how a young university could compete with well-established universities without entering a new field.

The young university made use of the reform wave of the early 1990s when everything new and unusual came into fashion. HSE positioned its brand as market orientation, timeliness, and nontraditionalism. When the well-established Russian universities opposed the introduction of the Bologna Process, HSE was one of the first to adopt a two-tier system and make it part of its public image (Chuchalin, Boev, Kriushova 2007). It was an ingenious move to take advantage of the high prestige of the

Soviet tradition in mathematics and physics and apply it to the social sciences. HSE associated its style of teaching economics with the style of teaching physics and mathematics. In doing so, HSE attached itself to a tradition that was of high repute at home and abroad.

Another distinctive feature of HSE's positioning was (and still is) its international engagement. Thanks to the grants from the European Union and some European governments, HSE established close ties with several leading universities. Those links became an important aspect of HSE's public image. The opportunity to participate in exchange programs and to study abroad became an important attraction for many Russian students.

Thus, HSE successfully identified its initial niche of modern, international, and innovative (as opposed to outdated, isolated, and traditional) economic education, focused on the realities of the market economy and pluralist democracy (as opposed to planned economy and totalitarian regime).

By 1995, it had become clear that advising the Ministry of Economy on social and economic reforms required expertise not only in economics, but also in social and political sciences and law. HSE leaders also realized that a modern research university should have a sufficient range of disciplines (as does the London School of Economics and Political Science). At the same time, researchers from other academic fields observed the new university with its attractive academic environment and approached its management with ideas for new areas of study and research. As a result, HSE management proposed to the government to broaden the scope of the institution's mission. The Ministry of Economy supported this move because it wanted to expand its influence and perspectives. In 1995, the government awarded HSE the status of university that signifies training and research in a wide range of areas including law, business, and humanities. In 1996, HSE began undergraduate programs in sociology, management, and law.

In this environment, the niche for content widened, primarily through the introduction of areas for study and research that either were absolutely new for Russian higher education or had rapidly increased in popularity. In the former, HSE not only forecasted, but also shaped the growing market (for example, in management studies). In the latter, HSE directly competed with well-established universities by stepping into traditional fields. From 1996 through 1999, HSE established faculties of law, sociology, management, psychology, and political sciences. The demand for training in these fields was quite high, so HSE could easily obtain second-class students. However, HSE positioned itself as an innovative university, even in these traditional fields, to attract the best students. Whereas most competitors continued to preserve their existing curricula as long as possible, HSE emphasized new content areas and curriculum structures. This emphasis worked as a marketing strategy, although in some cases its claims were not completely justified.

HSE sometimes tried to seize control over entry into new market segments from well-established universities that until then had monopolized certification of new specialties, programs, and textbooks. The master's degree programs in social sciences and economics are good examples of such aggressive competitive strategies. Because HSE was the first reputable university to open master's degree courses in a number of areas, it began claiming the control over the certification of such new programs and textbooks. The leading universities did not pay much attention to that approach, because the share of master's degree programs in Russian universities in the late 1990s equaled less than 3 percent. However, following Russia's accession to the Bologna Process in 1998 and enactment of the respective law, a large-scale transition to master's degree programs in social sciences and economics became a reality, with HSE acting as a leader and market-entry controller.

HSE used similar tactics in other cases. Its most audacious move was to establish and then legitimize completely new study areas. For instance, in 2001 the Ministry of Education authorized HSE to pilot business informatics training. It designed a new curriculum and enrolled students. Then, HSE lobbied for the approval of national standards for that field, based on the results of the pilot, and became a natural leader and a trendsetter in that area. HSE followed a similar approach when introducing new study areas such as logistics or statistics. Courage and intuition helped HSE effectively use these strategic opportunities.

A critical issue in niche identification was the focus on research. An important aspect of HSE's market positioning and its organizational identity was based on the idea of a research-intensive university. Why and how did HSE strengthen its emphasis on research? The main impetus for this focus was its initial affiliation with the Ministry of Economy, which considered HSE a think tank from the beginning. It often contracted with HSE for conducting empirical studies and applied analysis for economic reforms.

Another reason for focusing on research was the competition for students. Recent studies show that focusing on research increases universities' abilities to compete for students (Del Rey 2001; Warning 2007).

Therefore, HSE's focus on research helped it not only compete for research funding, but also attract the most productive students.

Identification of its size and scale of activity was another important component of HSE's market-penetration strategy. As a newly established institution, HSE was free to drastically increase student enrollment from the beginning. Yet it selected the strategy of "limited edition" to increase the attractiveness of its educational services by deliberately restricting the availability of these services. This strategy obviously helped maintain quality standards. However, it was also a well-considered move in the competitive struggle. The fact that HSE did not increase its enrollment and also did not open extramural or part-time departments contributed to its reputation as a high-quality higher education institution and stirred up interest among potential students. Such approaches enabled HSE to compete successfully both for good students (to fill budget-funded places) and for the financial resources of fee-paying students.

Competition for good students to fill budget-funded places. The struggle for high-quality students whose motivation and skills could become the young university's most empowering resource was the key competition field for HSE. In its first year, the university failed to attract even a suf-ficient number of applicants. As a result, the university needed to extend the enrollment deadlines for undergraduate programs. Later, the situation improved because in the early 1990s, more secondary school graduates rushed into economics and were looking for any higher education institu-tions or faculty specializing in economics (Egorshin, Abliazova, and Guskova 2007). Therefore, in general, entry into that growing market was not extremely difficult for universities. Moreover, traditional barriers to the higher education market entry—certification and licensing—stopped in the revolutionary chaos of the early 1990s. Yet, institutions' entry into the elite segment of the economics education market remained quite problematic.

To enter this segment, HSE decided to use its innovative brand and provide an explanation of its innovations to future applicants and their parents. Thus, the university used a multilevel (person-to-person) market-ing strategy in the first years of its operation. In 1994–97, HSE managers and teachers visited about 300 schools in Moscow and other cities to make presentations at parents' meetings, each attended by 300 people on aver-age. Their main message was that a "new economic order" required a new kind of training that could be provided only at new institutions. As a result, in 1994 the university received 4.5 applications for each student position.

However, a new positioning of economics (and then other social sciences) in secondary schools formed the truly strategic marketing move. In the past, only one social discipline—ideologically overburdened "social studies"—had been taught in secondary schools in the Soviet era, with a low status among teachers, students, and parents. HSE professors began promoting the introduction of new secondary school disciplines such as economics, political study, and law as early as 1993. To that end, they initiated the development and publication of school textbooks and workbooks in those disciplines. HSE found a business partner, a commercial publishing house interested in establishing and developing a new and rather profitable segment of the textbook market. Promotion of these disciplines (and the newly developed textbooks) in secondary schools was facilitated by the fact that the university launched an ambitious teacher retraining program to create a pool of teachers in economics. HSE professors also suggested another instrument to promote social and economic knowledge in secondary schools (All-Russia Academic Olympics in Economics). HSE organized the competitions, and many winners of the Academic Olympics were enrolled in HSE.

One of the most effective strategies for competing in a quasi-market is institutional transparency and informational support for students and their families (Woods, Bagley, and Glatter 1999). This strategy led HSE to develop the most informative website for potential students, according to the rating of the independent agency, Reitor (Reitor 2007).

HSE's approach to admissions to master's degree programs clearly demonstrates the key competition principle chosen by the young university: to predict market-development trends and to become the first institution to enter growing market segments. Since 1994, Russian higher education institutions could open two-level bachelor's and master's degree programs (four plus two years)—the Bologna model—parallel to the development of the traditional continental European model featuring the award of the specialist diploma (five to six years). Most leading institutions that competed with HSE vehemently opposed the Bologna Process and did not open master's degree programs. Unlike them, HSE took active steps to introduce the model, and in 1997, it became the first sizable university with a diversified and large-scale master's degree program. Therefore, HSE managed to attract gifted graduates from other universities, including those specializing in technical disciplines and sciences, which also contributed to significant diversification of the market.

It is interesting to note that such tactics failed in some segments of the education market. For instance, HSE was not able to become a leader in

PhD-level studies. HSE wanted to use aggressive marketing tactics and announced that it would offer non-fee-based PhD-level programs to maintain quality and integrity. However, graduates of other universities did not run to HSE because the PhD certification procedures were and still are controlled by the association of several traditional universities and the Academy of Sciences. This status prevented HSE from imposing a new set of specialties and new thesis standards. Therefore, HSE had to comply with the existing rules, which create implicit incentives for graduates to stay at their alma maters for their PhD-level training.

Competition in the market for fee-based education services. Development of HSE's brand facilitated its entry into the market for fee-based education. That market emerged simultaneously with HSE, and therefore, HSE and its potential competitors encountered about the same experience in such an environment. The young university pursued an aggressive policy, becoming one of the more expensive providers in the local market from the first years of its operation. Such policy was well in line with the general atmosphere in the market of goods and services, which saw the emergence of an expensive high-quality product segment in the early 1990s. Most players in the higher education market assumed that the sector of inexpensive, low-quality education was the most profitable and opted for price competition. Almost all institutions that provided fee-based education services in the social sciences and economics developed inexpensive programs, implemented as extramural or part-time courses. Demonstrating its special niche of high-quality fee-based education, HSE refused to follow an easy-money approach and declared that it was not going to have extramural or part-time departments for undergraduates.

Although charging high tuition fees, HSE was one of the first Russian universities to announce a system of discounts for applicants who demonstrated special achievements in one of the entrance exams or in the course of studies. It was one of the first institutions in Russia to begin cooperating with commercial banks on education loans for its students, which also led to the qualitative growth of students willing to pay for their education. Thus, HSE competed for quality rather than quantity. Because of this strategy, HSE retains its price leadership today, with tuition fees generating more than one-third of its budget.

Continuing education was another emerging sector in the market of educational services in the early 1990s. A rapid growth of the new economy sectors, with up to 50 percent of qualified specialists taking new occupations (mostly in the area of finance and business) has required a prompt retraining of tens of thousands of engineers and military personnel. Several niches emerged in continuing education as well. Many universities launched programs of accelerated, formal retraining that resulted in the issuance of a diploma or a certificate. Their competitors have offered some longer, more traditional programs. Within continuing education, similar to the basic education sector, HSE offered innovation products. HSE was among the first group of Russian universities offering their master of business administration programs and courses on project management and international finance. HSE management considered continuing education a stable and promising market. Therefore, a key element of HSE's approach was to establish a special department in charge of marketing and direct contacts with a corporate client to implement any continuing education program. Most competitors lacked a strategic attitude toward continuing education as a source of extra income. In their view, providing any continuing training services defined just a source of extra income for their professors rather than a separate and critical market segment. Thus, in the majority of competitive universities, extended education services were provided by the same units that provided basic education services.

Competition in the market of intellectual services and research. A sector of intellectual services (consulting, analysis, audit, and so forth) in social and economic areas emerged together with the market economy and political competition. However, in the early 1990s, this market remained as yet undeveloped. No Western consulting firms and think tanks were yet present in the market, and no mature Russian companies had been formed. The Russian government lacked the funds for commissioning studies and analytical work, and there was insufficient demand and supply. Under the above conditions, most universities did not treat any socioeconomic studies and analytical work as a promising market. Unlike other universities, HSE invested its earnings into public analytical work, which has contributed to its image as a well-known analytical and research center. Close contacts between HSE and the Ministry of Economy were critical in taking a strong competitive position in the intellectual services market. The university could see the areas where research and analysis were mostly needed. Gradually, the supply of analytical papers created a demand. As a result, in terms of the scope of work completed, by the end of the 1990s HSE had become a key Russian center for applied socioeconomic research and analytical work. Income from these contracts constituted at least 20 percent of HSE's total income. This result was important for capacity development in applied research. However, it did not help further develop a capacity for basic research at the international level. The decline of the Russian Academy of Sciences opened new possibilities for HSE's competitive positioning in basic economic and social research (Avtonomov et al. 2002). Many young researchers from the academy's institutions moved to HSE, which offered them a fast promotion, better income (including for those from contracts on applied research), and opportunities for international cooperation. However, the lack of external funding did not offer sufficient impetus for basic research. Bright graduate students and researchers preferred external contracts for applied studies. This situation did not stop HSE from becoming one of the leading research centers in Russia. Yet this procedure happened in the atmosphere of the general decline of basic research in the country.

Conclusions on the role of competition in forming the university's identity. The actions of the university under the conditions of competition were largely opportunistic and reactive. At the same time, literature suggests that strategic behavior is critically important for newcomers in overcoming entry barriers (Geroski, Gilbert, and Jacquemin 1990). What was the strategic element of HSE's competitive actions? The analysis shows that a certain interpretation of an ideal model of a research university preconditioned the entry into various sectors of the education market. The key element of university identity and image also included internationalization, innovations, and a predominant orientation toward elite and emerging markets.

Another important factor affecting many of HSE's decisions was its mission as an innovative university that supports Russian economic and social reforms. This ideology often justified aggressive actions by HSE (even arrogant, from the point of view of its competitors).

Likewise, marketization of higher education forced HSE to develop itself as an entrepreneurial university (Clark 1998) with strong and centralized management, diversification of financing sources, and a complex system of academic incentives. It became an interesting hybrid of models of both a research and an entrepreneurial university.

An interesting example of this combination of semistrategic, missionary, and opportunistic behavior was a (not planned) geographic expansion of HSE. HSE was offered facilities from the regional authorities in a few Russian cities to open educational programs there in 1996 and 1997. HSE used this new opportunity to expand its operations and to raise its national profile. Obviously, that procedure was not necessary for the development of HSE as a research university and even led to heated discussions within HSE's leadership. But HSE had a mission to promote innovative approaches in teaching economics and social sciences, which drove its geographic expansion.

However, in the early 2000s, after HSE reached the top of the Russian higher education system, the university's actual steps were traditional rather than innovative. Many innovations initiated by HSE were adopted by its competitors. Some critics noticed that HSE culture was becoming similar to the culture of traditional Russian universities, which meant stagnation for HSE leaders. To avoid the stagnation, the university had to move away from the opportunistic behavior toward more strategic positioning. There was no option to become another Moscow State University or to follow the international model of a research university. The decision was made. HSE announced its strategy "to become a research university of global standards" as early as 2002 (Higher School of Economics 2006).

Toward a Research University Model

It is not a coincidence that the new strategic direction appeared in the time of accelerated growth of the Russian economy, based on high oil prices. New resource opportunities and challenges for the Russian economy affected HSE's behavior. The institutional inertia pushed the university to quantitative expansion (the number of first-year students doubled between 1999 and 2004). The strategic vision required qualitative changes.

The strategic transformation will be examined using the framework by Jamil Salmi (2009). This framework includes three main conditions that are critical for any university to achieve world-class status: attraction of talents, sufficient resources, and effective governance and management systems. The analysis also includes a review of the research priorities important for understanding HSE's emerging identity as an international research university.

Attraction of Talents

HSE's strategy to attract the best students has been previously described. Because of that strategy, HSE has been attracting active and dynamic Moscow secondary school graduates. However, HSE initially fell behind leading Moscow universities in attracting academically oriented youth from other Russian regions. As a result of being the first to accept national university entrance exam results, an average number of HSE applicants from the region grew, and HSE has reached its major competitors.

HSE's leadership in promoting the master's degree–level training has been previously mentioned. However, it has been difficult to transform this advantage into a new inflow of talented graduates from other universities because the quality of training received at regional universities does not allow their graduates successfully to pass HSE's master's degree–level entrance examination. To solve this problem, in 2001, HSE established a system of free winter preparatory schools for the most talented final-year undergraduates from regional universities. In 2008, HSE actually extended its master's degree program for these students and began using an extra year (remedial) for their training. As a result, HSE has already outpaced some leading Russian universities in the number of graduate students. Today, the share of graduate students at HSE is 15 percent. In 2009, the intake of students for master's degree programs at HSE reached 1,500, one of the largest in Russia. In the next 10 years, HSE plans to increase the share of master's degree students up to 40 percent.

Once the best students are available, it is important to maintain their academic motivation and secure a fulfillment of their talents. HSE has developed a number of economic incentives for accomplished students by introducing special grants for free students and discounts for accomplished fee-paying students.

At the same time, poor infrastructure, lack of courses delivered in English language, and a low international reputation of Russian socioeconomic sciences have resulted in a low percentage of foreign students. Even the best Russian-speaking students from the former Soviet Union prefer studying at the universities of Western Europe and the United States. In recent years, the number of foreign students has reached only 3 percent.

A key element of the strategy to implement the world-class research university model has been the attraction of talented teachers and researchers. HSE has faced a lack of specialists available in Russia in some subject areas. Therefore, different approaches to establishing strong academic teams have been applied in various socioeconomic sciences. In the area of applied mathematics (applications to the economy), Russia has had its longstanding traditions and internationally acknowledged scholars. The majority of the scholars were employed by the Academy of Sciences, which experienced a dramatic funding decrease in the early 1990s. HSE was able to hire these specialists by offering them attractive contracts, which allowed it to establish academic teams working on an international level within a few specific research areas. This step was critical because these teams are to disseminate these standards in other research areas. No such capacity was available in other segments of socioeconomic sciences. Therefore, HSE had to choose between mobilizing foreign academics and nurturing a team of local researchers.

At about the same time, the New Economic School was established in Moscow. That institution has taken the first path demonstrating that the option of hiring internationally recognized academics would be efficient in allowing a new institution to participate effectively in global knowledge generation and international exchange networks. However, the above option could not be fully implemented given the absence of abundant financial resources, which were not available in Russia then. Therefore, HSE followed a more complicated strategy.

During the first two years, up to 30 percent of professional courses were taught by professors from foreign universities. As a matter of priority, young academics who had already established themselves at HSE took their short-term probation at foreign universities, where they could master the relevant courses and get acquainted with modern research methods. HSE supported both their lecturing activities and their research.

Aware that Russian science would not be able to compete with Western science in the areas of economic or sociological theory in the near decade, HSE decided to use a unique advantage of operating in Russia that was truly a "laboratory of a transitional economy." Western researchers had no easy access to such a laboratory. Therefore, HSE's specialists dealing with empiric studies of a transitional economy and social processes have become partners for leading foreign specialists in socioeconomic theory. In fact, the strategy of cultivating talented researchers was coupled with the method of cultivating modern socioeconomic science in Russia. HSE nurtured a group of young specialists who became unique among Russian universities. In the 1990s, the average age of lecturers was 33 years, and the average age of HSE managers was 36 years. Today, the average age of HSE lecturers is 43 years, which makes HSE the "youngest" public university in Russia. These young professors came mainly from the Russian Academy of Sciences and Moscow State University. They were attracted not just by career prospects, but also by opportunities to enter the world of modern social and economic sciences, escaping the Soviet ideological cave.

Another element of HSE's staffing strategy involved mobilizing foreign specialists on a temporary basis (usually for one semester). It was also aimed at developing certain training courses later commissioned to the Russian lecturers. Obviously, foreign professors taught in English, which was illegal because the existing regulatory framework did not permit teaching in a foreign language. HSE lobbied the changes in the regulatory framework that made this practice acceptable. Currently, even some Russian professors teach in English. The university aims to have sufficient courses in English to attract more foreign students.

One of the unique elements of the staffing strategy was the invitation of leading economists and politicians from the government to teach at the university. All ministers of economy and finance were professors at HSE. They brought the vision of real-world problems into the classrooms and research groups.

It was equally important both to attract and to retain talented professors at HSE. The key task was to secure their loyalty to HSE as their primary place of employment. Two factors made this a difficult task.

First, as previously mentioned, universities in the Soviet Union were not considered a natural place for research. This approach manifested itself in a high teaching load for lecturers (up to 700 hours per annum) that left no time for research work. Some leading universities had close contacts with the Academy of Sciences, which allowed its researchers to become part-time professors and actively engaged many students in research activities. Also, at the Moscow and the Saint Petersburg universities, the share of postgraduate students was high, which contributed to the research activities. However, this environment was an exception rather than the rule. Therefore, the key task of HSE was to make research and teaching equally prestigious goals for professors.

Another specific problem of higher education and science in Russia in the 1990s was the reduction in funding, resulting in a dramatic drop of academic salaries. Within one year, university professors revealed that their salaries did not maintain their former living standards and would not allow them to survive. In 1993, the monthly salary of a professor at an average Russian university was US$50, and the monthly salary of a professor at the major universities was US$100–120. This salary was much lower than a starting salary for many university graduates. As a result, practically every professor had to take several jobs and visit his or her base university only to lecture.

A critical task was to fight the trend of turning all professors into multiple jobholders. To cope with this problem, HSE management developed a special theoretical concept—the efficient contract (Kuzminov 2006). It is a system of mutual obligations, with an aggregate of incentives (primarily financial ones) for HSE to secure the loyalty of lecturers to the institution as their primary place of employment, including their engagement into basic and applied research. An efficient contract system did not mean that all professors of the same rank would receive an equal salary. For those employees who demonstrated international competitiveness, efficient contracts were a tool for earning an income similar to that at international universities. Professors holding a strong position at the local market would receive a different salary. An efficient contract system does not always mean a guaranteed payment for a standard scope of work. Normally, an efficient contract is related to the possibility to gain some extra income at the university by contributing to any fundamental and applied research and any high-cost training programs ordered by major corporations. This system also rests on a set of incentives such as salary supplements for regular publications in any reviewed scientific magazines, internal research grants, and special grants to young teachers.

Today, more than 30 percent of HSE professors are on efficient contracts, which secure their loyalty to HSE and their active engagement in research work. The efficient contract system allows professors to maintain a middle-class lifestyle.

Tenure contracts are not permitted under Russian legislation. HSE has tried to imitate tenure by introducing the internal status of "distinguished professor" supported by a higher salary, special rights, and an informal promise to extend the contract as long as the professor wants. However, HSE failed to introduce clear criteria, based on research productivity, for awarding this status. For many professors, their status became a comfortable retirement niche.

A quantitative expansion of HSE could not be ensured without an adequate supply of professors. The possibilities for an external search of candidates were almost exhausted. Gradually, HSE has begun to offer jobs to its own graduates rather than to mobilize talent from outside. This practice creates a risk of inbreeding and stagnation as well as low staff mobility. Despite the absence of a formal open-ended contract, there were almost no cases of the rejection of the contract extension initiated by the university.

To respond to these risks, HSE developed new staffing initiatives: inviting outstanding scholars as guest researchers or lecturers, reducing the teaching load for professors with the most remarkable achievements in research, and hiring specialists from the international labor market. During the past few years, HSE has been hiring three to five young PhD graduates annually from the leading universities. Still, the ratio of professors active in research and modern teaching methods is not high enough (about 40 percent).

Resource Conditions for Development

Since the day of its establishment, HSE has looked for any resources to secure the mobilization of talented academics and the conditions for their efficient work. As previously discussed, HSE used an entrepreneurial approach to diversify the sources of funding. Today, it has four sources of funding in addition to the federal budget: the basic higher education market, a continuous education market, research, and consulting.

During the past few years, on average, the federal budget allocation for the education of non-fee-paying students and capital investments compose about 33 percent of the university revenue, whereas 16 percent is generated from the fees of students attending on a cost-recovery basis. Continuing education programs contribute 19 percent, the research project portfolio gives 15 percent, grants and sponsor support compose about 13 percent, and other sources amount to about 2 percent.

The ratio between budgetary and nonbudgetary funding was 60 to 40. Most of HSE's income from educational activity has been invested in research. As a result, HSE has become a leader among Russian universities in its own investment into research. This situation led to a higher visibility of HSE and allowed the university management to argue for better budget funding.

In recent years, budget funding has increased. In 2006, HSE lobbied for additional funding from the government to support its basic research program. The government approved this additional annual funding, which reached US$15 million in 2009 and boosted research activity. It also had a reverse effect: some researchers who received funding for basic research from the university scaled down their efforts to get external grants. Despite a significant increase in funding (from 1993 through 2008, the funding per student increased by 15 times in comparable prices), HSE's resource provision (even in terms of purchasing power parity) has been well behind that of Western universities.

Organizational and Management Structure

Organizational and management issues cover a number of aspects of HSE's development: autonomy, organizational structure, hierarchy, and management culture. All public universities in Russia have similar management systems formally providing conditions for broad academic democracy and autonomy. However, the practical functioning of the management structures at various universities is different. Since the beginning, HSE has enjoyed much more autonomy than other universities because it reported to the Ministry of Economy rather than to the Ministry of Education. A high share of nonbudgetary income has also contributed to the culture of independence in the use of financial resources.

The internal governance and management culture combines high transparency and rigid vertical management under a rector. However, this system lacks checks and balances. The rector is elected by a senate (and approved by the government afterward). But the rector has strong influence on the senate composition and is not subordinated to any external body like a governing board. This centralization was crucial at the initial stage of the university's history. It helped in setting and keeping priorities and in focusing resources for a limited number of objectives. HSE leadership has been and continues to be a driving force of the innovative development, pushing changes into all university units. New ideas rarely come from the bottom of the institutional hierarchy. Because HSE founders, to a large extent, remain managers, the basic ideas of the institution's development strategy have been developed not by the senate (academic board) but by the rector's office. At the same time, transparency has secured the feedback from the staff and staff's engagement into policy discussions.

One of the critical functions of the centralized management system has been the efficient distribution of scarce resources for financing different types of contracts. The centralized system of incentives based on the experts' opinions has been noted as perhaps the most effective way of grading the researchers and professors in an uncertain academic environment (Diamond 1993).

Another critical function of the centralized management is to secure the patronage of the government, which forms an important condition for HSE's success. The government prefers to speak with the executive (the rector) rather than with an independent body like a governing board.

An interesting detail of the governance structure of HSE is the position of the academic leader of the university, who plays a major advisory role and carries out representation duties. This position is occupied by one of HSE's founders and a former minister of economy, Evgeny Yasin. The independent position assures the importance of research for the university. The academic leader reports to the senate directly.

Another important feature of HSE's governance system is the stability of the university leadership, which is still led mostly by the same leaders who founded the university. Professor Yaroslav Kuzminov has been the rector since the establishment of HSE and is still the major driving force and an ideologue of university strategic development. Theoretically, the stability of the university leadership team facilitates an institutional inertia. In reality, the opportunistic character of HSE's early development and the dynamic external environment did not allow its leaders to stop worrying.

The leadership team understands the risk of stability and therefore seeks external challenges. In early 2000, it lobbied for such a challenge— the government push for international competitiveness. In response to this challenge, the university leadership team accepted a new set of main performance indicators: (a) research performance and (b) the university's involvement in socioeconomic reforms. These indicators include primarily university publications in peer-reviewed journals, the scope of contractual research, and the influence of HSE's analytical materials on policy making. However, the centralized character of management and the lack of external accountability do not require systematic use and in-depth analysis of such data.

The transformation of HSE into a research-intensive university required a particular organizational structure. The separation between teaching (training) units and research and analytical institutes (centers) was adequate for aggressively and opportunistically entering the markets. However, this structure does not allow integrating teaching with research and innovation activity. It also hampers the transformation of HSE into a modern research university. In recent years, this problem has been recognized, and HSE stimulated the creation of new structures in which such integration happens naturally. These structures are called student research laboratories and student project groups, and they allow undergraduate students, postgraduate students, and professors to join teams under common themes or projects. The aim is to improve internal flexibility and provide opportunities for interdisciplinary research. However, barriers remain between the teaching and the research and development units.

Priorities of the Research University

The selection of the priorities is critical for any university positioning itself in the global educational market. A new university can follow well-established universities by importing researchers and participating in existing projects and networks. This type of strategy definitely creates results, and HSE followed it by joining a number of international comparative study projects and inviting Western scholars to introduce young Russian researchers into cutting-edge research areas. However, such an approach rarely leads to creating a unique research profile and to competing with international research universities.

So in addition to this approach, HSE is identifying specific niches where its capacity and expertise could be unique and internationally competitive. One of these multidisciplinary areas is the study of social and economic transition. By focusing on the transition, many HSE researchers have become widely known experts in the field. HSE has hosted a number of conferences of the international networks of researchers in this area. Such an orientation helped the young university to become a center of knowledge creation and exchange. At the same time, such a focus creates a risk of missing critically important cutting-edge areas.

Another approach to enter global research networks is based on appreciating the importance of empirical data. HSE invested its own resources and convinced the government to support large-scale empirical studies—including household surveys, monitoring of enterprises and innovative activities, empirical studies of civil society development, and so forth. This rich body of knowledge was expected to attract foreign scholars to work in cooperation with Russian researchers. However, huge investments in these studies did not fully pay off because the methodology of these studies was not always up to date. This situation confirmed that setting priorities could be a very difficult and risky task.

Happy Ending or New Challenges?

In August 2008, the Russian government decided to place HSE under the direct supervision of the Cabinet of Ministers (together with five leading universities) to ensure their important role in providing knowledge support for policy development. This decision required HSE to develop a strategy, up to 2020, to secure its competitive position compared to the major international research and educational centers in the areas of social sciences and economics. This external push became a strong factor for the transition to a new stage of HSE development, requiring a strict approach as opposed to an opportunistic one. This effort presents a choice between quantitative expansion and qualitative transformation.

The policy developed by HSE was approved by the government commission in October 2009. HSE was awarded a large grant to support the implementation of this strategy. It was also awarded a special status—National Research University. This status connotes more academic autonomy, higher responsibility for the results of research activities, recruitment of international students, and high-quality training. The challenge for HSE is not to obtain another award, but to become an international research university in reality.

Conclusion

This chapter has examined the roots of HSE's success as a national flag-ship university and a strong candidate to become a global research university. The factors that contributed to this success are as follows:

- An initial orientation toward a research-intensive university model that focuses on human resources and quality of research
- Deliberate implementation of an entrepreneurial university model and aggressive competition in emerging and elite markets
- Close ties with international universities and research networks, resulting in active adaptation of the best international curricula and modern research methodology in the specific environment of Russian education
- Use of issues of national significance (including major social and economic reforms) as subjects for research and analytical work
- Investments in the public image of HSE as a center of excellence in the area of social sciences and economics

This analysis confirms a conclusion that was based on the history of the London School of Economics and Political Science—the role of institutional entrepreneurs in university development is very important if they happen to be in the right place at the right time (Czarniawska 2009).

References

Altbach, Philip G., and Jorge Bálan. 2007. *World Class Worldwide: Transforming Research Universities in Asia and Latin America.* Baltimore: John Hopkins University Press.

Avtonomov, Vladimir, Oleg Ananyin, Yaroslav Kuzminov, Igor Lipsits, Lev Lyubimov, Rustem Nureev, and Vadim Radayev. 2002. "Economic Science, Education and Practice in Russia in the 1990s." *Problems of Economic Transition* 4 (9/10): 3–21.

Bezglasnaya, G. A. 2001. "Strukturnye sdvigi v rossiskov obrazovanii [Structural shifts in the Russian education]." In *Prepodavaniye sozialno-gumanitarnykh disziplin v vuzakh Rossii: sostoyzniye, problemy, perspectivy* [Teaching of socially humanitarian disciplines in high schools of Russia: Condition, problems, prospects], ed. L. G. Ionin, 23–31. Moscow: Logos.

Boldov, O., V. Ivanov, B. Rosenfeld, and A. Suvorov. 2002. "Resursny potential socialnoi sfery v 90-e gody [Resource potential of the social sector]." *Voprosy Prognozirovaniya* [Forecasting studies] 1: 23–30.

Canaan, Joyce E., and Wesley Shumar. 2008. "Higher Education in the Era of Globalization and Neoliberalism." In *Structure and Agency in the Neoliberal University*, ed. Wesley Shumar and Joyce E. Canaan, 3–30. London: Routledge.

Chuchalin, Alexander, Oleg Boev, and Anastasia Kriushova. 2007. "The Russian System of Higher Education in View of the Bologna Process." *International Journal of Electrical Engineering Education* 44 (2): 109–17.

Clark, Burton R. 1998. *Creating Entrepreneurial Universities: Organizational Pathways of Transformation*. Oxford: Pergamon.

———. 2004. *Sustaining Change in Universities*. London: Open University Press.

Czarniawska, Barbara. 2009. "Emerging Institutions: Pyramids or Anthills?" *Organization Studies* 30 (4): 423–41.

Del Rey, Elena. 2001. "Teaching versus Research: A Model of State University Competition." *Journal of Urban Economics* 49: 356–73.

Diamond, Arthur M. Jr. 1993. "Economic Explanations of the Behavior of Universities and Scholars." *Journal of Economic Studies* 20 (4–5): 107–33.

Egorshin, Alexander, N. Abliazova, and I. Guskova. 2007. "Higher Economic Education in Russia, 1990–2025." *Russian Education and Society* 49 (10): 30–52.

Froumin, Isak, and Jamil Salmi. 2007. "Rosiskie vuzy v konkurencii universitetov mirovogo klassa [Russian higher education institutions in global universities competition]." *Voprosy obrazovaniya* [Russian educational studies journal] 3: 5–45.

Geroski, Paul, Richard Gilbert, and Alexis Jacquemin. 1990. *Barriers to Entry and Strategic Competition*. New York: Harwood Academic.

Gokhberg, Leonid, L. Mindeli, and L. Rosovetskaya. 2002. *Higher Education in Russia: 2001. Data Book*. Moscow: Center for Science Statistics Publishing.

Higher School of Economics. 2006. *Universitetskie innovacicii: Opyt vyshei shkoly ekonomiki*. [Innovations in universities: The Higher School of Economics experience]. Moscow: Higher School of Economics Press.

Klyachko, N. L., ed. 2002. *Modernizatzia rossiyskogo obrazovaniya: ressursny potenzial I podgotovka kadrov* [Modernization of Russian education: Resource potential and a professional training]. Moscow: Higher School of Economics Press.

Kolesnikov, V. N., I. V. Kucher, and V. N. Turchenko. 2005. "The Commercialization of Higher Education: A Threat to the National Security of Russia." *Russian Education & Society* 47 (8): 35–48.

Kuzminov, Yaroslav I. 2006. "Vyshaya shkola ekomiki: Missiya I strategii ee realizacii [Higher School of Economics: Mission and its implementation]."

http://management.edu.ru/images/pubs/2007/07/17/0000309490/02 kuzminov-6-9.pdf. Accessed September 12, 2009.

Makasheva, N. 2007. "Ekonomicheskaya nauka v Rossii v epoku transformacii [Economic science in Russia in period of transformation]." In *Istoki* [Roots], 24–38. Moscow: Higher School of Economics Press.

Mohrman, Kathryn, Wanhua Ma, and David Baker. 2008. "The Research University in Transition: The Emerging Global Model." *Higher Education Policy* 21: 5–27.

Morgan, Anthony W., Evgeny Kniazev, and Nadia Kulikova. 2004. "Organizational Adaptation to Resource Decline in Russian Universities." *Higher Education Policy* 17 (3): 241–56.

Pehrsson, Anders. 2009. "Barriers to Entry and Market Strategy: A Literature Review and a Proposed Model." *European Business Review* 21 (1): 64–77.

Reitor. 2007. *Reiting universitetskikh saitov* [University Ratings Websites]. Moscow: Reitor.

Salmi, Jamil. 2009. *The Challenge of Establishing World-Class Universities.* Washington, DC: World Bank.

Shishikin, V. 2007. "Platnoe vyshee obrazovanie v Rossiskoi Federacii—osnovnue tendencii v 1990–2000 godakh [Privately paid higher education in the Russian Federation—Main trends in 1990–2000]." http://history.nsc.ru/snm/cohf2007.htm. Accessed September 12, 2009.

Titova, N. 2008. *Put uspekha I neudach: Strategicheskoe razvitie rossiskikh vuzov* [Way to Success and Failure: Strategic Development of the Russian Universities]. Moscow: Higher School of Economics Press.

Warning, Susanne. 2007. *The Economic Analysis of Universities: Strategic Groups and Positioning.* Cheltenham, U.K.: Edward Elgar.

Woods, Philip, Carl Bagley, and Ron Glatter. 1999. *School Choice and Competition: Markets in the Public Interest?* London: Routledge.

CHAPTER 11

The Road to Academic Excellence: Lessons of Experience

Jamil Salmi

In the past decade, the term *world-class university* has become a catch phrase to describe research universities at the pinnacle of the tertiary education hierarchy.[1] However, as Philip G. Altbach (2004) has accurately observed, the paradox of the world-class university is that "everyone wants one, no one knows what it is, and no one knows how to get one."

Becoming a member of the exclusive group of world-class universities is not something that can be achieved by self-declaration. This elite status—exemplified by U.S. Ivy League universities such as Harvard, Yale, or Columbia; the universities of Oxford and Cambridge in the United Kingdom; and the University of Tokyo—is usually conferred by the outside world on the basis of international recognition. Until recently, being deemed world class was based on a subjective qualification, mostly but not exclusively, of perceived reputation. However, no rigorous measures existed to quantify the inputs and processes that lead to the superior achievements and status of world-class universities in terms of training top graduates, producing leading-edge research, and contributing to dynamic knowledge and technology transfer. Even the higher salaries earned by those institutions' graduates could be interpreted as much as a signaling proxy to employers or the power of social capital in networking as the true value of their education.

The proliferation of international league tables in the past few years—extending the tradition of national rankings in the United States—has created more systematic ways of identifying and classifying world-class universities. The two most comprehensive world rankings, allowing for broad benchmark comparisons of institutions across national borders, are prepared by Shanghai Jiao Tong University (in 2003) and by Times Higher Education (since 2004). A third international ranking by Webometrics in Spain compares 4,000 tertiary education institutions and measures their visibility on the Internet as a proxy of the importance of the concerned institution. Since 2007, the Higher Education Evaluation and Accreditation Council of Taiwan has published a world ranking of universities based on academic performance and research output.

The international rankings have attracted even more attention than their producers originally anticipated, and the impact has been dramatic (Altbach 2006). In a small number of countries, the results are a source of national pride, but more often than not, they are a matter of great concern (Salmi and Saroyan 2007). The results are often dismissed by many critics as irrelevant exercises fraught with data and methodological flaws; boycotted or challenged legally by some universities that are angry about the results; and sometimes used by political opponents as a convenient way to criticize governing parties or, even, entire governments.[2] One thing is sure: they do not leave institutions and stakeholders indifferent.

Governments and institutions worldwide have responded to the university rankings with both words and concrete actions. At the national level, government reactions have ranged from plans to create alternative rankings to proactive policies in support of qualitative transformations in the university sector. At one extreme, RatER, the Russian Federation ranking agency, created an entirely new world ranking, which happened to place Moscow State University in fifth place ahead of Harvard University and the University of Cambridge (Smolentseva 2010). In 2008, during the French presidency of the European Union, the minister of higher education convinced the European Commission to launch a new European ranking that would be "more objective and more favorable to European universities."[3]

Rather than trying to circumvent the existing international rankings, some governments have provided additional funding to promote national elite universities with explicit or implicit designs to improve the institutions' position in the rankings. Those efforts are best illustrated by the various "excellence initiatives" taken in recent years in places as varied as China; Denmark; Germany; the Republic of Korea; Nigeria, Russia; Spain;

or Taiwan, China (Salmi 2009). In other cases, governments have encouraged top universities to merge to achieve economies of scale and to reach a better position to compete globally. The Russian government, for example, has promoted the merger of regional tertiary education institutions in Siberia and southern Russia into two federal universities and has provided additional funding to develop innovative programs in existing universities (Smolentseva 2010).

Significant behavioral changes have also been observed at the institutional level (Hazelkorn 2008). In some cases, colleges and universities have become more selective to fare better in rankings that measure the academic scores of incoming students. In many corners of the world, institutions are eagerly participating in the talent war to recruit top-level academics from the best universities internationally. As excellence tends to beget excellence, the effect of the rankings can be seen in the virtuous cycle, where the highest-ranked institutions can attract the best faculty and the best researchers, in turn, want to belong to and be validated by the highest-ranked universities. This cycle then extends to the best students wanting to study with the best faculty, which reinforces the institutional ranking, and so on. Ellen Hazelkorn (2008) also found that donors and philanthropists who offer scholarships for study abroad or funding for research look increasingly to the rankings to provide clues to excellence and to help make decisions about where to direct their resources.

But building a world-class institution requires much more than knee-jerk reactions to the rankings or massive infusions of government money. It is a complex and lengthy process that has only recently begun to receive careful attention (Altbach 2004; Salmi 2009). Not surprisingly, the top 10 universities in the Academic Ranking of World Universities were all founded before 1900, and two are more than eight centuries old (annex 11A).

In this book, the nine case-study chapters—covering 11 universities—illustrate the systematic efforts and multiple challenges faced by institutions trying to pursue the "road to academic excellence." This synthesis chapter attempts to identify common themes and preliminary lessons gleaned from the stories of these relatively young institutions, which have achieved outstanding results, shown promising signs of success, or faced reversals of fortune. After exploring the extent to which the findings of the case studies confirm or contradict the analytical model proposed in the introduction, this last chapter identifies important additional dimensions that should be taken into consideration to more accurately comprehend the success factors of top research universities. It proposes, in particular, to take a systematic look at the role of the tertiary education ecosystem, which represents the relevant external forces that directly influence—positively or negatively—the ability of research universities to prosper.

Testing the Model: Common Themes

Analyzing the experience of the 11 universities with a common framework allows, for the first time, a real-life testing of the three-sets-of factors model (talent, funding, and governance) developed by Salmi (2009) in *The Challenge of Establishing World-Class Universities.*

Talent

As all the case studies systematically illustrate, a key success factor in building a top research university is the ability to attract, recruit, and retain leading academics. Notably, what truly distinguishes the East Asian universities from the rest of the world is the marked emphasis on internationalization. Both Shanghai Jiao Tong University (China) and Pohang University of Science and Technology (the Republic of Korea) made a strategic decision to rely principally on Chinese or Korean academics trained in the best universities in North America or Europe and, to a large extent, to recruit highly qualified foreign faculty. Significantly increasing the percentage of courses taught in English is an integral part of this strategy, as well. It serves the dual purpose of making it easier to bring in foreign academics and gearing the curriculum toward training students for the global economy. A recent book, *The Great Brain Race* (Wildavsky 2010), provides a well-documented analysis of the rising international talent war. By contrast, because the University of Malaya (Malaysia) teaches courses predominantly in the national language (Bahasa Malaysia), it has a much more limited internationalization of programs, academic staff, and student body.

Hong Kong University of Science and Technology (Hong Kong SAR, China) has pushed this logic to the extreme. The rapid development and rise of the new university can be attributed, in large part, to its systematic policy of giving priority to outstanding Chinese from the diaspora for staffing the initial contingent of academics. This university's story contains another important lesson, as well; the university recognized that building a strong academic staff is not only about attracting experienced researchers but also about reaching a good balance between academics at the peak of their career and young researchers with promising prospects. Thus, it established recruitment processes in support of that objective.

Pohang University of Science and Technology's recruitment strategy has shown the same strategic concern of balance between experienced and promising researchers.

In other parts of the world (for example, Eastern Europe, India, and Latin America), staffing approaches have been characterized more by efforts to attract strong academics from the domestic market rather than from the full international arena. Indian Institutes of Technology followed a mixed approach by recruiting academics from the diaspora and local institutions. This strategy worked well for several decades but now that the Indian labor market has become more dynamic, private companies effectively compete for the most qualified professionals, and several Indian Institutes of Technology are facing serious staffing problems.

Similarly, Chilean universities seem to be limited by the fact that full-time professors represent less than half of their teaching staff. In Nigeria, as political troubles mounted under the successive military dictatorships, the University of Ibadan gradually lost its most talented researchers. Many left the country and the continent altogether, and the institution has not been able to replace them with equally qualified and experienced academic staff.

The quality of incoming students represents the second dimension when looking at "concentration of talent" as a key driver of success. In most cases, the institutions analyzed in this book have been very successful in attracting the best students in their country, such as National University of Singapore, Shanghai Jiao Tong University, Indian Institutes of Technology, Monterrey Institute of Technology in Mexico, the University of Chile and Pontifical Catholic University of Chile. In fact, Indian Institutes of Technology may well be the most competitive network of tertiary education institutions in the world, with an acceptance rate of only 1.6 percent (608 applicants for each place), compared, for example, with the all-time-low acceptance rate of 6.9 percent at Harvard for the incoming September 2010 class.

The 2002 admissions reform at the University of Malaya, which replaced the quota system with a meritocratic entrance procedure, reflects a genuine concern about attracting better-qualified students. The move was all the more important because the quality of secondary school graduates has been a preoccupation for the national education authorities. According to the Trends in International Mathematics and Science Study (TIMSS) 2007 results, Malaysian students perform below the average of all 49 participating countries and significantly below Singapore and other East Asian emerging economies.

The case studies of Pohang University of Science and Technology, Higher School of Economics (Russia), and Hong Kong University of Science and Technology illustrate a special challenge faced by new institutions that, by definition, have no comparative track record to boost their appeal and credibility among prospective students. Pohang University of Science and Technology faced the additional challenge of being located far from Seoul, where more than half the country's tertiary education infrastructure is concentrated. However, using innovative marketing approaches to showcase their operational excellence, the three institutions managed to overcome those obstacles and to establish themselves fairly rapidly as worthwhile options for students choosing from among the top institutions in the respective countries. The Higher School of Economics, for instance, ranks among the top three universities in Russia in terms of average scores of incoming students at the Unified State Examination. The University of Ibadan's decision to transform itself—for example, to have more graduate students than undergraduates—is an indication of its desire to strengthen its research focus and output, which is a key feature toward attaining world-class status.

At the same time, the high degree of admissions selectivity of emerging research universities raises a general equity issue, especially in the case of private institutions with high tuition fees. Unless they can pursue need-blind admissions policies and offer student aid to a significant proportion of incoming students, these universities risk operating as elitist institutions in terms of socioeconomic composition of the student body.

The balance between undergraduate and graduate students is an important dimension of this discussion on talent concentration. As expected, the more successful research universities tend to have a high proportion of graduate students, as illustrated by table 11.1, which allows the institutions to have a critical mass of research teams.

Institutions with a smaller proportion of graduate students are making deliberate efforts to increase the ratio, such as the Higher School of Economics (planning for 40 percent within 10 years), the National University of Singapore, and the University of Malaya. Even in some institutions with a high proportion of graduate students, the research nature of the institution is also reflected in the participation of undergraduate students in research projects as part of their regular curriculum and the important contribution that top researchers provide to undergraduate teaching.

Finally, it should be noted that the global financial crisis could play out as a positive factor for emerging research universities in many

Table 11.1   Importance of Graduate Students

Institution	Graduate students (%)
Indian Institute of Technology–Bombay	58
Pohang University of Science and Technology	55
Shanghai Jiao Tong University	42
Ibadan University	37
Hong Kong University of Science and Technology	36
University of Malaya	33
National University of Singapore	23
Higher School of Economics	15
University of Chile	15
Monterrey Institute of Technology	14
Pontifical Catholic University of Chile	13

Source: Author based on data from the chapters of this book.

developing and transition countries. First, institutions have the opportunity to reexamine their academic and financial models in ways that promote innovative thinking, creativity, and efficiency—because of scarcities that may not have been felt in times of abundant resources. Second, the severe budget cuts and resulting lack of employment opportunities in academic institutions in North America and Western Europe may make it easier for institutions in other parts of the world to keep their best academics home and to attract talented young academics away from the best universities in the West.

Resources

As expected, the findings of the case studies confirm that emerging research universities need to be well resourced to progress rapidly. This fact emerged appeared clearly from the East Asian cases, as well as from the comparison between the National University of Singapore and the University of Malaya. One reason behind the National University of Singapore's better performance overall is its ability to spend, year after year, two to three times as much per student as the latter. Similarly, Indian Institutes of Technology were always privileged in comparison with the leading public universities in India.

Abundant funding is indispensable not only for setting up first-rate facilities and an appropriate physical infrastructure but also for attracting and retaining high-level academics. The comparative data shown in annex 11B unequivocally show that the top performers in the rankings among the institutions included in this book have the highest level of annual per student funding, ranging from close to US$40,000 in the case of the National University of Singapore to US$70,000 for Pohang University of Science and Technology. At the other end of the spectrum, the financial limitations experienced by the Chilean universities or Higher School of Economics, for instance, are part of the challenge they face in upgrading the qualifications of their academic staff.

Most of the institutions reviewed in this book are public institutions, which reinforces the proposition of the difficulty in today's environment to consider establishing a new world-class institution using only private resources. Potentially, under special circumstances, this establishment might be achieved, as illustrated by the history of the three private institutions included in the book. But these experiences need to be understood within their specific contexts. The Pontifical Catholic University of Chile, for example, has been in the privileged position of receiving public funding to cover a nonnegligible part of its recurrent expenditures just like any other public university in Chile. As annex 11C shows, it receives the same percentage of its total annual income as the University of Chile (11 percent). Pohang University of Science and Technology has also obtained public subsidies (6 percent of its annual income) to complement the generous contribution from the Pohang Iron and Steel Company, the Korean steel giant (34 percent of annual budget). With an annual spending of about US$70,000 per student, Pohang University of Science and Technology compares favorably with Ivy League universities in the United States, all of which are private, nonprofit institutions receiving high levels of public funding—in many cases, more than some "official" public universities—through research grants and targeted student aid. Monterrey Institute of Technology, in addition to being well supported at the outset by wealthy industrialists, has enjoyed considerable resources through a popular lottery that the federal government allows it to run every year and through government scholarships for some of its graduate students. None of these high-quality private institutions subsists on private sources of funding alone.

Most of the universities showcased in this book have successfully diversified their funding sources by managing to mobilize significant additional resources beyond the direct subsidies they receive from government (see annexes 11C and 11D). The National University of Singapore's US$1 billion endowment is an impressive achievement. Part of the additional resources generated by successful institutions comes from donations, even though it takes time for new institutions to build up a solid funding base from alumni. The other part is usually linked to the university's ability to compete for public research funds. Hong Kong University of Science and Technology, for instance, obtained 72 percent of its research funding on a competitive basis in 2009. The availability of competitive research funding is indeed an important factor. In their comparative analysis of European and U.S. universities, Philippe Aghion and colleagues observed that regardless of the level of public funding and degree of management autonomy, the weak development of competitive funding mechanisms was one of the major differences identified to explain the much-lower performance of European research universities in international rankings (Aghion et al. 2009). Similarly, a recent report released by the League of European Research Universities attributes the inability of the old continent's universities to significantly contribute to the production of innovative products and services to inappropriate funding mechanisms. Instead of allocating research money in a competitive way, on the basis of criteria that reward excellence, most European countries display an "obsession with bureaucratic even-handedness" (LERU 2010, 3).

Finally, being well resourced in the early days of an institution is not sufficient for building a top-notch research institution. Funding must be sustained over the long term. The University of Ibadan's story shows that as the political situation deteriorated in Nigeria, so did economic conditions and the amount of budget resources available to the university. Similarly, in Russia, while the Higher School of Economics received a high level of funding when the new institution was launched, the government was unable to sustain its contribution, especially in terms of capital investment, during the financial crisis after 2007.

Governance

The case studies, which analyze a number of positive and less favorable governance situations, show that an appropriate regulatory framework, strong and inspiring leadership, and adequate management significantly influence the ability of research universities to prosper. Indian Institutes of Technology, for example, would not have operated as effectively as they do if they had been constrained by the same financial and administrative regulations that all other public tertiary education institutions must adhere to in India. They have also, by and large, been protected from political interference for the selection of vice chancellors and the recruitment of academics.

The comparison between the University of Malaya and the National University of Singapore illustrates in a striking way the differences in leadership and management approaches and their direct impact on the respective performance of the two institutions. Similarly, the University of Chile's status as a public entity prevents it from competing on a level playing field with the Pontifical Catholic University of Chile. Paradoxically, the latter is not subject to the same rules concerning administrative, procurement, and financial control as the former, even though the Pontifical Catholic University of Chile receives budget contributions from the state as other public universities do. The University of Chile is also handicapped by excessive decentralization, which undermines the power of the rector, and by not having a board with outside stakeholders that can help the university to respond better to the needs of society.

As private universities, Pohang University of Science and Technology and Monterrey Institute of Technology have enjoyed much more autonomy and flexibility than public universities in Korea and Mexico, respectively. And as just discussed, the Pontifical Catholic University of Chile has certainly benefited from its status as a private institution by enjoying the best of two worlds—the agility and independence of a nonpublic university, while obtaining public subsidies on a regular basis.

The key dimensions of autonomy brought out by the case studies include the ability to mobilize significant additional funding from a variety of nonpublic sources; to provide attractive remuneration packages for top academics; and to boost the international nature of the institution in terms of program content, language of instruction, and focus of the research.

The Hong Kong University of Science and Technology case study vividly illustrates the importance of leadership for achieving rapid progress. The deliberate decision to hire an experienced university president from the Chinese diaspora by the sponsors of the new university was undoubtedly a major factor contributing to the success of Hong Kong University of Science and Technology. Similarly, Monterrey Institute of Technology benefited from stability in terms of overall direction and management, with its founding entrepreneur remaining as chair of its governing board for 30 years and the same rector at the helm of the institution for the past 20 years.

One of the ways in which purposeful leadership manifests itself is through the talent of articulating an enticing vision for the future of the institution to all its stakeholders. Good salaries are not enough to attract and motivate high-performing academics; faculty members must feel that they are part of a significant project to ensure their full commitment toward the construction or renewal of the institution. In the words of the first president of Hong Kong University of Science and Technology about the qualities and motivation of his academic staff members, "they had talent, they had ability, but in the end what brought them here was their hearts." When Pohang University of Science and Technology was established, its leaders had the wisdom to carefully study the difficult experience of a new university established a few years before in Korea.

Finally, the comparisons between the University of Chile and the Pontifical Catholic University of Chile, on the one hand, and the University of Malaya and the National University of Singapore, on the other hand, serve to emphasize the importance of aligning the three sets of factors that, together, determine the performance of research universities: concentration of talent, sufficient funding, and good governance.

Paths of Development

The case studies explored in this book include established universities, which have made or are making deliberate efforts to upgrade their quality and effectiveness, and new institutions created from scratch with the ambitious vision of achieving world-class status. The four institutions that seem to have been the most successful, using the criterion of their position in the rankings of the Shanghai Academic Ranking of World Universities and the Times Higher Education rankings—namely, Indian Institutes of Technology, National University of Singapore, Hong Kong University of Science and Technology, and Pohang University of Science and Technology—are all relatively new institutions. Their trajectory would tend to demonstrate that it is easier to reach academic excellence by establishing a new research university than by attempting to upgrade an existing one. It is much less complicated, in particular, to set up a favorable governance framework for a new institution than to try to transform the mode of operation of existing institutions, as the Malaysian case clearly indicates.

Gerard Postiglione prefaced his chapter on Hong Kong University of Science and Technology with the reminder that "Rome was not built in a day." He stressed the important fact that building a world-class university is a lengthy and complex process that involves several decades of sustained determination and efforts. It has taken, for instance, five decades to bring Indian Institutes of Technology and the National University of Singapore to their present levels. In this respect, the long-term vision adopted by the Pontifical Catholic University of Chile (Horizon 2038) may be much more realistic than Nigeria's fixation on a 2020 target to have 20 globally ranked institutions.

Among all the case studies reviewed, Hong Kong University of Science and Technology is perhaps the institution that has enjoyed the most rapid ascension, because of a unique combination of favorable factors from the very beginning that may prove quite difficult to replicate. At a critical moment of transformation for the entire territory because of the handover to China, the new university was established with the benefit of a clear vision, strong leadership, an outstanding academic body, an innovative educational model, ample resources, and a supportive governance and management framework. This situation of "perfect star alignment" is not easy to replicate, let alone sustain, over the long term.

The case studies have also brought out a number of "accelerating factors" that can play a positive role in the quest for excellence. The first factor is relying extensively on the diaspora, especially when establishing a new institution. As illustrated by the experiences of Pohang University of Science and Technology and Hong Kong University of Science and Technology, convincing large numbers of overseas scholars to come back to their country of origin is an effective way of rapidly building up the academic strength of an institution. The second factor, using English as the main language of an institution, greatly enhances its ability to attract highly qualified foreign academics, as the National University of Singapore has managed to accomplish. Concentrating on niche areas, such as the science and engineering disciplines, is the third convenient manner of achieving a critical mass more rapidly. The fourth approach uses benchmarking as a guide to orient the institution in its upgrading efforts. Shanghai Jiao Tong University, for instance, anchored its strategic planning work in careful comparisons with leading Chinese universities first and then moved to include peer foreign universities in the benchmarking exercise.

The fifth factor is to introduce significant curriculum and pedagogical innovations. Hong Kong University of Science and Technology, for example, was the first U.S.-style university in Hong Kong, which made it distinct in comparison to the existing institutions operating according to the British model. Higher School of Economics was among the first institutions in Russia to offer a curriculum that integrates teaching and research and to establish a supportive digital library. Those kinds of innovative features—part of the "latecomer advantage"—are of great consequence for new institutions that need to be attractive enough to entice students away from existing universities and to get them to risk enrolling in an "unknown" program. Hong Kong University of Science and Technology's experience proves that, through a highly innovative academic model, new institutions can draw first-rate academics and students away from well-established universities.

The last point worth underlining regarding the "road to excellence" is the need for successful institutions to remain vigilant and to maintain a sense of urgency to avoid complacency. This factor implies continuous monitoring and self-assessment to identify tensions or threats and to act quickly to address them. The Indian Institutes of Technology, for example, are now faced with an issue of faculty renewal in an academic labor-force environment that has become increasingly competitive. The Pohang University of Science and Technology case study shows that integrating research and undergraduate education can be a significant challenge when academics are under pressure to publish in the top journals.

Emerging research universities also face a variety of equity challenges. Considerable financial resources are required to enforce a needs-blind admission system. Legally imposed affirmative-action programs may distort the meritocratic process. Highly competitive admissions procedures, including high-stakes admissions exams, may engender high levels of private coaching that favor students from richer families.

Importance of the Tertiary Education Ecosystem

Outstanding research universities do not operate in a vacuum. A common thread across all the case studies in this book is that analyzing what happens in the institutions alone is not sufficient to understand and appreciate the full dynamics of their relative success or failure. The analysis cannot be complete unless it also takes into consideration key forces at play at the level of what could be called the *ecosystem*, within which tertiary education institutions evolve. These forces can have a facilitating or constraining effect, depending on the circumstances. In Hong Kong, the creation of the University of Science and Technology fitted nicely with the ambitious plans of the new leadership after the transfer of authority from Great Britain to China. The new university benefited from a favorable governance framework, full academic freedom, and generous public funding. By contrast, in Chile, the absence of a national vision for the development of tertiary education, the limited leadership role played by the Ministry of Education, the lack of a modern governance structure for public universities, and the low level of financial support for the country's flagship research institution explain the modest results achieved by the University of Chile.

As illustrated in figure 11.1, the main dimensions of the ecosystem include the following elements:

- Macro environment: the overall political and economic situation of a country, together with the rule of law and the enforcement of basic freedoms, which influence, in particular, the governance of tertiary education institutions (appointment of university leaders), their level of funding, academic freedom, and safety in the physical environment
- Leadership at the national level: the existence of a vision and a strategic plan to shape the future of tertiary education and capacity to implement reforms

Figure 11.1   Understanding How the Ecosystem Influences the Performance of Top Research Universities

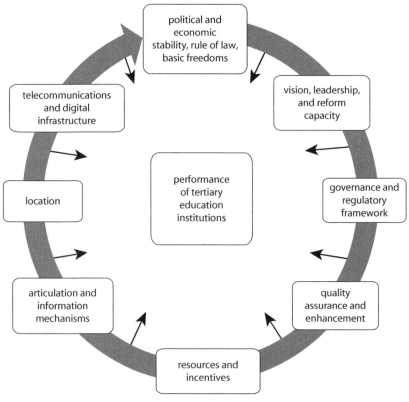

Sources: Jamil Salmi.

- Governance and regulatory framework: the governance structure and processes at the national and institutional levels that determine the degree of autonomy that tertiary education institutions enjoy and the mechanisms of accountability they are subject to (especially important from the viewpoint of the human resources policies and management practices that allow emerging research universities to attract and keep qualified academics)
- Quality assurance framework: the institutional setup and the instruments in place for assessing and enhancing the quality of research, teaching, and learning
- Financial resources and incentives: the absolute volume of resources available to finance tertiary education in a country (mobilization of public and private resources) and the mechanisms through which those resources are allocated to various institutions
- Articulation and information mechanisms: the links and bridges between high schools and tertiary education and the pathways and procedures integrating the various types of institutions that constitute a tertiary education system, all of which affect the academic characteristics of incoming students and their academic results as they move through the tertiary education system
- Location: the quality of economic, social, and cultural characteristics and infrastructures available in the specific geographical setting of a tertiary education institution that determine, in particular, its ability to attract outstanding scholars and talented students; these characteristics include public services, recreational amenities, housing, transportation, and environmental quality (Yusuf forthcoming)
- Digital and telecommunications infrastructure: the availability of broadband connectivity and end-user devices to support the delivery of educational, research, and administrative services of tertiary education institutions in an efficient, reliable, and affordable way

The case studies show several ways in which the tertiary education ecosystem affects the performance of individual institutions. The first general finding is that high-performing systems are characterized by a high level of alignment among the various dimensions, as highlighted by the Hong Kong SAR, China; Korea; and Singapore cases. The absence of some of the elements or the lack of alignment among the various dimensions is likely to compromise the ability of research universities to thrive and endure. In the Nigerian case, for example, the deteriorating governance situation during the dictatorship years had a directly adverse impact on the financing of the University of Ibadan. Moreover, it is doubtful that Nigeria, with its current digital infrastructure challenges, will achieve much progress toward its national objective of 20 world-class universities by 2020 without effective solutions to the problems of frequent power shortages and limited Internet access across the entire national university system.

Within this general principle, the second crucial finding is that some of the factors are absolute requisites, whereas others are quite relevant but not entirely indispensable. As discussed earlier, the governance framework and the availability of financial resources are definitely essential because they condition the degree of autonomy of research universities. Those factors influence the universities' ability to mobilize funding for recruiting and keeping top academics and for providing them with the appropriate teaching and research infrastructure, including the digital infrastructure that is becoming increasingly necessary for advanced research.

Other factors such as the rule of law, the level of democracy, the existence of a national vision for the future of tertiary education, articulation mechanisms, and location are certainly significant. Yet the jury is still out regarding the ability to determine, in a conclusive way, whether research institutions can excel without these supporting dimensions or whether these factors represent significant elements of vulnerability over the long term. The China case study is a good illustration of this dilemma.

China has been among the countries with the highest investing to upgrade their top universities through a series of targeted programs (the famous 211 and 985 Projects). The rapid rise of Chinese universities in the Academic Ranking of World Universities attests to the success of these efforts. In 2003, only 14 Chinese universities were included in the first edition of the ranking; by 2009, 24 appeared among the top 500 universities in the world. No other country in the world has made such progress. Increased funding has been coupled with more management autonomy to facilitate the development of Chinese universities. The tight political control in the country as a whole, however, translates into restrictions that could hamper the full development of flagship universities in the medium term.

The first element of tension comes from the dual governance structure that characterizes Chinese universities. Despite being the formal leader of the institution, the university president shares the authority to appoint members of the senior academic and administrative team with a

Communist Party secretary who, in many cases, is also the chair of the university board. This structure is not a problem when the two leaders see eye to eye, but it has the potential to undermine the ability of the university president to lead and manage the institution in a truly autonomous fashion. The success of the National Institute for Biological Sciences, which contributes half of the peer-reviewed publications in China, is attributed in part to the fact that it is the only research institute in China without a Communist Party secretary (Pomfret 2010).

Academic freedom is a second potential source of tension. It is not a significant constraint in the hard sciences—although government control of the Internet affects all scholars—but it certainly hinders the ability of social scientists to conduct scientific inquiries on issues that are politically sensitive. Finally, pressure from the local authorities may undermine the meritocratic admission process whenever a university is subject to a quota of local students. In the case of Shanghai Jiao Tong University, for example, at least 35 percent of incoming undergraduate students must be from the Shanghai region.

Generally speaking, the rule of law, political stability, and the respect of basic freedoms are important dimensions of the political context into which high-quality universities operate. Infringing on these basic tenets of democratic life is not conducive to a thriving intellectual environment. In Nigeria, for instance, substantial additional funding has been offered to a select group of federal universities. But the resurgence of sectarian and rebel violence and the lack of security in several states threaten the federal government's plans to build world-class universities. In early March 2010, hundreds of people were massacred in the state of Plateau, which raises questions about the country's image as a place where people of different beliefs can coexist peacefully and disagree in principle while still working together (Dickson and Abubakar 2010).

Malaysia is another country actively seeking to transform its top universities into flagship institutions. But recent disturbing political developments, from the burning of churches to the whipping of a woman for drinking beer in public, have cast a shadow on the country's image as an open and tolerant society that supports the freedom of expression and the separation of state and religion (Sta Maria 2010).

Even the United States, with its long democratic tradition, is not immune to restrictions on freedom of movement and to threats to academic freedom having a negative impact on the country's elite universities. Since September 11, 2001, the tighter visa regulations have prevented international graduate students from returning to finish their studies or new international doctoral candidates to enroll at a U.S. university. Some scholars who conduct academic research on the Middle East have been subject to selective harassment (Cole 2010).

With respect to leadership at the national level, research universities are more likely to prosper when their role is embedded in a national vision for the future of tertiary education, as in India and China (both mainland and Hong Kong SAR, China). But individual initiatives can also be successful without being framed within a national vision, as shown by Pohang University of Science and Technology, Monterrey Institute of Technology and Higher Education.

Location represents another factor that can facilitate or complicate the development of a research university. The vibrant economy and society of Hong Kong SAR, China, provide a serious setting to attract top academics and students. Singapore is ideally situated between China and India. By contrast, cities located in hardship zones, whether climate or political, will have much more difficulty attracting and keeping talented academics and students.

Of all the building blocks of the tertiary education ecosystem, quality assurance is perhaps the only one that can be found outside the national borders. When Pontifical Catholic University of Chile and Monterrey Institute of Technology and Higher Education were improving the quality of their course offerings in the absence of a national accreditation system, they successfully sought international accreditation for many of their programs to boost their academic standing. In fact, Monterrey Institute of Technology and Higher Education was the first non-U.S. institution to be accredited by a U.S. accreditation agency. Reaching out to foreign quality-assurance providers contributed significantly to raising the quality and to enhancing the prestige of these two Latin American institutions.

Conclusion

The trajectories of the 11 institutions analyzed in this book offer valuable insights into the complex transformation process that institutions striving to become world-class research universities are undergoing, whether they chose "upgrading" or the "starting anew" path to academic excellence. With proper leadership and vision, existing research universities can drastically improve the quality of their teaching and research. Alternatively, when talent, resources, and governance are adequately aligned from the beginning, new universities have the potential—though no guarantees can ever be given—to grow into high-quality research institutions within two or three decades. Even though the sample of institutions reviewed in this book is too small to be fully conclusive, the case studies seem to suggest that establishing a new institution is a relatively faster and more effective approach.

New research universities do face special challenges, however. To attract top academics and good students, they need to be sufficiently innovative to represent a convincing alternative to existing institutions. This difference seems to be more easily achieved with niche programs, as demonstrated by the experience of Indian Institutes of Technology, Pohang University of Science and Technology, Hong Kong University of Science and Technology, and Higher School of Economics.

Many valuable lessons can also be drawn from the African case study, which serves as a stern warning that success is fragile and that prestigious universities, like famous empires, are prone to fateful destinies should the fundamental enabling conditions disappear. These conditions, presented in the description of the tertiary education ecosystem within which universities can strive, are important to keep in mind.

All of the case studies in this book confirm the importance of maintaining the three sets of key factors put forward in the conceptual framework—concentrated talent, abundant resources, and favorable governance—well aligned. When it comes to transforming existing universities, however, leadership, governance, and management seem to be the key factors for starting a virtuous circle leading to momentous improvements. Indeed, visionary leadership, appropriate governance, and effective management make it easier to generate and manage additional resources, which, in turn, support building up a world-class group of professors and researchers and attracting talented students.

In his insightful book about highly successful companies, *From Good to Great*, Jim Collins (2001) studied the characteristics of leaders who played a catalytic role in bringing their firm to the top. Even though it is more difficult to define appropriate metrics of success for tertiary education institutions than for firms, whose results can be easily measured in terms of revenue and earnings, university leadership certainly warrants further research to understand the dynamics of change and progress in the academic world. The case studies unequivocally support the notion that exceptional leaders are at the heart of successful emerging research universities through their ability to formulate an inspiring vision for the future of the institution, to rally their academic and administrative staff behind this vision, and to implement the vision in an effective manner.

A significant new finding from the case studies is the weight of the tertiary education ecosystem in influencing the performance of research universities seeking to achieve world-class status. The various features of the ecosystem—from the macroeconomic and political situation to key dimensions of governance to resource mobilization and allocation to location and the digital infrastructure—have a strong effect on the ability of research universities to make progress on the road to academic excellence.

Finally, even top research universities face the challenge of achieving a harmonious balance between equipping their students with technical skills and rigorous methodologies and imparting the ethical values needed to pursue scientific inquiries in a socially responsible manner. Several of the case studies, especially Hong Kong University of Science and Technology and the Pontifical Catholic University of Chile, illustrate the concern to maintain a curriculum that blends a strong scientific training and a deep humanistic conviction. In the words of Sri Sri Ravi Shankar, the founder of a new university that is being established in the Indian state of Orissa, "only an education that can nourish inbuilt virtues can impart true intelligence" (Sri Sri University 2010).

Annex 11A   Age of the Top-Ranked Universities (2010 Academic Ranking of World Universities)

Ranking	Institution	Year founded
1	Harvard University (U.S.)	1636
2	University of California, Berkeley (U.S.)	1869
3	Stanford University (U.S.)	1891
4	Massachusetts Institute of Technology (U.S.)	1865
5	University of Cambridge (U.K.)	1209
6	California Institute of Technology (U.S.)	1891
7	Princeton University (U.S.)	1746
8	Columbia University (U.S.)	1754
9	University of Chicago (U.S.)	1891
10	University of Oxford (U.K.)	1096

Sources: Infoplease, http://www.infoplease.com/ipa/A0193904.html; University of California, Berkeley, http://www.ucberkeley.com; University of Chicago, http://www.uchicago.edu.

Annex 11B   Main Characteristics of Each Institution

Institution (year established)	Number of students (that graduate)	Student-to-faculty ratio	Share of direct public funding (%)	Endowment (US$)	Annual budget (US$)	Per student expenditure (US$)
University of Ibadan (1962)	19,521 (7,382)	16:1	85	0.2 million	46.7 million	2,390
Shanghai Jiao Tong University (1896)	43,000 (14,000)	15:1	40	120 million	700 million	16,300
Pohang University of Science and Technology (1987)	3,100 (1,700)	6:1	15	2 billion	220 million	70,000
University of Chile (1842)	30,702 (4.569)	9–15:1	11	0	520 million	17,000
Catholic University of Chile (1888)	22,035 (2,806)	8:1	11	0	453 million	20,500
Indian Institutes of Technology (first founded in 1950 in Kharagpur)	28,000 (12,000)	6:1 to 8:1	70	0	123 million	4,400
Hong Kong University of Science and Technology (1991)	9,271 (3,302)	19:1[a]	63	0.25 million	267 million	28,850
University of Malaya (1949)	26,963 (8,900)	12:1	60	0	271.6 million	14,000
National University of Singapore (1980)	27,396 (6,300)	14.4:1	58	1 billion	1.37 billion	39,000

(continued next page)

Annex 11B   Main Characteristics of Each Institution *(continued)*

Institution (year established)	Number of students (that graduate)	Student-to-faculty ratio	Share of direct public funding (%)	Endowment (US$)	Annual budget (US$)	Per student expenditure (US$)
Monterrey Institute of Technology (1943)	25,705 (3,600) (Monterrey campus)	12.2:1	0	1 billion	1.15 billion	10,200
Higher School of Economics (1992)	16,000 (2,400)	—	33	0	45.5 million	2,843

Source: Author based on data from the chapters of this book.
Note: — = not available.
a. A significant number of nonregular faculty members has been brought on recently to address the increased program diversity and has moved the student-faculty ratio in the direction of 15:1 to 14:1.

Annex 11C   Key Elements of the Strategic Approach Followed by Each Institution

Institution	Public/ private status	Direct public funding (%)	Autonomy	Student recruitment	Approach toward excellence
Ibadan University	Public	89	Low	Selective	Upgrading
Shanghai Jiao Tong University	Public	40	Medium	Selective	Upgrading
Pohang University of Science and Technology	Private	15	High	Highly selective	New institution
University of Chile	Public	11	Medium	Highly selective	Upgrading
Pontifical Catholic University of Chile	Private	11	High	Highly selective	Upgrading
Indian Institutes of Technology	Public	70	Medium	Highly selective	New institution
Hong Kong University of Science and Technology	Public	63	High	Selective	New institution
University of Malaya	Public	73	Low	Selective	Upgrading
National University of Singapore	Public	58	High	Selective	New institution
Monterrey Institute of Technology	Private	0	High	Highly selective	Upgrading
Higher School of Economics	Public	33	High	Selective	New institution

Source: Author based on data from the chapters of this book.

Annex 11D   Main Funding Sources of Each Institution

percent

Institution	Government budget	Tuition fees	Endowment income, donations, lottery, and corporate support	Competitive research funding	Consultancies, training, and contract research
University of Ibadan	85	1	1	2	10
Shanghai Jiao Tong University	40	10	5	15	30
Pohang University of Science and Technology	6	7	34	47	6
University of Chile	11	23	1	20	45
Pontifical Catholic University of Chile	11	30	7	4	48
Indian Institutes of Technology	70	5	5	5	10
Hong Kong University of Science and Technology	63	18	6	10	3
University of Malaya	73	11	10	0	6
National University of Singapore	58	—	—	—	—
Monterrey Institute of Technology	0	77	13	3	7
Higher School of Economics	52	25	3	10	10

Source: Author based on data from the chapters of this book.
Note: — = not available.

Notes

1. In this chapter, the terms *world class, flagship,* and *elite* are used indistinctly to describe research-intensive universities that are considered to operate among the top institutions in the world.

2. One of the most ironic manifestations of anger came from France. After the publication of the 2003 Academic Ranking of World Universities ranking, two French university presidents wrote a formal letter of complaint to the Chinese ambassador demanding from the Chinese government that it forbid Shanghai Jiao Tong University from continuing to publish its world rankings. It is paradoxical that representatives of a country that puts freedom (*liberté*) as the first of three principles in its national motto (*liberté, fraternité, égalité*) would encourage the Chinese government to limit academic freedom. In May 2010, the Education Commission of the French Senate organized a round table on international rankings with the title of "Forget Shanghai" (*Oublier* Shanghai).

3. See Minister Valérie Pécresse's declaration at the Conference on International Comparisons in Education held in Paris in December 2008.

References

Aghion, Philippe, Mathias Dewatripont, Caroline Hoxby, Andreu Mas-Colell, and André Sapir. 2009. "The Governance and Performance of Research Universities: Evidence from Europe and the U.S. National Bureau of Economic Research." Working paper 14851, National Bureau of Economic Research, Cambridge, MA.

Altbach, Philip. G. 2004. "The Costs and Benefits of World-Class Universities." *Academe* (January–February). http://www.aaup.org/AAUP/CMS_Templates/ AcademeTemplates/AcademeArticle.aspx?NRMODE=P/.

———. 2006. "The Dilemmas of Ranking." *International Higher Education* 42: 2–3.

Cole, Jonathan R. 2010. *The Great American University: Its Rise to Pre-eminence, Its Indispensable National Role, Why It Must Be Protected.* New York: Public Affairs.

Collins, James C. 2001. *From Good to Great: Why Some Companies Make the Leap—and Others Don't.* New York: Harper Business.

Dixon, Robyn, and Aminu Abubakar. 2010. "Survivors: Nigerian Attacks Planned." *Washington Post*, March 9.

Hazelkorn, Ellen. 2008. "Learning to Live with Leagues Tables and Ranking: The Experience of Institutional Leaders." *Higher Education Policy* 21 (2): 193–216.

LERU (League of European Research Universities). 2010. "Universities, Research and the 'Innovation Union.'" Advice Paper 5, October.

Pomfret, John. 2010. "China Pushing the Envelope on Science, and Sometimes Ethics." *Washington Post*, June 28, sec. A.

Salmi, Jamil. 2009. *The Challenge of Establishing World-Class Universities: Directions in Development*. Washington, DC: World Bank. http://portal.unesco .org/education/en/files/55825/12017990845Salmi.pdf/Salmi.pdf.

Salmi, Jamil, and Alenoush Saroyan. 2007. "League Tables as Policy Instruments: Uses and Misuses. *Higher Education Management and Policy* 19 (2): 31–68.

Smolentseva, Anna. 2010. In Search for World-Class Universities: The Case of Russia. *International Higher Education* 58: 20–22.

Sri Sri University. 2010. "Strategic Plan." Unpublished document. Sri Sri University, Orissa, India.

Sta Maria, Stephanie. 2010. "Academics Fear for the Future of Islam." *Free Malaysia Today*, May 28. http://www.freemalaysiatoday.com/fmt-english/ news/general/6125-academics-fear-for-the-future-of-islam.

Wildavsky, Ben. 2010. *The Great Brain Race: How Global Universities Are Reshaping the World*. Princeton, NJ: Princeton University Press.

Yusuf, Shahid. Forthcoming. *From Technological Catch-Up to Innovation: The Future of China's GDP Growth*. Washington DC: World Bank.

Index

CPSIA information can be obtained at www.ICGtesting.com
Printed in the USA
LVOW012149130613

338552LV00005B/126/P